AMERICA THE MAJESTIC

Pictorial Cook Book

WITH
SPECTACULAR AND
EASY TO PREPARE
RECIPES FROM
ALL MAJOR AREAS

To our Australian Reader

We take pride and pleasure being able to present this book to you.

It was developed and produced in Australia with every recipe tested and photographed by our Australian home economist in Manly, NSW.

Most ingredients are either freely available in Australia or substitutes are readily at hand.

Gaslight
PUBLISHING
PTY. LTD.
INCORPORATED in N.S.W.

MAJOR CREDITS

Published by:

GASLIGHT PUBLISHING Pty Limited
(Incorporated in N.S.W.)
Unit D-107-115 Asquith St.,
Auburn, N.S.W. 2144, Australia

Telephone: (02) 647 2899
Facsimile: (02) 647 2248
Telex No.: 121822 User Sy. 3909

CREATIVE DIRECTION of Art, Photography and Production:	**Jon Tarpstra**
ART AND ASSEMBLY:	Helen Reynolds Irene Harmsworth
FOOD WRITER:	Brian Crumblehulme
HOME ECONOMIST and Food Editor:	Ellen Argyriou
PHOTOGRAPHY (Food):	Hugh Scarlett
INTRODUCTIONS:	David Quick Joe Wolff (USA)
STYLIST AND PROPS:	Belinda Drew
PRODUCTION:	**Gas Graphics TGC** Pty Limited 173 Commonwealth St Surry Hills, N.S.W. 2010, Australia Phone: (02) 212 2522 Fax: (02) 212 6428 Griffin Press Limited 262 Marion Road Netley, S.A. 5037 Phone: (08) 292 2222 Fax: (08) 371 0503 Telex: AA89154

National Library of Australia
Cataloguing-In-Publication Data
The: "America The Majestic Pictorial Cooking Book"
Bibliography
Includes Index
ISBN 0 958812 2 5. 1 Cookery 2 United States –
Description and travel – 1981 – Views.
Copyright ©

COVER:
The majestic McLoud Reservoir in Northern California with the magnificent Bald Eagle.

Polar bear in the stark icy world of Alaska.

AMERICA THE MAJESTIC

Pictorial Cook Book

WITH
SPECTACULAR AND
EASY TO PREPARE
RECIPES FROM
ALL MAJOR AREAS

PUBLISHED BY

Gaslight

PUBLISHING
PTY. LTD.
INCORPORATED in N.S.W.

Capitol Hill in evening glow.

FOREWORD

America The Majestic in the Making

Roll a concise history of America into a first class cookbook and between the same covers add a practical manual on how to be the perfect host and hostess. What you have is the America The Majestic Pictorial and Cook Book, the first publication of its kind.

This magnificent book is no ordinary culinary reference work that will take its place on a kitchen shelf to be forgotten until you need a handy recipe. It is a genuinely rare mix of American recipes painstakingly drawn from every corner of the country. Add to this an unusual twist of American history garnished with photographs that illustrate both, and you have a truly unique work.

Think about it for a moment. From which single book would you get illustrated step-by-step instructions on the correct way to lay a formal table, how to open a champagne bottle, what cocktails to serve and how to mix them, a choice of unusual but easy recipes to suit every occasion along with conversational history directly relating to the area from which the recipe you have selected originates? There is only one and you are holding it in your hand right now.

America The Majestic is designed to be inspirational, the flash of genius you need to produce a meal that is stunningly different but easy and fast to prepare (recipes of an average 15 minutes preparation). It is a book for browsing and is far more than a simple "how to" cookbook. On every page you will learn something new presented in a light, entertaining and easily digested way.

This magnificent book is American, yet it was produced by a mix of nationalities, mostly Australian, working as a small but dedicated team in Sydney, Australia. To ask why, is to ask a fair question.

A pinch over two years ago, during one of many trips around the U.S.A., I discovered a collection of recipes written by Americans, that had been lovingly gathered (rather than amassed) over many years.

This collection of recipes was clearly different; flicking through them created an instant mental picture of different parts of America; of the different people who had adopted this magnificently vast country as a new homeland. The idea of producing a pictorial cookbook giving the reader digestible reference to the history behind the originating regions was born at that moment.

The concept of a book based on these recipes was to me obvious, though the finished work is actually greater in scope and glossy quality than even I had initially envisaged. I acquired the recipe collection which was to be the focus of the book and set about refining the work into a publication that would be something literally not seen before.

The logical step would have been to have produced America The Majestic with an American team in America. As is often the case, true logic is usually one thought beyond the obvious. Australians have an empathy with America and American people, a fact readily seen by the closeness between the lifestyles of the two countries.

The Australian production team viewed the complex production project, which has taken two solid years of work, as an enthralling challenge, the inherent risk of being jaded by being too close to the subject country was obviated by definition.

The result is a culinary compendium incorporating 320 pages in full color covering 17 sections. There are over 400 recipes, all of which have been tried and tested, 80 food color plates and 220 scenic color photographs by top photographers.

I know you will enjoy and give pride of place to this book in your home with the same pleasure and pride as we have in presenting the
America The Majestic
Pictorial and Cook Book to you.

MANAGING DIRECTOR

 **PUBLISHING** PTY. LTD.
INCORPORATED in N.S.W.

The Grand Canyon, a magnificent view of Colorado River from Lipan Point.

Historic Acorn Street, Beacon Hill, in Boston.

INTRODUCTION

America The Majestic is no ordinary cookbook, but an education in itself; an easily digestible blend of historical, culinary and useful facts as unique as many of the recipes to be found inside the 500 richly illustrated pages.

It is a literary and gastronomic stroll through the regional vastness of America with a chance to pause and learn a little of the history behind the astonishing variety of dishes to be found throughout the country, as well as discovering how to prepare, cook and serve them.

It is a rare compendium of vital but practical information to suit any and everybody from a busy mother to an aspiring high society hostess.

To cover every area, every ingredient, every dish and every recipe would be, of course, an impossible task in a single volume book.

America The Majestic is nevertheless a comprehensive selection — the pick of the best — from each region and subject.

Why did we cover regions and not states? The gastronomic borders of regional America are quite different from the geographic borders.

Texas and Mexico, for example, are from this viewpoint at least historically borderless, thus we cover both as the Tex-mex region.

Similarly, the Cajuns is a section focusing on the history of a people and not on an area, albeit that the Cajuns are predominantly settled in Louisiana, which is where this section takes us.

The dishes and recipes you will find in America The Majestic include obvious "standards" such as Onion Soup and Grilled Steak, but the emphasis throughout is on the speciality or unusual dishes indicative of each region.

Even the menu items which might be regarded as "standards" have a particularly regional twist. Grilled Steak from the Heartlands, for example, is actually Grilled Whiskey Steak with the difference from a normal grilled steak being that the meat is marinated in whiskey for about four hours before being rubbed with pepper and thyme immediately before cooking.

All facets of menu selection are covered, from exotic light snacks (Banana Soup and Toasted Mango Sandwiches from Hawaii is one example), to deliciously unusual main course meals such as Coffee-Glazed Crown Roast of Lamb with Golden Mushroom Sauce from the Sunbelt region.

This book provides the means to try something completely different in menu selection.

Salads can be, and often are, boring. Why not try the Orange and Herb Californian Salad with Mini Rolls, or the Chicken Melon Salad with Ginger Sauce found in the Pacific North West?

America is blessed with a huge coastline and abundant inland waterways which provide no less than 2200 different species of fish and seafood at the last count.

Each region has its own style of fish and seafood dishes, and few guests would fail to be impressed by a seafood meal comprising Shrimp Brochette with Aiole Sauce followed by Baked Red Snapper Mexican style.

If you really want to go to town, such a meal could start with homemade Turtle Soup as the Cajuns do it, with Irish Soda Bread on the side, baked by yourself with true New York flair. With America The Majestic, the possibilities of menu mix 'n' match are literally and delightfully endless.

Eating is fundamental and necessary to stay alive; but eating well should be part of social development and regarded as a quality-of-life art form. In this context, food as a subject takes on a whole new dimension.

With America The Majestic, however, you do not need to be a Cordon Bleu chef to achieve remarkable table results. Delightful and delicious meals can be selected for speed and ease of preparation, their exotic appeal, or simply to put more than a little zing into the family's diet.

Good table conversation is socially as vital as the meal itself and here, too, America The Majestic is an able companion.

Part of the fun of trying the many different dishes from each region in this book is discovering a little of the history behind the meal, the region and the people who live there.

This book is not intended to be a university degree course, but the foundation for social discourse.

How many people would know that were it not for Columbus discovering the Americas (who at the time was actually looking for a shorter route from Spain to India to give the Spanish an edge in the spice trade), the Italians would possibly not have had "their own" tomato sauce on the famous pizza, the French may have been without French Fries and the Austrian Gateau would probably not be covered with chocolate.

Did you know that the Spanish brought slavery to America as early as 1516, but it is thought to be the Dutch-brought slaves in 1619 who may have been responsible for the introduction of the curious Dutch Beet Eggs (see recipe in the Dixie section).

It is also interesting to note from the Dixie section that at the height of the slavery debate, only 5 per cent of the southerners actually had slaves and only half this number had more than five slaves. History may magnify perceptions, but nevertheless, for those interested in conversation around a lunch or dinner table, it offers many entertaining topics.

America The Majestic is designed to be a complete guide in the kitchen and you will find it invaluable as a reference work for many things.

The back of this book contains sections on everything from how to fold a napkin into a dazzling water-lily shape to the proper way to set a table and the socially correct seating positions for your guests.

Included in this section is much of what you need to know about herbs and spices — the varieties and their uses. There is even a whole section devoted to edible flowers; the characteristic of each flower, recommendations on how, when and with what to use them, complete with recipe ideas.

Also under the heading of useful information you will find sections on calorific values, planning menus for major occasions such as weddings, eating outdoors or setting up a buffet. Even the correct way to open a bottle of champagne is illustrated step-by-step.

Complete sections give you handy hints on selecting, serving and cooking with wines, with further sections covering recipes and tips from homemade lemonade to exotic hot punches.

Also included in these sections are recipes and recommendations for cocktails, hot and cold beverages (Iced Tea, Hot Chocolate, Milk Shakes, etc).

You will be amazed at the extent and range of valuable information included in America The Majestic, but as we said, it is not just another cookbook.

INTRODUCTION

Ellen Argyriou

HOME ECONOMIST

A young Miccosukee Indian holding an Alligator baby in the Everglades National Park.

CONTENTS

A sample of the abundance and richness of food in our Nation.

Alaska

ALASKA represents 20 per cent of the American land mass and is a place of many contradictions, so it should come as no surprise that the cuisine of this 49th State is of a similar ilk.

Here is a land poorly documented, largely unexplored and...

Autumn across the Matanuska Glacier, South-central Alaska.

ALASKA

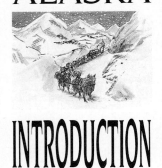

INTRODUCTION

despite its huge size of 586,400 square miles, of which a staggering 40,000 miles is coastline, is currently supporting less than half-a-million people.

From any normal viewpoint, much of Alaska is totally inhospitable to vegetation and human life, with about one-third of the State being within the Arctic Circle sporting a permanent mantle of severe frost and treeless 'tundra' (Russian for: trees won't grow here).

While the interior is largely frozen, much of the south coast and panhandle is at sea-level where mild summers and clear, dry winters are in sharp relief to the huge glacial regions and largely unexplored tundra.

Rainfall varies from 60 to 160 annual inches, which all adds up to an environment that should be great for growing things, at least in those areas not frozen solid.

Against this astonishing backcloth are active volcanos, desert sands, rain-forests and temperatures that can plummet to minus 60°F or soar to a sizzling 100°F.

It is also true that Alaska has some three million acres of tillable land, but a tiny population means much of it has yet to be cleared for use.

Although Alaska is one of the world's major fishing centers and grows some cool climate vegetables, about 90% of the dining-table produce for home consumption is imported from overseas.

Growing seasons, for those areas of the State that actually grow anything, are short. This is counterbalanced to a degree by long daylight hours.

In consequence, and all things considered, Alaska is surprisingly successful in growing wheat, oats, barley and rye but in limited quantities.

Perhaps the biggest contradiction of this tiny community is the curious mix of people that make up the population.

The indigenous people are Innuit Indians (Eskimos) and these people still figure strongly as about one-sixth of the population.

Then there's the Aluets, basically the descendants of immigrants and settlers.

America bought Alaska from the Russians in 1867 for a paltry two cents an acre. The Russians couldn't viably manage the place from Petersburg so America begrudgingly bought it. At the time, of course, neither side could foretell how valuable Alaska would become.

From a cuisine viewpoint, Alaskan food is today an unexpected mix of menu items some of which, like burnt apple borscht (recipe in this section), is a delightful heritage of the "Russian-American" period.

There is a strong influence of Chinese and Japanese genes in many of the people, but only a little sign of either in the cuisine (some dishes like vegetables in a nest of wild rice are in this section) despite the fact that the Alaskan salmon, its main produce, ranks with the best in the world, a logical target for Japanese gourmet treatment.

Similarly, you will find excellent recipes for things like tomato curry and even Madras curry powder, though there is virtually no trace of influence from either India or Pakistan in the people.

You will also find mouth-watering recipes that appear to have little connection with anything by family line but are thoroughly delightful for all that. Try the recipe for beer soup or radish onion flower with mustard cream, for example.

The Alaskans are also great people for unusual chutneys and hot pickles and with such a powerful line of seafood prevailing as both a resource and a historical ingredient, you can also expect to find seafood dishes that are temptingly different. If proof lies in the eating, have a go at making Crabzinni pie.

All this is a far cry from the original diet of hoof or paw as pursued by adventurers and traders, or the mono diet of "tail" favored by the Innuit, but because many of these dishes are instantly different, they are also an instant hit on the table.

Top: GAME HENS IN ORANGE SAUCE, Recipe page 26. *Middle left*: CARIBOU PIE, Recipe page 28.
Lower left: VEGETABLES IN NEST OF WILD RICE, Recipe page 21.

ALASKA

**APPETIZERS
SOUPS
SALADS
ENTREES**

Burnt Apple Borscht

PHOTOGRAPH PAGE 19

Preparation Time: 30 minutes
Cooking Time: 3 hours
Serves 6

4 Tbsp butter
2 lbs raw beets, peeled and chopped
2 stalks celery, chopped
3 leeks, chopped (white ends only)
1 cup cabbage, shredded
2 carrots, grated
2 onions, grated
1 clove garlic, minced
3–4 lbs (1½–2 kg) beef stewing bones
1 tsp salt
1 tsp pepper
2 bay leaves
1 tsp dried parsley
2 qts water
2 eggs, beaten
2 Tbsp lemon juice
2 sweet apples, peeled and sliced
sour cream for garnish

Melt the butter in a large heavy pan. Add the beets, celery, leeks, cabbage, carrots, onion and garlic. Sauté for 10 minutes, stirring frequently. Add the bones, salt, pepper, bay leaves, parsley and water. Cover and bring to a boil. Lower the heat and simmer for 2½ hours. Remove the soup bones. Put about half of the vegetables with 2 cups of stock into a food processor or blender. Add the eggs and lemon juice; puree until smooth. Return to the pan and stir well.

Ladle the soup into large ovenproof soup bowls and float several slices of apple on each one. Place under the broiler for 15 minutes at 400°F (200°C) until the apple starts to brown. Serve hot with dollops of sour cream.

Beer Soup

Preparation Time: 15 minutes
Cooking Time: 25 minutes
Serves 4

4 Tbsp butter
2 Tbsp flour
4 cups lager beer
pinch of salt, nutmeg, ginger, cinnamon
4 egg yolks, beaten
1 Tbsp sugar
1 cup white wine
1 Tbsp grated lemon peel
shredded lettuce
sliced radishes
sour cream

Melt the butter over medium heat and stir in the flour to make a smooth paste. Stir in the beer and spices; mix well and continue to heat. Beat the egg yolks in a bowl; gradually stir in a cup of the hot beer mixture. Return the egg/beer mixture to the pan and stir in the sugar, wine and lemon peel. Heat gently, stirring constantly; do not allow the soup to boil. Pour the hot soup into serving bowls and top each with shredded lettuce, radish slices and dollops of sour cream.

Rhubarb Soup

PHOTOGRAPH PAGE 19

Preparation Time: 10 minutes
Cooking Time: 25 minutes
Serves 8

2 lbs (1 kg) rhubarb, diced
8 cups water
1 stick cinnamon
2 slices lemon
1½ cups sugar
2 Tbsp cornstarch
2 Tbsp orange juice
whipped cream for serving

Place the rhubarb in a heavy pan with the water, cinnamon, lemon and sugar. Bring to a boil and simmer for 10 minutes until the rhubarb is very soft. Press the fruit through a sieve and return the liquid to the pan. Dissolve the cornstarch in the orange juice and stir it into the soup. Heat gently for 15 minutes stirring until it thickens and boils. Ladle into bowls and top with islands of whipped cream.

King Crab Royale

Preparation Time: 10 minutes
Cooking Time: 25 minutes
Serves 4

2 cups milk
½ lb (250 g) white fish fillets
1 lb (0.5 kg or 500 g) king crab meat
1 Tbsp butter
pinch of cayenne
1 tsp thyme
1 tsp sugar
2 cups chicken stock
½ cup heavy cream
¼ cup brandy

Poach the fish fillets gently in the milk for 10 minutes until they flake easily. Add half of the crab meat; add the butter, cayenne, thyme and sugar. Reheat to a simmer. Place the mixture in a blender or food processor and mix until smooth. Return to the pan. Add the chicken stock and the rest of the crab meat; bring to a boil. Reduce the heat to the lowest setting as you stir in the cream and brandy. Ladle into warmed soup bowls and serve immediately.

Top: BURNT APPLE BORSCHT, Recipe page 18. *Bottom*: RHUBARB SOUP, Recipe page 18.

Top: TOMATO CURRY, Recipe page 21. *Middle left:* CUCUMBER RAITA, Recipe page 22. *Middle right:* HOT PICKLES, Recipe page 22. *Bottom:* BANANA CHUTNEY, Recipe page 22.

Vegetables in Nests of Wild Rice

PHOTOGRAPH PAGE 17

Preparation Time: 20 minutes
Cooking Time: 45 minutes
Serves 4

3 Tbsp butter
1½ cups wild rice
3½ cups vegetable stock or water
2 cups tiny new potatoes or larger potatoes
    peeled and cut into ball shapes
1 cup baby carrots
1 cup pickling onions
1 cup melon balls

Glaze:
1 Tbsp butter
1 Tbsp sugar
1 tsp grated fresh ginger

Melt the butter in a heavy pan and sauté the rice for 5 minutes, stirring occasionally. Add the stock or water, stir and bring to a boil. Lower the heat then simmer, covered for 40 minutes or until all the liquid has been absorbed.

Meanwhile, in a large saucepan, heat water to a rapid boil. Scrub the potatoes and carrots and drop them into the boiling water. Cook for 5 minutes, then add the onions and cook for another 5 minutes or until the vegetables are tender. Add the melon balls and cook just long enough to warm them. Drain the vegetables and melon. Toss the vegetables in the butter, sugar and ginger until they are coated. Set them over very low heat until ready to serve.

When the rice is done, form it into nests on individual serving plates and arrange the vegetables on top.

Tomato Curry

PHOTOGRAPH PAGE 20

Preparation Time: 15 minutes
Cooking Time: 40 minutes
Serves 4

2 onions, chopped
¼ cup butter
3 Tbsp Madras curry powder (see page 22)
1 tsp cumin
1 cup chicken stock
½ cup raisins
8 cups chopped green tomatoes
1 apple, chopped
½ cup light brown sugar
2 Tbsp lemon juice
1 tsp paprika

Sambals (see page 22)

Sauté the onions in the butter for 10 minutes. Stir in the curry powder and cumin. Sauté for 2–3 minutes longer then add the next seven ingredients. Stir the mixture, cover it and simmer for ½ hour. Serve over rice with sambals on the side.

Radish & Onion Flowers with Mustard Cream

Preparation Time: 15 minutes
Standing Time: 6 hours

1 bunch globe radishes
1 cup small sweet onions
fresh radish flowers
fresh onion or chive flowers

Trim the stem ends of the radishes and stand them upright on the counter. Cut ¾ of the way through to the base in a cross pattern. Then cut ¾ of the way through in a square pattern around the edge.

Likewise trim the onions and cut them ¾ of the way through in a wedge or "petal" pattern, making 4 cuts across the onion (8 cuts if your are using larger onions). Place the radishes and onions loosely in a bowl. Cover them with cold water; allow them to stand for at least 6 hours or overnight to open. To serve, drain off the water and pat the "flowers" dry. Arrange them on a dish with the fresh radish and onion or chive flowers, which are also edible. Serve with a dip of mustard cream.

Mustard Cream

2 Tbsp olive oil
1 Tbsp powdered mustard
1 Tbsp cider vinegar
1 Tbsp honey
3 Tbsp heavy cream

In a blender, mix the olive oil and powdered mustard. Gradually add the other ingredients, blending continuously to form a creamy sauce. Serve as a dip with the salad vegetables.

ALASKA

APPETIZERS
SOUPS
SALADS
ENTREES

ALASKA

**APPETIZERS
SOUPS
SALADS
ENTREES**

Madras Curry Powder

*Preparation and Cooking Time: 15 minutes
Yield: ½ lb (250 g)*

When curried dishes are prepared, it is customary to combine specific spices chosen to produce a desired effect; the combinations are endless. However, for a quick curry sauce, or to warm up a soup, it is handy to have on the shelf a jar of the premixed spice that we in the West have come to know as "curry powder."

In a dry skillet over very low heat place:

8 Tbsp coriander seeds
6 Tbsp cumin seeds
1 Tbsp mustard seeds
1 Tbsp fenugreek seeds

Roast the seeds gently, shaking the pan occasionally, until they begin to pop. When about half the seeds have popped, add:

4 Tbsp ground cinnamon
8 Tbsp peppercorns
1 Tbsp ground nutmeg
1 Tbsp whole cloves
2 Tbsp ground cardamom
2 Tbsp turmeric
2 Tbsp ground ginger
1 Tbsp cayenne

Continue to heat and stir gently until the mixture is quite hot but not burnt. Pour into a dry blender or mill, or use a mortar and pestle. Grind the mixture to a fine powder. Pour into a clean dry jar, seal it and let it cool before using.

Sambals

PHOTOGRAPH PAGE 20

Sambals are cold, sometimes sweet or sharp side dishes used to complement a hot curry. The following are three examples:

Cucumber Raita

PHOTOGRAPH PAGE 20

1 cup cucumber, peeled and chopped
½ cup scallions, chopped
½ cup yoghurt or sour cream
fresh coriander
paprika

Combine all the ingredients in a bowl, mix well and top with a little chopped coriander or paprika.

Banana Chutney

PHOTOGRAPH PAGE 20

3 cups chopped onions
6 bananas, sliced

1½ cups chopped dates
1½ cups cider vinegar
1 cup crystallized ginger pieces
2 cups seedless raisins
2 cups pineapple juice
1 tsp curry powder

Combine all the ingredients in a saucepan and simmer, covered, for 20 minutes. Pour the mixture into sterilized jars and store in the refrigerator. Serve as a sambal with any curry or as a garnish with cold beef, chicken or ham.

Hot Pickles

PHOTOGRAPH PAGE 20

1½ cups cucumber, peeled and chopped
pinch of salt
1½ cups chopped carrots
4 tsp sugar
1 onion, chopped
4 green chilies, seeded and minced
¼ cup cider vinegar
pinch of turmeric

In a bowl, toss the cucumber with a sprinkle of salt and let mascerate for 10–15 minutes to draw out the water. Drain the cucumber, roll in a paper towel and pat dry. Return the slightly dried cucumber to the bowl and add the carrots, sugar, onion and minced chilies. Sprinkle the mixture with vinegar, toss well, cover and let stand for 2 hours at room temperature. Place in the refrigerator and chill. Serve cold as a side dish with a light dusting of turmeric.

Baked & Pickled Arctic Char

*Preparation Time: 15 minutes
Baking Time: 45 minutes
Preheat Oven: 400°F (200°C)
Serves 6–8*

1 small onion, chopped
¼ cup sweet pickle juice
½ cup chopped sweet pickles
¼ cup chopped hot pickles
2 Tbsp chopped fresh parsley or
    1 Tbsp dried parsley
3 Tbsp melted butter
5–6 lbs (2.5 kg–3 kg) Arctic char

Combine the chopped onion, pickles, pickle juice and parsley; mix well. Clean the fish and pat it dry. Brush the inside of the fish with melted butter and fill with the pickle mixture. Place the fish in a buttered baking dish and brush it all over with melted butter. Bake for 40–50 minutes. Serve immediately.

Game Paté

PHOTOGRAPH THIS PAGE

Preparation Time: 20 minutes
Cooking Time: 1¾ hours
Preheat Oven: 325°F (160°C)
Serves 8–10

at least 1 lb (500 g) leftover game meat — rabbit, duck,
    quail, etc.
1 lb (500 g) fatty pork
4–5 slices of bacon
2 cloves garlic, minced
15 black peppercorns
15 juniper berries
⅔ cup game or chicken stock
2 Tbsp brandy
bacon fat or lard

Chop, grind or mince the game, pork and bacon; mix together well. Mince the garlic; mix it in with the meat along with the peppercorns and juniper berries. Stir in the stock and brandy. Combine thoroughly.

Pour the meat mixture into a well-greased paté mold or small loaf pan. Stand the mold in a large pan of water in the oven and cook for 1¾ hours.

Remove the paté from the oven, cover it with waxed paper on foil and press it with a 2–3 lb (1 kg to 1.5 kg) weight until it is cold.

This paté will keep for up to 10 days in the refrigerator. Serve it cold with crackers and port.

Cranberry Catsup

Preparation Time: 15 minutes
Cooking Time: 20 minutes
Yield: 1 quart (1 lt)

1 lb (500 g) fresh cranberries
2 cups minced onion
3 cups light brown sugar
2 cups port wine
1 Tbsp grated orange peel
1 Tbsp cinnamon
1 Tbsp allspice
1 Tbsp pepper

Combine all the ingredients in a Dutch oven or heavy saucepan and bring them gently to a boil. Stir well, cover and simmer for 15 minutes. Serve hot or ladle into sterilized canning jars and seal. This catsup complements any poultry or game dish.

ALASKA

**APPETIZERS
SOUPS
SALADS
ENTREES**

Fishing boat moored in Whittier, Alaska.

ALASKA

MAIN COURSE

Koulibiac

Preparation Time: 30 minutes
Cooking Time: 50 minutes
Preheat Oven: 400°F (200°C)
Serves 6

1 cup short pastry dough (p. 50)
2 cups cooked white rice
1½ lbs (0.75 kg) salmon fillets, in 6 portions
3 hard-boiled eggs, chopped
1¼ cups chopped mushrooms
2 Tbsp chopped parsley or
   1 Tbsp dried parsley
3 Tbsp chopped chives
6 Tbsp melted butter
soy sauce
1 cup choux pastry dough

Divide the short pastry into 6 equal portions and roll out to 4-inch (10 cm) rounds. Pleace each in a 4-inch (10 cm) round pie dish. To assemble the koulibiac, spread 3 Tbsp of the cooked rice over each round of dough. Place a salmon fillet in the center of each and sprinkle with chopped egg, mushrooms, parsley and chives. Pour 1 Tbsp melted butter and a dash of soy sauce over the salmon and top with approximately 2 Tbsp of choux pastry. When all the pastries are assembled, bake in the preheated oven for 45–50 minutes until tops are golden. Serve immediately.

Koulibiac can be prepared in advance and kept in the refrigerator for a few hours until time for baking.

Game Hens in Orange Sauce

PHOTOGRAPH PAGE 17

Preparation Time: 20 minutes
Cooking Time: 35 minutes
Preheat Oven: 400°F (200°C)
Serves 6

3 large game hens
½ cup orange juice
1 Tbsp grated orange rind
¼ cup white wine
pinch of powdered ginger
pinch of pepper
1 tsp fresh rosemary or
   ½ tsp dried rosemary
1 tsp mace
1 tsp sugar
1 Tbsp flour
½ cup currants
10 prunes

Cut the game hens in half and place them in a large heavy pan. Cover them with boiling water and simmer for 10–12 minutes. Lift out the hens and arrange them in a clay baker or large casserole dish. Skim off the fat from the stock in which the game hens were simmered. Pour ½ cup of the stock into the blender; add the orange juice and rind, the wine, spices, sugar and flour. Blend until smooth. Sprinkle the fruit around the game hens and pour the sauce over. Bake for 20 minutes.

Sourdough Bread

PHOTOGRAPH PAGE 29

Starter: 3 days
Preparation Time: 30 minutes
Rising Time: 2½ hours
Baking Time: 30 minutes

Starter:
½ cup warm water
1 tsp sugar
1 package active dry yeast
4 cups warm water
1 Tbsp sugar
4 cups flour

Dough:
1 cup milk
¼ cup sugar
1 tsp salt
2 Tbsp shortening
7–8 cups flour

In a large, deep bowl or pot, dissolve the 1 tsp sugar and the yeast in ½ cup of warm water; let it froth for 10 minutes. When this liquor has a good "head," briskly stir in the remaining water, sugar and the flour. Mix well. Cover the container and let the starter stand for 3–4 days at room temperature. Stir daily.

To make the bread, scald the milk and stir in the sugar, salt and shortening. Take 3½ cups of the sourdough starter and mix it with the warm milk. Combine well and add 3–4 cups of flour. Beat vigorously by hand, in a food processor or with an electric mixer. Gradually add the remaining flour. Turn the dough onto a floured board and knead it well for 10 minutes until the dough is very smooth. Cover and let rise in a warm place for 1½ hours. Punch down the risen dough and divide it into 4 equal portions. Shape each portion into a loaf and place in individual greased loaf pans or on baking sheets. Brush the tops with melted butter and allow to rise for 1 hour. Bake the loaves in a preheated 375°F (190°C) oven for 30–35 minutes.

Note: To sustain the leftover sourdough mixture, add 3 cups of flour and 3 cups of warm water. Stir well and allow it to ferment for 3–4 days. Use the dough immediately or place it in the refrigerator and use once a week.

Baked Alaska Black Cod

Preparation Time: 10 minutes
Cooking Time: 40–50 minutes
Preheat Oven: 450°F (230°C)
Serves 6

5–6 lbs (2½–3 kg) black cod
¼ cup soy sauce
¼ cup peanut oil

Sauce:
¼ cup sesame oil
¼ cup chopped scallions
1 Tbsp grated fresh ginger root
¼ cup soy sauce
1 Tbsp cornstarch
2 Tbsp red wine vinegar
2 Tbsp orange juice
1 tsp sugar

Clean and trim the cod. Brush it liberally inside and out with soy sauce and peanut oil. Place the cod in a baking dish and bake it 10 minutes for each inch of thickness.

Heat the sesame oil in a saucepan; fry the scallions and ginger for 3–4 minutes. Dissolve the cornstarch in the soy sauce and stir it into the pan. Add the vinegar, orange juice and sugar; mix thoroughly. Remove the sauce from the heat as soon as it begins to thicken and pour it over the baked fish. Serve immediately.

Salmon Baked in Cedar

PHOTOGRAPH THIS PAGE

Preparation Time: 10 minutes
Cooking Time: 1 hour
Preheat Oven: 400°F (200°C)
Serves 5–6

a 5–6 lb (2½–3 kg) salmon
melted butter
cedar branches

Clean the salmon, trim it and brush it liberally inside and out with butter. Lay a piece of heavy duty aluminum foil on your workspace. The foil should be 4–5 inches (12–15 cm) longer than the salmon. Arrange a bed of fresh green cedar "leaves" on the foil. The branches should be small and light enough not to break through the foil. Place the fish on the cedar bed and cover it with additional cedar. Top with a second piece of foil.

Crimp all the edges securely then turn them up so that the juices will not escape. Bake in the preheated oven for 1 hour, or 45 minutes on a hot grill with a reflector cover. Remove the wrapping, discard the cedar and serve the salmon with wild rice. Salmon cooked in this way is very moist and has an aromatic bouquet.

ALASKA

MAIN COURSE

SALMON BAKED IN CEDAR, Recipe this page.

MAIN COURSE

Kidneys in Bacon & Red Wine Sauce

Preparation Time: 15 minutes
Cooking Time: 15 minutes
Serves 4

1 lb (500 g) veal or lamb kidneys
3 Tbsp butter
4 slices of bacon
½ tsp coriander seeds
½ tsp anise seeds
¼ cup red wine
2–3 Tbsp heavy cream

Trim the fat from the kidneys and remove any gristle. Slice crosswise into strips about ¼ inch (5 cm) thick. Sauté the slices in butter for 2–3 minutes on each side. Remove the kidney strips from the heat and place them in a chafing dish or shallow baking dish. Cover them with slices of bacon and broil for 10–12 minutes until the bacon is crisp. To the butter in the frying pan, add the coriander seeds, anise seeds and red wine. Simmer for 5 minutes. Remove from the heat and stir in the cream. Pour the sauce over the broiled kidneys and bacon.

Caribou Pie

PHOTOGRAPH PAGE 17

Preparation Time: 25 minutes
Cooking Time: 30 minutes
Baking Time: 25 minutes
Serves 4–6

2 lbs (1 kg) caribou or moose steak
3 Tbsp lemon juice
¼ cup flour
1 tsp chili powder
¼ cup pork fat or lard
½ tsp mace
3–4 bay leaves
½ tsp fresh lovage or celery seeds
1 cup red wine
rich pastry crust

Cut the meat into 1-inch (2.5 cm) cubes and roll them in lemon juice. Mix the flour and chili powder; dredge the meat cubes in the mixture. Heat the fat in a large skillet or heavy saucepan and brown the meat a few cubes at a time. When all the cubes are seared, return them to the pan; add the spices and red wine. Cover with cold water and bring to a boil. Lower the heat and simmer, covered, for ½ hour. Transfer the meat to a pie dish and top with the pastry crust. Bake at 400°F (200°C) for 20–25 minutes.

Crabzini Pie

Preparation Time: 10 minutes
Baking Time: 45 minutes
Preheat Oven: 300°F (150°C)
Serves 4

2 cups grated zucchini
1 lb (500 g) crab meat
2 Tbsp lemon juice
1 clove garlic, minced
2 Tbsp melted butter
½ tsp pepper
1 tsp sugar
½ cup sour cream
1 cup grated cheddar cheese

Combine the grated zucchini, crab, lemon juice, garlic, butter, pepper and sugar in a bowl; mix well. Stir in the sour cream and spoon the mixture into a casserole dish. Top with the grated cheese and bake for 45 minutes.

Caribou in the snowy wilderness of Alaska, with Mt. Drum in the background.

Top: SOURDOUGH BREAD, Recipe page 26.
Bottom: CORNED BEAR WITH HOT MUSTARD DILL SAUCE, Recipe this page.

Corned Bear with Hot Mustard Dill Sauce

PHOTOGRAPH THIS PAGE

Pickling Time: 3 weeks
Cooking Time: 4 hours
Serves 8–10

2 cups sea salt
¼ cup sugar
4 qts (3½ lt) hot water
2 Tbsp pickling spice
5 lbs (2½ kg) bear meat
3 cloves garlic, chopped

Dissolve the salt and sugar in hot water; stir in the pickling spice. Place the bear meat in a crock or casserole and sprinkle on the garlic. Cover with the salt water, put on the lid and allow to stand for 3 weeks in a cool place, turning the meat once a day.

To prepare for cooking, rinse the meat and soak it in clean water overnight. Pour off the water. Put it in a deep heavy pan or Dutch oven; add fresh cold water just to cover. Simmer for 4 hours.

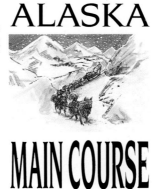

ALASKA

MAIN COURSE

Sauce:
2 Tbsp butter
1 Tbsp flour
1 Tbsp powdered mustard
pinch of pepper
1¼ cups bear stock
¾ cup half and half
¼ cup chopped fresh dill or
    2 Tbsp dried dill

Sauce:
Melt the butter in a saucepan; stir in the flour, powdered mustard and pepper. Add a few tablespoons of the hot stock and whisk to a smooth paste. Add the remaining stock. Stir and simmer for 5 minutes. Add the cream and chopped dill. Keep warm over low heat while the meat is being sliced. Serve hot.

Beautifully decorated AK-Totems at Ward Lake in Ketchikan, Alaska.

ALASKA

SWEETS

Graham Crackers

Preparation Time: 12 minutes
Cooking Time: 15 minutes
Preheat Oven: 350°F (180°C)

1 cup white flour
1 cup whole wheat flour
5 Tbsp sugar
pinch each of salt, baking soda, cinnamon
1 tsp baking powder
3 Tbsp butter
¼ cup shortening
2 Tbsp honey
1½ Tbsp molasses
1 tsp vanilla
¼ cup cold water

Sift all the dry ingredients into a bowl or food processor and combine well. Gradually cut in the butter and shortening until the mixture is crumbly. Add the honey, molasses, vanilla and enough cold water to make a stiff paste.

Spread the paste very evenly onto a 12-inch by 15-inch (30 cm x 35 cm) baking sheet. Score with a pattern of squares or rectangles of the desired size. Bake for 15 minutes. Allow the crackers to cool, then remove them from the pan and break along the scored lines.

Crab Apple Cream Pie

PHOTOGRAPH PAGE 33

Preparation Time: 40 minutes
Cooking Time: 50 minutes
Preheat Oven: 400°F (200°C)
Serves 4–6

Pastry:
1 cup all-purpose flour
½ cup shortening
pinch of salt
1 tsp mace
1 tsp cinnamon
cold water
milk

Filling:
4 cups crab apple chunks
2 cups sugar
1 tsp vanilla
1 egg, beaten
1 cup sour cream
1½ Tbsp flour

Topping:
2 Tbsp cold butter
¼ cup dark brown sugar
1 Tbsp ground ginger
¼ cup chopped walnuts

Put the flour into a bowl or food processor and cut in the shortening. Add the salt, mace and cinnamon; mix until crumbly. Gradually add 4–5 Tbsp cold water and mix until the dough just clings together. Roll out onto a lightly floured board and line a 9-inch (23 cm) pie dish. Trim and flute the edges and brush them with milk. Place the pie dish in the freezer for 10 minutes while you make the filling.

It should not be necessary to peel the crab apples but they will have to be cored. Toss well with the sugar, vanilla, egg, sour cream and flour; set aside.

In a separate bowl, combine the butter, brown sugar, ginger and walnuts; mix until crumbly.

To assemble the pie, spoon the filling into the chilled crust and press it down firmly. Sprinkle the topping thickly and loosely over the filling and bake for 50–60 minutes.

Alaska Tea

Preparation Time: 5 minutes
Steeping Time: 10 minutes
Serves 8–10

1 qt (4 cups) fresh cranberries
1 tsp cinnamon
juice of 1 lemon
2 cups orange juice
2 cups sugar
3 qts (3 lt) boiling water

Combine the cranberries, cinnamon, lemon juice, orange juice and sugar in a large saucepan and pour on the rapidly boiling water. Stir well and let the mixture steep for 10 minutes. Strain and serve hot.

The exotic-looking Skunk Cabbage flower, found on Perry Island, Alaska.

Rhubarb Pie

PHOTOGRAPH THIS PAGE

Preparation Time: 30 minutes
Cooking Time: 10 minutes
Preheat Oven: 350°F (180°C)
Chilling Time: 5 hours
Serves 6

Crust:
1½ cups Graham cracker crumbs
½ cup melted butter
2 Tbsp sugar

Filling:
3 cups rhubarb, diced
1 cup sugar
1 Tbsp grated lemon rind
2 Tbsp water
1 cup milk
1 package unflavored gelatin
1 cup heavy cream, whipped
strawberries and cream for garnish

ALASKA

SWEETS

Mix together the crumbs, butter and sugar. Butter a 9-inch (23 cm) pie plate and press the cracker mixture onto the base and sides. Bake for 8–10 minutes.

Place the diced rhubarb in a pan; add the sugar, water and lemon rind. Cover the pan and simmer the rhubarb for 10 minutes until just soft, cool to tepid. Dissolve gelatine in a little hot water, cool, then add to rhubarb. Stir in the milk. Refrigerate until it just begins to jell. Whip the cream and fold in. Pour the filling into the crust and chill it for 4–5 hours. Garnish the pie with more whipped cream and sliced strawberries.

Top: RHUBARB PIE, Recipe this page. Bottom: CRAB APPLE CREAM PIE, Recipe page 32.

Pacific Northwest

Tucking into a beer steak with hot mustard dill sauce, in some superbly isolated log cabin mountain restaurant, very much fits how many Americans perceive the Pacific North West region.

A clump of Huckleberry bushes seems to be on fire at the shore of Picture Lake on the foot of Mt. Shuksan, Washington.

PACIFIC NORTH WEST

INTRODUCTION

To those who haven't been there, the North West is a place where every man is assumed to be a kind of Grizzly Adams sporting giant lumberjack muscles under a hairy lumberjack shirt; where ladies dutifully duck between house and cowshed with buckets of milk in either hand.

In truth, this image fits some parts of the region like a glove. Both Oregon and Washington are states boasting towering mountains, tall-timbered forests, raging white-water rivers and small farm-towns.

This is a totally outdoors corner of America and a real magnet for vacationers looking to relax in the lap of nature, particularly in the back country laced with trails giving frequent and easy access to miles of saltwater beaches.

Freshwater fish abound in countless rivers and lakes, a veritable paradise for the cook who knows the value of a trout caught that morning and simply spit-grilled over an open fire for lunch an hour later.

But there is another, gentler and more sophisticated side to the North West to be found in cities like Seattle and Portland.

In these locales, elegant restaurants reflect elegant societies. In these environs, the he-man steak can be politely exchanged for Cream of Nettle Soup as a gastronomic prelude to, perhaps, Trout Wellington.

Or how about Cream of Sorrel Soup followed by Lamb with Rosemary and Hot Mint Salad nicely finalized with a delicate Apricot Soufflé with Orange Walnut Sauce (all of these delightful recipes can be found in this section of your book).

The Pacific North West is a spectacular display of nature, being both wild and tame simultaneously.

Vast areas of rugged mountain regions in Washington are enhanced by the soft contrast of Portland as "Rose City", a city noted for the finesse of its private parks and gardens where roses and rhododendrons are in numbers and types to be marveled.

The cuisine of this Pacific Ocean-bordering region is also both wild and tame, simultaneously producing dishes like Fish Roses and Ricotta Scallop Rolls.

Behind the cuisine variety lies the fact that this area boasts some of every kind of terrain and climate and virtually all of the flora and fauna areas are abundantly rich, especially in both salt- and freshwater resources.

The biggest single influence on Pacific North West diets probably originates from the early 1900s which saw 100,000-plus Europeans, mostly Scandinavians, Germans, Dutch and Swiss, arrive in search of a new land and a new life.

Until then, the eating habits of the area had been decided by the early trappers and traders whose requirements were hardy but basic. This was not really improved by the arrival of New England colonists or the pioneers retreating from the California gold rush in the mid-1800s.

The Europeans added their own distinctive agricultural stamp and the result, evolution of Pacific North West gastronomy, is reflected in the enticing list of recipes you will find in this section.

Selections from these will provide the culinary means to feed a number of guests with considerable style, or amaze "the boss" with your sophistication in the kitchen.

Top: LAMB WITH ROSEMARY & HOT MINT SALAD, Recipe page 47. *Middle*: CARROTS IN CINNAMON
SAUCE, Recipe page 44. *Bottom*: SMOKED SALMON WITH BACON & WATERCRESS CREAM, Recipe page 38.

Cream of Nettle Soup

Preparation Time: 10 minutes
Cooking Time: 30 minutes
Serves 4

3 strips bacon, chopped (optional) or
　　2 Tbsp melted butter
1 onion, chopped
1 medium potato, peeled and chopped
5 cups water
1 tsp pepper
½ tsp salt
½ tsp thyme
1 lb (500 g) fresh nettle tops
4 Tbsp heavy cream

Fry the chopped bacon and onion in a heavy pan for 10 minutes until quite soft. (Or cook the onion until soft in the melted butter). Add the potato, water and seasonings, cover and bring to a boil. Lower the heat and simmer for 15 minutes until the potato is soft. Puree the mixture in a blender or food processor until smooth. Return to the pan and add the nettle tops. Simmer for 5 minutes. Return to the blender and puree the nettles. Adjust the seasoning if necessary and keep hot until ready to serve. Ladle into individual dishes and gently swirl 1 Tbsp cream in each one.

Hot Apple Soup with Mushrooms

Preparation Time: 20 minutes
Cooking Time: 25 minutes
Serves 4

4 Tbsp butter
¼ cup scallions, chopped
2 slices of bacon, chopped
2 cups peeled and chopped apple
4 cups chicken stock
½ cup white wine
pinch each of nutmeg, pepper and salt
¼ lb (125 g) mushrooms, chopped
¼ cup heavy cream
cinnamon

In a large heavy pan, melt the butter and sauté the scallions and bacon for 5 minutes until transparent. Add the apple and 2 cups of the chicken stock. Bring to a boil, reduce the heat and cook for 10 minutes until the apple is soft. Pour the mixture into a blender and puree until smooth. Return to the pan and add the remaining stock, wine, nutmeg and seasonings to taste. Bring to a boil then reduce the heat to a simmer.

To serve, ladle the soup into bowls and place 1 Tbsp cream and 1 Tbsp chopped mushrooms in each one. Dust lightly with cinnamon.

Smoked Salmon with Bacon & Watercress Cream

Preparation Time: 15 minutes
Makes 1 snacking platter

4 strips bacon, chopped
½ lb (250 g) smoked salmon
½ lb (250 g) smoked oysters
6 egg yolks
2½ Tbsp water
1 cup vegetable oil
2½ Tbsp lemon juice
1 bunch watercress

Fry the chopped bacon bits until crisp. Drain and set aside. Slice the salmon thinly and roll it into tight fingers. Arrange the salmon and oysters attractively on a serving platter.

In a blender or food processor, beat the egg yolks and water. With the machine running on low speed, gradually add the vegetable oil and lemon juice, beating until smooth and creamy.

Blanch the watercress in boiling water for a few seconds then drop it into the blender with the creamed mixture. Puree until very smooth.

Pour the watercress cream into a bowl. Put the bacon bits in another bowl. To eat, dip a salmon roll or oyster first into the watercress cream then into the bacon bits.

Geoduck Chowder

Preparation Time: 15 minutes
Cooking Time: ½ hour
Serves 6

¼ cup vegetable oil
4 cloves garlic, minced
2 onions, chopped
2 cups celery, chopped
4 cups fish stock
1 lb (500 g) geoduck, chopped fine
3–4 potatoes, peeled and diced
2 carrots, sliced
1 bay leaf
1 tsp salt
1 tsp pepper
1 cup milk
2 Tbsp cornstarch

Heat the oil in a large heavy pan. Fry the garlic, onions and celery for 2–3 minutes. Add the stock, geoduck, vegetables, bay leaf and seasonings. Bring the mixture to a boil, lower the heat and simmer for 25 minutes. Dissolve the cornstarch in the milk and stir into the chowder. Reheat just until thickened and serve.

Left: CHICKEN MELON SALAD WITH GINGER SAUCE, Recipe this page.
Right: CREAM OF SORREL SOUP, Recipe this page.

Cream of Sorrel Soup

PHOTOGRAPH THIS PAGE

Preparation Time: 20 minutes
Cooking Time: 25 minutes
Serves 4

butter for frying
1 onion, chopped
3–4 scallions, chopped
1 potato, peeled and chopped
2 sprigs of parsley
3 cups liquid (water or light stock)
½ lb (250 g) sorrel
1 tsp sugar
salt and pepper to taste
¼ cup cream (optional)

Heat a large dab of butter in a soup pan; let it melt, then add the onion and scallions. Cook over medium heat, stirring, until tender, then add the potato, parsley and water or stock. Bring to a boil then lower the heat and simmer for 10–15 minutes. Remove from the heat and mash or blend this mixture for a few seconds.

Wash the sorrel and remove the stalks. Add it to the vegetable stock in the pan. Cook for 5 minutes. In a blender, blend the mixture at high speed to obtain a smooth, creamy soup.

Return the soup to the pan and reheat, adjusting to taste with the sugar, salt and pepper. Stir in the cream and serve.

Note: This soup should have a sharp taste, neither acidic nor sweet. The addition of cream raises it to ambrosia. Variations include spinach, lettuce or mixed herbs, but the piquant flavor of sorrel makes this version supreme.

Chicken Melon Salad with Ginger Sauce

PHOTOGRAPH THIS PAGE

Preparation Time: 10 minutes
Cooking Time: 5 minutes
Serves 4–6, or makes 1 snacking platter

1 lb (500g) cooked chicken, in 1-inch (2.5 cm) cubes
1 small honeydew melon, in 1-inch (2.5 cm) cubes
¼ cup honey
¼ cup lemon juice
1 Tbsp grated fresh ginger

Place the chicken and melon cubes in a bowl. For a party or gathering, arrange them on a platter on toothpicks.

In a small saucepan, combine the honey, lemon juice and ginger. Place over very low heat and stir for 5 minutes. Cool the dressing. Pour over the salad and toss gently.

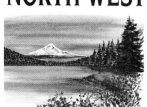

PACIFIC NORTH WEST

APPETIZERS
SOUPS
SALADS
ENTREES

A picturesque Seattle Waterfront on Elliott Bay in Washington.

PACIFIC NORTH WEST

MAIN COURSE

Ricotta Scallop Rolls

Preparation Time: 20 minutes
Cooking Time: 30 minutes
Preheat Oven: 375°F (190°C)
Yield: 20 rolls

¼ cup olive oil
1 cup fish stock or white wine
¼ cup lemon juice
1 tsp pepper
3 Tbsp heavy cream
20 nasturtium leaves
20 medium-sized scallops
1 cup ricotta cheese

Combine the olive oil, stock, lemon juice and pepper in a saucepan; bring the mixture to a boil. Reduce the heat and simmer for 5 minutes. Remove from the heat and stir in the cream. Set aside.

Wash the nasturtium leaves and remove the stems. Place them stem side up on a baking sheet. Put a scallop and 1 tsp of ricotta on each leaf. Roll up each leaf tightly and turn it over so that the loose edges are underneath. When all the leaves are rolled, pour the sauce over and bake the rolls for 30 minutes. Serve hot or cold.

Cod in Sour Cream

Preparation Time: 20 minutes
Cooking Time: 25 minutes
Preheat Oven: 400°F (200°C)
Serves 4

4 Tbsp butter
¼ cup chopped shallots
1 Tbsp chopped fresh dill or
   1½ tsp dried dill
1 Tbsp chopped fresh parsley or
   1½ tsp dried parsley
1 Tbsp chopped fresh basil or
   1½ tsp dried basil
½ tsp pepper
pinch of salt
1 lb (500 g) cod fillets
2–3 tomatoes
1½ cups sour cream

Melt the butter in a saucepan; add the shallots, herbs, salt and pepper. Fry for 3–4 minutes until the shallots are transparent.

Wash the fillets and pat them dry; arrange them in a buttered baking dish. Blanch the tomatoes for a few seconds in boiling water then remove the skins. Chop the tomatoes coarsely and stir them into the herbed sauce.

Heap the sauce over the fillets. Carefully spoon the sour cream over the top and bake for 25 minutes.

Hot and Sweet Yard-Long Beans

Preparation Time: 5 minutes
Cooking Time: 10 minutes
Serves 4

1 lb (500 g) yard long beans
3 Tbsp butter
1 Tbsp grated fresh ginger
1 Tbsp powdered mustard
2 Tbsp lime juice
2 Tbsp brown sugar
1 Tbsp cornstarch
1 Tbsp soy sauce
¼ cup finely chopped chives
¼ cup roasted salted peanuts, chopped

Trim the ends of the beans and place them in a large saucepan. Cover with boiling water and boil for 6–8 minutes until just cooked. Drain the beans and place in a serving dish; keep hot.

In a saucepan, melt the butter; stir in the ginger, mustard, lime juice, sugar, cornstarch and soy sauce. Stir these ingredients over low heat until dissolved then add the chives and peanuts. Continue to heat and stir the sauce until it thickens slightly. Pour the sauce over the hot beans and serve immediately.

Note: Yard-long beans are a traditional favorite in China and may be found in Chinese produce markets.

Hot Orange Celery

Preparation Time: 10 minutes
Cooking Time: 25 minutes
Preheat Oven: 400°F (200°C)
Serves 4

4 cups chopped celery
1 cup sour cream
1 Tbsp powdered mustard
1 Tbsp fresh orange juice
1 cup grated cheddar cheese
¼ cup sesame seeds

Place the celery in a saucepan, cover it with boiling water and boil for 3–4 minutes. Drain. Stir in the sour cream, mustard, orange juice and cheese; mix well. Pour into a small baking dish and top with sesame seeds. Bake for 20 minutes until the sesame seeds start to brown.

ARTICHOKE HEARTS & SNOW PEAS WITH SOUR CREAM & HONEY, Recipe this page.

Artichoke Hearts & Snow Peas with Sour Cream & Honey

PHOTOGRAPH THIS PAGE

Preparation Time: 10 minutes
Cooking Time: 35 minutes
Preheat Oven: 325°F (160°C)
Serves 4

4 fresh artichokes, or canned artichoke hearts
2 Tbsp lemon juice
1 lb (500 g) snow peas
2 Tbsp liquid honey
½ cup sour cream
pinch of rosemary
pinch of pepper

Discard the outer leaves of the artichokes. Place the hearts in a pan, add the lemon juice and cover with boiling water. Simmer for 25 minutes. Drain and cool. When cool enough to handle, cut the artichokes in half and remove the pith (choke). Arrange them in a 1-inch (2.5 cm) baking dish and cover with the snow peas. Whip together the honey, sour cream, rosemary and pepper. Spoon this mixture over the vegetables. Place in the preheated oven for 10 minutes until warmed through.

Note: Canned artichokes can be substituted in which case there is no need to precook; they can be placed directly in the baking dish with the peas.

Jerusalem Artichokes & Peas

Preparation Time: 10 minutes
Cooking Time: 10–12 minutes
Serves 6

1 lb (500 g) Jerusalem artichokes
½ lb (250 g) fresh green peas
2 Tbsp butter
1 small bunch scallions, chopped
1 Tbsp chopped fresh mint or
*   1½ tsp dried mint*
1 tsp sugar

Peel and slice the artichokes and place them in a heavy pan with the peas. Cover the vegetables with boiling water, bring to a boil, lower the heat and simmer for 3–4 minutes. Drain off the water. Add the butter, scallions, mint and sugar. Stir to mix well. Toss to coat the vegetables then place over low heat for 5–10 minutes. Serve hot.

PACIFIC NORTH WEST

MAIN COURSE

Leeks with Broccoli Sauce

Preparation Time: 10 minutes
Cooking Time: 15 minutes
Serves 4

1 lb (500 g) leeks
1 Tbsp butter
1 cup cooked broccoli
½ cup heavy cream
1 Tbsp lime juice
pinch of cayenne
2 Tbsp butter

Wash the leeks thoroughly, trim the roots, and chop the white ends and tender, pale green leaves. (Save the dark green tops for soups or stock.) Cover with water in a pan and simmer for 10–12 minutes until just soft. Drain the leeks, stir in 1 Tbsp butter, cover and keep warm until ready to serve.

Make sure the broccoli flowers and stalks are tender. Place the broccoli in a food processor or blender and puree until smooth. Add the cream, lemon juice and cayenne; mix well. Melt 2 Tbsp butter in a saucepan and add the broccoli puree. Heat slowly, stirring occasionally, until the sauce is hot. Serve over the leeks.

Carrots in Cinnamon Sauce

PHOTOGRAPH PAGE 37

Preparation Time: 4 minutes
Cooking Time: 10 minutes
Serves 4

1 lb (500 g) small whole carrots
1 Tbsp long grated coconut
2 Tbsp light brown sugar
½ tsp cinnamon
1 Tbsp soy sauce
1 Tbsp lemon juice

Scrub the carrots and place them in a small saucepan. Sprinkle on all the other ingredients. Add just enough boiling water to barely cover. Simmer for 7–8 minutes. Remove the carrots with a slotted spoon and keep warm. Vigorously boil the sauce for 2 minutes to reduce it. Pour the sauce over the carrots and serve.

Stir-Fried Sea Cucumbers

Preparation Time: 20 minutes
Cooking Time: 20 minutes
Serves 4

4 Tbsp peanut oil
1 cup sliced green peppers
1 cup snow peas
1 cup sliced mushrooms
1 cup bean sprouts
1 lb (500 g) sea cucumber fillets
1 Tbsp grated fresh ginger
1 Tbsp soy sauce
1 Tbsp cornstarch
¼ cup sesame seeds
oyster sauce
cooked rice

To fillet a sea cucumber, cut it lengthwise and open it flat. Remove and discard the viscera. Wash the sea cucumber in cold water. Cut the meat into long, thin strips, discarding the skin. Drop the fillets in boiling salted water and cook for 20 minutes. Remove from the heat, drain and pat dry.

To stir-fry, heat 1 Tbsp peanut oil in a wok or large skillet until very hot but not smoking. Add the pepper strips and fry them for 1 minute, stirring constantly. Remove the peppers and set aside. Add ½ Tbsp peanut oil to the wok and fry the snow peas, mushrooms and bean sprouts in turn for a few minutes each. Pour off the pan juices into a cup; add the remaining peanut oil to the wok. Stir-fry the sea cucumber fillets and the grated ginger for about 4 minutes. Drain and set aside.

In a cup, mix the vegetable juices, soy sauce and cornstarch; stir to dissolve. Pour the cornstarch mixture into the wok; add all the vegetables and the fillets. Stir briskly over medium heat until the vegetables and fillets are nicely glazed. Remove from the heat and sprinkle with sesame seeds. Serve immediately with rice and oyster sauce.

Abalone Steaks

Preparation Time: 7 minutes
Cooking Time: 6 minutes
Serves 6

1 lb (500 g) abalone meat
¼ cup all-purpose flour
pinch of cayenne
2 eggs, beaten
¼ cup shredded coconut
butter or oil for frying

Slice the abalone into small steaks, ¼-inch (6 mm) thick, cutting across the grain. Lay the steaks on a sheet of plastic wrap or waxed paper and cover them with a second sheet. Beat the steaks gently for 1 minute with a mallet or knife handle. In a skillet, heat the butter or oil to 375°F (190°C). Mix the flour and cayenne together. Dredge the steaks first in flour, then in the beaten eggs and finally in the coconut. Fry for 3 minutes on each side in the hot oil or butter. Drain the abalone steaks and serve hot with lemon wedges.

TROUT WELLINGTON, Recipe this page.

Trout Wellington

PHOTOGRAPH THIS PAGE

Preparation Time: 15 minutes (not including
    pastry)
Cooking Time: 30 minutes
Preheat Oven: 400°F (200°C)
Serves 4

2 Tbsp butter
2 Tbsp lemon juice
½ tsp pepper
1 cup shrimp meat
2 Tbsp sherry
2 Tbsp capers
4 trout, boned
puff pastry (p. 230)
1 egg, beaten

Melt the butter in a saucepan; add the lemon
juice, pepper and shrimp meat. Simmer for 5
minutes. Remove from the heat and add the
sherry. Process in a food processor to a smooth
paste. Stir in the capers.

Wash the trout and pat them dry. Place them on
a buttered baking sheet with at least 1-inch
(2½ cm) of space around them. Spread the shrimp
paste over the fish. Make the pastry and roll out ⅛-
inch (3 mm) thick. Cut the pastry into four sheets
and cover each fillet. Tuck in the sides firmly, brush
with beaten egg and bake for 30 minutes.

Fish Roses

Preparation Time: 20 minutes
Cooking Time: 30 minutes
Preheat Oven: 400°F (200°C)
Serves 4

¾ lb (375 g) sole fillets
¾ lb (375 g) spring salmon fillets
1 cup fish or chicken stock
½ cup dry white wine
1 Tbsp olive oil
1 Tbsp flour
1 tsp fresh tarragon or
    ½ tsp dried tarragon
3–4 drops concentrated rosewater
1 tsp pepper
1 Tbsp lime juice

Wash the fillets and pat them dry. The fillets should
not be larger than 10-inches by 2-inches (25 cm by
5 cm). If they are larger, cut them into diagonal
strips. Roll up each fillet tightly and arrange in a
shallow oven-to-table baking dish. (The rolled
fillets will resemble a bouquet of red and white
roses.) Combine the remaining ingredients in a
blender or bowl and mix until smooth. Heat the
mixture in a pan until it comes to a boil. Pour over
the fish and bake in the preheated oven for
25 minutes. Serve immediately.

PACIFIC NORTH WEST

MAIN COURSE

MAIN COURSE

Beef with Walnut-Orange Stuffing

PHOTOGRAPH THIS PAGE

Preparation Time: 10 minutes
Cooking Time: 30 minutes
Preheat Oven: 400°F (200°C)
Serves 4

1 Tbsp butter
1 bunch chives, chopped
¼ cup chopped walnuts
½ cup orange sections, chopped
1 Tbsp cornstarch
1 tsp powdered mustard
2 Tbsp red wine
1½ lb (750 g) beef fillet

Melt the butter in a saucepan; add the chives, walnuts and orange sections. Simmer for 5 minutes. Dissolve the cornstarch and mustard in the red wine and stir into the sauce. Simmer, stirring constantly, until the mixture is slightly thickened.

Trim any fat from the meat and cut the fillet almost in half lengthwise. Then cut each half almost in half again. This makes three equally spaced slashes. Fill these cuts with the orange stuffing and heap any remainder down the center. Lift up both sides of the meat until they meet at the top to form a roll and tie it a 1-inch (2.5 cm) intervals with a string. Place the roll, cut side down, in a narrow baking dish and brush the top with any remaining pan juices. Bake for 25-30 minutes, basting after 15 minutes to glaze the top.

To serve, lift out the meat and remove the string. Cut the beef crosswise into four serving pieces. The stuffing will have formed a star-shaped pattern through each steak. Top with a spoonful of juices.

Deep-Fried Red Chard

PHOTOGRAPH PAGE 46

Preparation Time: 10 minutes
Cooking Time: 10–12 minutes
Serves 4–5 as a side dish

1 lb (500 g) Swiss chard
1 egg
4 Tbsp flour
¼ tsp pepper
¼ tsp mace
oil for frying

Wash the chard and cut out the center rib of each leaf. Place in a lidded pan and stew in the moisture clinging to the leaves for 4–5 minutes. Do not drain. Chop the chard with a vegetable chopper or in a food processor or blender. Add the egg, flour, pepper and mace and mix well.

Heat 2 Tbsp oil in a skillet and drop spoonfuls of the chard batter into the hot oil to form small pancakes, about 2-inches (5 cm) in diameter. Fry for 3-4 minutes on one side then turn and fry for 2-3 minutes on the other. Lift out the chard cakes with a slotted spoon, drain them on a paper towel and keep them warm until all the batter is used up. Add more oil to the pan as needed.

Lamb with Rosemary & Hot Mint Salad

PHOTOGRAPH PAGE 37

Preparation Time: 10 minutes
Cooking Time: 25 minutes
Serves 4

8 loin or rib lamb chops
3 Tbsp butter
2 Tbsp chopped fresh rosemary or
    1 Tbsp dried rosemary
1 tsp pepper
1 pear
1 banana
small bunch fresh mint

Wash the lamb chops and pat them dry. Melt the butter in a large skillet; stir in the rosemary and pepper. Fry the chops for 10 minutes on each side. Remove them from the skillet and keep warm. Retain meat juices in skillet.

Peel and coarsely chop the pear and banana. Wash the mint and shake dry; pull off the leaves and chop them finely. Combine the mint and fruit.

Add the fruit to the meat juices in the skillet and heat, stirring constantly, for 2 minutes until warm.

Place a spoonful of fruit on each chop before serving.

Elephant Garlic Bread

Preparation Time: 5 minutes
Cooking Time: ½ hour
Preheat Oven: 400°F (200°C)
Serves 4

16 cloves elephant garlic
1 French loaf
butter

Separate the cloves and brush off any dirt. Leave the skins on. Place the garlic on a small baking sheet and bake for ½ hour. Remove the garlic from the oven and cool slightly. The garlic will be crisp on the outside and creamy soft inside.

Cut through a fresh, warm French loaf and butter the slices. Crack open the garlic skins and squeeze out the creamy insides, spreading liberally on the bread slices.

Serve as an accompaniment to almost any baked pasta or seafood dish.

Note: Elephant garlic is a giant variety of regular garlic with a mild, sweet garlicky flavor. It has a gorgeous creamy texture when baked and is much easier to eat in company than its smaller relative.

Octopus Fennel Stew

Preparation Time: 10 minutes
Cooking Time: 50 minutes
Serves 4

2 Tbsp butter
2 cloves garlic, minced
2 cups fish stock
1 lb (500 g) octopus
1 lb (500 g) fennel
1 small bunch fresh mint

In a heavy pan or Dutch oven, melt the butter and fry the garlic over medium heat for 5 minutes or until light brown. Add the stock and heat to a simmer. Skin the octopus tentacles (or ask your fish store manager to do this for you) and cut them into 1-inch (2.5 cm) pieces. Beat the meat with a mallet or tenderizer to soften it. Wash the fennel bulbs and cut them into 1-inch (2.5 cm) pieces. Stir the octopus meat, fennel pieces and mint leaves into the stock. Simmer, covered, over low heat for 45–50 minutes. Serve hot with elephant garlic bread (This Page).

PACIFIC NORTH WEST

MAIN COURSE

Freshly logged trees at one side of the many timber forests in the Pacific Northwest.

Rhubarb Sorbet

Preparation Time: 20 minutes
Cooking Time: 7–8 hours
Serves 6

2 cups rhubarb cut in 1-inch (2.5 cm) pieces
2 cups water
½ cup sugar
2 Tbsp lemon juice
1 Tbsp grated fresh ginger
2 egg whites, stiffly beaten

Combine the rhubarb, water, sugar, lemon juice and ginger in a heavy pan. Bring to a boil and simmer for 10–12 minutes until the rhubarb is very soft. Remove from the heat and sieve through a strainer into a bowl to eliminate the rhubarb fiber. Cool. When the mixture is completely cool, place it in the freezer for about 2 hours until it starts to freeze. Break up any ice and add the beaten egg whites. Mix well and return to the freezer. After 2 hours, again break up the ice and beat well. Pour the mixture into molds and freeze for 3–4 hours or overnight.

Serve the rhubarb sorbet after the main meat course and before a sweet dessert.

Note: If sorbets appear to be frozen too hard, they can be softened by placing them in the refrigerator for 15–20 minutes prior to serving.

Fried Peppermint Custard Creams

Preparation Time: 25 minutes
Cooking Time: 2 hours
Frying Time: 4 minutes
Yield: 15–20 creams

¼ cup sugar
¼ cup flour
3 eggs
3 cups milk
1 small bunch fresh peppermint
¼ cup brandy
1 egg
2 Tbsp sugar
1 cup chopped hazelnuts
oil for frying
heavy cream

Beat together the sugar, flour and eggs. Pour the milk into a saucepan with the mint and heat until scalded. Let cook over very low heat for 10 minutes. Discard the mint and gradually pour the flavored milk into the egg mixture. Combine well and return to the pan. Heat, stirring constantly, until the custard is quite thick. Remove from the heat and stir in the brandy. Flour an oblong or square pan or dish and pour the custard into it to a depth of about 1 inch. Cool then chill.

When the custard is firm, cut it into squares or rounds with a cookie cutter. Beat together the egg and 2 Tbsp of sugar. Dip the custards first in the egg mixture then in the chopped nuts.

Pour ½-inch (1.25 cm) of vegetable oil in a skillet and heat to 375°F (190°C). Fry the custard creams for 2-3 minutes on each side until golden. Drain and serve warm with heavy cream. These custards are also delicious served cold.

Plumskis

Preparation Time: 20 minutes
Cooking Time: 35 minutes
Preheat Oven: 350°F (180°C)
Yield: 12

12 perfect plums
¼ cup ground almonds
½ cup sugar
2 Tbsp bourbon

Pastry:
2 cups flour
1 cup butter
1 egg, beaten
2–3 Tbsp milk

Glaze:
1 egg, beaten
3 Tbsp lemon juice
½ cup ground almonds
2 Tbsp sugar

Whipping cream

Carefully halve the plums and pit them. Beat together the almonds, sugar and bourbon to make a thick paste. Spoon 1 tsp of the paste into each plum half and press the halves together.

Sift the flour and cut in the butter. Mix until crumbly then add the beaten egg. Add just enough milk to make a soft dough. Roll out on a lightly floured board ¼-inch (6 mm) thick. Cut the rolled dough into twelve 3-inch (7.5 cm) by 4-inch (10.2 cm) rectangles.

Cover each stuffed plum with pastry, carefully tucking in the ends to seal. Place the plum rolls 1 inch (2.5 cm) apart on a greased baking dish. Bake for 25 minutes.

Beat the egg, lemon juice, almonds and sugar together and brush the glaze over the hot plum rolls. Return to the oven and bake for 10 minutes longer. Allow the rolls to cool slightly. Serve warm or cold with lightly whipped cream. Do not chill.

Top: CIDER SYLLABUB, Recipe this page.
Bottom: APRICOT SOUFFLÉ WITH ORANGE WALNUT SAUCE, Recipe this page.

Cider Syllabub

PHOTOGRAPH THIS PAGE

Preparation Time: 3 minutes
Serves 4

2 Tbsp sugar
½ pt (1¼ cups) whipping cream
12 oz (360 ml) bottle dry cider, chilled
cinnamon

In a bowl, whip the sugar and cream until fairly stiff. Pour on ¼ bottle of cider and whip again. Pour on another ¼ bottle of cider and whip. Continue until all the cider is whipped into the cream. The drink will have the consistency of a thick milkshake and have a light, refreshing taste.

Pour into serving glasses, dust lightly with cinnamon and serve.

Apricot Soufflé with Orange Walnut Sauce

PHOTOGRAPH THIS PAGE

Preparation Time: 40 minutes
Chilling Time: 4 hours
Serves 6

Soufflé:
1 lb (500 g) fresh apricots
2 cups milk
¼ cup sugar
2 eggs
1 Tbsp grated orange rind
1½ cups heavy cream

Sauce:
2 Tbsp butter
2 Tbsp chopped walnuts
¼ cup sugar
¼ cup orange juice
¼ cup Amaretto

Soufflé:
Pit the apricots and drop the fruit halves into boiling water for 2–3 seconds to loosen the skins. Peel the apricots and place them in a saucepan with the milk. Gently heat to a simmer, cover and cook over low heat for 10–12 minutes until the apricots are soft. Pour the milk and apricots into a food processor or blender and puree until smooth. Blend in the sugar, eggs and orange rind. Return the mixture to the pan and cook gently, stirring occasionally, until the custard thickens. Cool. Whip the cream until thick and fold it into the cooled custard. Pour the mixture into individual molds and chill for at least 3–4 hours.

Sauce:
Melt the butter in a saucepan and add the walnuts, sugar and orange juice. Simmer the mixture for 7–8 minutes. Remove from the heat and stir in the Amaretto. Serve the sauce warm with the soufflé.

PACIFIC NORTH WEST

SWEETS

New England

The overall charisma of New England and the three states it comprises is a pervading sense of the delicate.

Much of this can be attributed to the Pilgrim Fathers (a visit to Boston to see the Mayflower is worthwhile if you get the chance)

The last traces of morning mist linger in the brilliant Autumn leaves at Vermont in East Corinth, New England.

NEW ENGLAND

INTRODUCTION

and the Irish, English and Scottish bloodlines that now reach out throughout virtually all New England communities.

Boston, capital of Massachusetts (the oldest of the three states), has also adopted the role of being the unofficial capital of the region.

Village greens or commons and spired tiny churches are the hallmark of England's (UK) rural areas and this is largely true of much of Massachusetts.

Indeed, New England's village commons are a British heritage, leftover from the 17th century when village greens (usually called The Common) were literally common land for the residents to graze livestock, hold community festivals, town meetings and generally provide a recreational focus.

The oldest known public park in America is Boston Common, though it contrasts curiously these days against a background of major ultra-modern architectural developments.

Some say New England is the root of American culture and the home of powerful brains, a debatable generalization, though with 13% of the nation's education and research resources, possibly not without foundation.

Nevertheless, New Englanders certainly know how to eat well, though typical menus for "elegant eating" have long since departed from the European strains of the people's origins. Culinary delights New England style tend to be delicate and sophisticated in keeping with how they like to view their lifestyles.

The cuisine has evolved over the last century to become identifiably "New England" with the major influence being an abundance of food resources, especially fish and seafood varieties.

The region is part of the world's richest fishing grounds with water that gradually gets colder from south to north (hence the wide varieties).

Fishing is carefully controled (they are almost paranoiac about over-fishing) and lobster, an expensive menu item in most parts of the world, is an especially abundant item.

Most of the major communities lie along the Atlantic coast (Vermont is an exception) which further accounts for a strong seafood bias.

Long chilly winters with short cool summers, plus a typical rainfall of between 32" (87½ cm) to 45" (1 mtr 125 cm) per annum, give a growing season of around 150 days.

Some 80% of New England is forest with trees towering up to an astonishing 240ft (7 mtrs 312 cm).

Coastal plains are a milder climate and the area is renowned for dairy farming plus a strong emphasis on poultry and fruit. New England cranberries and blueberries are among the finest in the world, as is New England maple syrup.

Adventurous cooks tend to lean towards French cuisine for dinner parties where a lofty social impression is more important than nourishment.

New England cuisine provides both, and it's a fair bet that many of the dishes you will find in this section will be new to your guests — which guarantees you the first 10 points of a high-scoring successful meal.

Who would fail to be impressed by dishes like pheasant with fruit stuffing or duck in kumquat sauce.

Top: ROSE PETAL HERB SALAD, Recipe page 58. *Bottom:* FLOUNDER IN MUSTARD & BURNT ALMONDS, Recipe page 64. **page 55**

Massachusetts Clam Chowder

Preparation Time: 20 minutes
Cooking Time: 35–40 min.
Serves 4

½ cup chopped salt pork or bacon
1 onion, chopped
1 cup peeled and diced potato
2 cups liquid (10 oz (315 g) can clam juice and white wine
to make 2 cups)
1 cup fresh or canned clams
1 cup milk
1 Tbsp fresh or dry thyme
1 Tbsp fresh parsley or
  1½ tsp dried parsley
pepper to taste

In a large heavy saucepan, fry the salt pork or bacon bits until crisp; toss in the onion, and cook for 5 minutes, stirring frequently to avoid sticking. Add the diced potato and clam juice, bring to a boil then reduce the heat and simmer for 10 minutes. If the clams are large, chop them (I use scissors) but don't mince. Add the clams, milk, thyme and parsley. Simmer for 5 minutes longer. Add pepper to taste and serve.   If you're not counting calories or cholesterol levels, a dollop of fresh butter on each serving will enhance the flavor.

Coriander Soup

Preparation Time: 10 minutes
Cooking Time: 20–25 minutes
Serves 4

1 potato, peeled and chopped
2 Tbsp butter
1 Tbsp ground coriander seed
1 tsp ground cumin
4 cups chicken stock or chicken consommé
juice of ½ lemon
1 tsp pepper
½ cup light cream
fresh coriander for garnish

Cook the potato in a small amount of water until soft enough to mash. Add the butter, coriander, cumin and stock to the mashed potato. Stir while simmering for 5 minutes. Add the lemon juice and pepper. Stir in the cream and gently reheat. Serve with chopped fresh coriander leaves.

Notes: If you substitute canned consommé for stock, omit the potato. You can also use prepared curry powder in lieu of the cumin and pepper, but it will introduce other flavors. A recipe for Madras style curry powder can be found on page 22.

Fresh coriander can often be obtained at local supermarkets and is a staple at Chinese groceries. To grow your own, throw a few whole coriander seeds in a pot or jar. Keep them at 60–70°F (30°–40°C) and slightly damp. The sprouts should be big enough to cut in 3–4 days.

Anadama Bread

Preparation Time: 15 minutes
Rising Time: 1 hour
Baking Time: 50–60 minutes
Yield: 2 loaves

If you haven't tried this unusual bread yet, you may enjoy the apocryphal story that goes with it and contributes in no small measure to the flavor. A New England farmer became so enraged with his wife's dull and repetitious fare of cornmeal and molasses that he mixed the two together along with flour and yeast and cooked it himself, muttering all the while, "Anna, damn her!"

2 cups water
1 cup yellow cornmeal
¼ cup vegetable oil
½ cup molasses
½ cup warm water
1 package active dry yeast
1 egg, beaten
3–4 cups all-purpose flour
salt to taste

In a saucepan combine the water, cornmeal, oil and molasses. Bring to a boil and boil gently for 1 minute, stirring constantly. Remove from the heat.

In a large bowl, stir together the yeast and warm water. Add half the flour and mix well. Pour in the warm cornmeal mixture and the beaten egg. Gradually add the rest of the flour until you have a soft, sticky dough.

Grease two loaf pans and divide the batter between them. Sprinkle the tops with a little extra cornmeal and allow to rise in a warm place uncovered for about 1 hour.

Bake at 375°F (190°C) for 50–60 minutes. Cool on a rack before slicing.

Top: ORANGE PUMPKIN SOUP, Recipe this page.
Bottom left: BOSTON BROWN BREAD, Recipe this page.

Orange Pumpkin Soup

PHOTOGRAPH THIS PAGE

Preparation Time: 15 minutes
Cooking Time: 25 minutes
Serves 5–6

2 Tbsp butter
½ onion, chopped
14-oz (410 g) can pumpkin
4 cups chicken stock
1 cup orange juice
½ cup heavy cream
1 tsp pepper
orange slices

In a heavy pan, melt the butter and gently fry the onion until golden. Add the pumpkin and stock, bring to a boil and simmer for 10 minutes, stirring occasionally. Blend the mixture in a blender for a few seconds then return it to the pan.

Stir in the orange juice, cream and pepper. Gently reheat but do not boil. Serve with an orange slice floated on top.

It is interesting to note that, weight for weight, pumpkin contains as much Vitamin A as spinach.

Boston Brown Bread

PHOTOGRAPH THIS PAGE

I offer this recipe in its original form as it was supposed to be boiled in a coffee can alongside the beans with which it was served.

Preparation Time: 15 minutes
Cooking Time: 2½ hours
Yield: 2 loaves

1 cup whole wheat flour
1 cup rye flour
1 cup cornmeal
1½ tsp baking soda
½ tsp salt
¾ cup molasses
2 cups sour milk
1 cup raisins

In a large bowl mix well the first five ingredients. Gradually add the molasses, sour milk and raisins, mixing all the time.

Liberally butter the insides of two clean 1-lb (500 g) coffee cans. Pour in the batter. Cover each tin with a sheet of wax paper and a square of aluminum foil. Secure with string.

Stand the cans upright on a rack in a deep pan and add enough boiling water to reach halfway up the tins. Cover the pan with a lid, bring the water to a boil, then lower the heat and simmer for 2½ hours.

To serve, remove the cans from the pan, take off the foil and paper caps, turn the cans upside down and remove the bottoms with a can opener. Then push out the loaves onto a bread board, slice and serve hot.

This bread is almost a meal in itself and rather resembles the old English boiled puddings, with which it no doubt shares a common ancestor.

NEW ENGLAND

APPETIZERS
SOUPS
SALADS
ENTREES

NEW ENGLAND

APPETIZERS SOUPS SALADS ENTREES

Summer Morning Apple Juice

Preparation Time: 5 minutes
Serves 4

8 juicy red apples
¼ cup lemon juice
2 Tbsp chopped fresh mint

Put the apples through a juice extractor. Mix with lemon juice and stir in the mint. Serve chilled.

Tomato Ice Cream

Preparation Time: 10 minutes
Chilling Time: 1½ hours
Serves 4

This unusual item makes a refreshing appetizer for a barbeque or late night supper party.

2–3 ripe tomatoes
2 tsp lemon juice
Tabasco sauce
salt and pepper to taste
1 cup heavy cream

Skin the tomatoes by dropping them in boiling water for a few seconds after which the skin will come away easily. Place the tomatoes in a blender or food mill; add the lemon juice and seasonings. (I put in a generous dash of Tabasco and a pinch of pepper but no salt.) Blend to a puree.

Whip the cream. Stir in the tomato puree, then whip again. Spoon the mixture into molds or dishes and freeze for a couple of hours until mushy.

Serve with Scotch or rye.

Note: Do not leave tomato ice cream in the freezer too long or it will set like ice.

Rose Petal Herb Salad

PHOTOGRAPH PAGE 55

Preparation Time: 15 minutes
Serves 4

1 cup fresh rose petals
1 small bunch chives
¼ cup fresh mint
1 sprig lemon balm
½ cup purslane
1 orange peeled and sectioned
3 fresh figs
1 tsp grated orange rind
¼ cup slivered blanched almonds
2 Tbsp olive oil
2 Tbsp cider vinegar
½ tsp sugar

Clean, rinse and gently pat dry the rose petals and herbs. Tear the herbs into small pieces; the rose petals may be left whole. Chop the orange sections and figs; add to the herb mixture along with the orange rind and almonds.

Blend the oil, vinegar and sugar in a blender for a few seconds. Pour over the salad, toss lightly and serve immediately.

A rose petal salad? Not as exotic as it may at first appear. Most of the ingredients are readily available. If you can't find lemon balm or purslane in the market, both are very easily grown from seed and are listed in most seed catalogues.

Cheese Watercress Salad

Preparation Time: 10 minutes
Serves 4

1 bunch watercress
1 lb tomatoes
1 package cream cheese
small bunch chives
2 Tbsp fresh thyme
large pinch of pepper
½ tsp sugar
½ tsp powdered mustard
2 Tbsp cider vinegar
1½–2 Tbsp olive oil

Wash, dry and pull apart the watercress. In a bowl, chop the tomatoes and add the watercress. Cut the cream cheese into pieces the size of sugar cubes and roll in a mixture of finely chopped chives and thyme. Add them to the cress and tomatoes.

In a blender, put the pepper, sugar, mustard, vinegar and oil. Blend for a few seconds. Pour the dressing over the salad and toss lightly until the ingredients are well coated.

Celery & Horseradish Cream

PHOTOGRAPH PAGE 59

Preparation Time: 15 minutes
Makes: 15-20 pieces

1 tsp sugar
1 cup cream cheese
½ cup sesame seeds
1 small bunch celery
¼ cup butter
½ cup heavy cream
½ cup grated fresh horseradish

Separate the celery stalks, wash and dry them.

Cream together the butter, cream, horseradish, sugar and cheese. Press the mixture into the hollow side of the celery stalks. Cut the stalks into 3-inch (8 cm) lengths and coat the filled side with the sesame seeds.

Chill; serve while fresh and crisp.

Scrambled Eggs with Sour Cream & Red Caviar

PHOTOGRAPH THIS PAGE

Preparation Time: 6 minutes
Cooking Time: 3 minutes
Serves 2

1 Tbsp butter
4 large eggs
¼ cup light cream
6 sprigs chives

½ tsp freshly ground pepper
4 hot, buttered, savory biscuits
4 tsp red caviar
4 tsp sour cream
1 lime

In a small iron skillet, melt the butter over medium heat. Beat the eggs and cream together until just mixed; do not overbeat. Pour the eggs into the hot pan and stir gently with a wooden spatula. Add the chopped chives and pepper; stir again. Cook quickly, stirring occasionally, until just set. Remove from the heat, stir once more, and mound over the hot buttered biscuits. Place 1 tsp of sour cream and 1 tsp of caviar on each mound. Serve at once with a lime garnish.

NEW ENGLAND

APPETIZERS
SOUPS
SALADS
ENTREES

Top: SCRAMBLED EGGS WITH SOUR CREAM & RED CAVIAR, Recipe this page.
Bottom: CELERY & HORSERADISH CREAM, Recipe page 58.

Restaurants, shops and produce market at Faneuil Hall Market Place in New England.

Shaker Bean Casserole

Preparation Time: 15 minutes
Cooking Time: 45 minutes
Preheat Oven: 350°F (180°C)
Serves 4–5

1½ lbs (750 g) green beans
2 Tbsp butter
1 onion, finely chopped or grated
1 Tbsp flour
1 tsp sugar
1 tsp pepper
1 cup sour cream
½ lb (250 g) cheddar cheese, grated
½ cup buttered bread crumbs or corn flakes

Slice the beans diagonally and boil rapidly in a small amount of water for 6–8 minutes or until almost cooked but still quite firm. Drain the beans and place them in a casserole or pie dish.

Melt the butter and sauté the onion for 2 minutes. Stir in the flour. Remove from the heat and stir in the sugar, pepper and sour cream. Pour the mixture over the beans and stir well. Spread the grated cheese over the top. Finish with a layer of breadcrumbs or crushed corn flakes. Bake for about ½ hour or until the top is golden and bubbly.

Sweet & Sour Pineapple Peppers

Preparation Time: 15 minutes
Cooking Time: 12 minutes
Serves 6

6 medium sweet red peppers
1 16-oz (500 g) can crushed pineapple
¼ cup white wine vinegar
¼ cup sugar
1 Tbsp powdered mustard
2 Tbsp cornstarch
1 bunch scallions, chopped

Remove the tops and seeds of the peppers. If the peppers have uneven ends, trim them so they will stand up, but be careful not to cut holes in the peppers or they will leak. Set aside.

Strain the pineapple, reserving the juice. In a bowl, mix the vinegar, sugar, mustard and cornstarch. Add the pineapple juice and mix until the sugar and cornstarch are completely dissolved. Add the pineapple pulp and chopped scallions. Stir the ingredients until they are well mixed and spoon into the peppers.

Stand the peppers close together in a pan half filled with hot water. (Take care not to get any water inside the peppers.) Gently poach the peppers for 12–15 minutes until cooked but not mushy; the filling should be syrupy.

Ginger Roasted Fennel

Preparation Time: 15 minutes
Cooking Time: 20 minutes
Preheat Oven: 400°F (200°C)
Serves 4

1 lb (500 g) fresh fennel
2 Tbsp water
2 Tbsp butter
2 Tbsp sugar
1 Tbsp ground ginger

Clean and trim the fennel. (Save the feathery tops for garnishing soups and salads.) Place it in a pan of slightly salted boiling water; boil for 10 minutes until almost soft.

Mix the remaining ingredients in a saucepan and bring to a boil. Continue to boil, stirring constantly, until the mixture is syrupy.

Remove the fennel from the water. Pat dry and place in a baking dish. Brush the fennel with the syrup until completely coated; pour over the rest of the syrup. Roast in the preheated oven for 10 minutes. (Baste after 5 minutes.) The syrup should be bubbling and golden brown. Serve hot.

Baked Beans

Preparation Time: 10 minutes
Cooking Time: at least 6 hours
Serves 12

½ cup molasses
4 cups dried navy or white beans
1 lb (500 g) fatty salt pork
1 onion
1 Tbsp powdered mustard
1 Tbsp powdered ginger
1 cup maple syrup
1 tsp salt
4 red apples
1 cup brown sugar
½ cup butter
½ cup rum

Place the beans and molasses in a pan; add enough boiling water to cover and allow to stand for an hour or more. Bring to a boil, reduce the heat and allow to simmer for 1½ hours.

In the bottom of a large bean pot or crock pot place the pork and the onion. Add the beans and cooking liquid. Stir in the ginger, mustard, maple syrup and salt. Place in a 300°F (150°C) oven and bake for 4 hours or more.

About 1 hour before serving, core and pare the apples and cut into rings. Put the apple rings on top of the beans. Add the brown sugar and butter; continue cooking. Just before serving, add the rum. Serve hot with an apple slice on each portion.

STUFFED BAKED LOBSTER WITH LIME, Recipe this page.

Stuffed Baked Lobster with Lime

PHOTOGRAPH THIS PAGE

Preparation Time: 30 minutes
Cooking Time: 50–60 minutes
Serves 6

1 onion
1 carrot
1 stick celery
1 bunch parsley
1 bay leaf
salt and pepper
2 qts (2 lt) water (approx.)
12 lobster tails
¾ cup butter
4 Tbsp flour
1 Tbsp paprika
pinch of dried tarragon
pinch of cayenne
salt and pepper
2 cups half and half
3 Tbsp lime juice
2 Tbsp butter
½ cup Parmesan cheese
½ cup bread crumbs

Put the onion, carrot, celery, parsley, bay leaf, and salt and pepper to taste in a large heavy pan. Add the water and bring to a boil. Add the lobster tails. Boil for 5 minutes (6–7 minutes if the tails are frozen.) Remove from the stock and allow to cool.

Carefully cut away the undershell of the lobster tails with kitchen scissors and pull the meat away from the shell. Save the shells for serving. Cut the meat into small chunks.

In a heavy saucepan melt the butter; add the lobster meat, and stir until coated. Gradually stir in the flour, paprika, tarragon and cayenne. Season to taste with salt and pepper. When the mixture is smooth, remove from the heat and add the half and half. Reheat, stirring constantly. Add the lime juice then remove from the heat again.

Arrange the shells close together in a baking dish. Support them with aluminimum foil so they do not fall over. Heap the filling into the shells. At this point the lobster may be cooked or kept refrigerated for up to a day.

To prepare for serving, preheat the oven to 350°F (180°C). In a saucepan, melt the 2 Tbsp of butter and stir in the cheese and bread crumbs. When the crumbs are thoroughly coated, spoon over the filling and bake 30-40 minutes until the topping is golden brown. Serve immediately.

NEW ENGLAND

MAIN COURSE

Lemon Linguini with White Clam Sauce

Preparation Time: 10 minutes
Cooking Time: 10 minutes
Serves 4

½ lb (250 g) lemon linguini
¼ cup olive oil
1 clove garlic, chopped
1 onion, chopped
1 lb (500 g) fresh clams
¼ cup chopped fresh parsley or
  2 Tbsp dried parsley
¼ cup chopped fresh basil or
  2 Tbsp dried basil
½ cup dry white wine
½ tsp pepper

Cook the linguini in slightly salted boiling water for about 10 minutes, stirring occasionally.

In a heavy skillet, heat the olive oil and sauté the garlic and onion until soft. Stir in the clams, parsley, basil and wine. Season to taste. Bring to a boil and simmer for 5 minutes.

Drain the linguini and serve immediately with the hot clam sauce.

Shark Teriaki

Preparation Time: 5 minutes
Marinate: 6 hours
Cooking Time: 20 minutes
Serves 4

4 shark steaks or fillets
¼ cup sesame oil
¼ cup soy sauce
¼ cup honey
2 Tbsp cider vinegar
1 clove garlic, minced
1 Tbsp grated fresh ginger
1 small bunch chives or scallions

Rinse the shark steaks and pat them dry.

Put all the other ingredients in a blender and mix well. Allow the steaks to marinate in this sauce for 4–6 hours.

Grill for 20 minutes, turning once. Baste frequently with the marinade.

Flounder in Mustard & Burnt Almonds

PHOTOGRAPH PAGE 55

Preparation Time: 15 minutes
Cooking Time: 25 minutes
Preheat Oven: 400°F (200°C)
Serves 2

2 small fillets of flounder or 1 large one
2 Tbsp butter
1 Tbsp flour
1 tsp powdered mustard
1 tsp heavy cream
pinch of salt
1 Tbsp sliced blanched almonds

Wash the fillets and pat them dry. Butter a shallow baking dish and arrange the fish on it.

Cream the butter and blend in the flour, mustard, cream and salt. Mix into a paste. Spread evenly over the fillets to form a thick topping. Sprinkle the almond slices over the paste and gently press them in.

Bake for 20–25 minutes or until golden brown. (The almonds may burn slightly along the edges.) Serve immediately.

Bluefin in Ginger Lime Sauce with Stir-Fried Vegetables

Preparation Time: 15 minutes
Cooking Time: 15 minutes
Serves 4

4 bluefin fillets
2 Tbsp butter
2 Tbsp lime juice
2 Tbsp soy sauce
1 Tbsp powdered ginger
1 tsp pepper
2 Tbsp butter
4 cups thinly sliced vegetables
  green, red or yellow peppers
  cauliflower
  broccoli
  onion
  bean sprouts
  green onions
  water chestnuts, etc.

Rinse the fillets and pat them dry. Melt the butter in a heavy skillet. At the same time, combine the lime juice, soy sauce, ginger, pepper and butter in a small saucepan and bring to a boil.

When the butter in the skillet is hot but not brown, add the fillets. Sauté for 5 minutes until the fish begins to brown at the edges, gently shaking the pan from time to time to ensure that the fillets do not stick. Turn the fillets carefully, pour 1 Tbsp of sauce over each one and sauté for five minutes longer. Carefully lift the fish onto a serving dish and keep warm.

Scrape loose any fish bits in the pan, add a little extra butter and sauce and quickly stir-fry the vegetables. Drain and serve immediately with the fish, steamed rice and jasmine tea.

Chicken & Creamed Curried Coconut

PHOTOGRAPH THIS PAGE

Preparation Time: 15 minutes
Cooking Time: 25 minutes
Preheat Oven: 400°F (200°C)
Serves 4

3 whole chicken breasts (or 6 halves)
2 Tbsp butter
1 small onion, finely chopped
1 Tbsp Madras curry powder (page 22)
1 tsp sugar
½ cup light cream
½ cup white wine
2 Tbsp long shredded coconut

Carefully bone the chicken breasts, or have your butcher bone them for you. Be sure the tendon is removed.

Melt the butter in a saucepan and add the chopped onion and curry powder. Sauté for about five minutes or until soft, stirring occasionally. Add the sugar, cream, wine and coconut; stir and reduce the heat.

Cut the chicken into lengthwise strips, about 1-inch (2.5 cm) thick and place in the sauce. Stir with a wooden spoon to ensure thorough mixing and simmer for 10 minutes. Do not boil.

Butter a shallow baking dish. Using kitchen tongs, remove the chicken strips from the sauce and arrange them on the dish. Strain the sauce over the chicken then spread the coconut and onion bits, which remain in the strainer, on top.

Bake for 10 minutes or until the coconut is just golden. Serve at once.

Duck in Kumquat Sauce

PHOTOGRAPH THIS PAGE

Preparation Time: 20 minutes
Cooking Time: 1½ hours
Serves 2

1 2–2½ lb (1–2 kg) domestic duck or 2 wild ducks
1 potato, coarsely chopped
1 onion, coarsely chopped
1 clove garlic, chopped
1 tsp pepper
1 cup fresh kumquats
½ cup brown sugar
¼ cup dry white wine

Cut the duck(s) in half down the center and place, skin side down, in a large pan. Add the potato, onion and garlic coarsely chopped, sprinkle with pepper and barely cover with cold water. Bring to a boil, lower the heat and simmer for 45 minutes. Remove from the heat and, using kitchen tongs, lift the duck out of the stock and arrange on a baking dish or platter.

Strain the stock and skim off the fatty layer from the top. In a blender or food processor, place the kumquats, brown sugar, wine and 1 cup of the duck stock. Blend for 2–3 seconds or until the kumquats are chopped but not pureed.

Pour the sauce over the duck and bake in a 375°F (190°C) oven for ½ hour or until the duck is well browned.

NEW ENGLAND

MAIN COURSE

Left: CHICKEN & CREAMED CURRIED COCONUT, Recipe this page.
Right: DUCK IN KUMQUAT SAUCE, Recipe this page.

NEW ENGLAND

MAIN COURSE

Veal Collops

PHOTOGRAPH THIS PAGE

Preparation Time: 15 minutes
Cooking Time: 10 minutes
Serves 4

4 veal collops (thin steaks)
1 clove garlic
1 cup mild paté (approx.)
4 thin slices ham
pinch of cayenne
3 Tbsp butter
dash of white wine and lemon juice
light cream (optional)

Rub the veal collops with the garlic and place on a floured board. Spread paté over each one and top with a ham slice. Sprinkle a pinch of cayenne over each, roll up and secure with string or a toothpick. Sauté in the butter until lightly browned. Remove the collops to a warm dish. To the pan gravy, add the wine and lemon juice. Bring to a boil, adding a touch of cream if you like, and pour over the collops.

Cod Provincetown

Preparation Time: 5 minutes
Cooking Time: ½ hour
Preheat Oven: 375°F (190°C)
Serves 2

2 fresh cod fillets
2 Tbsp butter
1 clove garlic
1 small onion
1 tomato, peeled
1 tsp fresh tarragon or
  ½ tsp dried tarragon
¼ cup white wine
salt and pepper
breadcrumbs or crushed cornflakes

Arrange the cod in a well-buttered casserole dish.

Put the garlic, onion, tomato, tarragon, wine and seasonings in a blender or food processor and blend for a couple of seconds. Pour the sauce over the fish. Top with the crumbs and bake 20–30 minutes depending on the thickness of the fish. When it flakes easily, it is done.

Turbot in Sorrel Sauce

Preparation Time: 15 minutes
Cooking Time: 15 minutes
Preheat Oven: 400°F (200°C)
Serves 4

4 fresh turbot fillets
2 Tbsp butter
1 grapefruit
2 Tbsp butter
2 scallions or green onions
½ cup white wine
1 small bunch sorrel, chopped
1 tsp cornstarch or arrowroot
1 tsp lemon juice
½ cup cream
salt and pepper

Wash the fillets and pat them dry. Arrange the fish on a well-buttered baking dish. Top with slices or sections of grapefruit. Bake for about 15 minutes.

Meanwhile, melt the butter in a saucepan and sauté the scallions. Add the white wine and sorrel leaves; bring to a boil. Remove from heat and whisk until smooth. Reheat. Make a paste of the cornstarch and lemon juice. Stir into the sauce.

Add the cream and season to taste. Pour the sauce over the fish and serve hot.

VEAL COLLOPS, Recipe this page.

Historical canons at Gettysburg National Military Park, in Gettysburg, New England.

PHEASANT WITH FRUIT STUFFING, Recipe this page.

NEW ENGLAND

MAIN COURSE

Pheasant with Fruit Stuffing

PHOTOGRAPH THIS PAGE

Preparation Time: 20 minutes
Cooking Time: 1½ hours
Serves 4

1 5–6 lb (2½–3 kg) pheasant
1 onion
1 carrot
1 stalk celery
1 leek, white part only
3 sprigs fresh thyme
3 sprigs fresh rosemary
1 tsp freshly ground pepper
3 cups game or chicken stock
2 Tbsp flour
2 Tbsp butter
½ lb (250 g) seedless green grapes
½ lb seedless green grapes
2 medium red apples, coarsely chopped
½ cup walnuts, chopped
¼ cup light cream
¼ cup Madiera

Clean and rinse the pheasant and place in a heavy pan. Cut the onion, carrot, celery and leek into chunks and add them to the pan along with the thyme, rosemary and pepper. Cover with stock. Bring to a boil, lower the heat and simmer for 1 hour.

Lift out the pheasant. Discard the herb sprigs. Put the remaining vegetables and stock in a blender, along with the flour, and puree.

In a heavy pan, melt the butter and stir in the chopped shallot. Sauté until soft. Remove the pan from the heat and add the grapes, apples and walnuts. Toss gently with a wooden spoon until the fruit and nuts are coated.

Stuff the pheasant with the fruit mixture and place in a baking dish or pan. Pour over about 2 cups of the vegetable puree to a depth of about ½ inch (1 cm), thoroughly moistening the outside of the bird. Bake at 400°F (200°C) for 25 minutes until the pheasant is browned and the sauce is thick and bubbly.

Remove the pheasant to a hot serving dish. Pour the sauce into a saucepan and stir in the cream and Madiera. Bring just to a boil; serve at once.

Pork Chops, Thyme & Honey

Preparation Time: 5 minutes
Cooking Time: 20 minutes
Serves 4

4 pork chops
1 Tbsp butter
2 Tbsp fresh or dried thyme
3 Tbsp honey

Melt the butter in a skillet. Wash the pork chops and pat them dry. Spread half the honey over one side of the chops, sprinkle with half the thyme and place, honey side down, in the skillet. Cook over medium heat for 10 minutes.

While the chops are cooking, spread the remaining honey and thyme on the top sides. After 10 minutes, turn and cook for another 10 minutes. Nudge the chops from time to time with a wooden spoon to prevent them from sticking to the skillet.

Remove the chops to a warm serving plate and pour the sauce over them. If the sauce is too thick, thin it with a bit of white wine. Serve hot.

Beef & Sweet Bean Sauce

Preparation Time: 15 minutes
Cooking Time: 5 minutes
Serves 6

2 lbs (1 kg) sirloin steak
⅓ cup soy sauce
3 Tbsp cornstarch
3 Tbsp rice wine
1 tsp sugar
1 tsp sesame oil
2 Tbsp peanut oil
1 bunch chives
¼ cup water
2 tsp sweet bean sauce
1 tsp powdered ginger
2 tsp hoisin sauce

Cut the steak across the grain into thin strips the size of French fries. Mix the soy sauce, cornstarch, wine, sugar and sesame oil in a bowl. Stir in the beef strips and marinate for 10 minutes.

Cut the chives into 3-inch (8 cm) lengths. In a wok or skillet, heat the peanut oil to medium temperature and stir-fry the chives for 2 minutes or until limp but not brown. Remove the chives from the wok and drain. Add the beef to the wok and stir-fry for 2 minutes or until just brown. Remove the beef and drain.

Thouroughly mix together the water, bean sauce, ginger and hoisin sauce. Pour into the wok, stir and bring to a boil. Add the beef and chives; again bring just to a boil. Remove to a warm serving plate and serve immediately.

Grilled Swordfish Steaks with Red Pepper Sauce

Preparation Time: 10 minutes
Cooking Time: 20 minutes
Serves 4

4 swordfish steaks (at room temperature)
1 Tbsp soft butter
2 cloves garlic
1 or 2 hot red chili peppers
2 tomatoes, peeled
2 Tbsp melted butter
1 small onion
2 Tbsp lemon juice

Gently rub 1 Tbsp butter over both sides of the fish steaks. Heat a barbecue grill. When the grill is hot, cut the garlic cloves in halves and drop onto the coals. Place the steaks on the grill, or use a fish grill, and cook for 10 minutes on each side.

While the fish is cooking, place the remaining ingredients in a blender and blend well. Pour into a saucepan and bring to a boil. Simmer for 10 minutes. Serve the sauce hot with the grilled steaks.

Grilled Morels, Peppers, Cheese & Beef on a Stick

Preparation Time: 15 minutes
Cooking Time: 20 minutes
Serves 2

6 small green or red sweet peppers
8 oz (250 g) package cream cheese
1 tsp caraway seeds
1 lb (500 g) beef sirloin
1 Tbsp butter
3 morels
1 sweet onion

Heat the cream cheese in a double boiler or saucepan over very low heat until it is runny. Remove from the stove and stir in the caraway seeds.

Carefully cut out the stalks and remove the seeds from the peppers. Fill them with the melted cheese. Allow them to cool.

Cut the beef into 6 2-inch (5 cm) steaks and, with your fingers, knead and rub the butter into both sides of each one. Cut the morels and onion in half. On a skewer, arrange the items as follows: ½ onion, ½ morel, steak, stuffed pepper, morel, steak, pepper, etc., finishing with the remaining ½ onion.

Make sure all the peppers are upright. Place on the grill and cook at medium temperature for 20 minutes.

Magnificent rock formations fan out from Pemaquid Lighthouse on the Main Coast, part of the State Park of New England.

NEW ENGLAND SWEETS

Strawberries in Mint

Preparation Time: 20 minutes
Cooking Time: 10 minutes
Serves 6 or more

½ cup water
2 cups sugar
1 small bunch fresh spearmint
1 qt (1 kg) fresh strawberries
¼ cup chopped fresh Corsican mint (optional)

Dissolve the sugar in the water, add the fresh spearmint and boil for 10 minutes. Remove the mint.

Dip each strawberry into the hot mint syrup then place on a tray or platter to cool. Top with finely chopped spearmint (or a sprinkling of Corsican mint) and a dusting of icing sugar. Chill before serving.

Of the dozens of types of mint, Corsican mint (Metha requieni) is the smallest variety. In my garden, it is a hardy perennial available year round. Its fresh "crème de menthe" flavor combines marvelously with berries. If it's not to be found in your area, substitute fresh spearmint.

Chocolate Crèpes with Bitter Orange Sauce

Preparation Time: 30 minutes
Cooking Time: 40–45 minutes
Serves 4–5

Crèpes:
1 Tbsp butter
1 oz (30 g) unsweetened chocolate
1½ cups milk
2 eggs
1 cup flour
butter for frying

In a double boiler or heavy pan, melt the butter and chocolate over low heat, stirring occasionally. Add half the milk and stir well. Pour the chocolate mixture, eggs and remaining milk into a blender and mix well. Gradually add the flour, mixing until the mixture is light and creamy.

To make the crèpes, melt 1 tsp of butter in a 6-inch iron skillet over medium high heat. Brush the pan to coat evenly; pour ¼ cup batter into the pan, tipping it to spread the batter over the entire base without touching the sides. Cook for about 2 minutes or until just set on top. Turn once and cook for a half minute more. Slide the crèpe onto a warm plate, cover and keep warm. Brush the pan with butter and repeat.

Filling:
1 oz (30 g) unsweetened chocolate
1 cup milk

2 eggs or 4 egg yolks
½ cup sugar
1 tsp vanilla
½ cup cream

Melt the chocolate as above; add half the milk and mix well. In a blender, combine the remaining milk, the chocolate/milk mixture, eggs, sugar and vanilla. Blend until smooth. Return to the pan and heat gently, stirring constantly until the custard thickens. Remove from the heat and stir in the cream.

Sauce:
2 Tbsp butter
grated rind of 2 oranges
juice of 2 oranges
¼ cup brandy
¼ cup golden sugar (topping)

In a small saucepan, melt the butter and add the orange rind and juice. Bring to a boil and simmer for 5 minutes. Remove from the heat and add the brandy.

To assemble:
Place a crèpe upside down on an ovenproof serving dish or plate. Place one large spoonful of custard filling in the center and roll up the crèpe, tucking the edge underneath. Continue until all the crèpes have been filled and rolled. Sprinkle the tops with golden sugar, pour over the orange sauce and place in a 400°F (200°C) oven. Bake for 5–7 minutes until the sugar begins to melt and the sauce is bubbling. Serve immediately.

This light but rich dish makes an excellent brunch with hot cheese biscuits and fresh fruit. For a dessert, the constituent parts can all be made earlier but should not be chilled, and the crèpes should not be allowed to dry out.

Wild Blueberry Sorbet

PHOTOGRAPH PAGE 73

Preparation Time: 10 minutes
Freezing Time: 6–8 hours
Serves 6

2 qts (1 kg) fresh wild blueberries
1½ cups sugar
¼ cup lemon juice
2 egg whites
1 cup heavy cream

Carefully pick over the blueberries and remove any leaves, stalks, etc. Place in a food mill or blender and blend until smooth.

Pour into a mixing bowl, add the sugar and lemon juice and mix until the sugar is completely dissolved. Beat the egg whites until stiff and fold into the blueberry mixture. Place in the freezer for 3–4 hours until frozen.

Top left: WILD BLUEBERRY SORBET, Recipe page 72.
Right: WHITE CHOCOLATE CHEESECAKE, Recipe this page.

Whip the cream. Remove the blueberry-egg mixture from the freezer and stir vigorously to break up the ice. (The egg whites will prevent the growth of large ice crystals.) Stir in the cream. Pour into a mold or bowl and return to the freezer for 3–4 hours or overnight.

White Chocolate Cheesecake

PHOTOGRAPH THIS PAGE

Preparation Time: 20 minutes
Cooking Time: 40 minutes
Chilling Time: 8 hours
Preheat Oven: 350° (175°C)
Serves 6

2 Tbsp butter
2 Tbsp sugar
1 cup chopped hazelnuts
1 cup Graham cracker crumbs
½ lb (250 g) white chocolate

8 oz (125 g) cream cheese
1 cup sour cream
1 cup sugar
3 eggs, separated
¼ cup cognac
dark chocolate curls
whipped cream (optional)

Cream the butter and sugar; stir in the nuts and Graham cracker crumbs. Line a 9-inch (23 cm) cheesecake pan and press the crumb mixture into the bottom. Set aside to chill.

Melt the white chocolate in the top of a double boiler over hot (not boiling) water. Beat the cream cheese until light and fluffy and stir into the melted chocolate. Add the sour cream and sugar, stirring until the sugar is dissolved. Beat the egg yolks until smooth then stir into the chocolate/cheese mixture. Whip the egg whites until soft peaks form and fold in. Add the cognac. Stir gently and pour into the crumb-lined pan. Bake for 40 minutes. Allow to cool, then chill for 8 hours. Before serving, cover with whipped cream if desired, garnish with curls of dark chocolate.

NEW ENGLAND

SWEETS

Heartland

The Midwest regions have given America much, from huge and highly successful motor car industries in Chicago and Detroit to quaint phrases that have somehow managed to slip into any country where English is spoken.

Night reflections over Chicago River.

HEARTLAND

INTRODUCTION

There would be few husbands and wives in the world, that haven't at some point had to patch up a tiff by "burying the hatchet".

The phrase was originally coined at Fort Ouiatonenon in Indiana where Chief Pontiac ended his war against the whiteman in 1766 by doing just that — burying his hatchet. Had the weary warrior known an automobile would later be named after him, he might have been tempted to dig it up again!

Today, most of our heavy industry products come out of the Midwest. Think of the Midwest and you think of iron and steel from areas like Ohio, Chicago and Detroit.

Yet Ohio, with some 45,000 miles of streams and rivers, including the Ohio River, sports another face apart from the industry focused in the eastern sector (the Wright brothers first "took to the air" from Dayton, now it's an aviation center).

It has huge flat plains in the Ohio valley dotted with picturesque villages and homesteads and a mix of farming well able to support a large section of America by itself.

Cleveland is the 11th largest metropolitan sprawl covering some 50 miles or so either side of the Cuyahoga River — not the sort of PR mileage to put the vast and delightful tracts of verdant countryside in high profile!

Ohio has more than it's fair share of both big and small farming with an unusual twist of profitable cottage industries.

It also has the largest Amish population in the world, and one of them, the Berlin community in Holmes County, trots visitors around Ohio's only working woolen mill with understandable pride.

Ohio is a sort of heaven for cheese freaks. It has some of the biggest cheese producers anywhere and is especially famous for Swiss cheeses.

Ohio's sister states also reveal a bias to Amish communities, largely a result of the New England Puritans who arrived there as settlers. It also has a strong German influence.

There are obvious exceptions, but generally Midwest areas like Illinois, Minnesota, Iowa, Wisconsin, Michigan, etc., boast huge areas of highly fertile farmland.

Summers tend to be hot, winters cold and tornadoes are common with between 30" and 40" of rainfall annually.

Despite the weather's vicissitudes, the Heartlands have a high percentage of ground under plough and their highly mechanized farming techniques are among the best in the world. As a result, the Midwest is the principal stockist of the nation's pantries.

Chicago, perhaps better known for producing high-speed beasts on wheels, used to be called "hog butcher to the world" — a four-footed beast that is still one of Chicago's strongest commodity markets.

Chicago is also our biggest producer of soybeans and second-largest corn producer.

Illinois, the Prairie State, home to President Abraham Lincoln and noted for steel production, is probably best described as provincially cosmopolitan, an expression that probably sits well on most Midwest areas with the exception of Chicago.

Chicago is internationally flavored through its world trade dealings as a transport and trading hub, and by a society of three million people speaking some 50 different languages and dialects.

Midwest cuisine has been honed over the decades and now provides menu items that are different but dependable. These are selections worth choosing for a dinner party where there may be a mix of tastes. Also a great choice to prove to the family that you really can cook when you put your mind to it!

It might be a hot meatball salad, a Cornish pasty Midwest style or a rhubarb omelette. Don't expect to have anything left on the plate to give the dog!

Top: ROAST GOOSE WITH SNOW APPLES, Recipe page 85. *Bottom:* SZEGED GOULASH, Recipe page 89.

Fava Beans with Bacon and Ginger Cream

Preparation Time: 15 minutes
Cooking Time: 15 minutes
Serves 4

4 slices bacon, chopped
¼ cup white wine
½ tsp ground cumin
½ lb (250 g) fava beans
½ cup heavy cream
1 Tbsp grated fresh ginger root

Fry the bacon in a saucepan until crisp. Remove the slices with a slotted spoon and set aside. Scrape the pan and add the wine and cumin to the bacon drippings. Bring to a boil and add the beans. Cook, covered, for 10 minutes until tender. Remove the beans and set them aside with the bacon. Cool the liquid. Add the ginger to the cream and whip until stiff. Gradually beat in the cooking liquid to make a soft cream sauce. Pour the sauce over the bacon and beans. Serve hot.

French-Toasted Eggplant

Preparation Time: 20 minutes
Cooking Time: 15 minutes
Serves 4

butter for frying
1 large eggplant, pared and sliced ½ inch (1 cm) thick
1 Tbsp lemon juice
½ cup chopped green onion
½ cup seeded and chopped green or red sweet peppers
½ cup Colby cheese, grated
1 tsp fresh chopped basil
1 tsp black pepper
1 egg
½ cup milk
1 Tbsp butter

Melt butter in a frying pan or skillet. Brush the eggplant slices with the lemon juice. Sauté on both sides for 2–3 minutes until almost cooked but still firm. Add more butter as needed. Remove from the pan and set aside.

In a bowl or processor, mix the onions, sweet peppers, cheese, basil and black pepper to make a coarse filling. In a separate bowl, beat the egg and milk together. Melt 1 Tbsp butter in the skillet. Heap half the eggplant slices with about 2 Tbsp of filling each then top with another slice of eggplant. Dip each "sandwich" into the egg/milk mixture and sauté for 2–3 minutes on each side until golden.

Beef Carpaccio

Preparation Time: 15 minutes
Serves 4

½ lb (250 g) fillet of beef
½ lb (250 g) tomatoes, finely chopped
1 bunch scallions, finely chopped
1 can anchovies fillets
2–3 chili peppers
¼ cup red wine vinegar
¼ cup olive oil
1 Tbsp chopped fresh parsley
1 loaf pumpernickel bread

Cut the raw beef into thin slices across the grain; this may be easier to do if the meat is partially frozen. Toss the tomatoes and scallions with the beef. Drain the anchovies and mix with the peppers, vinegar and oil. Pour this dressing over the salad, tossing gently. Sprinkle it with parsley. Serve chilled with buttered pumpernickel bread.

Hot Meatball Salad

PHOTOGRAPH PAGE 79

Preparation Time: 20 minutes
Cooking Time: 15 minutes
Preheat Deep Fryer: 400°F (200°C)
Serves 4

1 lb (500 g) ground beef
1 egg, beaten
1 small onion, chopped
1 hot pepper, minced or grated
1 cup pineapple juice
¼ cup cider vinegar
1 Tbsp powdered mustard
1 Tbsp soy sauce
2 Tbsp cornstarch
2 cups pineapple chunks
1 banana, sliced thickly
4 cups shredded lettuce
small bunch of chives, chopped

Beat together the ground beef, egg, onion and hot pepper. Shape the mixture into small (1-inch) (2.5 cm) balls. Fry the meatballs in a deep fryer or in 1-inch (2.5 cm) of oil in a skillet for 5 minutes. Drain them and keep them hot.

Blend together the pineapple juice, vinegar, mustard, soy sauce and cornstarch. Heat these ingredients gently in a saucepan, stirring occasionally, until the sauce thickens slightly. Add the meatballs, pineapple chunks and banana slices; reheat for 1 minutes.

On a serving platter, prepare beds of shredded lettuce. Pour the meat and fruit over the lettuce. Sprinkle with chives and serve.

Left: NASTURTIUM CHICKEN SALAD LOAF, Recipe this page.
Right: HOT MEATBALL SALAD, Recipe page 78.

Nasturtium Chicken Salad Loaf

PHOTOGRAPH THIS PAGE

Preparation Time: 20 minutes
Chilling Time: 2 hours
Serves 6

10 fresh nasturtium flowers
1 bunch chives
1 bunch watercress
1 cup grated red or green cabbage
3 cups diced cold cooked chicken
2 Tbsp chopped fresh tarragon
1 tsp chopped fresh mint
1 package unflavored gelatin
1 cup water
pinch of salt
1 tsp black pepper
1 tsp sugar
1 large, fresh country-style loaf of bread (white)
soft butter
½ cup sour cream

Place the nasturtium flower petals in a large mixing bowl, discarding the stems and centers.

Add the chives, cut into 2-inch (5 cm) lengths. Pull the leaves and tips from the watercress, adding this to the mixing bowl along with the grated cabbage. Mix in the chicken, tarragon and mint. Toss gently.

In a small pan, stir the gelatin into the cold water and heat slowly. When the gelatin is fully dissolved, remove the pan from the heat and stir in the salt, pepper and sugar. Allow the solution to cool.

Cut a ¾-inch (2 cm) slice from one end of the loaf, butter it and set aside. Using your hands, scoop out most of the soft center of the bread and rub the inside of the loaf with butter. Stir the sour cream into the gelatin solution then pour it over the salad ingredients. Toss well to coat thoroughly. Spoon the salad into the loaf, pressing it in firmly. Replace the buttered end slice. Stand the salad loaf on end in the refrigerator and chill for 2 hours or more until the gelatin is set.

To serve, place the loaf on a cutting board and cut into thick slices.

Hot Roast Corn

Preparation Time: 8 minutes
Cooking Time: 15 minutes
Serves 6

¼ cup butter
3–4 chilies, peeled and minced
2 cloves garlic, minced
1 Tbsp lemon juice
6 ears of fresh corn
aluminum foil

Cream the butter with the chilies, garlic and lemon juice. Rub the mixture generously over the corn. Wrap each ear in foil, twisting the ends to seal tightly. Place on a hot grill for 15 minutes, turning once, or bake in a 400°F (200°C) oven for 25 minutes.

HEARTLAND

APPETIZERS
SOUPS
SALADS
ENTREES

HEARTLAND

APPETIZERS
SOUPS
SALADS
ENTREES

Cabbage Hearts with Almond Butter

Preparation Time: 5 minutes
Cooking Time: 12 minutes
Serves 6–8

1 large, or 2 small, very firm heads of savoy or
    winter heart cabbage
¼ cup blanched, broken almonds
¼ cup butter
1 tsp lemon juice
black pepper, freshly ground
caraway seeds

Remove the outer leaves of the cabbage, leaving the solid heart intact. Place the heart in the very smallest saucepan that will hold it, cover it with boiling water and boil, covered, for 12–15 minutes, or cook 5 minutes in a pressure cooker. Remove the cabbage heart from the heat and drain it. Place the almonds in a blender and chop until fine. Cream the butter, almonds and lemon juice together in a bowl.

To serve, remove any loose outer leaves from the cabbage and cut it into large wedges. Place the cabbage wedges on a serving platter. Dot them with almond butter and sprinkle with pepper and caraway seeds.

Pumpkin Flower Fritters

Preparation Time: 12 minutes
Cooking Time: 4 minutes
Preheat Deep Fryer: 375°F (190°C)
Serves 4

12 large, firm flowers of pumpkin (or cucumber
    squash, etc.)
1 egg
1 cup milk
½ cup flour
1 tsp pepper
2 tsp finely chopped mint (optional)
¼ cup chopped salted peanuts

Heat a light vegetable oil in the deep fryer. Blend together the egg, milk, flour, pepper and mint to produce a very smooth, thin batter. The flowers should be clean and dry. Dip them in the batter coating completely. Sprinkle a pinch of chopped nuts into the center of each flower then drop them into the hot oil. Fry for 3–4 minutes until golden. Using a slotted spoon, gently lift out the flowers and drain them on a paper towel. Serve hot.

The life-giving sunshine over the wheatfields of South East Indiana.

Onion Soup I

Preparation Time: 10 minutes
Cooking Time: 15 minutes
Serves 2

2 Tbsp butter
2 cups finely chopped sweet onions
2½ cups beef stock (duck stock is even better)
1 loaf of French bread
6–8 Tbsp Gruyère cheese, grated
pepper

Melt the butter in a large pan, add the onions and cook over low heat for 10-15 minutes, stirring occasionally. Onions should become soft and rich brown colour. Add the stock and bring it rapidly to a boil. Lower the heat and simmer for about 10 minutes.

Meanwhile, cut the bread into thin slices; spread with butter and toast under the broiler until quite crisp. Arrange some of the toast on the bottom of an ovenproof soup tureen or bowl. Sprinkle the toast with half the grated cheese and season with pepper. Gently pour on the onion broth.

Float a second layer of toast on the broth, cover it with the remaining cheese and place the bowl under the broiler until the cheese begins to bubble and brown. Serve immediately.

Onion Soup II

Preparation Time: 20 minutes
Cooking Time: 15 minutes
Serves 2

2 Tbsp butter
2 cups coarsely chopped sweet onions
2½ cups beef or duck stock
1 cup milk
1 tsp sugar
2 tsp fresh thyme or
   1 tsp dried thyme
2 tsp pepper
1 egg, beaten
1 loaf French bread
½ cup grated Gruyère cheese
½ cup whipping cream

Melt the butter in a heavy pan over low heat then add the chopped onion. Cook gently for 10 minutes. Add the beef stock and bring to a boil. Lower the heat and simmer for 10 minutes.

Remove the soup from the heat and blend or process until the onion is finely chopped but not pureed. Return it to the pan. Add the milk, sugar, thyme, pepper and beaten egg. Stir the mixture and keep it warm over low heat.

Meanwhile, cut the loaf into 1-inch (2.5 cm) thick slices and toast them on both sides. Whip the cream.

Pour the soup into a clay baker, topping it with islands of toasted French bread carefully mounded with cheese. Place under the broiler until the cheese bubbles and starts to run.

Serve immediately with whipped cream on the side. Some cooks prefer to stir the cream into the soup just before topping it with the toast and cheese.

Wild Mushroom Soup

Preparation Time: 20 minutes
Cooking Time: 40 minutes
Serves 6

1½ lbs (750 g) wild mushrooms
¼ cup butter
6 cups game stock (or chicken & beef stock mixed)
1 leek, grated
1 carrot, grated
1 stick celery, grated
½ cup heavy cream
pinch of cayenne
12 tiny fluffy biscuits

Gently trim the mushrooms and brush them clean. Cut them into thin slices. Melt half the butter in a large heavy pan and toss in the mushrooms, reserving about ½ cup of the most attractive slices for garnish. (When using morels,

they should all be cooked.) Sauté the mushrooms gently for 5 minutes then add the stock. Bring to a boil, lower the heat and simmer for ½ hour. Unless you are fond of a strong mushroom flavor, strain the soup, discarding the mushrooms and retaining the consommé.

In a saucepan, melt the remaining butter and add the grated vegetables. Stir and sauté for 5 minutes. Add the vegetables to the consommé. In a small bowl, whip the cream with the cayenne.

To serve, split and butter the biscuits. On each biscuit half place ½ tsp whipped cream and a sprinkle of chopped raw mushroom. Ladle the soup into six bowls. Float the buscuit "boats" on the soup and serve immediately.

Zucchini on a Stick

Preparation Time: 30 minutes
Cooking Time: 5–10 minutes
Preheat Deep Fryer: 375°F (190°C)
Serves 8

8 zucchini, each about 7-inches (18 cm) long
1 Tbsp butter
1 onion, chopped
1 clove garlic, minced
1 green pepper, seeded and chopped
1 hot red pepper, seeded and chopped
1 cup firm cream cheese, diced
1 Tbsp chopped fresh dill
1 egg, beaten
8 thin slices ham
8 thin slices Mozzarella cheese

Batter:
1 egg
1 cup flour
1 cup beer

Trim the stalk end from the zucchinis, slice them in half lengthwise and remove the seeds, making a trench down the middle. Set aside. In a saucepan, melt the butter then add the onion, garlic and peppers. Stir for 5 minutes until just soft. Dice the cream cheese and stir it into the pepper mixture. Continue to cook, stirring constantly, until the cheese is melted.

Remove the mixture from the heat and add the dill and beaten egg. Stir until the mixture is sticky. Spoon the filling into the 16 zucchini halves. Join the matching halves together. Wrap each zucchini in a slice of ham and a slice of Mozzarella cheese, securing with a toothpick.

In a bowl or blender, beat the egg, flour and beer into a light batter. Dip each zucchini roll in the batter and deep-fry for 5 minutes until lightly golden. Drain and serve at once.

HEARTLAND

APPETIZERS
SOUPS
SALADS
ENTREES

This sunflower crop is almost ready for harvest on Wisconsin's Door Peninsula.

HEARTLAND

MAIN COURSE

Baked Potato Soufflé

PHOTOGRAPH THIS PAGE

Preparation Time: 30 minutes
Cooking Time: 1½ hours
Preheat Oven: 375°F (190°C)
Serves 6

6 large potatoes
2 Tbsp coarse salt
3 Tbsp butter
1 cup sour cream
1 tsp pepper
3 eggs

Clean the potatoes, prick them all over with a fork and roll them in the salt. Bake for 1 hour (or in a microwave according to directions) then remove from the oven. Taking each potato in turn, hold it firmly with an oven mitt and cut a slice off the top. With a spoon, scoop the pulp into a bowl, leaving about ¼ inch (0.5 cm) of pulp inside the skin to retain the shape. When all the potatoes have been hollowed out, mash the pulp and blend together with the butter, sour cream and pepper. Separate the eggs. Beat the whites until stiff, the yolks until creamy. Stir the egg yolks into the potato mixture then fold in half the beaten egg whites. Mix well then fold in the rest of the whites. Spoon the mixture back into the potato skins and rebake in a 400°F (200°C) oven for 20 minutes. Serve immediately.

Scotch Potatoes

Preparation Time: 5 minutes
Cooking Time: 15 minutes
Serves 2

4 slices of bacon
1 large potato
1 apple
2 Tbsp brown sugar

Fry the bacon in a heavy skillet until it is crisp. Remove to a warm dish and set aside.

Meanwhile, peel and slice the potato and apple into 5 silver-dollar-sized pieces. Stir these in the bacon fat until they are coated on both sides. Fry the potato and apple slices for 5 minutes then turn them over. Sprinkle with brown sugar. Reduce the heat and cook for about 10 minutes or until tender and golden. Serve immediately with the hot bacon.

Top: GOOSE & MUSHROOM PÂTÉ, Recipe page 85. *Bottom:* BAKED POTATO SOUFFLÉ, Recipe this page.

Goose & Mushroom Paté

PHOTOGRAPH PAGE 84

Preparation Time: 15 minutes
Cooking Time: 10 minutes
Serves 6–10

1 lb (500 g) butter
1½ lbs (750 g) mushrooms (preferably wild), sliced
½ cup goose gelatin
1 cup coarsely chopped filberts
2 Tbsp Worcestershire sauce
2 tsp pepper
¼ cup brandy
½ lb cooked goose meat

Melt the butter in a skillet. Add the mushrooms, goose gelatin, nuts, Worcestershire sauce and pepper. Simmer 10 minutes. Remove from the heat and pour in the brandy.

Butter a small loaf pan or paté mold and line the bottom with mushroom slices. Arrange alternate layers of paté and goose meat, ending with paté. Refrigerate for at least half a day.

To serve, place the mold in hot water for 2–3 seconds then invert onto a serving tray. Allow to stand at room temperature for a few minutes before serving.

Roast Goose with Snow Apples

PHOTOGRAPH PAGE 77

Preparation Time: 20 minutes
Baking Time: 3½ hours
Preheat Oven: 400°F (200°C)
Serves 6

10–12 lb (5–6 kg) goose, cleaned and trussed
black pepper
6 firm red apples
1 cup currants
½ cup chopped walnuts
1 Tbsp cinnamon
¼ cup honey
6 small sprigs rosemary
3 egg whites
1 Tbsp sugar
1 cup heavy cream

Rinse the goose and sprinkle the cavity liberally with pepper. Place the goose in a deep baking pan and prick the skin all over with a fork. Bake for 45 minutes then remove from the oven and pour off the accumulated fat. Reduce the oven heat to 350°F (180°C) and bake for a further 1½ hours. Add the snow apples to the pan and bake an additional 30–40 minutes.

Snow Apples

Core but do not peal the apples. Combine the currants, walnuts, cinnamon and honey and spoon the mixture into the center of each cored apple. Top each with a sprig of rosemary.

Whip the egg whites with the sugar until stiff. Spoon this "snow" over each apple and arrange the apples around the goose. (If the pan is too crowded, place on a separate baking sheet.) The apples are done when the "snow" turns golden. Drizzle with a bit of warmed cream before serving with the goose.

Sweet-Spicy Popcorn Balls

Preparation Time: 5 minutes
Cooking Time: 30 minutes
Yield: 5 quarts (4½ lt)

1½ cups popping corn
½ cup butter
1 lb (500 g) brown sugar
⅓ cup corn syrup
2 Tbsp caraway seeds
1 Tbsp cinnamon
1 Tbsp ground ginger
1 tsp white pepper (optional)

In a skillet, heavy pan or corn popper, make about 5 qts (4½ lt) of popped corn. Melt the butter in a heavy saucepan and stir in the sugar and syrup. When the syrup is hot but not boiling, add the spices and stir well.

In a large bowl, thoroughly mix the popped corn and syrup until the corn is well coated. Roll the popcorn into balls and cool them on waxed paper until set.

Brats 'n Beer

Preparation Time: 5 minutes
Cooking Time: 20 minutes
Serves 4–8

8 bratwurst
2 Tbsp butter
2 bottles or cans of beer
1 large sweet onion or 1 cup chopped chives
8 hot dog buns
mustard and relish

Grill or broil the bratwurst until crispy on the outside. Melt the butter in a pot, pour in the beer and bring to a boil. Peel and cut the onion into rings and drop it into the hot beer along with the bratwurst. Boil for 5 minutes until the onion is soft. Drain the onion rings and bratwurst. Serve on the hot dog buns with mustard and relish.

HEARTLAND

MAIN COURSE

Cornish Pasties
PHOTOGRAPH PAGE 87

Preparation Time: 25 minutes
Cooking Time: 1 hour
Preheat Oven: 375°F (190°C)
Serves 4

Pastry:
3½ cups flour
1 tsp salt
1½ cups cold shortening
cold water

Filling:
¾ lb (375 g) ground beef
¾ lb (375 g) ground pork
½ cup chopped onion
1 cup diced potato
½ cup diced or grated carrot
salt & pepper to taste
dash of HP sauce or mild tamarind sauce

Pastry:
In a bowl or pastry maker, sift together the flour and salt. Cut in the shortening. Add cold water, 1 Tbsp at a time, to produce a light, firm dough. Do not overprocess. Divide the dough into four portions. Roll out on a floured board to make four pastry circles about 9 or 10 inches (23-25 cm) in diameter. Grease and flour two baking sheets and place two of the pastry circles on each. (This way they will not have to be moved after they are filled.)

Filling:
Thoroughly mix together all the filling ingredients. If the meat is very lean, add a small amount of butter.

Pasties:
Spoon some of the filling mixture into the center of each pastry ring. Fold the pastry over the filling and crimp the edges. The pasties should resemble half moons.

Baking:
Brush each pastry with melted butter and bake for at least 1 hour until the crust is golden. Remove from the oven and cool slightly before lifting from the baking sheet. Serve warm.

Traditionally, pasties were made as a meal-in-one for Cornish miners. The pastry dough was rolled thick, the meat or cheese filling was placed left of center and fruit or jam was tucked in on the right. When the thick pastry was folded over, handles were formed on either side. The men could enjoy a hot savory dinner, move on to dessert, then throw away the pastry handles without having eaten any of the grime from their hands.

Ham Steak and Fiddlehead Greens
PHOTOGRAPH PAGE 87

Preparation Time: 15 minutes
Cooking Time: 20 minutes
Serves 4

2 Tbsp butter
4 ham steaks
1 tsp powdered mustard
½ lb (250 g) fiddleheads
1 Tbsp cornstarch
¼ cup water
1 Tbsp honey
2 Tbsp slivered almonds

Melt the butter in a large skillet. Wash the steaks and pat them dry. Rub them on both sides with the mustard. Place the steaks in the skillet and fry them for 10 minutes on each side. Gently shake the pan from time to time to prevent the meat from sticking.

Meanwhile, drop the fiddleheads into rapidly boiling water; boil for 3–4 minutes. Remove from the heat and drain.

Dissolve the cornstarch in the water; add the honey and simmer, stirring constantly, until the glaze thickens. Drop in the fiddleheads and almonds; toss gently to coat.

Place the ham steaks on a warm serving plate. Using a slotted spoon, remove the greens and almonds from the glaze and serve over the ham.

Plantation Spare Ribs
PHOTOGRAPH PAGE 87

Preparation Time: 10 minutes
Baking Time: 1½ hours
Preheat Oven: 425°F (220°C)
Serves 6–8

4 lbs (2 kg) pork Spare Ribs
½ cup corn syrup
½ cup beer
1 Tbsp powdered mustard
2 Tbsp Worcestershire sauce
2 Tbsp hot sauce
1 tsp thyme

Place the Spare Ribs on a rack in a baking dish and bake in the preheated oven for ½ hour. Combine all the other ingredients in a saucepan and bring to a boil. Pour off the fat from the spareribs and baste them liberally with the hot syrup. Reduce the oven heat to 350°F (180°C) and bake for 1 hour longer, basting every 15 minutes.

Top: PLANTATION SPARE-RIBS, Recipe page 86. *Middle:* HAM STEAK AND FIDDLEHEAD GREENS, Recipe page 86. *Bottom:* CORNISH PASTIES, Recipe page 86.

CALZONE, Recipe this page.

HEARTLAND

MAIN COURSE

Calzone

PHOTOGRAPH THIS PAGE

Preparation Time: 40 minutes
Rising Time: 2 hours
Cooking Time: 30 minutes
Serves 4

Calzone is a spicy turnover or "pizza loaf" which can be eaten hot, or cold, or can be reheated without its drying out.

Dough:
1 package active dry yeast
1 cup warm water
1 tsp sugar
2 cups flour
pinch of salt
¼ cup olive oil

Filling:
¼ cup olive oil
1 medium sweet onion, chopped
1 clove garlic, minced
1 red pepper, seeded and chopped (or hot peppers if you like)
1 small eggplant, peeled and chopped
½ lb (250 g) Feta cheese, diced
1 cup Parmesan cheese, grated
1 Tbsp Mozzarella cheese, grated
1 Tbsp chopped fresh sage
pepper to taste
1 egg, beaten
1 tsp sesame seeds

In a mixing bowl, combine the yeast, warm water, sugar and 1 cup of the flour. Allow the mixture to froth for 5–10 minutes then stir in the remaining flour, the salt and olive oil. Mix well to make a stiff dough, adjusting with additional flour or water as necessary. Turn the dough out on a floured board and knead by hand for about 5 minutes or until it is smooth and glossy. Place the dough in a clean bowl, cover and allow it to rise in a warm place for 1–2 hours until doubled in bulk.

To make the filling, heat the olive oil in a large saucepan. Add the chopped onion, garlic, peppers and eggplant. Fry this mixture for 5 minutes, stirring occasionally. Remove the saucepan from the heat and add the cheeses, sage and black pepper. Mix well.

When the dough has risen, punch it down and knead it again for 2 minutes. Roll the dough out into a rectangle roughly 10 inches (25 cm) by 15 inches (38 cm).

Heap the filling in the center of the dough. Lift and fold both sides of the dough over the filling and pinch together down the center. Tuck both ends of the dough underneath so that the "package" is completely sealed. Cover the calzone with a warm cloth and let it rise for 30–40 minutes. Score the top with a knife to allow steam to escape. Brush the calzone with the beaten egg and sprinkle it with sesame seeds. Bake at 400°F (200°C) for ½ hour until golden.

Partridge, Cherries & Thyme

Preparation Time: 10 minutes
Parboil: 30 minutes
Baking Time: 20 minutes
Serves 4

4 partridges
1 clove garlic, minced
1 stalk celery, finely chopped
1 Tbsp green peppercorns
1 bunch fresh thyme
1 cup chicken or game stock
½ lb (250 g) black cherries, pitted
2 Tbsp lemon juice
2 Tbsp light brown sugar
1 bunch fresh thyme flowers

Rinse the partridges and place them in a deep pot or Dutch oven. Add the garlic, celery, peppercorns, thyme and stock. Bring to a boil, lower the heat and simmer for ½ hour.

Remove the partridges from the stock and arrange them in a baking dish with the cherries. Discard the thyme. Add the lemon juice to the stock and puree in a blender until smooth. Pour over the partridges and cherries. Sprinkle with brown sugar and bake at 400°F (200°C) for 20 minutes. Garnish with fresh thyme flowers.

Grilled Whiskey Steak

Preparation Time: 10 minutes
Marinating Time: 3 hours
Cooking Time: 25 minutes
Serves 10

6 lbs (3 kg) sirloin steak, cut 2 inches (5 cm) thick
rye whiskey, at least 1 cup
1 tsp freshly ground black pepper
1 tsp fresh thyme
2 Tbsp butter
2 Tbsp sherry
2 Tbsp hot pepper sauce

Trim any fat from the meat. Rub the steak on both sides with whiskey. Cover and let marinate in the whiskey for 3–4 hours. Just before cooking, rub the steak again with whiskey, then on both sides with the pepper and thyme.

In a small saucepan, melt the butter; stir in the sherry and hot sauce. Remove from the heat. Brush one side of the steak and the grill of an outdoor barbecue wih the butter sauce. Set the steak on the hot grill. Baste every 5 minutes. Turn once after 12 minutes. Cook another 12 minutes for medium-rare.

Szeged Goulash

PHOTOGRAPH PAGE 77

Preparation Time: 30 minutes
Cooking Time: 1½ hours
Serves 6

3 Tbsp vegetable oil
1½ lbs (750 g) beef chuck, cubed
2 onions, chopped
2 cloves garlic, minced
1 lb (500 g) tomatoes, peeled and chopped
1 cup white wine
1 cup water
2 Tbsp caraway seeds
1 tsp pepper
1 tsp thyme
1 bay leaf
pinch of salt
¾ lb (750 g) sauerkraut
3 potatoes, peeled and chopped
2 tsp paprika
½ cup sour cream
¼ cup fresh dill, chopped

Heat the oil in a large heavy pan. Brown the meat in the hot oil for 5 minutes, stirring from time to time. Add the vegetables, wine, water, herbs and spices; mix well. Bring the mixture to a boil, cover and simmer for 40 minutes.

Rinse the sauerkraut in cold water and squeeze dry. Add the sauerkraut, potatoes and paprika to the pan. Stir then simmer for another 45 minutes. Serve hot with sour cream and fresh dill.

Rhubarb Omelet

Preparation Time: 10 minutes
Cooking Time: 5–7 minutes
Serves 4

2 egg yolks
6 Tbsp sugar
1 tsp lemon rind
6 egg whites, beaten
1 tsp butter
1½ cups cooked rhubarb, sweetened to taste

Blend the egg yolks, sugar and lemon rind until smooth. Beat the egg whites until stiff then fold them into the yolks.

Melt the butter in a large, heavy skillet, pour in the egg mixture, cover and cook gently over low heat for about 5 minutes until the meringue has set and the bottom can be lifted easily. Slide the omelet onto a hot serving platter. Pour the hot rhubarb over it and serve.

HEARTLAND

MAIN COURSE

A horse drinking at a water tower in Chicago while the driver and carriage wait patiently.

HEARTLAND SWEETS

Oat Cakes

Preparation Time: 15 minutes
Resting Time: 1 hour
Baking Time: 15–20 minutes
Yield: 12

4 cups rolled oats
¾ cup all-purpose flour
1½ tsp baking powder
pinch of salt
8 Tbsp butter
2–3 Tbsp milk

A food processor is ideal for preparing this recipe. Combine the oats, flour, baking powder and salt; process until fine and light. Add the butter and process until crumbly. Add sufficient milk to make a stiff dough. Place the dough on a floured board, cover it with a towel and let it rest for ½ hour.

Preheat the oven to 350°F (180°C). Roll out the dough until it is very thin, about ⅛-inch (0.25 cm), then cut it into 6-inch (15 cm) rounds or squares. Bake for 15 minutes.

At this point the cakes will resemble slices of oat bread and should be quite soft. They may be eaten warm with butter and preserves or cheese, or served cold. If you prefer a crisper cake, bake them for a further 5 minutes; or they may be stored and toasted at a later time.

Cherry Kirsch Cobbler

PHOTOGRAPH PAGE 93

Preparation Time: 20 minutes
Cooking Time: 25 minutes
Preheat Oven: 400°F (200°C)
Serves 6

3 cups black cherries, pitted
¼ cup water
½ cup sugar
1 Tbsp lemon juice
¼ cup kirsch
1½ cups flour
2 Tbsp butter
2 tsp baking powder
2 Tbsp sugar
⅓ cup milk
½ cup thick cream

Put the cherries in a pan; add the water, sugar and lemon juice. Bring just to a boil, stirring regularly to mix and dissolve the sugar. Remove the pan from the heat and stir in the kirsch. Pour the cherries into a deep 9-inch (23 cm) or 10-inch (25 cm) pie dish.

In a bowl or processor, mix the flour, butter, baking powder and sugar until the mixture has the consistency of cornmeal. Stir in the milk to make a very soft dough. On a floured board, roll the dough out to ¾-inch (2 cm) thickness. Cut into biscuit-sized pieces using a knife, glass or cookie cutter and place over the cherries. Bake for 25 minutes. Serve with thick cream.

Orange-Nut Pancakes with Honey Butter

PHOTOGRAPH PAGE 93

Preparation Time: 25 minutes
Cooking Time: 4 minutes per panful
Serves 4

Honey Butter:
¼ cup butter
¼ cup honey

Batter:
1 cup fresh orange pulp
2 Tbsp grated orange rind
½ cup corn flour
½ cup all-purpose flour
¼ cup chopped walnuts
2 eggs
1 Tbsp baking powder
¼ cup brown sugar
pinch of pepper
butter for frying

In a small bowl, cream the butter and honey until smooth. Pat it into a ball and cool in the refrigerator for 15 minutes while the pancakes are cooking.

Blend together all the batter ingredients in a blender or food processor; combine until smooth. The batter should be fairly thick; if necessary add an additional Tbsp of flour. Heat a griddle or large skillet and brush with butter. Using about 3 Tbsp of batter for each pancake, cook for 3 minutes on one side and 1 minute on the other side. Serve hot with honey butter.

Scottish Shortbread

Preparation Time: 10 minutes
Chilling Time: 1 hour
Cooking Time: 20 minutes
Yield: 30

1 lb (500 g) butter
1 cup fruit sugar
1 cup rice flour
3 cups all-purpose flour

Cream the butter and sugar. Add the flours and mix well. Roll out into a lightly floured board until the dough is ¼-inch (0.5 cm) thick; cut it into small rectangles or rounds. Place the shortbread on an ungreased baking sheet and refrigerate for at least 1 hour. Preheat the oven to 375°F (190°C) and bake for 20 minutes. Cool then store in an airtight container.

Top: ORANGE-NUT PANCAKES WITH HONEY BUTTER, Recipe page 92.
Bottom: CHERRY KIRSCH COBBLER, Recipe page 92.

D-L Farm one of the many farms which feed America in the Heartlands.

HEARTLAND SWEETS

Chocolate Mint Fondu

PHOTOGRAPH PAGE 95

Preparation Time: 20 minutes
Cooking Time: 10 minutes
Serves 2–6

Sauce:
2 Tbsp butter
1 lb (500 g) semi-sweet chocolate
1 cup finely chopped fresh peppermint

Coating:
hazelnuts, finely chopped
cocoa powder
crushed mint candies
cinnamon/sugar

For Dipping:
strawberries
Mandarin orange sections
bananas
marshmallows
hard-frozen ice cream balls
small cream puffs
candied ginger
pears
pieces of cake

Using a double boiler, heavy saucepan, fondu pot or crock pot, melt the butter and chocolate together very slowly. (Make sure the pot and ingredients are completely dry or the chocolate will turn grainy.) When the sauce has melted, stir in the chopped mint. Cover and leave over low heat until ready for use.

Since the ritual of making the dessert is half the fun of a fondue, the greater the variety of morsels to be dipped and of coatings to roll them in, the greater is the potential for enjoyment. The coatings can be set around the fondue pot in shallow bowls. For dipping, use only perfect fruit. Wash the fruit and pat it thoroughly dry. Bananas and pears should be sliced. Ice cream can be used, but if it is not frozen very hard, it will disappear in the chocolate pot.

Provide guests with fondue or dessert forks. Encourage improvization by securing a fruit section or morsel of cake, dipping it in the mint chocolate sauce and quickly rolling it in one of the coatings.

Note: Whipped cream will not stick to fondu items unless they are first allowed to cool.

CHOCOLATE MINT FONDU, Recipe page 94.

Hot Grapefruit

PHOTOGRAPH PAGE 97

Preheat Oven: 200°F (100°C)

grapefruit
wildflower or peppermint geranium honey
mint
caraway seeds

Cut the grapefruit in half, remove the seeds and precut the sections with a grapefruit knife. Spoon onto each half a dollop of wildflower or peppermint geranium honey. Arrange the grapefruit halves in a baking dish or tin (slice a strip from the bottom of each so they won't roll over) and place in a low oven for 10 minutes until the honey has thoroughly melted.

Serve in an attractive dish with a pinch of chopped mint or caraway seeds on top.

Choose very juicy grapefruit for this manner of serving; I prefer mine warm rather than hot. Another approach is to place the honeyed grapefruit under the broiler for a few minutes. The topping will be warm but the grapefruit will stay refreshingly cool.

Doughnuts with Kahlua Custard

PHOTOGRAPH PAGE 97

Preparation Time: 30 minutes
Rising Time: 2 hours
Cooking Time: 5 minutes
Yield: about 20 doughnuts

1 Tbsp sugar
¾ cup warm water
pinch of ground ginger
1 package dry yeast
1 cup milk
⅓ cup sugar
1 tsp salt
½ cup shortening
1 egg, beaten
5–6 cups flour

Doughnuts:

In a coffee mug, dissolve the sugar and ginger in the warm water. Stir in the yeast and let it stand for 10–15 minutes. Scald the milk in a saucepan then pour it into a large mixing bowl; add the sugar, salt and shortening. Stir in the egg and about 1 cup of the flour. By this time the yeast in the mug should have a good foamy head. Stir it into the flour/egg mixture. Add another cup of flour and beat well by hand until smooth. Gradually beat in the rest of the flour. Turn out onto a

floured board and knead well by hand for 10 minutes. The dough should be very smooth, satiny and light. Place the dough in a clean, buttered bowl. Brush the top with a little butter, cover it with a warm, damp cloth and put it in a warm place for at least 1 hour until it has doubled in size. Punch down the dough and roll it out on a floured board to ½-inch (1 cm) thickness. With a knife or pastry cutter cut the dough into 2-inch squares or 2-inch (5 cm) by 3-inch (8 cm) rectangles. Cover and let them rise until doubled in size — about 45 minutes. Heat clean vegetable oil in a deep fryer or large skillet to 375°F (190°C). Using a wide spatula, slide the doughnuts into the hot oil and fry until golden, turning once. Lift out and drain the doughnuts on a paper towel. When they are cool enough to handle, take each one in turn and, using a large kitchen syringe, inject each doughnut with about 1 oz (2 Tbsp) Kahlua custard. Then dip the doughnut into the sugar glaze and let cool on a wire rack. These must be eaten fresh!

Custard Filling:

Preparation Time: 10 minutes
Cooking Time: 12 minutes

1½ cups milk
⅓ cup sugar
2 eggs, beaten
½ tsp vanilla
¼ cup Kahlua

In a heavy saucepan, heat the milk until almost boiling. Stir in the sugar. Remove the sweetened milk from the heat and gradually add the beaten eggs, stirring constantly. Cook over low heat stirring steadily until the custard thickens. Remove the custard from the heat and stir in the vanilla and Kahlua. Cover and cool.

Glaze:

Preparation Time: 2 minutes

⅓ cup hot water
1 cup sugar
pinch of cinnamon

Blend all the ingredients together until smooth. Place them in a warm bowl or pan and keep the mixture tepid while dipping the doughnuts.

Left: DOUGHNUTS WITH KAHLUA CUSTARD, Recipe page 96.
Right: HOT GRAPEFRUIT, Recipe page 96.

Persimmon Cookies

Preparation Time: 15 minutes
Cooking Time: 20 minutes
Preheat Oven: 350°F (175°C)
Yield: 3 dozen

2 cups flour
1 tsp baking soda
1 tsp cinnamon
½ tsp mace
¼ tsp cloves
½ cup butter
½ cup sugar
1 Tbsp grated orange rind
1 egg
1 cup persimmon pulp
anise seeds

In a bowl, combine the flour, baking soda and spices. In a second bowl or food processor, cream the butter, sugar, orange rind and egg. Combine the dry ingredients with the creamed mixture. Lightly mix in the persimmon pulp. Drop the batter by the tablespoonful on a greased cookie sheet, sprinkle with anise seeds and bake for 15–20 minutes.

HEARTLAND

SWEETS

New York
(Eastern Seaboard)

New York, a world of its own and like no other place on earth; a place that visitors love or hate; where the term "middle of the road" doesn't exist and a city which, even if you hate it, has unenviable wicked charm by the bucketful

Touring Central Park in New York with a picturesque horse carriage.

NEW YORK

INTRODUCTION

Hardly surprising, then, that this giant human muddle of cosmopolitanism boasts eating habits also full of wicked charm.

Where else would you find potato chips with sour cream and caviar or deep-fried cream cheese (recipes for both will be found in this section) devoured with debauched gusto irrespective of cholesterol levels!

If it's true that a little bit of something naughty is good for you, this section of the book is probably the place where you will find a cuisine indulgence to lead your diet astray. Be warned, however, and take heed of the word "moderation".

Taking a bite out of the Big Apple can be tasty, but it is a mongrel diet born of fecklessness and a result of a population history that more threw itself together into a community format as the decades rolled by rather than evolving from any kind of historical order.

The original New York was only Manhattan Island. This tiny lump of land pointing at Europe across the Atlantic Ocean measures about 13 miles long by two miles wide.

It was originally settled by the Dutch and is thought to be the place of origin of the expression "going Dutch", where two people agree to split the bill.

Like the term "Big Apple" itself, which sports about 17 claimed origins at the last count, this should be taken with a pinch of salt.

By 1700, Manhattan had a 7000-strong population speaking 18 different languages. This is an astonishing number to boil down into one tongue which probably accounts for the reason why many Americans who don't speak another language, in many ways find it easier to communicate in Italy than they do in New York!

Today, New York has a population topping eight million and more than half of that figure are people either born in other countries or of foreign-born parents.

More than any other place in the world, New York is a genuine league of nations under one flag. Some 60 nationalities now call the Big Apple home and unswervingly vouch for it as not just the best city in the world, but the best planet in the universe.

Like everything else about New York, it is a place of extremes and eating New York style is no exception.

If you are going to have a burger, New York is the place to have the real thing (try the veal burger recipe).

It is also a place for sophistication, New York being probably one of the greatest international areas anywhere.

Chinese, Italian, German, Indonesian, French, Japanese, Thai, even African, are all nationalities that you will find in New York restaurants.

But what do you cook for yourself? Prosciutto and tomato salad has an Italian ring about it, but the New York dish has its own identity.

Have a try at seaweed cabbage with pigeon and wild rice plus bacon as a main meal. Don't you recognize it? Of course you don't. This is New York — the land of red currant blintzes and ginger-glazed pork chops, where anything goes.

In this section you will find devilled crab wonton, salmon in cream cheese pastry and baked ham with apricots (which is delicious).

As a last word, don't be afraid to mix the recipes into your own table presentation, but you will have to learn by experience which combination works for you — not everybody is a natural New Yorker!

Right: BAKED HAM WITH APRICOTS & CHINESE MUSHROOMS, Recipe page 113.
Left: ASPARAGUS IN TANGERINE SAUCE, Recipe page 104.

Tabbouleh

Preparation Time: 20 minutes
Chilling Time: 15 minutes
Serves 6

1 cup bulgur (cracked wheat)
1 cup chopped scallions
2–3 cups chopped fresh parsley
¼ cup chopped fresh mint
3 large tomatoes, chopped

Dressing:
¼ cup olive oil
¼ cup lemon juice
salt and pepper to taste
black olives
cucumber slices

Soak the bulgur in a bowl of warm water to cover for at least 15 minutes. Drain, then place on a paper towel and pat dry. Combine the bulgur with the scallions, herbs and tomatoes. Toss well and chill for 15 minutes.

Blend the olive oil, lemon juice, salt and pepper. To serve, toss the dressing with the salad and sprinkle with the olives and cucumber slices.

Purslane, Mint & Apple Salad

Preparation Time: 20 minutes
Serves 4

4 small green apples
¼ cup lemon juice
¼ cup water
1 large bunch purslane
2–3 sprigs fresh spearmint, finely chopped
¼ cup sour cream
1 Tbsp cider vinegar
1 Tbsp olive oil
¼ tsp pepper
½ tsp sugar

Core but do not peel the apples and cut them into thin wedges. Mix together the lemon juice and water; brush each apple wedge on both sides with the mixture. Arrange the apple wedges in a flower pattern on individual serving plates.

Pull apart the purslane, discarding the stalks. Heap equal mounds of purslane leaves in the center of each apple "flower." Sprinkle with the spearmint.

Blend together the sour cream, vinegar, oil, pepper and sugar. Drizzle the dressing over each salad. Serve at room temperature.

Chicken Lemon Soup

Preparation Time: 7 minutes
Cooking Time: 12 minutes
Serves 3

4 cups chicken consommé or broth
1 bunch chives, chopped
¼ cup cooked rice
1 egg
¼ cup lemon juice
pinch of cayenne

In a large saucepan, heat the consommé until boiling. Stir the chives into the broth along with the rice. Reduce the heat to a simmer.

Beat the egg with the lemon juice. Stir about a cup of soup into the egg/lemon mixture and beat well. Gradually return this mixture to the main stock in the pan. Add cayenne to taste. Continue to heat and stir until the soup takes on a glossy appearance.

Deep-Fried Herbs

Method I: Green Herbs

Preparation Time: 2 minutes
Cooking Time: 2 minutes each

Any of the following fresh herbs:
parsley, cilantro, coriander, sage, mint, marjoram, basil
light vegetable oil

In a skillet heat ½-inch (1 cm) of light vegetable oil to 375°F (190°C).

Take 2 or 3 sprigs of the herb, pick off any dead leaves but do not wash. Drop the sprigs into the hot oil for 3–4 seconds. When the herbs turn bright green, lift them out and drain them on a paper towel. Continue until you have the desired quantity. After a few seconds of cooking, the herbs set and become crisp. They are a tasty and colorful garnish to any meat or fish dish.

Method II: Tempura Herbs

Preparation Time: 7 minutes
Cooking Time: 5 minutes

parsley, cilantro, coriander, sage, mint, marjoram or basil
light vegetable oil

Batter:
1 egg
1 cup flour
1 tsp baking powder (optional)
1 cup ice water

Left: STUFFED ARTICHOKE SALAD, Recipe this page. *Right:* VILLAGE SALAD, Recipe this page.

Blend the egg, flour, baking powder (if desired) and water into a smooth, thin batter. Pour into a bowl. In a frying pan or skillet, heat 1 inch (1.5 cm) of light vegetable oil to 375°F (190°C) or use a deep fryer.

Take small sprigs of clean, dry herbs and drop them into the batter to coat. With a pair of tongs or chopsticks, lift out the herb sprigs and lower them into the hot oil. Fry until light golden, about 4 minutes. Drain and serve while hot as a garnish.

Village Salad

PHOTOGRAPH THIS PAGE

Preparation Time: 10 minutes
Serves 4

½ lb (250 g) feta cheese
2 large sweet onions
1 long English cucumber
½ lb tomatoes
1½ cups large black olives
2 Tbsp red wine vinegar
1 Tbsp dried oregano
2 Tbsp chopped fresh basil or
   1 Tbsp dried basil
½ lb (250 g) tomatoes

Dice the cheese into ½-inch (1 cm) squares (approximately). Coarsely chop the onions, cucumber and tomatoes. Mix with the cheese in a large bowl. Add the olives, vinegar, oregano and basil; toss gently. Pour on the olive oil, toss again and serve.

Stuffed Artichoke Salad

PHOTOGRAPH THIS PAGE

Preparation Time: 15 minutes
Cooking Time: 30 minutes
Serves 2

2 artichokes, cleaned and trimmed
2 Tbsp lemon juice
4 anchovys fillets
1 small bunch chives, chopped
1 Tbsp chopped fresh parsley
1 red pepper
3–4 oz (90-125 g) snow peas
2 Tbsp white wine vinegar
1 tsp honey
dash of Tabasco sauce
1 tsp sesame seeds

Place the artichokes and lemon juice in a pan, cover with boiling water, and boil for ½ hour until tender. Drain, cool, and cut the artichokes carefully lengthwise in halves. Remove the choke and place the heart halves, hollow side up, on salad plates.

Chop the anchovys and mix them with the chopped chives and parsley. Spoon this mixture onto the artichoke hearts.

Remove the stalk and seeds from the red pepper and cut it into thin strips. Trim the ends of the snow peas and cut the peas lengthwise into julienne strips. Arrange both vegetables around the artichokes.

Blend the vinegar, honey and Tabasco. Drizzle the dressing over the salad. Sprinkle with sesame seeds and serve.

NEW YORK

APPETIZERS
SOUPS
SALADS
ENTREES

NEW YORK

**APPETIZERS
SOUPS
SALADS
ENTREES**

Prosciutto & Tomato Salad

Preparation Time: 15 minutes
Marinate: 1 hour
Serves 4

½ lb (250 g) sliced prosciutto
¼ lb (125 g) hot cherry peppers
½ lb (250 g) cherry tomatoes
1 bunch scallions
1 clove garlic
¼ cup red wine vinegar
¼ cup olive oil
dash of red pepper sauce

Cut the prosciutto into 1-inch (2.5 cm) by 3-inch (8 cm) strips (approximately). Trim, core and wash the peppers and tomatoes. Cut them in halves. Fit half a pepper and half a tomato together, wrap a meat strip around each and secure with a toothpick. Continue until the peppers, tomatoes and meat strips are used up.

Cut the scallions into 1-inch (2.5 cm) lengths and place them in the blender with the garlic, vinegar, oil and red pepper sauce. Blend thoroughly. Pour the dressing over the salad and toss gently to coat. Allow it to rest for 1 hour. Toss the salad again lightly then drain it. Serve at room temperature.

Potato Chips with Sour Cream & Caviar

Preparation Time: 10 minutes
Soaking Time: 1–2 hours
Cooking Time: 20 minutes
Serves 3–4

2 large white potatoes
light vegetable oil
1 cup sour cream
3½ oz (100 g) black caviar

Peel the potatoes and discard the skins. Then continue to peel shavings off the potatoes into a large bowl until they are all sliced. Cover with a liberal quantity of unsalted cold water. Allow to soak for 1–2 hours.

Heat light vegetable oil in a deep fryer to 375°F (190°C). Lift the potato chips from the water and dry them on a towel. Drop them, a few at a time, into the hot oil. Make sure they do not stick together. Fry the potatoes for about 3 minutes until they are just golden. Lift them out with a slotted spoon and drain them. Place the chips in a bowl lined with a paper towel. Give them a light dusting of salt and keep warm in a 150°F (75°C) oven until all the chips are cooked

Serve warm with bowls of sour cream and caviar.

The modern expressions of the famous New York subway.

Asparagus in Tangerine Sauce

PHOTOGRAPH PAGE 101

Preparation Time: 7 minutes
Cooking Time: 8 minutes
Serves 6

4–5 fresh tangerines
¼ cup butter
1 Tbsp cornstarch
1½ lbs (750 g) fresh asparagus

Peel, remove the seeds and section the tangerines. Place about half the fruit in a blender and spin briefly.

Melt the butter in a saucepan. Add the blended tangerine pulp and stir in the cornstarch. Bring to a boil then stir in the whole tangerine sections. Lower the heat and simmer for 2 minutes.

Trim the asparagus and steam or boil in a small amount of water for 6–8 minutes, until just tender. Drain the asparagus and place in a hot serving dish. Pour the tangerine sauce over and serve immediately.

Seaweed Cabbage

Preparation Time: 2 minutes
Cooking Time:5 minutes
Serves 4

1 lb (500 g) dark green cabbage or mustard greens
3 Tbsp peanut oil
generous pinch each of sugar, salt, ground almonds and ground anise

Shred the cabbage or mustard greens very finely. Heat the oil in a skillet until almost smoking (425°F) (230°C). Stir-fry the cabbage until it just starts to brown at the edges. Remove from the heat and sprinkle with the sugar, salt, almonds and anise. Toss well and serve hot.

Marjoram & Cheese Omelet

Preparation Time: 5 minutes
Cooking Time: 5 minutes
Serves 2

3–4 eggs, separated
1 Tbsp milk
1 Tbsp butter
¼ cup ricotta or grated soft, mild cheese
2 Tbsp chopped fresh marjoram
large pinch of black pepper

Whip the egg whites until foamy. Beat the yolks and milk together until creamy.

Melt the butter in a 9-inch (23 cm) iron skillet over medium-high heat. When the butter is hot but not brown, brush it over the bottom and sides of the pan.

Stir the egg yolks into the whites and pour into the pan. Sprinkle the cheese, marjoram and pepper over the eggs; try to avoid getting the cheese around the edge of the pan. Cover the pan with a rounded lid, preferably one borrowed from a larger pan, and reduce the heat to moderate. Cook for about 4 minutes until the omelet is just starting to brown around the edge. Remove the pan from the heat, run a knife around the edge of the omelet and slide it onto a plate. Fold it in half and serve immediately.

Deep-Fried Cream Cheese

Preparation Time: 5 minutes
Cooking Time: 10 minutes
Preheat Deep Fryer: 375°F (190°C)
Serves 2

light vegetable oil
8 oz (250 g) package cream cheese, cubed
2 Tbsp flour
1 egg, beaten
1 cup toasted breadcrumbs

Dice the cream cheese into ¾-inch (2 cm) cubes (approximately). Roll the cheese cubes first in flour, then in the beaten egg and finally in the bread crumbs. Refrigerate for 1 hour. Drop a handful at a time into the hot oil and fry for 3–4 minutes until golden. Lift out with a slotted spoon or tongs and drain on paper towels. The cheese cubes will keep for a few minutes while you complete the cooking, but if left too long they will start to soften.

Serve the hot cream cheese tidbits with French fries or potato chips and a tossed green salad for a light lunch or brunch.

Potato Doilies

Preparation Time: 15 minutes
Cooking Time: 20–30 minutes
Serves 4

2 large potatoes
1 bunch chives
2 eggs
4 Tbsp flour
salt and pepper
butter

Peel the potatoes and cut them lengthwise into very thin slices using either a sharp knife or a potato peeler. Then stack and cut the slices lengthwise so that they resemble spaghetti. Dry the potato strips by carefully rolling them in a towel.

Clean the chives and cut them in half; they should be approximately the same length as the potato strips. Gently toss the potatoes and chives together.

In a blender, beat the egg, flour and seasonings until smooth; pour the batter into a shallow dish.

Melt about 2 Tbsp butter in a heavy skillet until bubbly. With a pair of chopsticks or fine-pointed kitchen tongs, pick up a small bunch of potato/chive strips, dip in the batter, then drop into the skillet to form a small lacy pancake. Fry for 5 minutes or until golden at the edges; using a spatula, turn and fry for a few minutes more. Remove to a warm plate. Continue cooking the rest of the potato/chive mix. Serve hot with a dab of sour cream.

Irish Soda Bread

Preparation Time: 15 minutes
Cooking Time: 40 minutes
Preheat Oven: 375°F (190°C)
Serves 4

3½ cups flour
1 tsp salt
1 Tbsp sugar
2 tsp baking soda
2 Tbsp soft butter
1¾ cups buttermilk

In a bowl, or using a food processor, mix all the ingredients lightly and quickly. Be careful not to overprocess the batter. Turn the dough out onto a floured board and mold it into a large, round loaf. Place the loaf in a greased 9-inch (23 cm) round pan and make an x in the top with a knife. Bake for 35–40 minutes or until golden. Cool the loaf on a rack.

NEW YORK

APPETIZERS
SOUPS
SALADS
ENTREES

Summer leisure on Bridle path in Central Park.

SHRIMP CRÈPES WITH LIME SAUCE, Recipe page 109.

Colorful traditional Chinese New Year celebrations in New York City Chinatown.

Shrimp Crèpes with Lime Sauce

PHOTOGRAPH PAGE 108

Preparation and Cooking Time: 1¼ hours
Preheat Oven: 400°F (200°C)
Serves 4

Crèpe batter:

2 eggs
1 cup flour
1 cup milk
1 Tbsp grated lime peel
2 Tbsp lime juice
butter for frying

Filling:

2 Tbsp butter
1 clove garlic, minced
1 tsp powdered mustard
dash of red pepper sauce
1 bunch scallions, coarsely chopped
1 lb (500 g) peeled shrimp

Sauce:

2 Tbsp white wine
3 Tbsp lime juice
2 Tbsp sherry
1 leek, chopped

Crèpes:

Blend the eggs, flour, milk, lime peel and lime juice until smooth and creamy. In a 6-inch (15 cm) iron skillet, melt 1 tsp butter over medium-high heat until it bubbles; brush the butter around the pan thoroughly. Pour in about 2 Tbsp of batter, tilting the pan to allow it to cover the bottom. Cook for 3 or 4 minutes until just set. Turn the crèpe over and cook for a minute longer. Remove the crèpe to a side platter and keep warm. Repeat this process continuing to make crèpes until all the batter has been used. (There should be about 12 crèpes.)

Filling:

In a saucepan, melt the 2 Tbsp of butter. Add the garlic and cook for 5 minutes. Stir in the mustard and red pepper sauce. Add the shrimp. Stir well and cook for 2 minutes until hot. Using a flat, oven-proof platter or serving dish, put one crèpe, the most attractive side down, at one end. Place 2 generous Tbsps of shrimp filling in the center of the crèpe and fold it over. Continue with the rest, lining the crèpes up side by side. If there is any filling left over, arrange it around the crèpes. Put the stuffed crèpes in the preheated oven for 10 minutes until they just start to bubble.

Sauce:

Combine the wine, lime juice, sherry and chopped leek in a saucepan and boil for 5 minutes until the leek is soft. Puree the sauce in a blender until creamy; return it to the pan and bring to a boil. Serve immediately over the crèpes.

NEW YORK

MAIN COURSE

NEW YORK

MAIN COURSE

Salmon in Cream Cheese Pastry

Preparation Time: 25 minutes
Cooking Time: 30 minutes
Preheat Oven: 375°F (190°C)
Serves 4

4 salmon fillets
2 Tbsp butter
2 Tbsp lemon juice
dash of Tabasco sauce

Pastry:
¼ cup butter
1 cup cream cheese
1 cup grated cheddar cheese
1 cup flour

Wash the fillets and pat them dry. Butter a baking platter and arrange the fillets in such a way that there is at least 1-inch (2.5 cm) of space around each one. Melt the butter and stir in the lemon juice and Tabasco. Brush the lemon mixture over the fillets.

In a pastry maker, food processor or bowl, cream the butter and cheeses. Add the flour until the dough just forms a ball. Divide the dough into 4 portions and roll out on a floured board until it is about ⅛-inch (0.2 cm) thick.

Carefully cover each fillet with a pastry shell, tucking it in at the edges and trimming off any excess. Bake for ½ hour or until golden. Serve immediately.

Pasta with Ham & Fresh Figs

Preparation Time: 7 minutes
Cooking Time: 12 minutes
Serves 2

2 Tbsp butter
¼ cup shallots, chopped
1 clove garlic, minced
½ lb (250 g) cooked ham, diced
½ lb (250 g) fresh figs, sliced
1 tsp pepper
¼ cup white wine
¼ cup heavy cream
½ lb (250 g) tomato pasta
1 Tbsp butter or olive oil

In a large saucepan, melt the butter; stir in the shallots and garlic. Cook for 5 minutes. Add the ham and figs; stir and simmer for 2 minutes. Add the pepper, wine and cream. Bring to a simmer and cook for 5 minutes.

Cook the pasta in 2 qts (2 lt) unsalted boiling water for 10 minutes or until tender. Drain and stir in the butter or olive oil. Serve immediately with the sauce.

Lobster Bisque
PHOTOGRAPH PAGE 111

Preparation Time: 10 minutes
Cooking Time: 20 minutes
Yield: 4½ cups

4 cups chicken stock
1 small carrot, grated
½ stalk celery, grated
¼ cup butter
pinch of salt
1 tsp fresh or dried thyme
1 3-lb (1½ kg) lobster
3 Tbsp brandy
¼ cup rice wine
pinch of cayenne

Combine the first 7 ingredients in a large pot and bring to a boil. Reduce the heat and simmer for 10 minutes. Remove the lobster and cool. In a blender, thoroughly blend the stock and vegetables until smooth. Return to the pot. When the lobster is cool enough to handle, remove the meat from the shell, chop the meat coarsely and return it to the stock. Stir in the brandy, wine and cayenne. Reheat but do not let boil.

Devilled Crab Wonton
PHOTOGRAPH PAGE 111

Preparation Time: 15 minutes
Cooking Time: 15 minutes
Serves 4

1 Tbsp butter
1 Tbsp flour
1 tsp powdered mustard
pinch of cayenne
pinch of black pepper
1 cup shredded crabmeat
½ lb (250 g) won ton envelopes
4 cups lobster bisque
small bunch watercress, coarsely chopped

Melt the butter in a saucepan and stir in the flour to make a smooth, light paste. Add the mustard, cayenne, pepper and crabmeat. Stir well and simmer for 5 minutes.

Remove the pan from the heat and, using a teaspoon, stuff the won ton envelopes with the crab mixture.

Heat the lobster bisque to boiling. Drop in the won tons and let boil for 5 minutes. Ladle the soup into the serving dishes and sprinkle with watercress.

Top: LOBSTER BISQUE, Recipe page 110. *Bottom:* DEVILLED CRAB WONTON, Recipe page 110.

Taxis scrambling for customers in New York's fast lane night-life.

NEW YORK

MAIN COURSE

Pigeon with Wild Rice & Bacon

Preparation Time: 15 minutes
Cooking Time: 40 minutes
Serves 2

3 cups water (approximately)
½ cup wild rice
pinch of salt
4 pigeons
2 tsp fresh or dried thyme
4 strips of bacon

Bring the water to a boil, add the salt and wild rice, lower the heat and simmer covered for 40 minutes. When done, the rice should be fluffy, dry and curled.

Meanwhile, wash the pigeons and pat them dry. Sprinkle ½ tsp of thyme in the cavity of each bird. Wrap each one with a strip of bacon and skewer onto a rotisserie spit side by side. Tie the wings with string if necessary. Roast over a hot barbecue grill or under a 450°F (230°C) broiler for 30–40 minutes until the bacon is crisp and the birds are just beginning to char. Serve immediately with the wild rice and asparagus tips or fiddlehead greens.

Ginger-Glazed Pork Chops

Preparation Time: 7 minutes
Cooking Time: 20 minutes
Serves 4

4 pork chops
1 tsp powdered mustard
1 Tbsp peanut oil
2 Tbsp butter
1 Tbsp ground ginger
1 Tbsp light brown sugar
dash of Hot Sauce (page 148)

Wash the pork chops and pat them dry. Rub both sides of the meat with the mustard.

Brush a barbecue grill with peanut oil and cook the chops for 15–20 minutes over medium heat, turning once.

While the chops are cooking, melt the butter in a saucepan. Stir in the ginger, sugar and pepper sauce. Heat to a simmer but do not boil.

When the chops are done, remove them to a serving platter and brush with the ginger glaze. Serve with red pepper, corn and new potatoes.

Veal Burgers

PHOTOGRAPH THIS PAGE

Preparation Time: 5 minutes
Cooking Time: 8 minutes
Serves 2–3

1 lb (500 g) veal or top round steak
2 Tbsp lemon juice
¼ cup scallions, chopped
¼ cup Dijon mustard
¼ cup cream
1 Tbsp lemon juice
butter

Grind the meat, or have your butcher do so. Blend in the lemon juice, add the chopped scallions and form into firm patties. Fry quickly in butter to your preferred degree of doneness. Remove to a hot dish.

Put the mustard, cream and lemon juice in the cooking pan and stir well. Bring to a boil, remove from the heat and pour over the veal burgers. Serve hot.

Baked Ham with Apricots & Chinese Mushrooms

PHOTOGRAPH PAGE 101

Preparation Time: 20 minutes
Cooking Time: 2½ hours
Preheat Oven: 450°F (230°C)
Serves 6

4–5 lb (2–2½ kg)
2 Tbsp butter
3 Tbsp light brown sugar
1 Tbsp powdered mustard
2 Tbsp flour
water
½ lb (500 g) fresh apricots
½ cup water
¼ cup sugar
1 cup Chinese mushrooms, chopped
1 tsp ground ginger
1 tsp cider vinegar

Rinse the ham and pat it dry. Melt the butter in a saucepan, add the sugar and stir until the sugar is dissolved. Blend in the mustard and flour. Mix well, adding water 1 Tbsp at a time to produce a smooth paste.

Set the ham in a baking dish and spread the paste all over the meat, making it a little thicker at the top. Place in the preheated oven for ½ hour until the paste has set then reduce the heat to 350°F (180°C) and bake for a further 1½ hours.

Cut the apricots in half and remove the stones. Place the fruit in a pan, add the water and sugar, and simmer for 10 minutes until the apricots are tender but not mushy. Remove them from the liquid with a slotted spoon and set aside.

To the remaining liquid add the mushrooms, ginger and vinegar. Boil for 10 minutes until the sauce is reduced and slightly thickened.

Remove the ham from the oven and decorate it with the apricot halves. Spoon the glaze over the ham and fruit then return to the oven for 20 minutes.

NEW YORK

MAIN COURSE

Long Island Duck with Burgundy Jelly

Preparation Time: 20 minutes
Cooking Time: 2 hours
Preheat Oven: 400°F (200°C)
Serves 3

1 fresh duck (5–6 pounds)
1 tart apple, coarsely chopped
1 cup raisins
1 Tbsp grated orange peel
salt and pepper

Clean the duck thoroughly, rinse, pat dry and singe the pin feathers if necessary. In a bowl, toss the apple, raisins, orange peel and seasonings. Stuff the duck with the fruit mixture. Prick the skin all over with a fork and place the duck on a roasting rack in a pan. Roast for ½ hour then lower the heat to 325°F (160°C) and roast for 1½ hours more. When done, the skin should be crisp. Serve with Burgundy Jelly.

Burgundy Jelly

Preparation Time: 10 minutes
Chilling Time: 2–3 hours

1 cup red currant jelly
½ cup burgundy
1 Tbsp powdered mustard

Melt the jelly in a heavy saucepan and stir in the wine and mustard. Mix well and continue to heat for 2–3 minutes. Pour the jelly into a 1½ cup mold, allow to cool then chill until set.

NEW YORK SWEETS

New York Trifle

PHOTOGRAPH PAGE 115

Preparation Time: 20 minutes
Cooking Time: 10 minutes
Serves 6

1 sponge cake or ½ lb (250 g) Savoy biscuits
1 cup dry sherry
4 cups custard
1 lb (500 g) macaroons
½ cup sliced almonds
2 cups fresh raspberries
1 cup heavy cream, whipped
candied violets

Cut the cake in half lengthwise then into sections to fit the bottom of a glass bowl. Or line the bowl with biscuits. Sprinkle with sherry and spread over the cake or bicuits a layer of custard. Sprinkle with ½ cup macaroons, almonds and a layer of raspberries. Repeat the layers until the dish is almost full. Top with whipped cream and decorate with candied violets.

Custard

3 cups milk
¾ cup sugar
6 egg yolks
1 tsp cornstarch
¼ cup brandy
½ tsp vanilla

Scald the milk in a heavy pan. Beat together the sugar, egg yolks and cornstarch and stir into the hot milk. Combine well then add the brandy and vanilla. Cook over low heat or in a double boiler, stirring constantly, until the custard thickens. Allow to cool before using.

From *The Universal Recipe Book* by a society of gentlemen in New York, 1814

Sponge Cake

Preparation Time: 15 minutes
Baking Time: 1 hour
Preheat Oven: 350°F (180°C)

4 eggs, separated
½ tsp cream of tartar
¾ cup sugar
¼ cup cold water
1 tsp lemon juice
1 tsp vanilla
¾ cup flour

Beat the egg whites and cream of tartar together until the egg whites are stiff but not dry. Beat in half the sugar. Set aside. Beat the egg yolks until smooth then gradually beat into them the rest of the sugar, the water, lemon juice and vanilla. Blend in the flour gradually. When all the flour has been added, fold in the egg whites.

Pour the mixture into an 8-inch (20 cm) ungreased tube pan and bake for 1 hour. Invert the pan on a rack and cool the cake. Run a knife around the edge of the pan to loosen the cake before removing it.

Macaroons

Preparation Time: 10 minutes
Cooking Time: 10 minutes
Preheat Oven: 350°F (180°C)
Yield:

4 egg whites
1¼ cup sugar
¾ cup flour
pinch of salt
1 tsp vanilla
2½ cups shredded coconut

Beat the egg whites until stiff then gradually beat in the sugar, flour, salt and vanilla. Fold in the coconut.

Drop the batter by the tablespoonful about 2-inches (5 cm) apart on a buttered cookie sheet. Bake for 10 minutes, until lightly browned.

Christmas at the world famous Rockefeller Centre in New York City.

Left: PASSIONFRUIT & ICE CREAM, Recipe this page. Right: NEW YORK TRIFLE, Recipe page 114.

Passionfruit & Ice Cream

PHOTOGRAPH THIS PAGE

Preparation Time: 30 minutes
Freezing Time: about 6 hours
Serves 6

1 qt (1 lt) vanilla ice cream
1 cup coconut milk
1 cup passion fruit juice
2 Tbsp sugar
¼ cup water
1 Tbsp lime juice
1 cup heavy cream
3 Tbsp long shredded coconut, toasted
2 Tbsp passion fruit juice
1 Tbsp white rum
1 Tbsp sugar

In a bowl, stir the ice cream until soft. Beat in the coconut milk. Spoon the mixture into a 1½ qt (1½ lt) mold, leaving a hollow in the center. Return the ice cream to the freezer.

Blend or mix well 1 cup of passion fruit juice, 2 Tbsp sugar, the water and lime juice; freeze this mixture for 2–3 hours. When the juices are frozen, but still mushy, beat them in a bowl. Whip the cream until thick then fold it into the frozen juices. Return the juice/cream mixture to the freezer for an hour or until set.

When the passion fruit mixture has set, spoon it into the center of the ice cream mold. Return the mold to the freezer until ready for serving.

To serve, unmold the ice cream onto a platter. Sprinkle over it the shredded coconut. Puree the 2 Tbsp passion fruit juice, white rum and sugar. Warm this mixture very slightly and pour over the ice cream. Serve immediately.

NEW YORK

SWEETS

NEW YORK SWEETS

Tarte Tatin
(Upside Down Pear Pie)

Preparation Time: 25 minutes
Cooking Time: 45 minutes
Preheat Oven: 375°F (190°C)
Serves 6

½ cup butter, divided
2 lbs (1 kg) Anjou pears (about 8 medium)
½ cup sugar
½ cup butter
1⅓ cups flour
1 egg
pinch of salt
heavy cream

In a heavy 9-inch (23 cm) iron skillet, put ¼ cup butter and set over medium heat. Peel and core the pears. Cut them into large pieces, add them to the melted butter and sauté for 5 minutes. Roll the pear pieces over so they are coated with the butter; add the remaining ¼ cup of butter and sprinkle on the sugar. Cover and cook for a further 10–12 minutes until the sugar starts to brown.

In a bowl, cream the ½ cup butter. Add the flour, egg and salt. Add a spoonful of water if necessary to hold the dough together and mix by hand just enough to make a soft pastry. Roll out the pastry ¼-inch (0.5 cm) thick and place over the cooked pear in the skillet. Trim and tuck in the edges. Place in the preheated oven and bake uncovered for ½ hour.

To serve, run a knife around the edge of the skillet. Invert a serving plate over the pan, then turn the plate and pan over so that the plate is now on the bottom. When you remove the pan the golden brown pears will be on top. Serve hot with a drizzle of heavy cream.

Traditional Strawberry Shortcake
PHOTOGRAPH PAGE 117

Preparation Time: 20 minutes
Cooking Time: 25 minutes
Steeping Time: 1 hour
Serves 5–6

about 1 qt (1 lt) strawberries (wild ones if you can find them)
1 cup fruit sugar or powdered sugar
2 cups flour
3 tsp baking powder
pinch of salt
4 Tbsp shortening
¾ cup milk
1 cup heavy cream, whipped
¼ cup wildflower honey

Hull the strawberries, cut them in halves and toss them gently with the sugar in a bowl. Allow to mascerate for 1 hour.

Meanwhile, in a bowl, food processor or pastry maker, sift the flour, baking powder and salt. Cut in the shortening. Pour on the milk and mix briefly to obtain a soft dough. Divide the dough in half, sprinkle with flour and roll out to ¾-inch (2 cm) thick rounds. Place one round on a floured baking sheet, brush with a little melted butter and place the second round on top. Bake for about 25 minutes in a 425°F (220°C) oven.

To serve, split the shortcake and spoon half the strawberries and half the whipped cream over the bottom layer, drizzling lightly with honey. Replace the top of the shortcake and cover with the remaining strawberries, cream and honey.

Red Currant Blintzes
PHOTOGRAPH PAGE 117

Preparation Time: 30 minutes
Cooking Time: 30 minutes
Preheat Oven: 350°F (180°C)
Serves 4–6

Batter:
¾ cup all-purpose flour
pinch of salt
1 cup milk
2 eggs
butter for frying

Filling:
2 cups ricotta cheese
2 Tbsp sugar
½ tsp vanilla
½ tsp mace

Sauce:
1 lb (500 g) fresh red currants
4 Tbsp sugar
1 tsp lemon juice
¼ cup sweet white wine

Combine the flour, salt, milk and eggs in a blender and mix until smooth. Heat a 6-inch (15 cm) skillet and brush with butter. Pour in 2–3 Tbsp of batter and fry until just set. Turn once and fry briefly on the other side. Remove from the pan, set aside and continue until all the batter is used. This should yield 12 very soft blintzes.

Beat together the ricotta, sugar, vanilla and mace. Place a generous Tbsp of filling on each blintz, fold them and stack in a baking dish. Warm the blintzes in the preheated oven for 10–15 minutes.

Put the red currants, sugar, lemon juice and wine in a saucepan and bring the mixture to a boil. Lower the heat and simmer for 5 minutes. Pour the sauce over the blintzes and serve hot.

Left: RED CURRANT BLINTZES, Recipe page 116. *Right:* TRADITIONAL STRAWBERRY SHORTCAKE, Recipe page 116.   **page 117**

California

Recipes Touched by the Sun.
In every golden Californian
orange there's a real piece of
sunshine, which probably
accounts for the sunny
disposition of the typical
bronzed Californian.
California is ideal growing
country with long hot summers,
wet winters and

Multi-colored flowers and a deep blue sky frame this famous span of the Golden Gate Bridge in San Francisco.

CALIFORNIA

INTRODUCTION

a climate ambience where extremes of either are not the norm.

One result of this is that the 26 million Californians who live in this 40,481 square kilometre Garden of Eden traditionally eat higher-quality fresh home-grown fruit and vegetables than almost anywhere else in the world.

Apart from being the biggest agricultural-producing state in America, the fortunate Californians have the benefit of fresh supply virtually all year round. Rarely, if ever, is what you want "out of season".

The list is impressive, Flagship fruits from a world market-viewpoint are, of course, grapes (Californian wines rate with the best in the world) and oranges.

In addition to this add lemons, figs, dates, peaches, plums, nectarines, pomegranates, kiwi fruit, walnuts, avocados, tomatoes, artichokes and lettuce to name just some of the prize-winning produce which Californians grow in huge quantities with relative ease.

From a gastronomic viewpoint at least, Californians have always had more than a fair share of nourishing wealth.

A pointer to this heritage is the large number of towns better known by the individual crop each specializes in.

Castroville, for example, bills itself as the artichoke capital of the world while Salinas takes a leaf out of the same book by calling itself "Lettuce Town."

Similarly, there are Grape Towns, Peach Towns and even Raisin Towns.

A superb list of natural ingredients growing under Californian feet is historically enhanced by a cosmopolitan cuisine showing distinct Mediterranean bias.

Spanish missionaries were largely responsible for the introduction of Mediterranean-style crops.

Missions tend to be modest places in most parts of the world but not in early California where they were actually large and usually very prosperous agricultural estates.

The estates were shrewdly managed by the Spanish friars who labored in combination with Indian converts. The work was demanding, but at least all concerned ate extremely well.

It was also Spaniards arriving from the South who introduced the taste for Mexican foods to California.

Barbecue beans, guacamole, chili powder and piquant salsas are now commonplace in Californian cuisine. All originated across the border.

California's cuisine rapidly expanded with the arrival of ethnic groups from all over the world and now constitutes one of the most cosmopolitan diets anywhere.

In California you will find an abundance of menus offering steamed or sautéed vegetables Chinese style, sushi, after the Japanese palate, and even Russian piroshki.

Speciality Italian and French dishes go without saying, as many of the first restaurants in California were either one or the other opened by enterprising European immigrants.

It isn't possible to pin-point any dish and say this is Californian food, as there is no indigenous diet. The cuisine is too cosmopolitan for that.

The international influences are apparent though, and can fairly be called Californian.

Sauces tend to be light, vegetables are only briefly cooked, meat is lightly seared and, naturally, there is predominant use of Californian wines.

Californian seafood cooking is also distinctive, being much influenced by Japanese sushi techniques.

These recipes are a delight to create, as preparation is relatively simple and the cooking time brief.

Try the recipe for that magnificent Italian-style shellfish and fish stew, cioppino, an excellent menu choice for something a bit different, with minimum fuss in the making.

There are recipes for pizzas to be proud of, frisky frittatas, and salads that will genuinely turn heads at the table.

Portions and variations will enable you to plan a total menu with complete freedom to produce luncheon main meals, entrées or first courses with a host of fruit-base desserts that make the most of California's superlative natural produce.

That's one of the glories of Californian cooking; there's something to appeal to everybody — and that's precisely what California is all about.

GINGER MELON SALAD, Recipe page 122.

Buttermilk & Watercress Soup

Preparation Time: 5 minutes
Chilling Time: 2 hours
Serves 4

2 cups buttermilk
1 bunch watercress
1 small bunch chives
½ cup apple juice
2 cups carbonated water
lemon slices

Combine the buttermilk, watercress, chives and apple juice in a blender. Mix until very smooth and chill thoroughly. To serve, mix with soda and garnish with lemon.

Velvet Garlic Soup with Thyme Cream

Preparation Time: 20 minutes
Cooking Time: 20 minutes
Serves 4

5 cups chicken consommé
6 cloves garlic, chopped
1 large sprig fresh sage
1 egg
1 Tbsp lemon juice
1 tsp cornstarch
½ cup heavy cream
1 tsp sugar
1 Tbsp fresh thyme, very finely chopped
½ tsp freshly ground black pepper

Heat the stock, garlic and sage together in a heavy pan and simmer for 15 minutes. Pour into a blender and puree for 10 seconds. Strain the soup back into the pan through a fine kitchen sieve. In a blender, blend the egg, lemon juice, cornstarch and sugar together. Add 1 cup of the soup and blend again. Add this mixture to the soup in the pan and reheat but do not boil.

Whip the cream, finely chopped thyme and pepper until firm but not overly stiff.

Ladle the soup into bowls and float 1 Tbsp of the thyme cream on each.

Ginger Melon Salad

PHOTOGRAPH PAGE 121

Preparation Time: 10 minutes
Cooking Time: 1 hour
Serves 4

1 honeydew melon, cut into balls
¼ cup honey
¼ cup lemon juice
1 Tbsp grated fresh ginger root
1 Serrano pepper, seeded and minced

Place the melon balls in a bowl. Melt the honey in small saucepan; add the lemon juice, ginger and minced pepper. Stir and simmer for 2–3 minutes. Cool slightly and pour over the melon. Marinate for 1 hour in the refrigerator, stirring occasionally. Serve in individual stem glasses.

Salad Pizza

PHOTOGRAPH PAGE 123

Preparation Time: 30 minutes
Rising Time: 1 hour
Baking Time: 40 minutes
Serves 4

Crust:
2 tsp olive oil
2 tsp cornmeal
1 package active dry yeast
1 tsp sugar
1½ cups flour
warm water

Topping:
1 Tbsp olive oil
2 Tbsp lemon juice
¼ cup cold water
2 cups Japanese eggplant, peeled and chopped
1 cup chopped onion
1 large sweet red pepper, seeded and chopped
1 Tbsp chopped fresh sage or
    1½ tsp dried sage
1 Tbsp dried oregano
½ cup grated Parmesan cheese

Salad:
1 cup shredded lettuce
2 tomatoes, chopped
1 hot pepper, minced or grated
1 cup grated or crumbled Feta cheese
½ cup grated Mozzarella cheese
2 Tbsp olive oil

Crust:
Combine all the crust ingredients except the water in a bowl or food processor. Mix well and add sufficient water to make a stiff dough. Turn the dough onto a lightly floured board and knead for 10 minutes until smooth. Cover the dough and set it aside in a warm place for 1 hour. Knead again for 2 minutes then roll out the dough to a large round about ¼ inch (0.5 cm) thick. Place it on a greased baking sheet or pizza plate and brush the top with olive oil and stand in a warm place for 5 minutes.

Left: SALAD PIZZA, Recipe page 122.
Right. ORANGE & HERB SALAD WITH MINI ROLLS, Recipe this page.

Topping:

Mix the oil, lemon juice and cold water together in a bowl. Add the eggplant and toss until well coated. Shake the eggplant dry and place it on the dough. Sprinkle on the onion, pepper, sage, oregano and Parmesan cheese. Bake at 425°F (220°C) for 25–30 minutes.

Remove the pizza from the oven and add the salad topping: lettuce, tomatoes, hot pepper, feta and Mozzarella cheeses. Sprinkle with olive oil and place under the broiler for 10 minutes at 400°F until bubbly.

Orange & Herb Salad with Mini Rolls

PHOTOGRAPH THIS PAGE

Preparation Time: Dough—2½ hours
Assembly—10 minutes

Serves 4

Rolls:
1 recipe of sweet bread dough (page 217)
1 cup pitted dates
1 cup fresh figs
¼ cup whole blanched almonds

Salad:
3 oranges, peeled and sectioned

1 small bunch spinach, torn in pieces
sprig of tarragon
sprig of lemon balm
sprig of parsley
sprig of chervil

Dressing:
2 Tbsp olive oil
2 Tbsp red wine vinegar
pinch of sugar
pinch of pepper

Make one batch of sweet dough according to the recipe on page 217. After the first rising, punch the dough down and roll it out ¼-inch (0.5 cm) thick on a lightly floured board. With a knife, cut the dough into straws ½-inch (1 cm) thick and 3–4 inches (5–10 cm) long. Wrap some of the straws around the dates, figs and almonds; tie the remainder into knots or roll them into balls. Place them on a baking sheet to rise for 1 hour. Bake at 400°F (200°C) for 15–20 minutes until golden and quite crisp.

Place the orange sections and spinach pieces in a bowl. Chop the fresh herbs and toss with the oranges and spinach. Add the bread/fruit straws and mini rolls. Blend the olive oil, vinegar, sugar and pepper. Sprinkle the dressing over the salad. Toss well and serve immediately.

CALIFORNIA

**APPETIZERS
SOUPS
SALADS
ENTREES**

CALIFORNIA

APPETIZERS
SOUPS
SALADS
ENTREES

Cauliflower with Huntingdon Sauce

PHOTOGRAPH THIS PAGE

Preparation Time: 5 minutes
Cooking Time: 5 minutes
Serves 4

1 medium cauliflower
2 Tbsp butter
2 tsp curry powder
½ tsp grated fresh ginger root
1 clove garlic, minced
2 tsp chopped fresh parsley
3 Tbsp heavy cream

Trim the leaves and stalk from the cauliflower and place the head in a pot. Cover it with boiling water and quickly return to the boil. Cover, lower the heat and simmer for 3–4 minutes.

Meanwhile, melt the butter in a small saucepan and stir in the curry powder, ginger, garlic and parsley. Simmer for 3–4 minutes. Stir in the cream; reheat for 1 minute but do not boil. Drain the cauliflower and place it on a hot serving dish. Pour the sauce over and serve immediately.

Escargot with Brie

Preparation Time: 30 minutes
Cooking Time: 10 minutes

1 French loaf
½ cup melted butter
2 cups canned snails
½ cup chicken stock
1 tsp chopped fresh or dried thyme
1 tsp chopped fresh tarragon or ½ tsp dried tarragon
½ cup sour cream
1 Tbsp brandy
½ cup heavy cream
large pinch of cayenne
1 lb (500 g) Brie cheese
1 bunch of chives, chopped

Cut the bread into 1-inch (2.5 cm) thick slices. Brush both sides with the melted butter. Heat in a 350°F (180°C) oven for 10–12 minutes until golden.

Chop the snails; mix them in a saucepan with the stock, thyme and tarragon. Bring to a boil, lower the heat and simmer for 10 minutes. Remove from the heat and stir in the sour cream and brandy. Combine well.

CAULIFLOWER WITH HUNTINGDON SAUCE, Recipe this page.

Whip the cream with the cayenne.

To assemble, spread a layer of Brie on each bread slice; sprinkle on the chopped chives. Spoon on about 2 Tbsp of the herbed snail mixture and top with 1 tsp of seasoned cream.

Note: These may be served hot or cold, but do not assemble until just before serving, as the bread will become soggy.

Spinach & Pear Rolls

Preparation Time: 30 minutes
Cooking Time: 40 minutes
Serves 6

1 lb (500 g) fresh spinach
2 Tbsp melted butter
1 cup ricotta cheese
¼ cup grated Parmesan cheese
1 egg
1 tsp pepper
1 tsp nutmeg
1 Tbsp chopped fresh mint
1 tsp caraway seeds
2 large pears

Pastry:
1 cup semolina
2 cups flour
3 eggs
2 Tbsp grated fresh ginger root

Topping:
1 cup bacon bits

Wash the spinach thoroughly and steam it for 3–4 minutes in a tightly covered saucepan. Chop the undrained spinach well. Add the butter, cheeses, egg, pepper, nutmeg, mint and caraway seeds. Mix well and set aside. Peel, core and quarter the pears.

Pastry:
Combine the semolina, flour, eggs and ginger. Add enough cold water to make a firm dough. Roll out the dough ⅛-inch (0.3 cm) thick on a floured board. Spread it thickly with the spinach filling, leaving 1 inch (2.5 cm) around the edges. Place the pear sections in rows across the spinach. Carefully shape the dough to form a large, sausage-shaped roll. Pinch the ends closed and wrap the roll in muslin or cheesecloth, cut to size. (Aluminium foil will also work, but not as well.) Place the wrapped roll in a large pot or steamer. Cover it with boiling water, lower the heat and simmer for ½ hour.

When the roll is cooked, drain it and remove the wrap. Cut the roll into 1-inch (2.5 cm) thick slices and lay them on a baking sheet. Sprinkle the slices with bacon bits and broil in a 400°F (200°C) oven for 10 minutes.

Piroshkis with Crab Sauce

Preparation Time: 45 minutes
Chilling Time: 1 hour
Baking Time: 15 minutes
Yield: 25

Pastry:
3½ cups flour
1 tsp baking powder
pinch of salt
½ cup cold butter
2 eggs
1 cup sour cream
1 egg, beaten

Filling:
¼ cup butter
1 lb (500 g) mushrooms, chopped
1 tsp flour
4 Tbsp sour cream
salt and pepper to taste
1 Tbsp lemon juice
1 Tbsp chopped fresh chives
1 Tbsp chopped fresh tarragon or
    1½ tsp dried tarragon
chicken stock or white wine

Sauce:
2 Tbsp butter
½ lb (250 g) crab meat
1 tsp curry powder
¼ cup heavy cream

Pastry:
Combine the flour, baking powder and salt; cut in the butter until the mixture is crumbly. Beat in the eggs and sour cream. Turn the dough onto a floured board and knead it a little until smooth. Cover and chill the dough in the refrigerator for 1 hour.

Filling:
Melt the ¼ cup butter in a saucepan; stir in the mushrooms and flour. Cook, stirring, for 2 minutes. Add the sour cream, seasonings, lemon juice, chives and tarragon. Stir in a little chicken stock or white wine and simmer for 2 minutes.

Preheat the oven to 400°F (200°C). Roll out the chilled dough ¼-inch (0.5 cm) thick and cut it into 3-inch (8 cm) rounds. Place a generous tablespoon of the filling on each round. Fold the rounds in half and pinch the edges with a fork. Brush with a beaten egg and bake for 15 minutes until golden.

Sauce:
To serve, melt the remaining 2 Tbsp of butter in a saucepan and stir in the crab meat and curry powder. Simmer for 3 minutes. Stir in the cream; reheat and pour over the piroshkis.

CALIFORNIA

**APPETIZERS
SOUPS
SALADS
ENTREES**

Beautiful Mexican dancers at "Cinco De Mayo" in Los Angeles.

CALIFORNIA

MAIN COURSE

Stuffed Squid & Tomato Salad

Day Before:
Preparation Time: 30 minutes
Cooking Time: 30 minutes
Chilling Time: overnight

Serving Day:
Preparation Time: 10 minutes
Serves 4

1 lb (500 g) small fresh squid

Stuffing:
1 large egg
2 Tbsp lime juice
1 tsp pepper
pinch of sugar
½ cup chopped fresh mushrooms
¼ cup finely chopped almonds
heavy cream

Sauce:
1 cup white wine
¼ cup olive oil
1 Tbsp chopped fresh mint or
  1½ tsp dried mint
1 Tbsp cornstarch
1 cup fish stock
1 lb (500 g) tomatoes
fresh salad greens

Thoroughly clean and wash the squid. Remove the tentacles and set them aside. Dry the squid inside and out. In a bowl or food processor, combine the egg, lime juice, pepper, sugar, mushrooms and nuts; mix well. Add enough heavy cream to make a thick paste. With a piping bag or basting syringe, fill each squid about ¾ full of the paste. Fasten each with a toothpick.

In a saucepan, combine any leftover stuffing with the squid tentacles. Add the white wine, olive oil, mint, cornstarch and stock; mix well. Simmer, stirring occasionally until the sauce begins to thicken. Add the stuffed squid. Baste it with the sauce then cover and simmer for 25 minutes. Cool then refrigerate overnight.

To serve, arrange a bed of fresh, crisp salad greens of your choosing. Remove the squid from the sauce with a slotted spoon, discard the toothpicks and slice the squid into bite-sized pieces. Cut the tomatoes into quarters or eighths. Place the tomato and the squid slices on the salad leaves and pour the sauce over.

Low-Calorie Seafood Sausages

Preparation Time: 15 minutes
Cooking Time: 15 minutes
Serves 4

½ lb (500 g) crab meat
½ lb (500 g) halibut fillet, coarsely chopped
1 cup ricotta cheese
3 Tbsp sour cream
2 Tbsp lemon juice
3 Tbsp chopped fresh dill or
  1½ Tbsp dried dill
2 Tbsp pine nuts
pinch of garlic salt
1 tsp pepper
1 egg, beaten

Sausage casings, soaked then rinsed in cold water

Combine all the ingredients (except casings) in a bowl and mix them together with a wooden spoon. (If you use a food processor, take care not to overmix.) The stuffing should be well-combined but coarse in texture, not smooth and pasty. Tie and knot the casing at one end and stuff firmly with the seafood mixture. Twist and tie off the sausages at 4-inch (10 cm) intervals. Heat the links in boiling water for 15 minutes. The drained sausages can then be pan-fried, or broiled. They will also keep well for several days if refrigerated. Serve with hollandaise sauce or sour cream and Tabasco sauce and grapefruit.

West Coast Sushi

Preparation Time: Sushi: 10 minutes each
            Rice: 15 minutes
Chilling Time: 30 minutes
Serves 2–3

Sushi is a snack food from Japan which consists of a variety of fillings often accompanied by a sticky rice and rolled in nori seaweed.

Sushi Rice

1 cup short-grain rice
1 cup cold water
4 tsp rice vinegar

Place the rice in a saucepan and add the cold water. Cover and bring to a boil. Lower the heat and simmer for 12 minutes then cool. Stir in the rice vinegar and use with the various fillings to make sushi rolls.

Right: GINGER PRAWN SUSHI, Recipe this page. *Lower left:* SMOKED SALMON AND AVOCADO SUSHI, Recipe this page. *Top left:* MELON AND CHIVE SUSHI, Recipe this page.

Ginger Prawn Sushi

PHOTOGRAPH THIS PAGE

1 *sheet nori*
½ *cup sushi rice*
¼ *cup shelled prawns, cooked*
1 *tsp grated fresh ginger root*
1 *tsp lemon juice*

Lay the nori on the counter and spread the rice down one side of the full length of the sheet. Place the prawns in the rice and sprinkle with ginger and lemon juice. Roll the nori up into a tight cylinder and cut it into 2-inch (5 cm) sections.

Smoked Salmon and Avocado Sushi

PHOTOGRAPH THIS PAGE

1 *sheet nori*
2–3 oz (60–90 g) *smoked salmon, sliced*
½ *cup sushi rice*
1 *avocado, peeled and mashed*
1 *tsp lemon juice*
1 *Tbsp sesame seeds*

Place the nori on the counter and lay the salmon slices down the length of it. Cover the nori with sushi rice and spread with the mashed avocado. Sprinkle with lemon juice and sesame seeds. Roll into a tight cylinder. Cut into 2-inch (5 cm) slices.

Melon and Chive Sushi

PHOTOGRAPH THIS PAGE

1 *sheet nori*
½ *cup sushi rice*
½ *cup honeydew melon slices*
small bunch of fresh chives
1 *tsp grated fresh ginger root*
1 *Tbsp oyster sauce*

Place the nori on the counter and spread it with rice. Place on it a line of melon slices and whole chives. Sprinkle with ginger and oyster sauce; roll into a tight cylinder. Cut into 2-inch (5 cm) slices.

Chill the sushi for at least a half hour. Serve with soy sauce and extra rice.

CALIFORNIA

MAIN COURSE

CALIFORNIA

MAIN COURSE

San Francisco Cioppino

Preparation Time: 20 minutes
Cooking Time: 45 minutes
Serves 6

2 Tbsp olive oil
1 small onion, minced
2 cloves garlic, minced
2 Anaheim peppers, seeded and chopped
1 lb (500 g) tomatoes, peeled and chopped
1 cup tomato paste
1 cup dry red wine
3 Tbsp chopped fresh parsley or
    4½ tsp dried parsley
2 Tbsp chopped fresh basil or
    1 Tbsp dried basil
1 Tbsp dried oregano
½ lb (250 g) fresh clams, shucked
½ lb (250 g) fresh shrimp meat
1 lb (500 g) sole fillets

In a large skillet, heat the olive oil and sauté the onion, garlic and peppers for 5 minutes. Stir in the tomatoes, tomato paste, wine and herbs; bring to a boil. Lower the heat, cover and simmer for 20 minutes. Add the clams and shrimp; cook gently for 10 minutes. Cut the sole fillets into 1-inch (2.5 cm) pieces and lightly stir in. Simmer for an additional 10 minutes and serve.

Chapatis with Cauliflower, Zucchini & Onion

Preparation Time: 30 minutes
Cooking Time: 20 minutes
Serves 4

Chapatis:
1 potato
1 cup water
1 cup whole wheat flour
½ tsp cumin
1–2 cups white flour
hot oil for frying

Sauce:
1 cup chicken stock
1 clove garlic, minced
¼ cup currants
1 Tbsp flaked almonds
1 Tbsp grated fresh ginger root
pinch of ground cardamom
pinch of ground ginger
1 tsp turmeric
1 tsp pepper
1 tsp sugar
¼ cup plain yoghurt

Vegetables:
1 small cauliflower
4 small zucchini
1 large sweet onion
1 egg, beaten
½ cup finely chopped salted peanuts

Chapatis:

Peel and slice the potato. Boil it in 1 cup of water for 10 minutes or until soft. Mash the potato thoroughly in the cooking water. Stir in the whole wheat flour and cumin; mix well. Stir in as much plain white flour as it takes to make a fairly dry but soft dough. Divide the dough into four portions and roll out each one on a lightly floured board. The dough should be about ¼-inch (0.5 cm) thick.

Heat the oil in a skillet to at least 400°F (200°C). Fry each chapati until golden on one side (about three minutes); turn and fry for 2 minutes on the other side. Drain well on a paper towel. The chapatis should be light, puffy and almost crisp around the edges.

Sauce:

In a saucepan, combine all the sauce ingredients except the yoghurt. Simmer for 15 minutes. Just before serving, stir in the yoghurt.

Vegetables:

Remove the leaves and stem from the cauliflower. Break the head into small flowerets and place in a deep saucepan. Cover with boiling water. As soon as the water returns to a boil, remove the pan from the heat immediately, cover the pan and allow the cauliflower to remain in the hot water until you are ready to serve.

Cut the zucchini into ½-inch (1 cm) thick slices; cut the onion into rings. Pat dry, then dip the zucchini slices and onion rings first in the beaten egg then in the chopped peanuts. Drop them into the hot oil used for frying the chapatis. Fry for 2–3 minutes until brown and crisp.

To serve: drain the cauliflower and pour the sauce over it. Serve with the chapatis, the fried vegetables and steamed rice.

Chicken Chapatis

PHOTOGRAPH PAGE 131

Preparation Time: 30 minutes
Baking Time: 40 minutes
Preheat Oven: 375°F (180°C)
Serves 4

CHICKEN CHAPATIS, Recipe this page.

Chapati:

2 cups flour
½ cup shortening
½ cup onion, grated
1 tsp thyme
1 tsp cumin
½ tsp turmeric
1 egg, beaten
cold water
extra flour
4 chicken breasts, boned
2 Tbsp butter, melted
4 Tbsp yoghurt

Sift the flour and cut in the shortening. Add the onion, thyme, cumin and turmeric. Mix well, then add the egg and sufficient cold water to make a smooth dough. Do not overwork the dough. Divide it into 4 balls, roll them in flour and chill for a few minutes.

Butter a baking sheet. Place the chicken breasts 2 inches (5 cm) apart on the sheet. Brush the chicken with the melted butter and put 1 Tbsp yoghurt on each breast. Roll out the dough balls into 4 rounds and cover each piece of chicken. Tuck the edges of the dough around the chicken breasts and bake for 40 minutes.

Coast Oyster Pie

Preparation Time: 15 minutes
Cooking Time: 40 minutes
Serves 2

2 cups chopped oysters
1 cup scallops
1 cup chopped almonds
½ cup shelled pistachios
1 cup fish stock
1 cup chopped celery
½ cup chopped, pitted dates
½ cup chopped fresh apricots
1 tsp pepper
1 tsp coriander
½ cup white wine
1 Tbsp sugar
1 cup fine dry breadcrumbs

Combine all the ingredients except the breadcrumbs in a flame-proof dish. Stir well to mix then cover and let simmer on top of the stove for ½ hour. Remove the lid and sprinkle with the breadcrumbs. Place under the broiler for 10 minutes.

CALIFORNIA

MAIN COURSE

POMEGRANATE BEEF STEAK, Recipe page 133.

Pomegranate Beef Steak

PHOTOGRAPH PAGE 132

Preparation Time: 10 minutes
Cooking Time: 14 minutes
Serves 4

4 sirloin steak fillets
2 Tbsp butter

Sauce:
½ cup pomegranate juice
1 Tbsp lemon juice
1 Tbsp cornstarch
dash of Tabasco sauce
1 sweet yellow pepper, thinly sliced
small bunch of chives

Trim the steaks. Rub them well with the butter, kneading it into the meat. Let the steaks rest for 15 minutes then place them on a hot grill (barbecue) and cook for 6–7 minutes on each side.

Mix together the pomegranate juice, lemon juice, cornstarch and Tabasco in a saucepan; heat gently until the sauce just thickens. Stir in the sliced peppers and chives; heat for 1 minute. Pour over the steaks and serve immediately.

Jalapeño Jelly

Preparation Time: 5 minutes
Cooking Time: 5 minutes
Yields 2½ cups

2 cups apple jelly
2 jalapeño peppers, minced
1 sprig of fresh mint

Melt the jelly in a saucepan and stir in the jalapeños. Simmer for 5 minutes. Allow to cool to room temperature. Strain the mixture into a sterilized jar. Add a sprig of mint. Seal the jar and store in the refrigerator. Serve with lamb, pork, ham and the dark meat of poultry.

Marigold Pie

Preparation Time: 30 minutes
Baking Time: 30 minutes
Preheat Oven: 325°F (170°C)
Serves 4

Pastry:
pinch of saffron
2–3 tsp hot water
1 egg yolk
2 cups flour
2 Tbsp shortening
2 Tbsp butter
2–3 Tbsp cold water

Filling:
1 apple, peeled, cored and chopped
¼ cup milk
½ cup fresh marigold petals or
   ¼ cup dried petals
2 eggs
1 egg white
⅓ cup cottage cheese
pinch of mace
fresh marigold flowers for garnish

Pastry:
Soak the saffron in the hot water for a few minutes then blend in the egg yolk. Cut the shortening and butter into the flour and mix together well until crumbly. Add egg and sufficient cold water to make the pastry cling. Roll out the dough ⅛-inch (2.5 mm) thick on a lightly floured board and press it into a 9-inch (23 cm) pie dish. Trim and flute the edges then chill in the freezer for 15 minutes or until the filling is ready.

Filling:
Place the chopped apple, milk and marigold petals in a saucepan; bring them to a boil. Lower the heat and simmer for 10 minutes until soft. Mash the mixture or puree it in a blender until very smooth. Stir in the eggs and egg white, cottage cheese and mace; mix well. Pour the marigold mixture into the prepared pie crust and bake for ½ hour. Cool slightly and serve warm or cold. Garnish with fresh marigold petals.

Versions of this recipe are at least 400 years old and come to us from a time when flowers were used frequently for color and flavor. The marigold referred to in the recipe is the Calendula or pot marigold, not the French or African marigold of the Tagetes species. For variety, you might substitute rose, violet, nasturtium or chive flowers.

CALIFORNIA

MAIN COURSE

Buena Vista, one of the many wineries of California.

The magnificently colored Iceplant clings to the cliffs at Pacific Grove in California.

CALIFORNIA

SWEETS

Stuffed Dates

Preparation Time: 5 minutes
Cooking Time: 6–7 minutes
Yield: 12 stuffed dates

12 whole dates
12 blanched almonds
⅓ cup honey
1 Tbsp cinnamon
pinch of pepper

Carefully remove the pits from the dates, replacing each one with a whole almond.

Pour the honey into a heavy saucepan and place it on low heat. When the honey is liquid, add the cinnamon and pepper; stir well. Put the stuffed dates in the honey and stir gently to coat. Leave on *very low* heat for 5 minutes until the dates are hot. Watch the sauce so that it doesn't boil or even simmer. Serve hot.

Grape & Kiwi Slice

Preparation Time: 30 minutes
Baking Time: 15 minutes
Preheat Oven: 350°F (170°C)
Serves 8

4 large eggs, separated
½ cup powdered sugar
2 Tbsp corn syrup
½ cup ground almonds
3 Tbsp sugar
1 Tbsp lemon juice
1 cup heavy cream
½ lb (250 g) seedless grapes, washed and stemmed
3–4 kiwi fruit, peeled and sliced

Blend the egg yolks with the sugar until smooth and lemony. Whip the egg whites until very stiff. Beat the corn syrup into the egg whites and fold into the yolk mixture. Stir in the ground nuts to make a batter.

Line a 10-inch by 12-inch (25 by 30 cm) baking sheet or pan with waxed paper and spread the batter evenly over the bottom of the pan. Bake for 15 minutes then cover the cake and cool in the pan.

To assemble, dust a sheet of waxed paper with icing sugar. Turn the cake over onto the waxed paper. Cut the cake in half lengthwise. Add the sugar and lemon juice to the cream and whip until stiff. Spread half of the cream on half of the cake. Arrange the grapes over the cream and cover with the second half of the cake. Spread the remaining cream over the upper layer of cake and decorate with kiwi slices.

Rose Straffole

Preparation Time: 15 minutes
Chilling Time: 15 minutes
Cooking Time: 8 minutes
Serves 8–10

3 cups flour
2 eggs
2 Tbsp soft butter
¼ cup sugar
3–4 drops rosewater concentrate
¼ cup sweet white wine
lemon sugar

In a bowl or food processor, combine all the ingredients except the lemon sugar. Mix lightly; avoid overprocessing. Roll the dough into a ball and chill for 15–20 minutes.

When you are ready to cook the straffole, heat oil in a deep dryer to 375°F (180°C); or heat 1½ inches (3.5 cm) of oil in a skillet. Roll the dough out ¼-inch (0.5 cm) thick on a lightly floured board. With a pastry cutter or sharp knife, cut the pastry into ¼-inch (0.5 cm) strips. Tie the strips into bows, knots or other shapes to suit your fancy. Fry a few at a time until golden brown, about 3–4 minutes. Drain well on paper towels and dredge in lemon sugar while the straffole are still hot. Cool before serving.

Lemon Sugar

2 cups sugar
2 Tbsp freshly grated lemon rind

Mix the sugar and lemon rind together and store in a covered container for 24 hours until the sugar has taken on a lemon bouquet.

Yoghurt Cheese with Hot Nut Topping

PHOTOGRAPH PAGE 137

Preparation Time: Day Before: 10 minutes
Serving Day: 10 minutes
Serves 4

4 cups fresh yoghurt
¼ cup honey
1 tsp ground cardamom
½ tsp nutmeg
½ tsp cinnamon
2 Tbsp honey
1 cup mixed nuts—pistachios, peanuts, almonds, etc.

Pour the yoghurt into a cheesecloth-lined colander over a bowl. Cover and leave it overnight at room temperature.

Left: POLVORONES (Spanish Cookies), Recipe this page.
Right: YOGHURT CHEESE WITH HOT NUT TOPPING, Recipe page 136.

The next day, discard the liquid whey and place the yoghurt "cheese" in a bowl. Add the honey, cardamom, nutmeg and cinnamon; mix well. Chill the cheese spice mixture in the refrigerator.

Just before serving, heat the 2 Tbsp honey gently in a saucepan and stir in the nuts. Heat on low temperature for 2–3 minutes until the nuts are hot and well coated.

Spoon the cheese mixture into serving bowls, pour the nut sauce over and serve immediately.

Polvorones (Spanish Cookies)

PHOTOGRAPH THIS PAGE

Preparation Time: 25 minutes
Baking Time: 30 minutes
Preheat Oven: 325°F (160°C)
Yield: 7 dozen

1 tsp cinnamon
1 Tbsp sesame seeds, toasted
½ cup blanched almonds, toasted
1½ cups sugar

9 cups all-purpose flour
1 lb (500 g) lard
2 Tbsp grated lemon rind
2 eggs
¼ cup sugar
¼ cup orange juice

Place the cinnamon, sesame seeds and almonds in a food mill or blender and grind until fine. Pour the powdered mixture into a large bowl; mix in the sugar and flour. Cut in the lard with a pastry blender or two knives; add the lemon rind and mix well. Turn the dough onto a floured board and knead for 5 minutes. Divide the dough into two portions. Line two baking sheets with waxed paper and roll out each piece of dough ½-inch (1½ cm) thick on the baking sheets. Score the tops in 1-inch by 2-inch (2½ cm by 5 cm) rectangles and bake for 20 minutes.

Beat the eggs, sugar and orange juice together. Liberally brush the top of the cookies with the orange glaze. Bake for a further 10 minutes. Cool slightly, then break along the scored lines. These cookies will keep for two weeks if stored in an airtight tin.

CALIFORNIA

SWEETS

CALIFORNIA SWEETS

Ruby-Throated Hummingbird Cake

PHOTOGRAPH THIS PAGE

Preparation Time: 30 minutes
Baking Time: 1 hour
Preheat Oven: 350°F (180°C)
Cooling Time: 1 hour
Serves 6

Cake:
1½ cups flour
3 tsp baking powder
pinch of salt
⅓ cup sugar
½ cup vegetable oil
6 egg yolks
1 8-oz (250 g) can crushed pineapple
2 Tbsp lemon juice
6 egg whites
pinch of cream of tartar
½ cup sugar

Filling:
¼ cup water
1½ Tbsp cornstarch
⅓ cup sugar
2 Tbsp white rum
1 cup chopped strawberries

Icing:
½ cup butter
1 8-oz (250 g) package cream cheese
1 tsp vanilla
1 lb (500 g) icing sugar
milk
1 sweet red grapefruit
fresh flowers such as rose petals, violets, nasturtiums

Cake:
In a mixer, food processor or large bowl, sift together the flour, baking powder, salt and sugar. Blend in the oil, egg yolks, pineapple and lemon juice. Mix well. In a separate bowl, beat the egg whites, cream of tartar and sugar together until

RUBY-THROATED HUMMINGBIRD CAKE, Recipe this page.

very stiff. Fold the cake mixture into the meringue and stir until well blended. Pour the mixture into an ungreased 10-inch (25 cm) tube pan and bake for 1 hour. Remove from the oven and cool upside down on a rack. When cool, remove to a serving plate.

Filling:

Stir the cornstarch into the cold water and heat gently in a saucepan until it just starts to thicken. Stir in the sugar and rum; beat until smooth and shiny. Stir in the chopped strawberries.

Icing:

In a food processor, combine the butter, cream cheese, vanilla and icing sugar. Process to a smooth, spreadable paste. Adjust the texture with a little milk if necessary.

To assemble, spoon the strawberry filling into the hollow center of the cake. Spread the icing over the cake including the sides. Decorate the top with grapefruit sections and fresh flowers.

Espresso Creams

Preparation Time: 15 minutes
Chilling Time: 1½ hours
Yield: 24

3 Tbsp unflavored gelatin
¾ cup coffee liqueur
3 cups hot espresso coffee
¾ cup sugar
2 cups heavy cream, whipped
24 chocolate-covered Graham wafers
1 cup heavy cream, whipped
cocoa powder

Combine the gelatin and liqueur in a bowl. Gradually add the hot coffee and sugar; stir until the gelatin and sugar are dissolved. Cool for ½ hour until the mixture has thickened slightly. Whip the 2 cups of cream until stiff. Fold into the coffee jelly. Pour the mixture into two ice cube trays and chill it for at least 1 hour but do not freeze. To serve, unmold the "coffee cubes" and place each one on a chocolate Graham cracker. Top with whipped cream and dust with cocoa powder.

Frittata with Cheese and Fresh Herbs

Preparation Time: 10 minutes
Baking Time: 30 minutes
Preheat Oven: 375°F (180°C)
Serves 4

1 small bunch of chives
1 small bunch of chervil

3–4 fresh mint leaves
1 sprig fresh thyme
6 eggs
1 tsp pepper
2 Tbsp butter
½ cup Colby cheese, grated
¼ cup fine breadcrumbs

Finely chop all the herbs and place them in a bowl with the eggs and pepper. Beat well. Butter a shallow baking dish and pour in the mixture. Sprinkle on the cheese and top with breadcrumbs. Bake for ½ hour.

CALIFORNIA SWEETS

Pêches Crème Brulée

Preparation Time: 30 minutes
Cooking Time: 15 minutes
Chilling Time: 1 hour
Serves 8

4 large ripe peaches
whole nutmeg, grated
dark rum
2 cups milk
½ cup sugar
⅓ cup flour
pinch of salt
½ cup cold milk
4 egg yolks, well beaten
2 tsp vanilla extract
1 Tbsp butter
½ pt (300 mls) heavy cream
1 cup light brown sugar, packed

Drop the peaches into boiling water for a few seconds. Lift, drain and rub off the skins. Cut the peaches in half, remove the stones and lay the halves, cut side down, in a shallow ovenproof serving dish. Dust the peaches with freshly grated nutmeg and sprinkle with a little rum.

Scald the 2 cups of milk. Set aside. Combine in a saucepan or double boiler the sugar, flour and salt. Slowly blend in the cold milk, stirring until smooth. Add the hot milk. Place this mixture over medium heat and bring to a boil, stirring constantly. Remove from the heat. Stir a little more than half of the hot mixture into the beaten egg yolks. Pour back into the saucepan and continue cooking until the mixture reaches the boiling point (it will coat a silver spoon). Cool the custard slightly then add the vanilla and butter, cool completely.

While the custard continues to cool, whip the cream until stiff. Fold it into the vanilla custard. Spoon over the peaches, levelling the top. Sift the brown sugar evenly over the custard, making a layer at least ¼-inch (0.5 cm) thick. Place the dish under the broiler about 3 inches (6 cm) from the heat just until the sugar is melted. Refrigerate until serving time.

CALIFORNIA

SWEETS

Café Diable

Preparation Time: 5 minutes
Cooking Time: 3 minutes
Serves 8

8 tsp sugar
4 whole cloves
1 cinnamon stick
grated rind of 1 orange
1 Tbsp orange juice
½ cup cognac
8-cup pot strong hot black coffee

In a chafing dish or stainless steel saucepan, combine all the ingredients except the coffee; heat until simmering. Ignite the contents of the dish or pan and add the hot coffee. Strain into serving cups.

Chocolate Cake with Tangerine Curd

Preparation Time: 30 minutes
Baking Time: 30 minutes
Preheat Oven: 350°F (170°C)
Serves 8

Cake:

10 oz (315 g) unsweetened chocolate
¼ cup butter
6 eggs, separated
¾ cup sugar
1 cup flour

pinch of salt
2 Tbsp grated orange rind

Curd:

3 tangerines, juice and grated rind
½ cup sugar
¼ cup butter
3 eggs

Break the chocolate into pieces and place in a dry saucepan with the butter. Heat gently, stirring occasionally, until the chocolate has melted. Beat the egg yolks and sugar together until creamy, then stir in the flour. Add the salt, orange rind and melted chocolate. Beat the egg whites until stiff and fold half of them into the cake batter. Mix thoroughly. Fold in the second half of the egg whites and mix lightly. Butter a 9-inch (23 cm) round cake pan and pour in the batter. Bake for ½ hour. Cool for 10 minutes then turn the cake out onto a wire rack. Cool completely.

To make the curd, combine the tangerine juice and rind, sugar and butter in the top of a double boiler and heat. Beat the eggs then strain them into the juice mixture. Heat the mixture for about 15 minutes, stirring constantly, until it begins to thicken. Remove from the heat and cool.

To serve, set portions of the cake onto individual plates and spoon or pipe the curd over each one. Do not decorate the whole cake unless you are sure it will all be eaten at once, as the curd will soak into the cake during storage.

If the curd is not used immediately, it should be poured into a sterilized jar, sealed and stored in the refrigerator.

With a ride in one of San Francisco's famous trams we'll take you to the next chapter.

PAVLOVA, Recipe this page.

Pavlova

PHOTOGRAPH THIS PAGE

Preparation Time: 20 minutes
Cooking Time: 50–60 minutes
Preheat Oven: 325°F (160°C)
Serves 8

6 egg whites
1½ cups sugar
1½ tsp vanilla extract
1½ tsp flour
1½ tsp vinegar
1 pt (600 mls) heavy crea
sliced fresh fruit (kiwi, st
pears, pineapple, bananas,

Beat the egg whites until foamy. Gradually beat in the sugar, a little at a time. Continue beating the mixture until it is stiff and glossy. Fold in the vanilla, flour and vinegar. Spread the mixture into a well-greased 10-inch (25 cm) round cake pan, making the sides about 1 inch (2.5 cm) higher than the center. Bake for 1 hour. The Pavlova should be crisp and golden brown on the surface and soft inside. Let cool.

When the Pavlova is room temperature, fill the center with whipped cream and arrange the well-drained fruit on the top. Decorate with more whipped cream if desired.

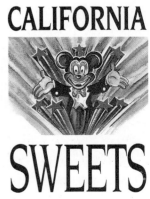

CALIFORNIA

SWEETS

Tex-Mex

Everything about Texas is big, at least it is according to tourism folklore, and in truth the adage bears enough foundation to justify the claim made almost without exception by every Texan.

Not least of the "big things" in Texas is Texan pride.

This colorful Mardi Gras event attracts over 250,000 to the Strand district in Galveston.

TEX-MEX

INTRODUCTION

One Texan landowner boasted to an English farmer while visiting the UK that it took three days to drive around his property "back home" in Texas.

Despite the dry response from the Englishman (he said he had owned an unreliable car like that at one time) this is exactly what Texas is all about. With approaching three million acres of land, and that's bigger than many European countries, Texas throws up a few surprises faster than gushing oil wells.

To start with, it has more than 600 miles (960 km) of coastline edging the Gulf of Mexico providing ample seafood — from oysters to shrimp and red snapper to kingfish — though this is presumably of poor comfort to the folks living in places like Amarillo, some 800 miles (1287 km) north. With the exception of freshwater fish, places like this don't get the benefit of "that morning's" catch as a matter of form.

Contrary to what many people believe, the mighty Lone Star state is far from being totally arid inland. The "western" movie-famous arid tracts, and they are undeniably vast, are counterbalanced by a diversity of land and climate ranging from subtropical around the Rio Grande on the Mexican border to a damp, cool ambience in the northwest. These areas make possible a wide range of fruit and vegetables, plus the fact that Texans are, dare we say it, big in irrigation programs.

Also big in Texas is the influence of the Spanish who, having created Mexico, slipped across the border taking with them what was to become the start of the big Texas cattle industry (the famous longhorns) and a fondness for spicy foods.

Mexico these days tends to be thought of as a poor relative to Texas, though the Mexican influence began with the indigenous pueblo Indians whose culture was carried into Texas by the Spanish in the 17th century. Spanish priests set up missions like Mission San Jose and these, either as a matter of policy or colonizing evolution, were quickly followed by Spanish military.

By the 18th century, the Spaniard's highly developed prowess as soldiers and seemingly insatiable habit for pinching anybody's gold they could get their hands on, began to stick in the gullet of the newly established United States. By 1821, Mexico had broken away from Spain, become its own country and had made Texas a part of itself as an area of the Mexican republic.

This uneasy situation didn't last long. It took only 10 years for the Texans to take control of their own destiny as a republic, becoming an independent nation following famous battles such as the Alamo.

A decade later, Texas joined the United States but the indelible, and very edible traces of Spanish tastes, had already been stamped on Texans' methods of cooking which, along with traditional dishes, means this part of America has probably a greater variety of "their own" table dishes to offer guests than most other states.

The Lone Star state boasts the simple word "friendship" as its motto and Texas is big in this, too. In few other states will you find a warmer or more generous welcome.

You have never been hugged in genuinely warm rib-crushing greeting on the doorstep until you have been greeted by a Texan. What's more, they mean it. Texans aren't good at pretending, they are more inclined to show what they feel, there and then, and if you are a friend, be prepared for sore ribs!

If you are having Texans over for dinner, give them something spicy. With Texans you rarely have to worry that your guests won't be able to cope with a hot chili, though most Texans will be surprised that you have come to grips with something like Texas Green Chili Stew (recipe in this section) as they tend to think the rest of America hasn't achieved furnace level cuisines yet.

Alternatively, a dish like Shrimp Brochette with Aiole Sauce Texan-style is a safe bet to delight guests from any part of the world and between courses let on that you know a little of how Texas started.

Top: TOMATO-TORTILLA SOUP, Recipe page 146. *Middle left:* HUEVOS RANCHEROS, Recipe page 148.
Bottom: CHEESE ENCHILADAS, Recipe page 153.

TEX-MEX

**APPETIZERS
SOUPS
SALADS
ENTREES**

Creamed Corn Soup & Crab

Preparation Time: 30 minutes
Cooking Time: 1 hour
Serves 6

6 ears fresh corn
¼ cup butter
1 onion, chopped
1 bay leaf
2 whole cloves
1 tsp fresh rosemary or
  ½ tsp dried rosemary
1 tsp fresh or dried thyme
6 cups chicken broth
pinch of nutmeg
1 tsp pepper
½ lb (250 g) crab meat
1 cup heavy cream
2 Tbsp cornstarch

Scrape the corn kernels from the cobs into a bowl. In a large saucepan, melt the butter and sauté the onion for 5 minutes. Add 2 cups of corn kernels. Place the bay leaf, cloves, rosemary and thyme in a cheesecloth bag and add it to the pan. Add the chicken broth, nutmeg and pepper and stir well. Bring to a boil then lower the heat and simmer for 45 minutes.

Remove the cheesecloth bag and discard it. Strain off most of the liquid from the soup mixture and set aside. Put the remaining mixture in a blender and puree until smooth. Return the pureed mixture to the stock. Add the crab meat and reheat; let simmer for 5 minutes. Dissolve the cornstarch in the cream and stir it into the soup. Heat for 10 minutes, stirring occasionally, until the soup has thickened slightly.

Tomato-Tortilla Soup

PHOTOGRAPH PAGE 145

Preparation Time: 20 minutes
Cooking Time: 30 minutes
Serves 4

1 lb (500 g) tomatoes, chopped
3 cloves garlic
1 onion, chopped
1 Tbsp Hot Sauce (page 148)
5 cups chicken stock
4 Tbsp sherry
4—4-inch (10 cm) flour tortillas, toasted
1 cup shredded lettuce
½ cup chopped scallions
½ cup grated Mozarella cheese
½ cup sour cream
dash of hot sauce

Combine the tomatoes, garlic, onion, hot sauce and stock in a heavy pan. Bring to a boil, lower the heat and let simmer for 15 minutes. Place the mixture in a blender and puree for 30 seconds. Pass the puree through a sieve.

Divide the strained soup into 4 serving bowls and add 1 Tbsp sherry to each one. Float one toasted tortilla on each bowl of soup. Top the tortillas with shredded lettuce, scallions, Mozarella cheese and sour cream. Sprinkle with hot sauce. Place the soup bowls in a 400°F (200°C) oven for 10 minutes until the cheese melts.

Chicken Potato Soup

Preparation Time: 20 minutes
Cooking Time: 1 hour
Serves 6

3 lbs (1.5 kg) chicken, cut into small pieces
2 cups chopped onion
1 tsp salt
1 tsp cumin
1 tsp coriander seeds
1 lb (500 g) white potatoes, peeled and coarsely chopped
½ lb (250 g) sweet potatoes, peeled and coarsely chopped
1 lb (500 g) fresh or canned baby corn
1 cup shredded lettuce
½ cup chopped fresh tarragon
1 cup half & half

Place the chicken pieces in a large heavy pan, cover with cold water and bring to a boil. Remove from the heat and skim off the fat. Return to the stove; add the onion and spices. Simmer for 20 minutes. Add the white and sweet potatoes and cook for 20 minutes longer. Stir in the corn, lettuce, tarragon and cream. Simmer 5 minutes more, then serve.

Curried Shrimp Slaw

Preparation Time: 20 minutes
Cooking Time: 5 minutes
Serves 4–6

1 cup shredded red cabbage
1 cup cauliflower pieces
1 bunch scallions, chopped
2 green apples, chopped
1 lb (500g) cooked shrimp meat
¼ cup butter
1 Tbsp curry powder
½ tsp garlic powder
¼ cup heavy cream

Toss the cabbage, cauliflower, scallions, apples and shrimp together in a bowl and chill. Melt the butter in a saucepan; stir in the curry and garlic powders. Cook gently for 5 minutes, being careful not to burn. Remove from the heat, cool and stir in the cream. Pour the sauce over the slaw, toss and serve.

Left: CAUSA (Sweet Potato Salad), Recipe this page.   Right: MEXICAN SALAD CAESAR, Recipe this page.

Causa (Sweet Potato Salad)

PHOTOGRAPH THIS PAGE

Preparation Time: 30 minutes
Cooking Time: 20 minutes
Chilling Time: 1 hour
Serves 6

3 lbs (1½ kg) sweet potatoes, peeled, cooked and mashed
1 Tbsp lemon juice
pinch of salt
2 garlic cloves, mashed
½ cup minced onion
¼ cup chopped pitted green olives
1 head crisp lettuce, shredded
1 bunch radishes
½ lb (250 g) cherry tomatoes
¼ cup chopped fresh parsley
3 Tbsp light oil
3 Tbsp red wine vinegar
3 Tbsp Hot Sauce (page 148)

Combine the sweet potatoes, lemon juice, salt, garlic, onion and olives. Mix thoroughly. Scoop the mixture into balls about the size of golf balls, place them on a tray and chill. Arrange the chilled shredded lettuce in a salad bowl. Add the radishes, tomatoes and potato balls. Blend together the parsley, oil, vinegar and hot sauce. Dress the salad and serve immediately.

Note: This salad can be turned into a meal by adding cold cooked shrimp, sliced ham and sliced hard-boiled eggs.

Mexican Salad Caesar

PHOTOGRAPH THIS PAGE

Preparation Time: 30 minutes
Serves 4–6

1 clove garlic
pinch of salt and pepper
⅓ cup olive oil
¼ cup lemon juice
1 Tbsp red wine vinegar
1 egg
dash of Worcestershire sauce
1 head iceburg lettuce
1 head Romaine lettuce
1 bunch radicchio
1 cup white croutons sautéed in butter
1 cup whole wheat croutons sautéed in olive oil
1 can anchovy fillets
1 bunch globe radishes

Rub a salad bowl with the garlic. In the same bowl, combine the salt, pepper, olive oil, lemon juice, vinegar, egg and Worcestershire sauce. Beat until creamy. Tear the chilled lettuces and radicchio into small pieces and place in the salad bowl. Add the croutons and toss. Wrap an anchovy around each radish and secure with a toothpick. Scatter over the salad, and serve immediately.

TEX-MEX

APPETIZERS
SOUPS
SALADS
ENTREES

TEX-MEX

**APPETIZERS
SOUPS
SALADS
ENTREES**

Mexican Hot Sauce (Salsa Fria)

Preparation Time: 10 minutes
Yield: Approx 2 cups

3 large tomatoes, peeled and chopped
2 onions, minced
3 cloves garlic, minced
4 Tbsp red wine vinegar
½ tsp oregano
1 sweet green pepper, minced
3 red chili peppers, minced
1 tsp Tabasco sauce
1 tsp chopped fresh coriander leaves

Combine all the ingredients and mix well. This will keep for up to 1 month if stored in a covered jar in the refrigerator.

Hot Sauce

Preparation Time: 20 minutes
Cooking Time: 35 minutes
Yield: about 2½ cups of sauce

4 dried red chilies
3 cups boiling water
¼ cup shortening
⅓ cup flour
pinch of salt
1 Tbsp sugar (optional)
1 tsp fresh dried thyme (optional)

Rinse the chilies and boil them gently in the water for 5 minutes. Remove from the heat and allow them to sit for an hour to soften.

Remove the chilies from the water, saving the water. Cut out the stems, discard the seeds and rinse the chilies under cold water. Put them in a blender with ½ cup of the chili water and puree until smooth. Push the pulp through a fine sieve to remove the skins. Rinse the blender with the remaining chili water. Pour this water through the sieve and add to the puree. Discard the strainings.

In a heavy pan, melt the shortening and stir in the flour, salt, sugar and thyme. Stir well and cook for 5 minutes to obtain a smooth paste. Add the chili puree. Stir, then simmer for 20 minutes, stirring occasionally. Use in any recipe calling for hot sauce.

Scrambled Eggs with Beef

Preparation Time: 8 minutes
Cooking Time: 12 minutes
Serves 2

2 Tbsp vegetable oil
1 small onion, chopped
2 fresh red chilies, chopped
2 cups chopped cold cooked beef
6 eggs
1 cup fresh tomato sauce

In a large skillet, heat the oil and sauté the onions and chilies for 2–3 minutes. Stir in the beef. Cover and simmer for 5 minutes. Break the eggs into the beef mixture and cook for 2–3 minutes, stirring occasionally until the eggs are just cooked. Serve immediately with fresh tomato sauce.

Fresh Tomato Sauce

Preparation Time: 5 minutes
Yields: 1 cup

2 large tomatoes
small bunch fresh chives
small bunch fresh coriander
1 tsp sugar
1 tsp olive oil

Coarsely chop the tomatoes by hand and place them in a bowl. Chop the herbs and combine them with the tomatoes. Add the sugar and oil. Mix thoroughly but do not puree. Serve with Scrambled Eggs and Beef.

Huevos Rancheros

PHOTOGRAPH PAGE 145

Preparation Time: 10 minutes
Cooking Time: 30 minutes
Preheat Oven: 350°F (180°C)
Serves 6

3 Tbsp olive oil
1 onion, chopped
1 sweet pepper, chopped
1 hot pepper, seeded and chopped
2 cloves garlic, minced
3 Tbsp chili powder
½ tsp cumin
½ tsp oregano
1 tsp Tabasco sauce
2 cups tomatoes, peeled and chopped
6 eggs
¼ cup grated Mozarella cheese

Fry the onion, peppers and garlic in the olive oil for 5 minutes. Add the spices and tomatoes. Stir, then simmer the mixture for 10 minutes. Pour the sauce into a shallow baking dish. Gently break the eggs into the sauce. Sprinkle with the cheese and bake for 15–20 minutes until the eggs are set.

Left: MEXICAN PIZZA, Recipe this page. *Bottom right*: GUACAMOLE, Recipes this page.

Mexican Pizza

PHOTOGRAPH THIS PAGE

Preparation Time: 15 minutes
Cooking Time: 15 minutes
Preheat Oven: 375°F (190°C)
Serves: 4

1 12-inch (30 cm) tortilla
oil for frying
⅓ cup refried beans
8 cherry tomatoes, cut in half
2 green onions, chopped
3–4 black olives, pitted and sliced
¼ cup sliced sweet peppers
1 cup grated Monterey Jack cheese
¼ cup taco salsa
2 Tbsp olive oil

Heat 1 inch (2.5 cm) of oil in a skillet. Soften the tortilla in the hot oil for a few seconds. Drain it on a paper towel and lay it flat on a plate or baking sheet.

Cover the tortilla with refried beans. Decorate it with tomatoes, onions, olives and peppers. Top with cheese and salsa. Sprinkle with the olive oil. Bake for 15 minutes.

Guacamole I

PHOTOGRAPH THIS PAGE

Preparation Time: 10 minutes
Serves: 6-8

2 large avocados, peeled and pitted
2 Tbsp lemon juice
1 clove garlic, minced
dash of Tabasco sauce
pinch of cumin
2 tomatoes, peeled and chopped
½ onion, chopped
2 green chilies, seeded and minced
fresh coriander leaves

Thoroughly blend the first five 5 ingredients to a smooth paste. Add the chopped tomatoes, onions and chilies; stir in with a spoon but do not mash. Sprinkle with fresh coriander leaves and serve.

Guacamole II

Preparation Time: 3 minutes
Serves: 6-8

Mash the pulp of 2 avocados with 3 Tbsp of Mexican hot sauce. (Recipe page 148.)

TEX-MEX

APPETIZERS
SOUPS
SALADS
ENTREES

A magnificent Longhorn steer at the TX-YO Ranch in Texas.

TEX-MEX

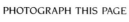

MAIN COURSE

Baked Red Snapper

PHOTOGRAPH THIS PAGE

Preparation Time: 20 minutes
Cooking Time: 30 minutes
Preheat Oven: 375°C (190°C)
Serves 4

¼ cup olive oil
1 onion, chopped
1 Tbsp coriander seeds
1 Tbsp cumin seeds
pinch of cayenne
½ cup chopped dates
1 cup chopped sweet pepper
2 tomatoes, chopped
½ cup lime juice
½ cup dry white wine
2 lbs (1 kg) whole red snapper

In a medium saucepan, heat the oil and sauté the onion, coriander, cumin and cayenne for 5 minutes. Blend well then return to the pan. Stir in the remaining ingredients, except the snapper, and bring to a boil.

Wash and pat the fish dry. Place it in a deep, buttered baking dish and pour the sauce over it. Bake for ½ hour or until the fish flakes easily.

Shrimp Brochette with Aiole Sauce

Preparation Time: 15 minutes
Marinating Time: 20 minutes
Cooking Time: 5 minutes
Serves 4

1½ lbs (750 g) shrimp
¼ cup olive oil
¼ cup light vegetable oil
3 cloves garlic
2 tsp chopped fresh parsley or
* 1 tsp dried parsley*
1 tsp pepper
1 egg
2 Tbsp lemon juice
toast
1 tsp paprika

Clean and devein the shrimp. In a blender, thoroughly blend the oils, garlic, parsley and pepper. Pour the mixture over the shrimp in a bowl. Toss to coat well and marinate for 15–20 minutes. Skewer the shrimp tightly, 4 or 5 together, and grill or broil over high heat for 2–3 minutes on each side. Return the remaining marinade to the blender and add the egg and lemon juice. Blend until very smooth. Strain the sauce and serve it on the side. Arrange the shrimp on toast wedges and sprinkle with paprika.

BAKED RED SNAPPER, Recipe this page.

Grilled Shrimp with Sweet Almond Fish Cakes

Preparation Time: 30 minutes
Marinating Time: 1 hour
Cooking Time: 7 minutes
Serves 4

12 large shrimp, cleaned and deveined
¼ cup olive oil
1 tsp pepper
¼ cup red wine
1 Tbsp powdered mustard
1 tsp ground ginger
milk for poaching

1½ lbs (750 g) fish fillets (swordfish, cod, etc.)
½ cup chopped onion
2 eggs, beaten
2 Tbsp flour
1 Tbsp slivered almonds
2 Tbsp liquid honey

Arrange the shrimp in a flat bowl or cake pan. Blend the olive oil, pepper, wine, mustard and ginger until smooth; pour this mixture over the shrimp. Cover and marinate for at least 1 hour. Turn the shrimp occasionally.

Pour ½-inch (1½ cm) of milk into a saucepan or skillet and heat to a simmer, but do not let it boil. Lay the fish fillets in the milk and poach for 10–12 minutes, turning once. When the fish is just done, remove to a plate. Flake with a fork and re-move skin and bones. Place flaked fish in a mixing bowl, add the onion, eggs and flour and mix thoroughly. (If the mixture appears to be too dry, moisten it with a spoonful of milk from the pan.) Shape the fish mixture into small patties and roll in the slivered almonds.

Remove the shrimp from the marinade. Pour the marinade into a small saucepan, add the honey and heat gently.

Grill or broil the fish cakes and shrimp for 6–7 minutes, turning once. Baste frequently with the hot marinade.

Cheese Enchiladas

PHOTOGRAPH PAGE 145

Preparation Time: 15 minutes
Cooking Time: 12 minutes
Preheat Oven: 350°F (180°C)
Serves 4

12—6-inch (15 cm) corn tortillas
oil for frying
2½ cups red chili enchilada sauce
2 cups grated cheddar cheese
1 cup grated Monterey Jack cheese
½ cup chopped scallions
1 cup sour cream
1 cup shredded iceburg or other head lettuce

In a skillet, fry the tortillas one at a time in about 1 inch (2.5 cm) of hot oil for a few seconds until soft. Drain them on paper towels. Using four oven-to-table serving plates, prepare the enchiladas as follows: on each plate put 2 Tbsp enchilada sauce; top with a tortilla; add 2 Tbsp sauce, 2 Tbsp cheddar, 1 Tbsp Monterey Jack, 1 tsp scallions, 2 Tbsp lettuce and 1 Tbsp sour cream. Repeat twice more on each plate. Sprinkle on any remaining cheese and heat in the oven for 12 minutes.

Enchilada Sauce

Preparation Time: 5 minutes
Cooking Time: 20 minutes
Yield: 2½ cups

2 cloves garlic, minced
2 Tbsp bacon fat
2 Tbsp flour
2 Tbsp chili powder
pinch of salt
1 tsp dried oregano
1 tsp cumin seeds
½ cup tomato sauce
2 cups cold water

Melt the bacon fat in a saucepan and sauté the garlic for 5 minutes. Add the other ingredients, stir well to mix and simmer for 15 minutes, stirring occasionally.

Chicken Peach Rolls

Preparation Time: 40 minutes
Cooking Time: 20 minutes
Preheat Oven: 400°F (200°C)
Serves 12

Pastry:
1 cup white flour
½ cup whole wheat flour
3 Tbsp bran
2 Tbsp wheat germ
4 Tbsp baking powder
⅓ cup sour cream
⅔ cup milk

Filling:
1 Tbsp butter
2 Tbsp flour
¼ cup sherry
¼ cup milk
2 cups chopped cooked chicken
½ cup chopped fresh chives
¼ cup chopped fresh tarragon

Topping:
12 peach halves
1 cup cottage cheese
1 lb (500 g) snow peas

Glaze:
2 Tbsp butter
3 Tbsp sugar
dash of hot sauce

Pastry:
In a bowl or food processor, combine all the pastry ingredients to make a soft dough. On a floured board, roll out to a 12-inch by 15-inch (30 by 38 cm) rectangle.

Filling:
In a saucepan, melt the butter and stir in the flour. Remove from the heat and add the sherry, milk, chicken and herbs, mixing well. Spread the mixture over the pastry. Roll up the filled pastry as you would a jelly roll. Cut it into ¾-inch (2 cm) slices. Place the slices flat on a baking sheet about ½-inch (1½ cm) apart.

Topping:
Fill the center of each peach half with cottage cheese and invert over each roll. Decorate the roll with snow peas.

Glaze:
Melt the butter in a saucepan and stir in the sugar and hot sauce. Brush the peach halves and snow peas with the glaze.

Bake for 15–20 minutes until the rolls start to brown. Remove them from the oven and cool. Brush over a second layer of glaze and serve warm or cold.

TEX-MEX

MAIN COURSE

TEX-MEX

MAIN COURSE

Chicken & Herb Sausages

Preparation Time: 1 hour
Cooking Time: 10 minutes
Serves 6

2 lbs (1 kg) raw chicken meat
¼ cup bacon drippings, melted
1 cup grated onion
2 green chilies, minced
1 tsp chopped fresh sage or
    ½ tsp dried sage
4 tsp chopped fresh marjoram or
    2 tsp dried marjoram
¼ cup chopped fresh tarragon or
    2 Tbsp dried tarragon
1½ cups seedless green grapes
A sausage casing, rinsed under running water

Thoroughly combine all the ingredients except the grapes. This may be done very effectively in a food processor, adding the meat and drippings last. The mixture should be quite doughy. If it is still crumbly, add butter 1 Tbsp at a time. When the mixture is well blended and moist, spoon it into a bowl and add the grapes. Stuff the mixture into the sausage casing until it is filled. Try to avoid leaving air spaces. Tie up both ends of the casing. Make sausages by twisting the casing every 4–5 inches (12–15 cm) to form links. The sausages may be broiled, fried or grilled.

Note: If sausage casings are not available, oven-proof plastic wrap may be used as a substitute. Lay the wrap out on a workspace, "fill" with the sausage meat and roll up tightly. Remove the wrap after cooking.

Chili Con Carne

Preparation Time: 30 minutes
Soaking Time: overnight
Cooking Time: 2½ hours
Serves 8–10

1 cup dried pinto and/or red kidney beans
¼ cup olive oil
2½ lbs (1¼ kg) beef, cubed
½ lb (250 g) capacollo sausage, sliced
1 cup chopped onion
2 cloves garlic, minced
1 sweet green pepper, chopped
1 sweet red pepper, chopped
1 bay leaf
1 Tbsp dried oregano
3 Tbsp chili powder
1 tsp cumin
¼ tsp cayenne
½ tsp pepper
1 Tbsp paprika

½ tsp cinnamon
2 red chilies, minced
1½ qts (1½ lt) beef stock
2 Tbsp sugar

Place the beans in a bowl, cover them with cold water and let soak overnight. Drain the beans and put them in a pan. Cover them with fresh cold water and gradually bring to a boil. Reduce the heat and simmer for 45 minutes until the beans are tender. Drain the beans and discard the water.

In a large heavy pan, heat the olive oil. Add the beef, sausage, onion and garlic. Fry for 5 minutes, stirring constantly. Add all the other ingredients; mix well, bring to a boil and simmer covered for at least 2 hours. Add the beans, stir well and reheat to a simmer. Serve with corn bread.

Texas Long Loaf

Preparation Time: 10 minutes
Cooking Time: 10 minutes
Serves 2 heavy eaters or 4 light eaters

1 French loaf
2 cups chili con carne
4 wieners

Grill the wieners. Cut the French loaf in half lengthwise. Place the wieners along the loaf. Pour the hot chili over the wieners, close the loaf and cut it in half.

Corn Dog

Preparation Time: 15 minutes
Cooking Time: 7 minutes
Preheat Deep Fryer: 350°F (180°C)
Serves 4

1½ cups yellow cornmeal
2 eggs
1 Tbsp baking powder
1 Tbsp powdered mustard
1 tsp pepper
12-oz (375 g) can or bottle of beer
8 wieners
oil for deep-frying
corn syrup

In a mixing bowl or blender, combine the cornmeal, eggs, baking powder, mustard, pepper and sufficient beer to make a thick batter. Wipe the wieners with a paper towel and skewer them on bamboo skewers, leaving a handle at each end. Roll each one in the batter and deep-fry for 6–7 minutes until golden. Remove and drain on paper towels. Serve drizzled with warm corn syrup.

Texas Green Chili Stew

PHOTOGRAPH THIS PAGE

Preparation Time: 20 minutes
Cooking Time: 1 hour
Serves 4

3 Tbsp bacon fat or lard
1 lb (500 g) lean pork
1 lb (500 g) beef chuck
3 ears fresh corn
1 onion, chopped
2 stalks celery, chopped
2 potatoes, sliced

2 large tomatoes
5 green chilies, seeded and roasted
3 juniper berries
1 Tbsp dried oregano
6 oz (180 ml) beer (½ can or bottle)

Melt the fat in a large stewing pan. Cut the pork and beef into cubes and fry for 10–15 minutes until well browned. Scrape the corn kernels from the cobs and add them to the meat. Add the remaining ingredients. Stir well, adding a little more beer if necessary. The stock should just cover the meat and vegetables. Cover the stew and simmer for 45 minutes.

Left: GORDITAS, Recipe this page. *Right*: TEXAS GREEN CHILI STEW, Recipe this page.

Gorditas

PHOTOGRAPH THIS PAGE

Preparation Time: 20 minutes
Cooking Time: 25 minutes
Preheat Deep Fryer: 375°F (190°C)
Serves 4

Gorditas:
2 cups masa harina (cornmeal flour)
2 Tbsp meat drippings or lard
pinch of salt
pinch of cayenne
cold water

Filling:
¼ cup olive oil
1½ lbs (750 g) lean beef, chopped or ground
1 clove garlic, minced
1 onion, chopped
1½ cup grated cheddar cheese

1 lb (500 g) tomatoes, chopped
2 cups shredded lettuce
1 cup sour cream
hot sauce (page 148)

Gorditas:
Combine the masa harina, drippings, salt and cayenne. Mix well. Gradually add cold water, mixing to form a thick paste. Pull off golf ball-sized pieces and roll out very thin on a floured board. Deep-fry for 2–3 minutes.

Filling:
Heat the olive oil in a skillet and add the chopped beef, garlic and onion. Fry for 10 minutes stirring occasionally. Stir in the grated cheese and tomatoes. Simmer for 15 minutes, stirring occasionally.

To serve, place 1 gordita on a plate and cover it with ½ cup shredded lettuce. Dot with sour cream and pour the meat filling over. Serve with hot sauce.

TEX-MEX

MAIN COURSE

Red Chili Pot Roast

Preparation Time: 10 minutes
Marinate: overnight
Cooking Time: 3 hours
Serves 4

3–4 lbs (1½–2 kg) beef pot roast
2½ cups red chili sauce (page 148)
2 cloves garlic, minced
1 Tbsp dried oregano
1 tsp cumin
1 onion, chopped
cold water

Day before:
Wash and trim the roast, place it in a deep baking dish or clay baker and add the sauce, garlic, oregano, cumin and onion. Add sufficient cold water to cover the meat. Stir the ingredients to mix them then cover the baking dish and marinate the roast overnight in the refrigerator.

Serving day:
Remove the roast from the refrigerator and let it come to room temperature. Place it in a 325°F (160°C) oven and roast for at least 3 hours until very tender.

Melon Chutney

PHOTOGRAPH PAGE 157

Preparation Time: 20 minutes
Cooking Time: 40 minutes
Yield: 4 qts (4 lt)

4 qts (4 lt) peeled cantaloupe
½ cup seedless raisins
½ cup chopped apricots
1 onion, chopped
1 clove garlic, minced
¼ cup grated fresh ginger
1 jalapeño pepper, seeded and minced
3 cups light brown sugar
5 cups vinegar
½ cup mustard seeds
bunch of fresh mint

Chop the cantaloupe into small chunks. Combine with the rest of the ingredients except the mint in a large saucepan. Stir the mixture and place it over moderate heat. Simmer gently for ½ hour. Ladle the chutney into sterilized jars adding a sprig of mint to each jar. Place the jars in a steamer and steam for 10 minutes, or process in a boiling water bath for 15 minutes. Seal and cool before storing the chutney.

Oil rig in the Gulf of Mexico.

Left: MELON CHUTNEY, Recipe page 156.
Right: BAKED LAMB WITH HERB SAUCE, Recipe this page.

Baked Lamb with Herb Sauce

PHOTOGRAPH THIS PAGE

Preparation Time: 15 minutes
Cooking Time: 1½ hours
Preheat Oven: 350°F (180°C)
Serves 4

2–3 lbs (1–1½ kg) lamb roast
1 tsp coriander seeds
1 tsp cumin seeds
1 tsp celery seeds
1 tsp caraway seeds
2 Tbsp honey
1 onion, chopped
1 cup water

Sauce:
1 cup beef stock
1 Tbsp olive oil
¼ cup red wine
1 tsp pepper
1 tsp ground ginger
2 tsp cornstarch blended with 1 Tbsp water

TEX-MEX

MAIN COURSE

Trim the lamb, wash and pat it dry. If there is a layer of fat, score it with a knife. Combine the herb seeds and honey in a saucepan and warm slightly. Liberally brush the meat on all sides with the herbed honey. Place it in a baking dish and sprinkle it with the chopped onion, add the water to the dish. Bake uncovered for 1 hour.

Combine the sauce ingredients in a saucepan and bring them to a boil. Pour the sauce over the lamb and bake, covered, for a further 30 minutes. Remove the lamb roast to a heated platter. Skim off the fat from the pan juices, add extra stock to make up to 1 cup if necessary. Scrape up all dried on juices. Place over heat, add blended cornstarch and stir until sauce thickens. Serve the sauce with the lamb.

Skyline of Dallas

Skyline of Fort Worth

Skyline of Houston

Skyline of Austin

Tequila with the worm, Mexico

TEX-MEX

SWEETS

Deep-Fried Chocolate Truffles

PHOTOGRAPH PAGE 161

Preparation Time: 20 minutes
Freezing Time: 3 hours, or overnight
Cooking Time: 30 seconds
Serves 4

1 pt (600 ml) chocolate ice-cream
¼ cup Grand Marnier
¼ cup heavy cream
½ cup crushed hazelnuts
1 cup chocolate Graham cracker crumbs
1 egg

In a bowl, beat the ice-cream, Grand Marnier and cream until smooth. Freeze for at least 1 hour until firm. Use a scoop to form the ice-cream into 1½-inch (2.5 cm) balls; place on a cookie sheet and refreeze for 1 hour.

Mix the hazelnuts and Graham cracker crumbs together in a bowl. Roll each ice cream ball in the crumb mixture, coating well. (Only part of the crumb mixture will be used up.) Return the truffles to the freezer for ½ hour.

Beat the egg. Dip each truffle in the egg then again in the remaining crumb mixture to coat a second time. Return to the freezer.

To serve, heat clean oil to 375°F (190°C) in a deep fryer or skillet and fry the ice-cream truffles for 20–30 seconds until dark brown. Drain on paper towels and serve immediately.

The truffles may be made a day ahead and deep-fried just before serving.

Buñelos (Cinnamon Fritters)

PHOTOGRAPH PAGE 161

Preparation Time: 20 minutes
Chilling Time: 1 hour
Cooking Time: 5 minutes
Serves 6

1 cup hot water
⅓ cup shortening
2 cups flour
½ cup sugar
1 Tbsp cinnamon
salt
2 Tbsp baking powder
oil for deep frying
¼ cup cinnamon
½ cup castor sugar

Melt the shortening in the hot water. Stir in the flour, sugar, cinnamon, salt and baking powder. Mix well, roll into a ball and chill the dough for at least 1 hour.

Heat 1 inch (2.5 cm) of vegetable oil to 375°F (190°C) in a deep fryer or skillet. Break off small lumps of dough and roll into balls. Deep-fry the buñelos for 3–4 minutes until brown. Lift out of the hot fat with a slotted spoon. Drain on paper towels and cool for a few minutes on a rack.

Mix the cinnamon and castor sugar together in a bowl. Roll the warm buñelos in the sugar mixture to coat them completely. Serve warm.

Fruit in Coffee

PHOTOGRAPH THIS PAGE

Preparation Time: 10 minutes
Cooking Time: 20 minutes
Chilling Time: 1 hour
Serves 4

½ cup sugar
1 pt (½ lt) strong black coffee
2 large Bartlett pears
4 small bananas
1 cup heavy cream, whipped
chocolate-covered coffee beans

In a deep saucepan, dissolve the sugar in the coffee and bring to a boil. Peel and halve the pears, removing the core. Place the pears in the coffee syrup and poach gently for 10–15 minutes, until just tender. Remove the pan from the heat. Peel the bananas and add them to the pears. Baste the fruit gently then allow to cool in the syrup. Remove the fruit from the syrup and chill thoroughly in the refrigerator.

To serve, boil the syrup with the lid off, reducing it in volume until it thickens slightly. Arrange a pear half and a banana on each of 4 serving plates. Pour the hot syrup over the fruit. Garnish with the whipped cream and chocolate coffee beans.

TEX-MEX SWEETS

Top left: DEEP-FRIED CHOCOLATE TRUFFLES, Recipe page 160. *Bottom left*: BUNELOS (Cinnamon Fritters), Recipe page 160. *Right middle*: FRUIT IN COFFEE, Recipe this page.

Cajun

Take a look at the map of Louisiana and what do you see? Several clues to illustrate the effects the French have had on that state; place names like Lafayette (after the French general and politician 1757-1834), Baton Rouge and New Orleans

The French Quarter, typical of New Orleans, Louisiana.

CAJUN

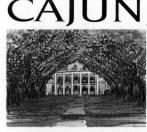

INTRODUCTION

(Orleans in France is pronounced "or-lay-or" with a heavy accent on either end).

Real Cajun country is the south-east end of Louisiana where bayous (swampy creeks) form a watery network lacing inland from the Mexican Gulf coast.

A potted if simplistic history of how the Cajun came to be both what and where they are, will make great after-dinner conversation following the Almond-Glazed Rum Babas (see recipe this section) so here it is:

Short of having a retrospective crystal ball, it is impossible to say what influence the French would have had on the area, or even if we would now have Cajun, had it not been for the Nova Scotians falling out with Britain in 1750.

Nevertheless, the Nova Scotians did fall out with Britain, and the French people in the Arcadian region were promptly expelled for placing their sympathies firmly on the wrong side, at least that is how history says the British saw the matter.

Thousands of French settlers subsequently made the journey from Arcadia to Louisiana to start a new life and thousands more returned to France only to be brought back to Louisiana by the French Government who then owned the territory "by discovery" in 1682, founding Louisiana in 1699.

Although France ceded Louisiana to Spain in 1762, the fiercely French Arcadians, who were no more fond of the Spanish than they were of the British, rebelled and generally gave the Spaniards such a hard time that in less than 40 years the Spanish gave it back to the French in 1800.

Then followed a busy period for the Arcadians. In 1812 Louisiana became the 18th state, following the completion of purchase by the United States some nine years earlier. This was followed by the battle of New Orleans only three years later in 1815 when the British were beaten by Andrew Jackson. Still less than happy with the way things were going, Louisiana seceded from the Union in 1861 only to be occupied by U.S. troops a year later, bringing Louisiana back into the Union in 1868.

Several thousand French people had settled primarily around southern Bayous and Lafourche a century earlier

and brought with them renewed vigor to the colony. Established locals were impressed by the new arrivals. Clearly these were a hardworking, dedicated people who set about establishing sugarcane, rice and cattle farming making good use of the Mississippi delta and sub-tropical climate.

The area was, and still is, rich in wildlife which the Cajuns used to supplement both their diet and their incomes. First class trapping skills acquired in Canada were soon at work catching beaver, deer, foxes, possums, rabbits and wild hogs.

Traditions die hard, if at all, and as history demonstrates, the Cajuns do not let go of what they hold precious very easily. Trapping is still a major way of life in these areas.

The convoluted coastline provides oysters, shrimp, jackfish, king mackerel, tarpon, bass catfish and gasperegon — all of which make excellent eating.

The most typical Cajun areas are the bayous regions and these bear a reputation for fine country lifestyles, fine foods and superb plantation homes. Swampboats are still used extensively to transverse the backwaters, though these days as much for ferrying tourists around as for personal and hunting transport.

The area has a high English-plus-French speaking population, a large negro population and descendants of the state's only indigenous Indian tribe, Chitimacha.

This area also boasts the site of the world's most famous Tabasco factory and, with the help of a sub-tropical climate and exceptional growing seasons (up to 300 days a year), specializes in out-of-season and rarer produce. These include peppers, strawberries, rice and tobacco.

If you are looking for a menu specifically to suit guests who have tried everything, even French guests, then this is an excellent section in which to find it.

Pleasing the gastronomic whims of anybody just arrived from Paris can be a daunting task. Most Frenchmen will have had Turtle Soup (Cajun recipe in this section), but not so many will have tried Crawfish Gumbo or Possum and Chestnuts.

Top: LIME MANGO BEIGNETS, Recipe page 176.
Middle: CRAWFISH GUMBO, Recipe page 172. *Bottom:* STUFFED PEPPERS, Recipe page 168.

CAJUN

**APPETIZERS
SOUPS
SALADS
ENTREES**

Sweet Potatoes & Black Walnuts

Preparation Time: 20 minutes
Cooking Time: 30 minutes
Preheat Oven: 350°F (180°C)
Serves 6

6 sweet potatoes
1 large sweet onion
3 Tbsp soft butter
1 cup light cream
½ cup sugar
1 cup crushed black walnuts
pinch of salt
2 Tbsp melted butter
1 tsp black pepper

Peel and slice the sweet potatoes; slice the onion. Boil the vegetables for 10 minutes; drain and mash them. Add the butter, cream, sugar, walnuts and salt. Combine well and pour the mixture into an ungreased baking dish. Pour the melted butter over the top and sprinkle with pepper. Bake for ½ hour until the top is dark and crusty.

Green Corn Pudding

Preparation Time: 30 minutes
Cooking Time: 45 minutes
Preheat Oven: 325°F (160°C)
Serves 4

12 ears of green corn (full size)
2 cups milk
4 egg yolks
4 egg whites
1 tsp sugar
salt and pepper to taste
2 Tbsp flour
1 Tbsp butter

Scrape the soft corn kernels from the corncobs into a saucepan. Add the milk and let simmer for 15 minutes. Remove the milk and corn from the heat and stir well, or blend in a blender. Pour through a strainer to remove any bits of corn skin or silk. Beat the egg yolks and stir into them a little of the corn milk. Stir in the remaining corn milk and add the sugar, salt and pepper. Blend the flour into the butter and stir it into the mixture. Beat the egg whites and fold all together.

Pour the mixture into a deep 9-inch (23 cm) buttered baking dish or soufflé mold and bake for 45 minutes.

Turtle Soup

Preparation Time: 1 hour
Cooking Time: 2 hours
Serves 6–8

1 large yellowbellied cooter or 4 terrapins
¼ lb (125 g) butter
1 cup chopped onion
¼ cup flour
salt and pepper to taste
2 Tbsp fresh or dried thyme
1 tsp mace
½ cup sherry
¼ cup brandy
½ cup cream (optional)

Plunge the turtle into a large pot of boiling water and boil it for ½ hour, much as you would a crab or a lobster. Remove, drain and cool the turtle. Discard the water. Pry off the shell, remove the meat and chop it into small pieces. In a large heavy pan, melt the butter then add the onion and turtle meat. Sauté for 10–15 minutes until the meat is well browned. Stir in the flour, salt, pepper, thyme and mace, along with about 2 qts (2 lt) of water. Bring slowly to a boil, lower the heat and simmer for 1 hour. Stir in the sherry and brandy. If desired, add ½ cup cream before serving.

Turnip & Ginger Soup

PHOTOGRAPH PAGE 167

Preparation Time: 20 minutes
Cooking Time: 25 minutes
Serves 4

1 lb (500 g) white turnips
½ lb (250 g) potatoes
3 Tbsp butter
4 cups chicken stock
2 oz (60 g) fresh ginger root, grated
pinch each of salt, pepper and sugar
½ cup chopped walnuts
1 Tbsp white wine vinegar
1 Granny Smith apple
sprig of fresh mint

Peel and slice the turnips and potatoes. In a large pan, combine the vegetables with the butter, stock and ginger root. Bring this mixture to a boil, lower the heat and simmer covered for 20 minutes. Mash or puree the mixture until smooth then return to the pan. Add seasonings to taste. Stir in the walnuts and vinegar. Grate the apple, or chop it into small pieces, and stir into the soup. Simmer for 2 minutes longer then ladle into bowls. Sprinkle each serving with chopped fresh mint.

TURNIP & GINGER SOUP, Recipe page 166.

CAJUN

**APPETIZERS
SOUPS
SALADS
ENTREES**

Crawfish with Redfish Crust

Preparation Time: 15 minutes
Cooking Time: 30 minutes
Serves 4

1 pt (570 ml) heavy cream
½ pt (280 ml) white wine
1 cup chopped onion
1 Tbsp fresh basil or
  1½ tsp dried basil
1 Tbsp fresh oregano or
  1½ tsp dried oregano
1 cup chopped parsley
1 lb (500 g) crawfish tails
2 Tbsp butter
1 Tbsp powdered mustard
½ lb (250 g) redfish fillets
pepper and nutmeg to taste

In a heavy saucepan, combine the cream, wine, onion and herbs. Bring to a simmer and add the crawfish tails. Simmer uncovered for 20 minutes; do not let boil.

In a small skillet, melt the butter and stir in the mustard. Add the redfish fillets and fry until golden on both sides. Then use a spatula to break up the fillets into approximately 1-inch (2.5 cm) chunks. Arrange the crawfish tails on a shallow oven dish. Pour over the sauce then place the redfish chunks in the center. Season liberally with pepper and nutmeg. Place under the broiler for 10–12 minutes until the top starts to brown and bubble.

Stuffed Peppers

PHOTOGRAPH PAGE 165

Preparation Time: 15 minutes
Cooking Time: 40 minutes
Preheat Oven: 375°F (190°C)
Serves 8

4 Tbsp butter
2 cloves garlic, minced
½ cup chopped celery
½ cup chopped onion
¼ cup chopped fresh parsley
½ lb (250 g) ground beef
½ lb (250 g) shrimp meat
1 Tbsp chopped fresh or dried thyme
1 tsp sugar
salt and pepper to taste
8 large sweet peppers
1 cup fresh breadcrumbs

In a skillet, melt the butter; sauté the garlic, celery, onion and parsley for 5 minutes. Stir in the beef and shrimp; sauté for 5 minutes longer. Remove from the heat and add the thyme, sugar and seasonings. Mix well.

Remove the tops from the peppers and wash out the seeds. Fill the peppers with the meat/shrimp mixture and stand them in a shallow baking dish. Top each with breadcrumbs. Add about 1-inch (2½ cm) of hot water to the baking dish. Cover dish with a large sheet of aluminum foil to form a tent. Bake for ½ hour. Remove foil and bake 10–15 minutes more.

The preservation H. jazz band, one of the many music bands of New Orleans, Louisiana.

WATERMELON PICKLES, Recipe this page.

Watermelon Pickles

PHOTOGRAPH THIS PAGE

Preparation Time: about 3 hours
Soaking Time: overnight
Cooking Time: 4 hours
Yield: about 1 gallon (4½ lt)

7 lbs (3½ kg) watermelon rind, cleaned
1 cup quicklime
4 lbs (2 kg) sugar
1 qt (1 lt) vinegar
2 Tbsp cinnamon
1 Tbsp cloves
1 Tbsp allspice

To prepare the watermelon rind, scrape off any red meat from the inside and peel off the outer green skin. Cut the remaining white rind into small pieces and place them in a bucket. Dissolve 1 cup of quicklime in 2 gallons (4 lt) of cold water and pour the solution over the rinds. Cover the bucket and let it stand overnight.

Next day, pour off and discard the quicklime solution. Rinse the rinds liberally with cold water. Place them in a large pot, cover with water and bring to a boil. Lower the heat and let simmer for 2–3 hours until the rind is tender. Drain off the water.

In a large saucepan, combine the sugar, vinegar and spices. Heat gently, stirring constantly, until the sugar is dissolved. Add the watermelon rinds to the syrup and simmer for 20 minutes. Cool them. Store in a large earthenware jar.

Note: Quicklime is slightly corrosive; avoid contact with the skin and keep it out of the reach of children.

Persimmon Brandy Conserve

Preparation Time: 2 hours
Cooking Time: 1 hour

8 cups very ripe persimmons (2 qts (2 lt) pulp)
1½ cups orange juice
6 cups sugar
brandy

Fill a steamer or large pot with ripe persimmons and heat very gently, or steam, for ½ hour until the fruit is pulpy. Press the pulp through a strainer and measure the volume. For every 2 quarts (2 kg) of persimmon pulp add ½ pt (1½ kg) orange juice and 1½ qts (1½ kg) sugar.

Put the mixture in a heavy pan or jelly pan and simmer uncovered for ½ hour, stirring every 10 minutes. When the mixture begins to thicken, remove from the heat. Stir in ¼ cup brandy for each qt (lt) of marmalade. Pour the marmalade into sterile jars and seal. Cool before storing.

CAJUN

APPETIZERS
SOUPS
SALADS
ENTREES

One of the famous Mardi Gras parades of New Orleans, Louisiana.

CAJUN

MAIN COURSE

Quail Pie

Preparation Time: 20 minutes
Cooking Time: 25 minutes
Preheat Oven: 400°F (200°C)
Serves 2

1 cup flour
¼ cup butter
½ tsp dried thyme
½ tsp powdered sassafras
1 tsp baking powder
½ cup half & half
¼ cup butter
1 lb (500 g) quail, cleaned and dressed
½ cup sherry

Combine the flour, butter, thyme, sassafras and baking powder. Mix until crumbly. Add the cream; mix into a dough. Roll out on a floured board to make a ½-inch (1 cm) thick pastry crust. Melt the butter in a skillet. Cut the quail into pieces and fry in the butter for 5 minutes, stirring occasionally. Arrange the quail in a baking dish. Stir the sherry into the pan juices and pour over the quail. Top with the crust. Prick the crust with a fork and bake for 20 minutes until golden.

Crawfish Gumbo

PHOTOGRAPH PAGE 165

Preparation Time: 25 minutes
Cooking Time: 1½ hours
Serves 4–6

Paste:
4 Tbsp lard
1 lb (500 g) okra, chopped
10-oz (315 g) can tomato sauce

Roux:
3 Tbsp lard
5 Tbsp flour

Gumbo:
2 onions, chopped
1 green pepper, chopped
3 stalks celery, chopped
1 clove garlic, minced
2½ qts (2 lt) water
salt, pepper and cayenne to taste
1½ lbs (750 g) crawfish meat
¼ cup chopped scallions
2 cups long-grain white rice, cooked
3 Tbsp chopped fresh parsley or
 1½ tsp dried parsley

In a saucepan, melt the 4 Tbsp lard; stir in the okra and tomato sauce. Simmer very slowly for at least ½ hour until the okra is soft. Remove the mixture from the heat and mash or puree until it is very smooth.

In a small saucepan, prepare the roux. Melt the 3 Tbsp lard and stir in the flour. Cook over very low heat for 10 minutes, stirring from time to time.

In a large pot, combine the onions, green pepper, celery, garlic, water and seasonings. Bring to a boil and simmer for ½ hour. Add the crawfish and scallions. Continue to simmer for 20 minutes. Stir in the tomato/okra paste and the roux. Mix well and reheat to a simmer. Serve the gumbo over steamed rice; sprinkle with chopped parsley.

Opossum & Chestnuts

Preparation Time: 40 minutes
Cooking Time: 1½ hours
Preheat Oven: 375°F (190°C)
Serves 2

1 medium opossum
salt and pepper
1 cup chopped sweet chestnuts
1 cup chopped apple
1 cup soft bread crumbs
1 large sweet potato
½ cup lemon juice
¼ cup brown sugar
¼ cup butter
1 cup boiling water

Skin the opossum and clean very thoroughly. Be sure to remove the glands. Place it in a large pot. Cover with boiling water and let boil for 10 minutes. Drain and discard the water. Liberally rub the opossum with salt and pepper.

Combine the chestnuts, apple and bread-crumbs and stuff the opossum. Place it in a deep baking dish or casserole. Peel and slice the sweet potato; layer the slices over the opossum. Combine the lemon juice, brown sugar, butter and water. Mix well and pour over the sweet potato slices. Bake covered for 1½ hours.

Shrimp Jambalaya

PHOTOGRAPH PAGE 173

Preparation Time: 1 hour spread over 2 days
Final Cooking Time: 1 hour
Serves 12

Stock I:

1 bottle dry white wine
1 cup chicken stock
juice of 1 lemon
1 bay leaf
2 cloves garlic
1 tsp salt
6 peppercorns

SHRIMP JAMBALAYA, Recipe these pages.

4 sprigs parsley
1 small bunch celery, chopped
1 onion, sliced
1 carrot, sliced
dash of hot sauce
2 lbs (1 kg) raw shrimp

Stock II:

6 strips bacon, chopped
1½ lbs (750 g) ham, diced
3 large onions, chopped
2 cloves garlic, minced
28-oz (875 g) can pimientoes
½ lb (250 g) pepperoni, sliced
3 sweet peppers, chopped
2 tsp fresh thyme or
   1 tsp dried thyme
2 tsp fresh tarragon or
   1 tsp dried tarragon
¼ cup chopped celery
¼ cup chopped parsley
1 bay leaf
salt and cayenne to taste
3 Tbsp butter
2 cups long grain white rice
1 lb (500 g) raw scallops

Day Before:

In a large pot, combine the first 12 items for Stock I and bring them to a boil. Reduce the heat and simmer for ½ hour. Add the shrimp and cook for 5 minutes longer. Remove from the heat, cool and refrigerate overnight.

In a separate heavy skillet, fry the bacon strips until the fat is rendered. Add the chopped ham, onions and garlic. Fry for 10–15 minutes until quite soft. Combine the remaining ingredients for Stock II, stir them, bring to a boil, lower heat and let simmer for ½ hour. Remove the mixture from the heat, cool then refrigerate overnight.

Serving Day:

Strain off the liquid from Stock I and add it to Stock II in a very large pot. Set over medium heat. Separate the shrimp from the strained vegetables. Discard the vegetables; shell and devein the shrimp. Set aside.

In a heavy pan or skillet, melt the butter and add the rice. Stir well to coat; fry for 10–15 minutes, stirring often, until the rice begins to brown. Add the rice to the stock. Wash the scallops and add them to the pot. Stir well, bring to a boil, lower the heat and simmer gently for ½ hour.

CAJUN
MAIN COURSE

CAJUN

MAIN COURSE

Catfish Balls with Lemon and Sour Cream

Preparation Time: 10 minutes
Cooking Time: 4 minutes
Preheat Deep Fryer: 375°F (190°C)
Serves 4

2 cups catfish, cooked and flaked
2 cups mashed potato
2 eggs
1 Tbsp chopped fresh parsley or
   1½ tsp dried parsley
1 hot red pepper, seeded and minced
1 Tbsp sugar
1 tsp fresh or dried thyme
lemon wedges
sour cream

In a bowl, combine all the ingredients except the lemon and sour cream. Mix until stiff. Shape into balls and deep fry for 3–4 minutes until brown. Drain on a paper towel and serve hot with lemon and sour cream. These catfish balls are also good served cold.

Fin 'n Feathers

Preparation Time: 15 minutes
Cooking Time: 25 minutes
Serves 4

4 large fresh trout
½ lb (250 g) butter
1 cup sliced shiitake mushrooms
½ cup peeled and sliced sweet chestnuts
½ lb (250 g) cooked chicken meat, chopped
2 Tbsp flour
1 cup heavy cream
½ cup sherry
1 sweet red pepper cut in strips
salt and pepper to taste

Wash the trout and pat them dry. Melt half of the butter in a large skillet and fry the trout for 5 minutes on each side. Remove the fish, cover them and keep warm.

Melt the remaining butter in the skillet. Stir the sliced mushrooms and chestnuts into the butter along with the chicken meat. Cook over low heat for 5 minutes then stir in the flour. Add the cream and sherry; reheat and remove from the stove. Arrange the trout on an ovenproof platter; decorate with strips of red pepper and

pour the sauce over. Place the platter in a preheated oven for 10 minutes until the sauce begins to bubble.

Note: Chestnuts will peel easily once they are cooked. Prick each shell with a pin, drop the nuts in boiling water and let cook for 5 minutes. Remove from the heat and drain. Let cool before peeling.

Cajun sign, typical of the French Quarter in New Orleans, Louisiana.

CATFISH WITH PECAN RICE, Recipe this page.

Catfish with Pecan Rice

PHOTOGRAPH THIS PAGE

Preparation Time: 20 minutes
Cooking Time: 1 hour
Preheat Oven: 500°F (250°C)
Serves 4

½ cup cornmeal
garlic, salt and pepper to taste
4 small catfish, cleaned and skinned
¼ cup peanut oil

In a shallow bowl, combine the cornmeal and seasonings. Pat the catfish dry and dredge it in the cornmeal mixture. Arrange the fish on a baking sheet and drizzle with peanut oil. Bake for 15–20 minutes until flaky. Serve over Pecan Rice.

Pecan Rice

Preparation time: 30 minutes
Cooking time: 1 hour
Serves: 4

1½ cups brown rice
3 Tbsp butter
1 medium onion, chopped
1 cup chopped pecans
¼ cup chopped fresh parsley
1 Tbsp grated fresh ginger root
1 Tbsp chopped fresh basil or
* 1½ tsp dried basil*
salt and pepper to taste

Steam the rice for 45 minutes until cooked. Set aside. Melt the butter and stir in the onion. Sauté for 5 minutes. Combine with the rice, pecans, herbs and seasonings. Stir and simmer for 10 minutes.

CAJUN

MAIN COURSE

CAJUN

SWEETS

Lime Mango Beignets
PHOTOGRAPH PAGE 165

Preparation Time: 30 minutes
Rising Time: overnight
Cooking Time: 20 minutes
Yield: 18 beignets

¼ cup sugar
¾ cup warm water
1 package active dry yeast
pinch of salt
1 egg, beaten
½ cup heavy cream
3½ cups flour

Glaze:
1 cup sugar
½ cup mango juice
2 Tbsp lime juice

In a mixing bowl, dissolve the sugar in the warm water and stir in the yeast. When the yeast begins to froth, add the salt, beaten egg, and cream; gradually stir in the flour. Mix well. Turn the dough onto a floured board and knead for 10 minutes. Roll the dough into a ball, brush with oil and place it in a clean bowl. Cover the bowl and put it in the refrigerator. Let the dough rise slowly overnight.

The following morning, turn out the dough and knead it for 2 minutes to soften. Roll it out ½-inch (1 cm) thick. Cut it into 2-inch (4 cm) triangles and let them rest for ½ hour. Deep-fry the beignets for 5 minutes at 375°F (190°C) until they are lightly golden.

In a saucepan, dissolve the sugar in the mango and lime juices and heat until just warm. Remove from the heat. When the beignets are done, drain them on paper towels for 1 minute then dip in the warm glaze. Set on a rack to cool.

Jelly Roll
PHOTOGRAPH PAGE 177

Preparation Time: 20 minutes
Cooking Time: 20 minutes
Preheat Oven: 375°F (190°C)
Serves 6

4 egg yolks
½ cup sugar
1 tsp vanilla
4 egg whites
⅓ cup sugar
¾ cup flour
1 tsp baking powder
1 cup blackberry jelly
⅓ cup icing sugar

Grease a 15 inches by 10 inches by 2 inches (38 cm by 25 cm by 5 cm) jelly roll pan. Line it with greased wax paper. Beat the egg yolks until creamy and lemon-colored. Gradually beat in the ½ cup sugar and the vanilla.

Beat the egg whites to soft peaks then beat into them the ⅓ cup sugar. Fold the egg whites into the yolk mixture. Add the flour and baking powder. Beat the batter well then pour into prepared jelly roll pan. Bake 15–20 minutes until pale golden. Turn onto a cloth or a paper towel. Trim the edges, removing any crust, and spread the roll with jelly. Roll it up into a log and allow it to cool. Sprinkle the jelly roll with icing sugar. Slice to serve.

Blackberry Pie
PHOTOGRAPH PAGE 177

Preparation Time: 20 minutes
Cooking Time: 1 hour
Preheat Oven: 450°F (230°C)
Serves 6

Pastry:
2 cups flour
pinch of salt
pinch of baking powder
1 Tbsp light brown sugar
¾ cup shortening
1 egg
1 tsp white vinegar
¼ cup cold water

Filling:
4 cups blackberries
2 Tbsp flour
¾ cup sugar
a few whole blackberries for garnish
1 beaten egg
2 Tbsp sugar

Sift the dry ingredients together and cut in the shortening. If you are using a food processor, be careful not to overprocess the pastry or it will be tough. Beat in the egg and vinegar. Add just enough water to make the dough cling together. Form the dough into a ball and chill for 15 minutes. Divide the dough into two portions and roll one of them out to a 12-inch (30 cm) round. Place it in a 9-inch (23 cm) pie dish and trim the edge. Half fill the pie with rice or dried beans and bake for 6 minutes. Remove from the oven and discard the rice. (It can be kept for reuse with other pie shells.) Leave the oven at 450°F (230°C).

Gently toss the blackberries with the flour and sugar. Pour them into the pie shell. Roll out the remaining dough to a 12-inch (30 cm) round. Make 1-inch (2.5 cm) cuts in this crust in rows 1½ inches (3.5 cm) apart, alternating the slashes. Stretch over the pie, which will cause the slashes to open slightly. Trim and flute the edge. Place a whole blackberry in each open cut. Brush the pastry with the beaten egg and sprinkle with the 2 Tbsp sugar. Bake for 10 minutes then reduce the heat to 350°F (180°C) and bake for 50 minutes longer.

Bottom: JELLY ROLL, Recipe page 176. *Top:* BLACKBERRY PIE, Recipe page 176.

CAJUN

SWEETS

Stuffed French Toast

PHOTOGRAPH PAGE 179

Preparation Time: 15 minutes
Cooking Time: 4 minutes
Serves 4

1 banana
1 apple
1 pear
¼ cup pecans
¼ cup light brown sugar
2 eggs
1½ cups milk
½ cup flour
1 tsp cinnamon
½ tsp mace
⅛ tsp cloves
4 1-inch (2.5 cm) thick slices white toasting bread
4 Tbsp butter

Peel and slice the fruit and chop the nuts; combine, sprinkle with the sugar and set aside. In a bowl or blender, combine the eggs, milk, flour and spices; beat until creamy. Set aside. Cut each slice of bread almost in half crossways leaving about a 1-inch (2.5 cm) "hinge" along the bottom. (It is easier to do this while the slice is still attached to the loaf.) Carefully open up the slices and rub 1 Tbsp of butter on each one. Fill the cavities with the fruit and nut mixture; press the halves of each slice together. Dip the bread on both sides in the batter and fry as with regular French toast, turning once.

Lemon Delight Bread Pudding

PHOTOGRAPH PAGE 179

Preparation Time: 30 minutes
Baking Time: 35–40 minutes
Preheat Oven: 325°F (140°C)
Serves 4–6

2 egg yolks
3 Tbsp soft butter
⅔ cup sugar
1 cup fresh white breadcrumbs
pinch of salt
1¾ cups light cream
1 tsp vanilla
juice and rind of 1 lemon
2 egg whites, stiffly beaten
whipping cream
grated orange rind

Beat together the egg yolks, butter and sugar until very smooth and creamy. Stir in the breadcrumbs, salt and cream. Heat the mixture in a heavy saucepan, stirring frequently, until the custard starts to thicken. Beat until well mixed.

Remove from the heat and add the vanilla, lemon juice and rind. Beat again. Delicately fold in the stiffly beaten egg whites. Pour the pudding mixture into a baking dish and set the dish in a pan containing 1-inch (2.5 cm) of hot water. Place in the preheated oven and bake for 35–40 minutes until golden. Serve warm with lightly whipped cream sprinkled with orange rind.

Rum Babas with Almond Glaze

PHOTOGRAPH PAGE 179

Preparation Time: 1 hour
Rising Time: 2½ hours
Baking Time: 15 minutes
Soaking Time: 30 minutes
Makes 8–10

Babas:
1 package active dry yeast
¼ cup warm water
2 Tbsp sugar
4 Tbsp butter
2 eggs
1½ cups flour

Syrup:
1½ cups water
1 cup sugar
¾ cup dark rum

Glaze:
¼ cup sugar
1 Tbsp rum
1 Tbsp water
1 cup slivered almonds
whipped cream

Babas:
In a coffee mug, dissolve the yeast in the warm water with the sugar. Set aside. Melt the butter and pour it into a mixing bowl. Add the eggs and beat until smooth. Stir in half the flour. When the yeast has a good head of froth, pour it over the flour mixture and combine well. Gradually add the remaining flour until the dough has lost most of its stickiness. Turn it out onto a floured board and knead for 10 minutes. The dough should be very soft, light and elastic in texture. Roll the dough into a ball, place it in a clean, greased bowl, cover with a damp cloth and set to rise in a warm place for about 1½ hours until doubled in bulk.

After the first rising, turn the dough out onto a lightly floured board and knead gently for 1 minute then roll it into a sausage-like shape. Slice the dough into sections and shape each one into a ball slightly smaller than a golf ball. Place the balls on a greased baking sheet or in a

Middle right: STUFFED FRENCH TOAST, Recipe page 178, *Top left:* LEMON DELIGHT BREAD PUDDINGS, Recipe page 178. *Bottom left:* RUM BABAS WITH ALMOND GLAZE, Recipe page 178.

muffin pan and let rise a second time for about 1 hour.

When the dough balls have doubled in size, bake at 375°F (190°C) for 15–20 minutes until just browned. Remove and cool on a wire rack.

Syrup:

Place the water in a saucepan and bring it to a boil. Remove from the heat and stir in the sugar. When the sugar is dissolved, stir in the rum.

When the babas are cool enough to handle, lightly prick them all over with a fork and arrange them in a dish or flat bowl. Pour the syrup over the babas, and let them soak for ½ hour, basting occasionally to ensure that they are thoroughly and evenly soaked.

Glaze:

Drain off any syrup that has not soaked into the babas and reheat it in a saucepan. If there is not enough syrup for a glaze, add the extra sugar, water and rum. Bring the syrup to a simmer then remove from the heat. The glaze should be stickier than the syrup. Place the slivered almonds in a shallow bowl. Roll the babas, one at a time, in the glaze and then in the almonds. Place in individual serving dishes. Serve slightly warm with whipped cream.

CAJUN

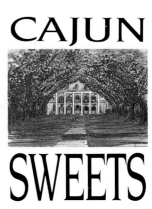

SWEETS

Dixie

The Heart of the South, Dixie conjures images of gracious lifestyles, hominy grits, negro slaves, and civil war. But did you know it was a favorite haunt of Black Beard and Daniel Boone? That Kitty Hawk was the site of the Wright Brothers first successful flight?

Paddlewheel boat on the Mississippi River in Mississippi.

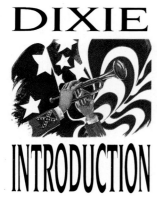

DIXIE
INTRODUCTION

That the cotton gin was invented here and that it is known as the Birth Place of Presidents? This area covers Virginia, North & South Carolina, Georgia, Tennessee, Alabama and Louisiana.

There are many explanations for the name Dixie, many pure conjecture, but some with perhaps a grain of truth. One, that a Louisiana bank issued a ten dollar note with 'dix' (French for ten) on it. Another, that a man called Dix or Dixy, living in Manhattan, had slaves whom he treated well and when he had to send them south, they were homesick for 'Dixy's Land'. All myth, perhaps.

In 1584, Queen Elizabeth I granted the area from, what is now Pennsylvania to South Carolina and west indefinitely, to Sir Walter Raleigh. In 1587 he sent a small group of new settlers to Roanoke Island in North Carolina to establish a permanent colony. With the Spanish Armada attempting a take-over bid in England, no ships could be spared to care for the tiny colony and when finally in 1590 a ship could be spared, no trace of this unlucky group of colonists was ever found, although some believe they intermarried with the Hatteras Indian tribe.

Virginia, named after the 'Virgin Queen', saw the first permanent English speaking settlement at Jamestown in 1607 and four years later the colonists were allowed to operate farms for their own profit. One of these was John Rolfe who successfully established the first tobacco farm and improved his lot further by marrying the legendary Pocahontas.

Spain held great tracts of land around the Gulf of Mexico which led to war between Britain and Spain in 1740.

French claims to the Tennessee area also found Britain embattled in 1743 but England gained control and with later 'to-ing and fro-ing', the area slowly came under the wing of the United States at the end of the 18th, and beginning of the 19th century.

With the success of cotton, tobacco, peanuts and other crops, the south developed huge farms unlike its northern cousins and inventions such as the cotton gin saw the south become a wealthy and necessary part of the United States' economy. The only way these plantations could be maintained was with a large and cheap work force. Slavery in the New World had started as early as 1516 with the Spanish and had flourished throughout the area. The Dutch brought slaves to the British colonies in 1619 (perhaps when Dutch Beet Eggs were first tried — see recipe in this section).

Although slavery flourished throughout the colonies, by 1808 the government abolished the importation of slaves to the United States. This, however, did not change the lot of those already in America.

Northern sympathy for the slave was not purely a human rights issue, but also the unprofitability of slave labor in factories and on the north's small farms, where they would have to be housed and fed. It is interesting to note that at the height of the slavery debate, only five percent of the Southerners had slaves and only half of these had more than five slaves.

This continuing conflict came to a head in 1861 with the Civil War, and as with all civil war, great bitterness and hardship were suffered by all. Although the South was defeated, its huge plantations continued to produce cotton and other important crops which aided in the recovery of the area.

Dixie is famous for many products, amongst these her cotton, fruits, peanuts, vegetables and, of course, Tennessee's horses — none better known than the Bluegrass. Wonderful seafood is also available off the coastline of this area and even Coca Cola comes from the region — Georgia.

The recipes on the following pages will give you a feel for the old South — whether it be Hot Peanut Soup, Charleston Red Rice, Ham & Black-Eyed Peas or Shoo Fly Pie. They will all conjure up memories of a time gone by when gracious living and beautiful homes were a part of everyday life.

Now you have the opportunity to re-create some of these delicious dishes and serve them to friends and family with good old Southern hospitality.

Top right: VIDALIA & HOT WATERMELON SALAD, Recipe page 184. *Bottom*: CAROLINA CORN SHRIMP PIE, Recipe page 188. *Top left*: SHOO FLY PIE, Recipe page 194.

DIXIE

**APPETIZERS
SOUPS
SALADS
ENTREES**

Hot Peanut Soup

Preparation Time: 10 minutes
Cooking Time: 10 minutes
Serves 3

2 Tbsp butter
1 medium onion, chopped
½ tsp black pepper
1 Tbsp powdered mustard
1 tsp fresh thyme or
   ½ tsp dried thyme
½ cup smooth peanut butter
3 cups chicken stock
3 Tbsp heavy cream

In a soup pan, melt the butter and sauté the onion until it is transparent. Add the pepper, mustard, thyme and peanut butter; stir until smooth and creamy. Add the stock, stir and bring the mixture to a boil. Lower the heat and simmer for 5 minutes. Add the cream just before serving.

Vidalia & Hot Watermelon Salad

PHOTOGRAPH PAGE 183

Preparation Time: 15 minutes
Chilling Time: 1 hour
Serves 4

2 Vidalias, or large sweet onions, cut into very thin slices
¼ cup lime juice
1 lb (500 g) watermelon, in 1-inch balls
Tabasco sauce

Place the thinly sliced Vidalias in a bowl and sprinkle with the lime juice. Cover and chill for at least 1 hour, stirring occasionally.

Place a drop of Tabasco on each watermelon ball and place in a separate bowl. Cover and chill for at least 1 hour, turning occasionally.

When thoroughly marinated, drain and toss the onions and melon balls together.

Arugula & Onion Salad

Preparation Time: 10 minutes
Serves 4

1 bunch arugula
1 large sweet red onion
¼ cup slivered almonds
¼ cup pitted chopped dates

Dressing:
2 Tbsp olive oil
2 Tbsp tarragon vinegar
1 clove garlic
1 Tbsp orange juice
pepper and sugar to taste

Pull the leaves from the arugula and place them in a bowl. Peel the onion and cut it into thin rings. Add the onion to the arugula along with the almonds and dates.

Put the dressing ingredients in a blender and blend thoroughly. Pour over the salad, and toss gently. Serve at room temperature.

Arugula or roquet is a popular fragrant herb with a mild peppery taste. It is available in many grocery stores or is easily grown from seed.

Jalapeño Hush Puppies

Preparation Time: 10 minutes
Cooking Time: 10 minutes
Preheat Deep Fryer: 375°F (190°C)
Serves 6

1 cup yellow cornmeal
½ cup flour
1½ tsp baking powder
1 medium onion, minced
4 jalapeño peppers, seeded and minced
pinch of garlic powder
1 egg
⅓ cup milk
oil for deep frying

In a mixing bowl, combine all the ingredients except the oil to a smooth, thick paste. Drop the batter into the hot oil by spoonfuls a few at a time and fry until golden, turning once. Drain on paper towels and serve hot.

Cracklin' Cornbread

Preparation Time: 5 minutes
Cooking Time: 25 minutes
Serves 6–8

2 cups white cornmeal
1 tsp baking soda
pinch of salt
2 eggs, beaten
2 cups buttermilk
¼ cup bacon dripping
1 cup cracklings

In a mixing bowl, combine the cornmeal, soda, salt, eggs and buttermilk until smooth. In a 9-inch or 10-inch (23 cm or 25 cm) heavy iron pan, heat the bacon fat and cracklings until hot, almost smoking. Pour in the batter, cover with a lid and cook over medium heat for about 25 minutes until firm. Serve hot straight from the pan.

Dutch Beet Eggs

Preparation Time: 10 minutes
Cooking Time: 45 minutes
Yield: 8

1 lb (500 g) beets
2 qts (2 lt) water
8 eggs, at room temperature

Remove the tops of the beets (if young, save to use as a separate vegetable), peel the beets and drop them into a pan of hot water to cover. Boil for ½ hour or until the beets are cooked through but are still firm. Remove from the water with a slotted spoon and set aside to cool.
Use for Pickled Beets.

Put the eggs in the beet water and slow boil them for 6–7 minutes. Remove the pan from the heat and lift out the eggs with a slotted spoon. Carefully crack the shells all around to form a crazed pattern then return the cracked eggs to the beet water for 2–3 hours. Remove the eggs and pat dry. Serve cold with a salad. The shells will be bright red in color and the whites of the eggs will be patterned with red lines.

Pickled Beets

Slice the cooled beets and put them into a 1-qt (1 lt) jar. Add a hot pepper and fill the jar with cider vinegar. Allow to stand for at least a week before using. Serve the pickled beets with salad or as a garnish with ham or lamb.

DIXIE

APPETIZERS
SOUPS
SALADS
ENTREES

Left: BABY CARROTS BOURBONAISSE, Recipe this page. *Right*: HOT MUSTARD BEANS, Recipe this page.

Baby Carrots Bourbonaisse

PHOTOGRAPH THIS PAGE

Preparation Time: 10 minutes
Cooking Time: 12 minutes
Serves 4

⅔ cup orange juice
¾ lb (375 g) baby carrots
2 Tbsp butter
2 Tbsp brown sugar
2 Tbsp bourbon
1 tsp fresh chopped dill

Heat the orange juice in a saucepan. Clean the carrots and put them in the hot juice. Boil them for 7–10 minutes until just tender. Lift out the carrots and set aside. Stir the butter and sugar into the hot juice and heat until the butter is melted and the sugar dissolved. Lower the heat and stir in the bourbon and carrots. Stir briefly and remove to a serving dish.
Sprinkle with fresh dill.

Hot Mustard Beans

PHOTOGRAPH THIS PAGE

Preparation Time: 10 minutes
Cooking Time: 10 minutes
Serves 4

1 lb (500 g) green or yellow snap beans
½ cup beef stock
1 Tbsp honey
1 tsp powdered mustard
1 tsp cornstarch
¼ cup pine nuts

Trim and slice the beans, if desired. Place them in a saucepan, cover with boiling water and let boil for 5 minutes. Drain the beans. Blend together the stock, honey, mustard and cornstarch. Pour the sauce over the beans. Reheat gently stirring occasionally, until the beans are glazed. Garnish with pine nuts.

The old Grist Mill spills heavily into the swift waters of Glade Creek at Babcock State Park in West Virginia.

Hominy Grits & Okra

Preparation Time: 8 minutes
Cooking Time: 30 minutes
Serves 4

4 slices of bacon
1 lb (500 g) boiled hominy or 16-oz (500 g) can hominy grits, drained
½ tsp pepper
½ lb (250 g) fresh okra, coarsely chopped

With a pair of scissors, cut the bacon into small strips then fry in a large skillet until crisp. Remove the bacon bits with a slotted spoon. Add the hominy grits to the skillet and cook over medium heat until golden and crisp underneath, about 15 minutes. With a wooden spoon or spatula, break up the hominy. Stir in the pepper, bacon bits and okra. Cover and cook for 5–7 minutes longer. Serve at once, preferably with scrambled eggs and hot biscuits.

Sweet Potato Pone

Preparation Time: 25 minutes
Cooking Time: 2 hours
Preheat Oven: 300°F (150°C)
Serves 4–6

1 lb (500 g) sweet potatoes (or yams)
⅓ lb (160 g) butter
1 cup sugar
1 Tbsp ground ginger
5 eggs
1 tsp baking powder
½ cup sour milk or buttermilk

Peel the potatoes and grate them by hand or in a food processor, using the shredding disc. Process until very fine.

In a bowl, cream the butter and sugar until smooth. Add the ginger and stir in the eggs, one at a time, mixing after each addition. Add the sweet potato and the baking powder. Stir in the milk to make a thick smooth batter. Pour into a 9-inch (23 cm) cake pan and bake for 2 hours.

Tilghman Island Crab Cakes

Preparation Time: 10 minutes
Cooking Time: 10 minutes
Serves 4

1 lb (500 g) backfin crab meat
1 Tbsp chopped fresh parsley
1 small onion, minced
1 Tbsp powdered mustard
1½ cups soft white breadcrumbs
1 tsp Worcestershire sauce

salt & pepper to taste
¼ cup butter for frying

In a bowl or food processor mix together all the ingredients until well blended. Form into small 1-inch (2.5 cm) by 3-inch (8 cm) cakes and fry in butter for 5 minutes on each side. Serve hot.

Ham & Black-Eyed Peas

Preparation Time: 15 minutes
Soaking Time: overnight
Cooking Time: 1¼ hours
Serves 8

1 lb (500 g) dried black-eyed peas
4–5 lbs (2–2½ kg) smoked ham
3 cups chopped onion
2 cloves garlic, minced
pinch of cayenne
1 tsp pepper
2 Tbsp honey
½ tsp dried thyme
½ tsp dried oregano
1 cup chopped scallions
1 lb (500 g) tomatoes, skinned and chopped
1 lb (500 g) fresh okra

Place the peas in a large bowl and cover with boiling water. Soak them overnight.

The next morning, place the ham in a large heavy pan or Dutch oven and add the peas, onion, garlic, cayenne, pepper, honey, thyme and oregano. Add just enough water to barely cover and bring to a boil. Lower the heat and simmer for 1 hour. Add the scallions, tomatoes and okra. Simmer for 15 minutes.

To serve, place the ham on a platter and arrange the vegetables around it.
Serve hot with rice.

Baked Vidalias & Peanuts

Preparation Time: 25 minutes
Cooking Time: 15 minutes
Preheat Oven: 400°F (200°C)
Serves 4

4 large Vidalias or sweet onions
¼ cup crunchy peanut butter
¼ cup shelled peanuts, roasted
1 tsp black pepper
3 Tbsp heavy cream

Peel the onions and trim the bottoms so that they will stand. Place them in a pan of hot water and boil them for 5 minutes until soft but not mushy.
In a bowl, mix the remaining ingredients. When the Vidalias are cooked, drain them and carefully make a hollow in each one. Stuff the hollows with the peanut mixture and place the onions on a baking sheet. Bake for 10 minutes. Serve hot.

DIXIE

MAIN COURSE

Carolina Corn Shrimp Pie

PHOTOGRAPH PAGE 183

Preparation Time: 20 minutes
Cooking Time: 70 minutes
Preheat Oven: 350°F (180°C)
Serves 6

¼ cup butter
¼ cup chopped onion
½ cup chopped celery
3 cups milk
2 cups fresh corn
1 tsp Tabasco sauce
1 tsp Worcestershire sauce
1 tsp powdered mustard
1 tsp pepper
salt to taste
3 eggs, beaten
2 lbs (1 kg) shrimp, shelled and deveined
2 Tbsp butter
2 cups fine cracker crumbs

In a large saucepan, melt the butter. Sauté the onion and celery in the butter for 5 minutes. Stir in the milk and corn. Heat but do not boil. Remove from the heat and add the seasonings and beaten eggs. Stir well then add the shrimp meat.

In a separate pan, melt the 2 Tbsp butter and mix into it the cracker crumbs. Press the crumbs onto the bottom and sides of a casserole dish to form a crust. Spoon in the filling, topping with more cracker crumbs, if desired. Bake for 1 hour until just set.

Chicken Livers in Madeira Sauce

Preparation Time: 10 minutes
Cooking Time: 12 minutes
Serves 4

1 lb (500 g) chicken livers
2 Tbsp butter
1 tsp freshly ground black pepper
1 leek, finely chopped
1 Tbsp butter
¼ cup heavy cream
½ cup Madeira
¼ cup chopped mushrooms

Wash the livers and pat dry. Melt the butter in a skillet and sauté the livers for 5 minutes, turning once. Lift out the livers with a slotted spoon and set them aside. Scrape the pan to loosen any bits of liver and add the pepper, leek and 1 Tbsp butter. Cook for 3–4 minutes, stirring occasionally, until the leek has softened. Stir in the cream, Madeira and mushrooms. Add the livers and reheat, stirring constantly, for 2–3 minutes but do not let boil. Serve hot.

Charleston Red Rice

Preparation Time: 10 minutes
Cooking Time: 30 minutes
Serves 6

4 slices of bacon
1 cup chopped onion
½ cup chopped green pepper
2 cups water
1 8-oz (250 ml) can tomato sauce
1 Tbsp brown sugar
pinch of salt
1½ cups long-grain white rice

Cut the bacon into bits and fry in a large skillet or heavy pan. When the pan is well greased, add the chopped onion and green pepper. Continue frying until the onion is golden and the bacon crisp. Add the water, tomato sauce, sugar, salt and rice. Cover and bring to a boil. Lower the heat and cook for about 20 minutes until the liquid is absorbed and the rice is tender.

Grilled Shrimp & Snow Peas in Ginger Glaze

PHOTOGRAPH PAGE 189

Preparation Time: 30 minutes
Marinating Time: 3–4 hours
Cooking Time: 8 minutes
Serves 6

4 cloves garlic
1 cup peanut oil
½ cup chopped fresh basil or
    ¼ cup dried basil
1 Tbsp Worcestershire sauce
1 Tbsp hot sauce
½ cup dry red wine
36 large shrimp, peeled and deveined
36 large snow peas
1 Tbsp cornstarch
1 Tbsp grated fresh ginger root
¼ cup sesame seeds

In a blender combine the garlic, oil, basil, Worcestershire sauce, hot sauce and wine; blend until smooth. Pour the blended mixture into a bowl and add the shrimp; toss gently then marinate for 3–4 hours, stirring occasionally.

To assemble: wrap a snow pea around each shrimp and skewer to hold in place. Arrange 6 wrapped shrimp on each skewer. Baste well with the marinade and grill or broil for 3–4 minutes on each side until the snow peas start to blister.

Meanwhile, dissolve the cornstarch and ginger in the cold marinade. Pour into a saucepan and bring to a boil, stirring constantly, until the sauce thickens to a glaze. When the shrimp and peas are cooked, dip or brush them liberally with the glaze and sprinkle with sesame seeds.

GRILLED SHRIMP & SNOW PEAS IN GINGER GLAZE, Recipe page 188.

Red, white and pink Azaleas are shaded from the tall trees and blossoming Dogwoods
at the beautiful Elizabethan Gardens in North Carolina.

DIXIE

MAIN COURSE

Ham & Red-Eye Gravy

Preparation Time: 20 minutes
Cooking Time: 15 minutes
Serves 2

2 Tbsp bacon fat or lard
2 ham steaks
1 tsp powdered mustard
1 small red chili
1 Tbsp corn flour
½ cup strong black coffee

Heat the bacon fat in a skillet until it crackles. Fry the ham steaks for 5 minutes on each side; set the steaks aside and keep them warm.

Scrape the pan to loosen any bits of meat and stir in the mustard and flour. If you like your chilies hot, mince the whole chili and add it to the pan; otherwise, remove the seeds before mincing. Pour in the coffee and stir well. Bring the mixture to a boil and simmer for 5 minutes. Serve the red-eye gravy over the ham steaks.

Steak with Mushrooms in Phyllo Pastry

Preparation Time: 30 minutes
Cooking Time: 35 minutes
Preheat Oven: 400°F (200°C)
Serves 4

1–1½ lbs (500 g–750 g) filet mignon at room temperature
1 Tbsp red pepper sauce
2 Tbsp melted butter

Sauce:
2 Tbsp butter
1 Tbsp flour
2 Tbsp grated Vidalia or sweet onion
¼ cup chopped pecans
¼ cup chopped mushrooms
1 tsp grated orange rind
2 Tbsp port wine
8 sheets of phyllo pastry
2 Tbsp melted butter

Rub the melted butter and pepper sauce into the meat, kneading it with your fingers. Oil a grill or broiler rack and cook the meat for about 7 minutes on each side until well seared on the outside and very rare inside.

In a saucepan, melt the 2 Tbsp butter, blend in the flour, then add the onion and pecans and cook for 5 minutes, stirring occasionally. Remove the pan from the heat and add the mushrooms, orange rind and Port. Stir and set aside.

Carefully separate the sheets of phyllo pastry and fold each sheet in half. Cut the filet mignon into 8 small thick steaks and place each one in the center of a pastry sheet. Spoon some sauce over each steak. Then fold the pastry over the meat and tuck it underneath to seal each package. Place on a baking sheet and brush with melted butter. Bake for 15–20 minutes until the pastry is golden.

Bourbon & Praline Ham

Preparation Time: 10 minutes
Marinating Time: 2–3 hours
Cooking Time: 2 hours
Serves 12

6–8 lb (3–4 kg) precooked ham, fat left on
1½ cups bourbon
2 Tbsp butter
1 cup maple syrup
½ cup brown sugar
½ cup ground or finely chopped pecans
½ cup pecan halves

Score the skin and fat of the ham and rub it liberally with bourbon. Place it in the smallest baking dish that will hold it and pour over the rest of the bourbon. Marinate for 2–3 hours, basting every ½ hour. Pour off the excess whiskey and bake the ham, skin side up, for 2 hours at 325°F (160°C).

In a saucepan, melt the butter. Stir in the bourbon marinade, maple syrup, sugar and pecans. Bring the mixture to a boil. Pour the glaze over the ham and brush well with a pastry brush. Decorate with pecan halves and bake for an additional 15–20 minutes.

Kielbasa Stew

PHOTOGRAPH PAGE 193

Preparation Time: 20 minutes
Cooking Time: 25 minutes
Serves 4

¼ lb (125 g) bacon, chopped
2 cloves garlic
3 cups coarsely chopped cabbage
3 cups peeled and chopped potato
2 Tbsp brown sugar
1 tsp chili pepper
1 tsp caraway seeds
1 lb (500 g) kielbasa sausage, cut into 1-inch (2.5 cm) pieces

Fry the bacon and garlic in a large skillet for 10 minutes until browned and crisp. Add the chopped cabbage, potato, sugar, chili pepper and caraway seeds; pour over just enough hot water to cover. Bring the mixture to a boil, lower the heat and simmer for 10 minutes. Stir in the kielbasa and simmer for 5 minutes longer.

Left: PLANTATION STEW, Recipe this page. Right: KIELBASA STEW, Recipe page 192.

Plantation Stew

PHOTOGRAPH THIS PAGE

Preparation Time: 20 minutes
Cooking Time: 2 hours
Serves 6–8

3½ lbs (1½ kg) lamb shoulder
½ cup olive oil
2 qts (2 lt) chicken stock
6 potatoes
2 red sweet peppers
1 tsp sugar
1 tsp fresh or dried thyme
1 Tbsp vinegar
1 Tbsp lemon juice
1 Tbsp orange juice
1 Tbsp Worcestershire sauce
1 Tbsp chopped fresh parsley or
    1½ tsp dried parsley
¼ cup sherry

Cut the lamb into large chunks. Heat the olive oil in a large heavy pan and add the meat. When the lamb is well browned on all sides add the stock. Bring it to a boil then lower the heat and simmer covered for 1½ hours. Peel and slice the potatoes, chop the peppers and add the vegetables to the stock. Stir in the remaining ingredients except for the sherry. Simmer for another ½ hour. Remove the stew from the heat, stir in the sherry and serve.

DIXIE

MAIN COURSE

DIXIE

SWEETS

Oatmeal Orange Muffins

Soaking Time: 15 minutes
Preparation Time: 20 minutes
Cooking Time: 20 minutes
Preheat Oven: 350°F (180°C)
Yield: 14 muffins

1 cup rolled oats (not instant or quick cooking)
½ cup orange juice
½ cup boiling water
½ cup butter
½ cup white sugar
½ cup brown sugar
2 eggs, beaten
½ cup sultanas
½ cup chopped walnuts
handful of coconut
1¼ cups flour
1 tsp baking powder
1 tsp baking soda
½ tsp salt
2 tsp vanilla

Soak the oats in the orange juice and water for 15 minutes. In a bowl, cream the butter and sugars. Add the eggs and sultanas; stir in the oat mixture. In a separate bowl, mix together the nuts, coconut, flour, baking powder, baking soda and salt. Add the dry ingredients to the creamed mixture stirring just enough to combine well. Stir in the vanilla. Pour the batter into well-greased muffin tins and bake for 20 minutes. Serve warm.

Shoo Fly Pie

PHOTOGRAPH PAGE 183

Preparation Time: 10 minutes
Cooking Time: 25 minutes
Preheat Oven: 400°F (200°C)
Serves 6

¾ cup corn syrup
¼ cup molasses
1 cup hot water
1 tsp baking soda
1 egg
1 cup flour
2 Tbsp butter
⅔ cup brown sugar
9-inch (23 cm) pastry pie shell (page 176), unbaked

In a bowl or food processor, mix together the corn syrup, molasses, water, soda and egg. Reserve about half of this mixture. To the rest add the flour, butter and brown sugar. Mix well then pour into the pastry shell. Carefully top with the reserved syrup and bake for 25 minutes. Allow to cool then chill the pie before serving.

Sally Lunn Coffee Cake

PHOTOGRAPH PAGE 195

Preparation Time: 25 minutes
Cooking Time: 30 minutes
Preheat Oven: 400°F (200°C)
Serves 8

½ cup shortening
½ cup sugar
1 tsp lemon juice
2 eggs
1½ cups flour
2¼ tsp baking powder
½ tsp salt
¾ cup milk

Topping:
1 Tbsp butter
⅓ cup sugar
⅛ tsp nutmeg
1 Tbsp grated lemon rind

In a mixing bowl, cream the shortening and sugar. Stir in the lemon juice and eggs, one at a time, beating well after each addition. Sift together the flour, baking powder and salt. Add the dry ingredients alternately with the milk to the creamed mixture to make a thick batter. Do not overmix. Pour into a greased 9-inch (23 cm) cake pan.

To make the topping, melt the butter and stir in the sugar, nutmeg and lemon rind. Sprinkle the topping as evenly as possible over the cake batter. Bake for ½ hour. Serve warm.

Bourbon Pecan Pie

PHOTOGRAPH PAGE 195

Preparation Time: 15 minutes
Cooking Time: 40 minutes
Preheat Oven: 375°F (190°C)
Serves 6

3 eggs, beaten
1 cup sugar
½ cup light corn syrup
½ cup dark corn syrup
⅓ cup butter
¼ cup bourbon
1 cup chopped pecans
¼ cup pecan halves
9-inch (23 cm) sweet pastry shell (page 176), unbaked

In a bowl or food processor, mix the eggs, sugar, syrups, butter and bourbon until smooth. Sprinkle the pastry with the chopped pecans then carefully pour in the filling. Coat each pecan half by dipping in the filling then arrange on the top. Bake for 40 minutes. Cool until set.

Top: SALLY LUNN COFFEE CAKE, Recipe page 194. *Bottom:* BOURBON PECAN PIE, Recipe page 194.

DIXIE SWEETS

Orange & Cream Cheese Brandy Snaps

PHOTOGRAPH PAGE 197

Preparation Time: 20 minutes
Cooking Time: 10 minutes
Preheat Oven: 325°F (160°C)
Serves 6

¼ lb (250 g) butter
3 Tbsp maple syrup
1 Tbsp brandy
¾ cup flour
¾ cup icing sugar
1 Tbsp ginger juice
⅓ cup crushed pecans

Filling:
½ lb (250 g) cream cheese
2 Tbsp sugar
⅓ cup orange sections
2 tsp Grand Marnier

In a heavy saucepan, melt the butter. Remove the pan from the heat and stir in the maple syrup and brandy. Add the flour, sugar, ginger juice and pecans; mix well. (Ginger juice may be obtained by pushing ginger root through a garlic press.) Drop the batter onto a buttered cookie sheet, 1 Tbsp at a time, 6 inches (15 cm) apart. Bake for 10 minutes until golden. Remove the snaps from the oven and allow to cool for a few seconds.

With a knife edge or spatula, lift each one and roll it into a cone or cylinder shape. Allow the snaps to cool. Brandy snaps may be kept unfilled for up to a week in a cookie tin.

Filling: In a bowl or food processor, blend all four ingredients into a smooth cream. Fill each brandy snap with the cream cheese mixture, using a kitchen syringe or a small spoon.

Grilled Fruit with Burnt Brandy Glaze

PHOTOGRAPH PAGE 197

Preparation Time: 20 minutes
Cooking Time: 20 minutes
Serves 4

2 lbs (1 kg) mixed fruit—at least 4 different fruits such as apples, figs, bananas, pears, peaches, persimmons, green seedless grapes, etc. Avoid citrus fruits, overripe fruits or those that are very moist.

Glaze:
2 Tbsp butter
½ cup sugar
1 Tbsp grated orange rind
sprig of fresh mint
pinch of white pepper
¼ cup brandy

Wash the fruit, peel it if you wish, and cut it into bite-sized chunks. Pat it dry.

In a saucepan, melt the butter; add the sugar, orange rind, mint and pepper. Stir to dissolve the sugar then bring the mixture to a boil. Lower the heat and simmer for 10 minutes. Discard the mint sprig and stir in the brandy. Arrange the fruit sections on 4 skewers, alternating the fruits. Dip or liberally brush the fruit kebabs with the glaze and grill or broil at a medium-hot temperature for 4–5 minutes on each side, basting frequently. The kebabs are done when the sugar begins to carmelize or brown.

Fish roasting at the ramps in Cosby.

Top left: ORANGE & CREAM CHEESE BRANDY SNAPS, Recipe page 196. *Top right:* GRILLED FRUIT WITH BURNT BRANDY GLAZE, Recipe page 196. *Bottom:* WATERMELON MOUSSE, Recipe this page.

Watermelon Mousse

PHOTOGRAPH THIS PAGE

Preparation Time: *15 minutes*
Freezing Time: *5 hours*
Serves 6–8

1 qt (1 lt) watermelon flesh with seeds removed
1 package of unflavored gelatin
½ cup sugar
2 Tbsp lemon juice
pinch of cayenne or white pepper
1 cup heavy cream
sprig of fresh mint

Blend the watermelon in a blender or food processor until liquid. Pour it into a pan and heat gently. Add the gelatin and stir to dissolve. Remove from the heat and stir in the sugar and lemon juice. Mix well and let cool. Place the mixture in the freezer for 2–3 hours until mushy.

Add the pepper to the cream and whip until thick. Stir into the watermelon ice. Pour into molds and return to the freezer for 1½–2 hours until set. Unmold the mousse and serve garnished with fresh mint. If the mousse freezes too hard, it can be softened by placing for ½ hour in the refrigerator just prior to serving.

DIXIE

SWEETS

Sunbelt

Here, it is said, the six C's reign supreme — cattle, cotton, citrus fruit, copper, crude oil and climate. Not a bad combination for what is generally considered to be a desert. Arizona, New Mexico and Texas — the Sunbelt.

The ancient beauty of the Arizona desert is even more apparent during sunset.

SUNBELT

INTRODUCTION

Indian history in this region is ancient, with their arrival in the Southwest near the end of the Ice Age. Being originally cave dwellers, they later lived in small villages where they developed their agricultural skills. With a more community based lifestyle came the beginnings of the beautiful pottery and weaving craft work which has developed here.

As early as the 8th century some of these Indians had developed a complex community while others did not reach their zenith until the 11th and 12th centuries with irrigation, road systems, organized government and magnificent buildings some five stories high.

These Indians were called Pueblo by the Spanish to distinguish their village lifestyle from the nomadic Apache and Navajo tribes, which had come from the north.

The first Spanish foray into the area was an unsuccessful search by Coronado for the legendary Seven Cities of Gold. The timing of the arrival of Spanish colonists (namely Jesuit priests) in the southern part of the U.S. can be visualized with the knowledge that they established Santa Fe in 1610, ten years before the Pilgrim Fathers arrived at Plymouth. The area they governed at that time was so large and unknown that even they did not know its boundaries.

Their control of the area came to an end in 1822 with Mexico's independence. Arizona, New Mexico and Texas became part of the new republic.

This tie with Mexico did not last long, however, and by 1845 Texas had become a state. The rest of this area was ceded to the U.S. in 1848, New Mexico achieved statehood in 1912 and Arizona followed only 39 days later.

Although not states at the time, New Mexico and Arizona were involved in the large migration of settlers to the southwest during the mid 1800s. These people included miners, gold prospectors, trappers, railroad workers and cowboys. Although there was a steady stream willing to try their luck in this new wilderness, population remained low in some areas and Indian hostility continued well into the 1880's.

The Sunbelt has an array of terrain from mountains to flat valleys, mesas to incredible gorges (such as the magnificent Grand Canyon) and desert basins.

With many of the early settlers coming from the southeastern states, cotton was brought into the area and became an important crop. Cattle can be seen grazing on the open plains and have always been an important asset to the farmers of this area. The Santa Gertrudis cattle are a breed developed in Texas and have world-wide popularity. (Steak Benedict with Hollandaise Pepper Sauce is worthy of any table — recipe this section.)

This area was also the scene of the Range Wars of the 1880's. By the end of the Civil War, the number of cattle were too great to be supported by the available land. Sheep farmers began to move into the plains and their animals cropped the grass too short for the cattle. (Coffee-Glazed Crown Roast of Lamb with Golden Mushroom is a good example — recipe this section.)

With the building of the Coolidge and Hoover Dams, huge tracts of land were irrigated to produce some of the best fruit (particularly citrus) and vegetables in the U.S. (try the Almond Soufflé with Orange Sauce or Stuffed Peaches in this section).

It is a region of great mineral wealth, with copper mining beginning in 1854, and oil developed from 1901.

If you have not been to this part of the U.S., the recipes in this section will give you a taste of what to expect when you do get there.

The delights range from Pepper Mousse & Apples to Tongue with Almond, Gooseberry and Mint Truffles. A tasty selection which encompasses the variety of the region.

Top left: COFFEE-GLAZED CROWN ROAST OF LAMB WITH GOLDEN MUSHROOM SAUCE, Recipe page 208.
Top right: DEVILLED NUT SALAD, Recipe page 205. *Bottom*: STUFFED PEACHES, Recipe page 218.

SUNBELT

**APPETIZERS
SOUPS
SALADS
ENTREES**

Chilled Cream of Pear Soup

Preparation Time: 10 minutes
Cooking Time: 30 minutes
Chilling Time: 3–4 hours
Serves 4

1½ lbs (750 g) pears, peeled and sliced
4 cups clarified chicken stock or chicken consommé
½ cup sugar
2 Tbsp ground cardamom
1 Tbsp lime juice
½ cup sherry
pinch of cayenne
½ cup heavy cream
fresh mint

Place the pear sections in a saucepan, cover them with the chicken stock and add the sugar and cardamom. Simmer the pears for ½ hour until very soft. Puree the pears in a blender or food processor until very smooth. Stir in the lime juice and sherry. Cool then chill the soup.

Stir the cayenne into the cream and pour into a sectioned ice-cube tray. Place in the freezer.

To serve, ladle the soup into individual bowls. Float 1 or 2 frozen cream cubes on each serving and garnish with fresh mint leaves.

Note: To clarify stock, chill it overnight in the refrigerator. The fat will rise to the top and solidify. It can then be easily skimmed off and discarded.

Nut Omelet

Preparation Time: 6 minutes
Cooking Time: 5 minutes
Serves 2

2 Tbsp butter
4 eggs
2 Tbsp light cream
3 Tbsp sour cream
¼ cup chopped cashews
salt & pepper to taste
4 slices bacon, chopped and crisp fried

Melt the butter in a 6-inch (15 cm) iron skillet, liberally brushing the butter around the sides of the pan. Combine the eggs and light cream in a bowl and beat for a few seconds. Pour the mixture into the pan and cook over medium heat for 2–3 minutes. Spoon on the sour cream, cashews and seasoning; cook for 2–3 minutes longer, until the omelet is set but still very moist on the top. Fold the omelet in half and turn it onto a serving plate. Top with the crisp bacon.

Pesto Bread

PHOTOGRAPH PAGE 203

Preparation Time: 30 minutes
Rising Time: 2½ hours
Baking Time: 30 minutes
Serves 4–6

Basic Dough (*see page 88*)

Pesto:
½ cup chopped fresh basil
2 Tbsp chopped fresh parsley
3 cloves garlic
½ cup olive oil
¼ lb (125 g) cheddar cheese
½ cup pine nuts
½ cup poppy seeds

Prepare the Basic Sweet Dough recipe as directed. After the first rising, roll out the dough on a lightly floured board until it is a ½-inch (1.5 cm) thick 12-inch (30 cm) by 15-inch (38 cm) rectangle.

Combine the basil, parsley, garlic and oil in a blender and blend until smooth.

Cut the cheese into ⅓-inch (2 cm) wide fingers. Place a line of cheese fingers across the narrow edge of the dough. Then spoon a line of pesto sauce across the dough about 2-inches (5 cm) from the cheese. Repeat with another row of cheese and another line of pesto to make 4 parallel rows approximately 2-inches (5 cm) apart. Sprinkle the top liberally with pine nuts. Starting from one end, roll up the dough like a jelly roll, trying not to spread the sauce out more than is absolutely necessary.

Sprinkle the workspace with poppy seeds and roll the loaf over them to press them in. Place the loaf in a baking tin, cover it and let it rise for 1 hour. Bake at 375°F (190°C) for ½ hour until lightly golden.

Tomato Ice

Preparation Time: 10 minutes
Chilling Time: 2 hours
Serves 6–8

1 lb (500 g) tomatoes
1 tsp Worcestershire sauce
1 Tbsp Tabasco sauce
¼ cup chopped fresh basil

Blanch the tomatoes in boiling water for 30 seconds then peel. Combine all the ingredients in a food processor or blender; puree until reasonably smooth. Pour into small molds or into an ice cube tray. Freeze for 2 hours. Serve the ices between courses with crackers or tortillas and some crisp celery.

Left: PESTO BREAD, Recipe page 202. Bottom: PEPPER MOUSSE & APPLES, Recipe this page.

Pepper Mousse & Apples

PHOTOGRAPH THIS PAGE

Preparation Time: 20 minutes
Cooking Time: 10 minutes
Chilling Time: 2–3 hours
Serves 4

2 Tbsp butter
3–4 jalapeño peppers, seeded and finely minced
¼ cup shallots, minced
1 tsp sugar
¼ cup white wine
1½ cups beef consommé
1 envelope unflavored gelatin
2 Tbsp chopped fresh mint
½ cup heavy cream
2 Granny Smith or other green apples
1 Tbsp lemon juice
¼ cup cold water
paprika
fresh mint leaves

Melt the butter in a saucepan and stir in the peppers, shallots and sugar. Sauté for 10 minutes. In a separate pan, combine the wine, consommé and gelatin; heat gently to dissolve the gelatin. Pour the consommé mixture into the pan with the peppers and shallots. Add the chopped mint and set the mixture aside to cool.

Whip the cream and stir it into the cooled mixture. When well combined, pour the mousse into individual molds. Chill in the refrigerator several hours until set.

To serve, quarter the apples but do not peel. Remove the cores and slice the apples into crescents. Combine the lemon juice and water; dip the apple slices into this mixture. Shake them dry then arrange on individual serving plates in a circle. (They will look like petals.) Unmold the mousse onto each apple "flower." Sprinkle lightly with paprika and garnish with whole mint leaves.

SUNBELT

**APPETIZERS
SOUPS
SALADS
ENTREES**

Playing prairie dogs in the Sonora Desert at Tucson, Arizona.

SUNBELT Phyllo Cheese Rolls

**APPETIZERS
SOUPS
SALADS
ENTREES**

Preparation Time: 20 minutes
Baking Time: 20 minutes
Preheat Oven: 400°F (200°C)
Yield: 20

1 lb (500 g) ricotta cheese
2–3 ripe sweet pears, peeled and sliced
1 cup mango chutney
1 cup roasted peanuts
¾ cup melted butter
pinch of cayenne (optional)
10 sheets of phyllo pastry

Before handling the pastry, set out on the workspace dishes of the various fillings. Phyllo pastry is quite easy to work with, but it is paper thin and must not be allowed to dry out.

With a sharp knife or scissors, cut the 10 phyllo sheets into approximately 5-inch by 8-inch (12 cm by 20 cm) pieces. Place 1 Tbsp of ricotta cheese on each piece and add any one of the other fillings: pear, chutney, peanuts, etc. Quickly fold in the sides of the rectangle and roll up. Place the rolls on a baking sheet, seam side down. Melt the butter and stir in the cayenne. Brush the rolls liberally with melted butter and bake for 20 minutes. Serve hot.

Devilled Nut Salad

PHOTOGRAPH PAGE 201

Preparation Time: 8 minutes
Baking Time: 20 minutes
Preheat Oven: 350°F (180°C)
Serves 4

2 Tbsp butter
1 Tbsp chili powder
pinch of salt
1 cup pecan halves
1 cup blanched almonds
2 cups shredded lettuce
1 apple, cored and chopped
½ cup seedless raisins
1 Tbsp lemon juice

Melt the butter in a saucepan; stir in the chili powder and salt. Mix well. Remove from the heat and add the pecans. Stir the nuts in the seasoned butter until thoroughly coated. Spread them on a baking sheet and bake for 20 minutes. Toss the lettuce with the chopped apple, raisins and lemon juice until well mixed. To serve, combine the hot nuts and the cold salad. Toss lightly and serve at once.

Cheese with Quince & Leeks

Preparation Time: 15 minutes
Chilling Time: overnight
Serves 4

½ lb (250 g) feta cheese
1 Tbsp green peppercorns
1 Tbsp chopped pimientos
1 Tbsp chopped black olives
1 tsp cumin seeds
1 tsp caraway seeds
1 lb (500 g) quinces, peeled and halved
½ cup chopped leek
1 Tbsp olive oil
1 Tbsp orange juice
2 Tbsp honey
¼ cup white wine
½ tsp pepper

Mash the feta with the peppercorns, pimientos, olives, cumin and caraway seeds. Form into a small cake; cover and chill overnight.

Next day: Remove the cheese cake from the refrigerator and bring to room temperature. Meanwhile, place the quince halves in a saucepan; cover them with water and simmer for 30 minutes until tender. Drain. Add the leek, olive oil, orange juice, honey, wine and pepper. Mix and simmer gently for 10 minutes. To serve, pour the hot sauce over the cheese cake.

Giant Horseradish Popovers

Preparation Time: 8 minutes
Cooking Time: 50 minutes
Preheat Oven: 425°F (220°C)
Serves 8

2 Tbsp oil or melted butter
4 eggs
2 cups milk
2 cups flour
pinch of salt
2 Tbsp grated horseradish
¼ cup sesame seeds

Liberally brush 8 individual popover cups or muffin tins with the oil or butter. *Note:* If you use a muffin tin, be sure to grease the top as well. Place the popover cups on a tray in the oven to warm.

Combine the eggs, milk, flour, salt and horseradish in a blender and beat until very smooth. When the cups are hot, remove the tray from the oven. Quickly fill the cups ⅔ full with the batter and sprinkle with sesame seeds. Return to the oven and bake for 15 minutes; reduce the heat to 375°F (190°C) and bake for a further 35–40 minutes until the popovers are crisp on the outside. Serve at once.

Peanut Potato Salad

Preparation Time: 15 minutes
Chilling Time: 1 hour
Serves 4

2 lbs (1 kg) potatoes, peeled, cooked and diced
½ cup chopped garlic chives
½ cup smooth peanut butter
1 cup apple juice, heated
¼ cup sour cream
1 tsp pepper
1 cup salted peanuts
¼ cup sliced pimientos
celery stalks, chopped

Toss together the potatoes and garlic chives; cover and chill. Blend together the peanut butter, hot apple juice, sour cream and pepper. Chill this mixture.

To serve, toss the potato salad with the dressing and salted peanuts. Mound on a plate. Top with strips of pimiento and surround with crisp chopped celery.

Note: If garlic chives are unavailable, rub the salad bowl with a clove of garlic and substitute regular chives.

SUNBELT

APPETIZERS
SOUPS
SALADS
ENTREES

Ruins of an old Indian civilization (Pueblo Bonito) at Chaco Canyon NHP.

SUNBELT

MAIN COURSE

Pucheroo

Preparation Time: 30 minutes
Cooking Time: 1½ hours
Serves 8

2 lbs (1 kg) lamb, cut into chunks
1 chicken, cut into small serving pieces
½ lb (250 g) bacon, chopped
water to cover
½ lb (250 g) capocollo sausage, sliced
1 cup chopped fennel
1 lb (500 g) small whole carrots
4 stalks celery, chopped
2 lbs (1 kg) potatoes, peeled and chopped
1 lb (500 g) sweet potatoes, peeled and chopped
1 lb (500 g) baby corn (fresh or frozen)
1 lb (500 g) white chicory, chopped
1 lb (500 g) yellow squash, cut up
2 cups kidney beans, cooked, or 1 15-oz (470 g) can
½ cup shelled pistachios

Combine the lamb, chicken and bacon in a large heavy pan and fry for 10 minutes. Cover with water; bring to a boil, lower the heat and simmer covered for 1½ hours. Skim the fat from the top of the stock and add all the other ingredients. Stir then let simmer for 20 minutes until the vegetables are just tender. Remove the meat and vegetables with a slotted spoon. Serve the soup in separate bowls, together with the meat and vegetables.

Note: When preparing the vegetables, they should be cut into large chunks.

Coffee-Glazed Crown Roast of Lamb with Golden Mushroom Sauce

PHOTOGRAPH PAGE 201

Preparation Time: 15 minutes
Baking Time: 1 hour
Preheat Oven: 350°F (180°C)
Serves 8

1 crown roast of lamb

Glaze:
1½ cups strong black coffee
1 cup honey
1 Tbsp fresh or dried thyme

Sauce:
2 Tbsp butter
¼ cup shallots, minced
1 tsp chopped fresh sage or
   ½ tsp dried sage
1 tsp powdered mustard
1 Tbsp ground saffron

1 cup sherry
2 egg yolks, beaten
1 cup whole white button mushrooms
3 red oranges, peeled and sectioned

Place a double rack of lamb chops around an oven-proof bowl (8-inch or 10-inch (20 cm or 25 cm) size) turned upside down on a roasting pan. Secure the meat with string if necessary. This is your crown.

Simmer the coffee in a saucepan with the honey and thyme until well blended. Liberally brush the crown roast with the coffee glaze. Bake the roast for 1 hour, basting every 15 minutes, until the chops are cooked. They will have a dark chocolate-brown glaze and be very moist.

Twenty minutes before the roast is done, melt the butter in a saucepan; sauté the shallots for 5 minutes. Stir in the sage, mustard and saffron. Add the sherry and beaten egg yolks. Heat gently, stirring frequently, until the sauce starts to thicken. Add the mushrooms and orange sections. Stir the sauce and cook over very low heat for 3–4 minutes. Do not let it boil.

To serve, place the roast on a heated platter, decorate it with the warmed orange sections and pour the sauce around it.

Chicken Poached in Plum Sauce

PHOTOGRAPH PAGE 209

Preparation Time: 12 minutes
Cooking Time: 40 minutes
Preheat Oven: 400°F (200°C)
Serves 4

4 deboned chicken breasts
2 Tbsp grated fresh ginger root

Sauce:
1 cup pitted prune plums
¼ cup water
1 Tbsp sugar
1 tsp powdered mustard

Wash the chicken breasts and pat them dry. Carefully score the top side of each breast in a diamond pattern and rub the grated ginger into the slits. Arrange the chicken in a shallow baking dish.

Combine the plums, water, sugar and mustard in a blender or food processor; process until the plums are coarsely chopped. Pour the plum mixture into a saucepan and bring it to a boil. Pour the hot sauce over the chicken, being careful not to wash out the ginger. The sauce should barely cover the chicken. Bake uncovered for 40 minutes. Add a little extra water to the dish during cooking if necessary. Serve on a warm platter.

Top: CHICKEN POACHED IN PLUM SAUCE, Recipe page 208. Bottom: STEAK BENEDICT WITH HOLLANDAISE PEPPER SAUCE, Recipe this page.

Steak Benedict with Hollandaise Pepper Sauce

PHOTOGRAPH THIS PAGE

Preparation Time: 10 minutes
Cooking Time: 10 minutes
Broiler or Grill
Serves 4

4 small fillets of beef, ½-inch (1.5 cm) thick
1 Tbsp butter
1 sweet red pepper, seeded and sliced
2 English muffins, split
4 soft poached eggs

Sauce:
4 egg yolks
2 Tbsp red wine vinegar
pinch of cayenne
¼ lb (125 g) butter
¼ cup beef consommé

Hot Sauce (*page* 148)

Trim the steaks, wash and pat dry. Rub the butter onto both sides of the steaks. Knead the meat with your fingers for a few minutes to soften it. Put the steaks on a rack and broil them for 3–4 minutes on one side. Turn them over, cover them with pepper slices and broil for an additional 3–4 minutes.

Sauce:
Blend the egg yolks, vinegar and cayenne until very smooth then pour the mixture into a saucepan or double boiler. Heat over low heat, stirring constantly. When the eggs just start to thicken, beat in the butter and consommé. Continue heating and stirring until the sauce has thickened.

Poach the eggs; toast and butter the muffins.

To serve, place a steak on each half of a buttered muffin. Top each steak with a poached egg. Garnish with the red pepper slices, and pour the sauce over all. Serve with Hot Sauce.

SUNBELT

MAIN COURSE

WALNUT YEAST WAFFLES, Recipe this page.

Orange Mint Butter

1 *cup butter*
½ *cup light brown sugar*
1 *Tbsp grated orange rind*
1 *Tbsp finely chopped fresh mint*

Combine all the ingredients and blend well. Shape into a square or put into a butter mold; chill overnight.

Mint Pesto with Saffron Pasta

Preparation Time: 1 hour
Cooking Time: 12 minutes
Serves 2

Pasta:
¾ *cup semolina*
¾ *cup all-purpose flour*
1 *Tbsp olive oil*
1 *tsp pepper*
1 *Tbsp ground saffron*
1 *egg*
cold water
4 *qts (4 lt) briskly boiling water*

Sauce:
¾ *cup olive oil*
2 *Tbsp chopped fresh basil leaves*
2 *cloves garlic, minced*
1 *Tbsp chopped fresh parsley*
½ *cup chopped fresh mint*
½ *cup grated Parmesan cheese*
⅓ *cup pine nuts*
⅓ *cup finely chopped mushrooms*

Pasta:

In a bowl or food processor combine all the pasta ingredients, except the water, until well blended. Gradually add 2–3 Tbsp cold water to form a stiff dough. Turn the dough out onto a floured board and knead well for 10 minutes until it is smooth and light. Let the dough rest for 10 minutes. Knead it again for 2 minutes. Either by hand or with a pasta machine, gradually roll out the dough until it is ¹⁄₁₆-inch (0.15 cm) thick. Leave the rolled dough uncovered on the counter for 15–20 minutes to dry. Then, again by hand or by machine, cut the dough into narrow strips and drop them into a large pot of boiling salted water. Simmer for 10–20 minutes until "al dente".

Sauce:

In a food processor, combine all the ingredients except the pine nuts and mushrooms. Blend until very smooth.

To serve, drain the pasta and stir in a spoonful of butter or olive oil to prevent it from sticking. Arrange pasta on a plate, pour the pesto sauce over it and sprinkle with pine nuts and mushrooms.

SUNBELT Walnut Yeast Waffles

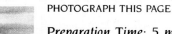

PHOTOGRAPH THIS PAGE

Preparation Time: 5 minutes
Standing Time: overnight
Cooking Time: 20 minutes
Serves 4

2 *eggs*
1½ *cups milk*
1 *Tbsp sugar*
1 *tsp mace*
1 *package active dry yeast*
¼ *cup shortening or oil*
2 *cups flour*
¼ *cup walnut pieces*

Combine all the ingredients in a food processor; using the metal blade, mix until the batter is smooth and the nuts are finely chopped. Refrigerate the batter overnight.

Remove the batter from the refrigerator ½ hour before cooking. Briefly mix again then bake the waffles in a lightly buttered waffle iron until golden. Serve hot with Orange Mint Butter and bacon slices.

Nature has carved its own sculpture and the smoothness of Slickrock Canyon is clearly shown here near Page, Arizona.

In a bowl or food processor, combine the first 7 ingredients. Chop or process thoroughly. Heat the chicken consommé in a saucepan until it boils. Form the pork mixture into small balls and drop, a few at a time, into the consommé. Let simmer for 10 minutes. Remove the pork balls and keep them warm. Reserve 1 cup of the broth for the sauce.

Note: If the pork balls are not to be cooked right away, they may be lightly rolled in flour and kept in the refrigerator.

Sauce:
Put the cup of reserved broth into a saucepan. Dissolve the cornstarch in the wine and stir it into the broth along with the mushrooms. Heat gently, stirring occasionally, until the sauce begins to thicken. Serve the sauce and meat balls with a watercress garnish. For special occasions, roll each pork ball in a nasturtium leaf and secure with a toothpick.

Tongue with Almond Gooseberry Sauce
PHOTOGRAPH PAGE 213

Preparation Time: 15 minutes
Cooking Time: 3 hours
Serves 6–8

5–6 lbs (2½–3 kg) fresh beef tongue
1 onion, chopped
2 Tbsp chopped fresh parsley or
    1 Tbsp dried parsley
1 Tbsp dried oregano
1 Tbsp whole peppercorns
2 bay leaves
1 tsp whole cloves
salt to taste

Sauce:
1 cup fresh or frozen gooseberries
½ cup tongue broth
1 Tbsp sugar
1 Tbsp lemon juice
¼ cup slivered almonds
1 tsp pepper
1 tsp cinnamon

Place the tongue in a heavy pan, add the onion, herbs and spices and cover with cold water. Bring to a boil, lower the heat and simmer covered for 2½–3 hours. Remove the tongue, rinse, peel and slice. Set the tongue aside to keep warm. Skim the broth.

Combine all the sauce ingredients in a saucepan. Stir gently to mix then let simmer for 5–6 minutes. Do not mash or puree the sauce. Serve hot with the sliced tongue.

The beautiful Claret Cup Hedgehog in the desert.

SUNBELT Pork & Green Peppercorn Balls
PHOTOGRAPH PAGE 213

MAIN COURSE

Preparation Time: 15 minutes
Cooking Time: 20 minutes
Serves 4

¼ lb (125 g) lean ground pork
1 clove garlic
small bunch of chives
¼ cup green peppercorns
½ tsp ground sage
1 Tbsp lemon juice
1 egg
2 cups chicken consommé

Sauce:
1 cup reserved broth
1 Tbsp cornstarch
¼ cup port wine
¼ cup chopped mushrooms
Bunch of watercress or nasturtium leaves

Top: TONGUE WITH ALMOND GOOSEBERRY SAUCE, Recipe page 212.
Bottom: PORK & GREEN PEPPERCORN BALLS, Recipe page 212.

Buff cliffs at South Yaki Trail overlook, frame this view from the Grand Canyon's South Rim.

Top: PLUM SCROLL, Recipe page 217. *Bottom*: CANNOLI, Recipe this page.

SUNBELT SWEETS

Cannoli

PHOTOGRAPH THIS PAGE

Preparation Time: 30 minutes
Cooking Time: 5 minutes
Preheat broiler: 400°F (200°C)
Serves 6

Dough:

4 cups flour
¼ cup light brown sugar
1 Tbsp cinnamon
½ cup crushed pecans
2 eggs
1 cup sherry
butter for frying

Filling:

1 lb (500 g) fresh peaches, peeled
1½ cups light brown sugar
1 lb (500 g) ricotta cheese

Dough:

Combine the flour, sugar, cinnamon and pecans in a mixing bowl or food processor. Add the eggs and sherry. Mix to a fairly stiff dough. Adjust with a Tbsp of flour or milk if necessary. Turn onto a floured board and roll the dough into a sausage shape about 2 inches (5 cm) thick. Cut into 2-inch (5 cm) sections and roll each piece out into rounds, about 6 inches (15 cm) across. Put 1 Tbsp butter in a small skillet and fry each cannoli for 3–4 minutes on one side then 1–2 minutes on the other. Set them aside.

Filling:

Cut the peaches into sections and mix them with the sugar. Place a cannoli on a baking dish, cover with sweetened peaches and top with 1 Tbsp cheese. Roll up the cannoli and put it to one side of the dish. Continue until all the cannoli are filled. Place under a broiler for 10 minutes until crisp on top.

Plum Scroll

PHOTOGRAPH PAGE 216

Preparation Time: 30 minutes
Rising Time: 2½ hours
Baking Time: 25 minutes
Yield: 12 sections

Dough:
½ cup hot milk
¼ cup sugar
½ tsp salt
¼ cup shortening
1 tsp sugar
⅓ cup warm water
1 package active dry yeast
pinch of ground ginger
1 egg, beaten
2½ cups flour

Filling:
3 Tbsp butter
1 tsp cinnamon
½ tsp pepper
¼ cup sugar
¼ cup chopped filberts

Topping:
12 large plums, halved and pitted
¼ cup brown sugar
¼ cup chopped filberts
1 Tbsp firm butter

Dough:
Combine the hot milk, ¼ cup sugar, salt and shortening in a mixing bowl. In a small bowl or mug, mix the 1 tsp sugar, warm water, yeast and ginger together; let stand for 10 minutes until frothy. Carefully beat the egg and 1 cup of the flour into the milk mixture. Stir in the yeast mixture. Gradually stir in the rest of the flour to make a smooth, light dough. Turn it onto a floured board and knead well for 10 minutes until the dough is very smooth and satiny. Roll the dough into a ball; place it in a clean bowl and cover with a damp cloth. Let the dough rise in a warm place for about 1½ hours until doubled in bulk.

Gently push down the dough and knead for 2 minutes. Roll it out on a lightly floured board to a ½-inch (1.5 cm) thick rectangle.

Filling:
Melt the butter in a saucepan and stir in the cinnamon, pepper, sugar and ¼ cup filberts. Spread this mixture evenly over the dough, leaving about 1-inch (2.5 cm) uncovered at the bottom edge. Carefully roll the dough from the top down like a jelly roll; transfer it to a baking sheet. With a pair of kitchen scissors, cut almost through the roll to make 12 sections. Twist and lay each slice down alternately to the left and to the right to form a scroll pattern.

Topping:
Lay a plum half in the center of each scroll. Mix the brown sugar, filberts and butter together until crumbly; sprinkle this mixture over the scroll. Set the scroll aside to rise for 1 hour. Bake at 400°F (200°C) for 25 minutes.

Tart Apple Tarts

Preparation Time: 15 minutes
Baking Time: 20 minutes
Preheat Oven: 425°F (230°C)
Serves 8

8 puff pastry tart shells (see page 230)
6 Granny Smith apples or
*   similar tart green apples*
¼ cup water
¼ cup heavy cream
2 Tbsp lemon juice
2 Tbsp sugar
icing sugar
cinnamon

Peel, core and chop 2 of the apples. Place them in a saucepan with the water and simmer for 8–10 minutes until tender. Remove from the heat and blend in the cream, lemon juice and sugar. Beat this mixture until creamy. Core and slice but do not peel the remaining 4 apples.

Place 1 Tbsp of apple cream in each tart. Arrange 4 or 5 slices of apple on top and add a second spoonful of apple cream over the slices. Bake the tarts for 15–20 minutes until the pastry is golden. Cool then dust lightly with icing sugar and cinnamon. Serve slighly warm.

Mint Truffles

Preparation Time: 15 minutes
Cooking Time: 10 minutes
Chilling Time: 2 hours
Yield: 30

⅔ cup heavy cream
10 oz (315 g) semi-sweet chocolate
6 Tbsp crème de menthe liqueur
grated chocolate or grated coconut

In a heavy saucepan, scald the cream and add the chocolate. Keep the pan over moderate-low heat, stirring the mixture occasionally, until the chocolate has melted. Remove from the heat and stir in the liqueur. Mix well then cool. Chill until the mixture is firm.

Dry your hands thoroughly. With an ice cream scoop, take out small portions of the chocolate cream and form it into 1-inch (2.5 cm) balls. Roll the balls in the grated chocolate or coconut (or both) to coat; store in the refrigerator or freezer.

SUNBELT SWEETS

SUNBELT

SWEETS

Fig Custard Cups

Preparation Time: 5 minutes
Cooking Time: 10 minutes
Serves 4

2 cups milk
1 tsp vanilla
4 egg yolks
¼ cup sugar
½ cup heavy cream
8 fresh figs
4 tsp kirsch

Simmer the milk gently in a saucepan and stir in the vanilla. Beat the egg yolks and sugar together until smooth; add a little of the milk to the yolk mixture. Stir and add the mixture to the pan. Heat gently, stirring constantly, until the custard thickens. Stir in the heavy cream. Cut open the figs and arrange 2 in each of four individual serving dishes. Sprinkle the figs with Kirsch and pour the custard over the fruit.

Stuffed Peaches
PHOTOGRAPH PAGE 201

Preparation Time: 10 minutes
Cooking Time: 30 minutes
Preheat Oven: 325°F (160°C)
Serves 6

3 large peaches
4 egg whites
½ cup sugar
½ tsp almond extract
6 Tbsp kirsch
¼ cup slivered almonds

Drop the peaches into boiling water for a few seconds. Lift out, drain and rub off the loose skins. Cut the peaches in half and remove the stones. Set each peach half in a serving dish or glass. Beat the egg whites until soft peaks form.

Add the sugar and almond extract to the whites and beat again until stiff. Put 1 Tbsp Kirsch in the center of each peach half. Spoon on the egg white mixture and decorate with slivered almonds. Bake for 30 minutes until the meringue is crisp and brown.

Orange Cups

Preparation Time: 30 minutes
Chilling Time: 2–3 hours
Serves 8

8 large oranges
2 envelopes unflavored gelatin
½ cup cold water
1½ cups sugar
3 Tbsp cognac
1½ cups heavy cream
1 Tbsp light brown sugar
1 Tbsp grated orange rind

Cut the tops off the oranges and scoop out the pulp using a grapefruit knife and spoon. Flute the edges of the orange shells and place them side by side in a shallow dish. Chop or process the orange pulp. Press it through a strainer to remove all the pith and skin. This should yield 3 cups of juice; if it does not, make up the quantity with additional freshly squeezed orange juice.

Mix the gelatin and cold water; gently heat it in a heavy saucepan or in the top of a double boiler. When the gelatin has dissolved, stir in the orange juice, sugar, cognac and 1 cup of the cream. Pour the well-combined mixture into the orange cups. Chill in the refrigerator for 2–3 hours.

To serve, whip the remaining cream. Garnish each cup with a dollop of whipped cream and a sprinkle of brown sugar and orange rind.

The influence of Christianity is very nicely shown in this robust
St. Augustine Cathedral Mission Church, downtown in Tucson, Arizona.

ALMOND SOUFFLÉ WITH ORANGE SAUCE, Recipe this page.

Almond Soufflé with Orange Sauce

PHOTOGRAPH THIS PAGE

Preparation Time: 30 minutes
Cooking Time: 40 minutes
Preheat Oven: 400°F (200°C)
Serves 6

Soufflé:

1 cup milk
½ cup sugar
1 cup ground almonds
5 egg yolks
1 Tbsp butter, melted
3 Tbsp flour
5 egg whites
pinch of salt
pinch of cream of tartar
2 Tbsp flaked almonds

Sauce:

2 Tbsp butter
2 Tbsp grated orange rind
½ cup orange juice
1 tsp cornstarch
¼ cup brandy

Soufflé:

In a saucepan, heat the milk. When warm, stir in the sugar and almonds. Simmer very gently for 15 minutes; do not allow to boil. Remove from the heat, cool slightly and beat in the egg yolks, butter and flour. Beat well by hand or in a blender until the mixture is very smooth. In a separate bowl, beat the egg whites with the salt and cream of tartar until they form stiff peaks. Spoon about ¼ of the egg whites into the custard and stir well. Fold in the rest of the egg whites. Butter 6 small soufflé cups or glass molds and spoon the soufflé mixture into them. Sprinkle with flaked almonds and bake for 15 minutes until golden on top.

Note: The unbaked soufflé mixture may be kept at room temperature for up to 1 hour before baking or may be frozen for later use. In the latter case, thaw the soufflé for 1 hour before baking.

Sauce:

In a saucepan, combine the butter, orange rind, orange juice and cornstarch. Mix well. Simmer, stirring constantly, until the sauce begins to thicken. Remove from the heat and stir in the brandy. Spoon the sauce over the hot soufflés and serve at once.

SUNBELT

SWEETS

Florida

Step four centuries back in time and the big attraction with Florida was drink rather than food, though to be fair it was a rather special kind of drink guaranteed to take years off the consumer.

Alligator at Mississippienis Wakulls springs in Florida.

FLORIDA

INTRODUCTION

A few hundred years later and the closest thing we have to the mystical, mythical fountain fluid is probably bottled mineral water. Yet today Florida has one of the highest retiree populations of any state,

Florida may not have the Fountain of Youth, but it does have an energizing climate with an average of 220 sunny days year-round, pleasantly cooled by breezes from both the Atlantic and the Gulf of Mexico. Add to this a reasonable 53 inches (108 cm) of annual rainfall and you have the ideal elixir for a fun, if not a young, lifestyle.

Colonists brought to the area by de Leon in 1521 would probably not have shared this comfortable view of modern Florida as they had a hard time making a go of things.

With simple wisdom the Indians regarded the newcomers as intruders and sent them packing as often and as uncomfortably as possible. These poor souls may well have created a dish "On the Rocks" (recipe this section).

Florida is, and always was, the kind of place to entice interest with temptations of one sort or another. Narvaez set forth in search of the rich delights of Florida as did De Soto, whose name was somewhat more widely respected in those days of the "discovery club", than it was to be centuries later as a make of automobile. Unhappily, the fabled gold under every footfall proved equally elusive. A better discovery is the "Golden Cheese Puffs" (recipe this section).

Frenchmen were the first settlers in the region, building a colony on the St. Johns River. The Spanish were not too pleased about this, however, and a year later (1565) founded St. Augustine. In what now seems to have been a fit of petulance, the Spanish proceeded to kill most of the French they found in the area.

Florida remained in Spanish hands for another 200 years.

In the early 1800s, American settlers were growing tired of Spanish control of the area and in 1814 General Andrew Jackson captured Pensacola. This victory, supported by a lot more harassment, resulted in Spain happily selling Florida to the United States for a mere $5 million, handing over control in 1821.

Florida became a state in 1845, but, being a slave state, became bitterly embroiled in the Civil War.

The need for slave labor prompted Florida to be the third state to join the Confederacy. However, because of its vast coastline, it wasn't long before Union forces captured most of the coastal towns however, inland fighting was fierce and Tallahassee was the only Confederate state capital not captured by federal troops. Florida was not re-admitted to the Union until 1868.

By the 1880's, large deposits of phosphate were found when swamplands were drained to increase farming potential. Citrus farmers planted great groves of trees that would eventually serve the markets of America and the world.

With such a magnificent climate and rich, fat lands on which to farm, it is no great surprise that Florida manages to produce some of the most delicious fruit and vegetables in the world (Peppered Strawberries will give you some idea — recipe this section).

If this isn't enough, Florida also has more than 1200 miles (1920 km) of coastline to provide some 600 types of fish including grouper, pompano, sea trout, shrimps, Florida lobsters, oysters, crayfish, scallops and conchs (savor Raw Conch Salad or Shrimp Turnovers — recipe this section). Florida's vast inland waters, not to be outdone, provide bass, trout, bream, mullet and catfish to name but a few.

With or without the Fountain of Youth, life in Florida is enviable. If you can't be one of the five million visitors who go there each year, use this section to at least get a taste of it, if not for it. Try delights like Egg Lime Soup, Cream-filled Seafood Puffs or Avocado Ice Cream — all easy to prepare. You can even 'resort' to Oysters in Cumin Sauce or Orange Scampi. Whichever recipe you try in this section, you will be guaranteed a taste of sunshine and the good life.

Top: MANGO STUFFED CHICKEN IN PUFF PASTRY, Recipe page 230.
Bottom: ORANGE SCAMPI, Recipe page 227.

FLORIDA

**APPETIZERS
SOUPS
SALADS
ENTREES**

Callaloo Soup

Preparation Time: 20 minutes
Cooking Time: 1 hour
Serves 4

¼ lb (125 g) pork roast, in 1-inch (2.5 cm) chunks
2 Tbsp peanut oil
1 sweet onion, chopped
1 clove garlic, minced
1 Tbsp fresh thyme
4 cups fish stock
½ lb (250 g) callaloo
½ lb (250 g) okra
½ lb (250 g) shrimp meat
½ cup coconut milk
½ cup heavy cream, whipped
hot sauce (page 148)

In a large pot or heavy pan, heat the oil and fry the pork, onion and garlic for 10 minutes. Add the thyme and the stock; bring to a boil. Chop the callaloo leaves and stir them in. Simmer for ½ hour. Cut the okra into chunks and add it along with the shrimp. Simmer for 10 minutes then stir in the coconut milk. Heat but do not boil. Pour the soup into serving dishes. Top with dollops of whipped cream and liberal dashes of hot sauce.

Note: Callaloo—also called taro or poi—is a large-leaved vegetable best known for its rich, starchy tubers which contribute to the diet of many south sea islanders. Occasionally callaloo can be found in North American supermarkets, and the plants are often grown as ornamentals in the warmer regions of North America.

Creole Shrimp Paté

Preparation Time: 10 minutes
Cooking Time: 20 minutes
Chilling Time: 2 hours
Serves 4

¼ lb (125 g) butter
3 Tbsp lime juice
1 tsp dry thyme
1 tsp powdered sassafras
1 jalapeño pepper, seeded and chopped
½ lb (250 g) shrimp meat, coarsely chopped
1 tsp sugar

Melt the butter in a saucepan and stir in the lime juice, thyme and sassafras. Stir in the jalapeño pepper and simmer for 5 minutes. Add the shrimp meat and sugar. Simmer and stir for 10 minutes. Butter a paté mold and fill with the mixture. Cool, then chill. To serve, unmold and arrange on a plate; serve with toast and raw vegetable slices.

Egg Lime Soup

Preparation Time: 20 minutes
Cooking Time: 30 minutes
Serves 4

2 Tbsp butter
1 cup chopped sweet onion
½ cup chopped celery
1 cup grated carrot
6 cups chicken stock
salt and pepper to taste
1 Tbsp chopped fresh parsley or
    1½ tsp dried parsley
1 Tbsp chopped fresh dill or
    1½ tsp dried dill
3 egg yolks
1 Tbsp cornstarch
1 cup milk
¼ cup lime juice

In a large pot, or heavy pan, melt the butter and add the onion and celery. Sauté for 5 minutes. Add the carrot, stock, seasonings and herbs. Bring to a boil, lower the heat and simmer for 20 minutes.

In a blender, combine the egg yolks, cornstarch, milk and lime juice; blend until very smooth. Add 1 cup of the hot soup stock to the egg sauce and combine thoroughly. Then pour the egg mixture into the pot, stir the soup and reheat but do not boil.

Nasturtium Leaf Rolls

PHOTOGRAPH PAGE 225

Preparation Time: 10 minutes
Chilling Time: overnight
Serves 4

½ lb (250 g) cream cheese
small bunch of chives
sprig of fresh mint
sprig of fresh basil
1 tsp caraway seeds
1 Tbsp grated orange peel
1 tsp sugar
8 large nasturtium leaves

Cream the cheese. Chop the herbs and beat together with the caraway seeds, orange peel and sugar. Combine well with the cheese. If you are using a processor, place the herbs in the machine and chop for a few seconds, then add the caraway seeds, peel and sugar. Blend in the cheese last. Place the mixture in a bowl and refrigerate overnight.

Wash the nasturtium leaves. Divide the cheese mixture into 8 "fingers" and roll a leaf around each; secure with toothpicks. Garnish with nasturtium flowers.

Left: NASTURTIUM LEAF ROLLS, Recipe page 224. Right: SERENATE, Recipe this page.

Serenate

PHOTOGRAPH THIS PAGE

Preparation Time: 20 minutes
Cooking Time: 20 minutes
Chilling Time: 1 hour
Serves 4

Salad:

4 cups water
1 bay leaf
pinch each of pepper, salt, dried thyme and dried parsley
1 lb (500 g) cod or whitefish
¼ cup chopped fresh parsley
2 sweet onions, chopped
3 tomatoes, chopped
small bunch of watercress

Dressing:

½ cup olive oil
1 clove garlic
¼ cup lime juice
fresh pepper to taste

In a large heavy pan, add the seasonings to the water and bring to a boil; add the fish, reduce the heat and simmer for 15 minutes until the fish flakes easily. Remove it from the stock and cool. (Reserve the stock for other recipes.)

In a salad bowl, combine the parsley, onions, tomatoes and watercress. Break the fish into chunks, discard any bones and add the fish to the salad.

In a blender, blend the olive oil, garlic and lime juice until smooth. Pour over the salad and toss gently. Chill for at least 1 hour. Grind fresh pepper over the top and serve.

Raw Conch Salad

Preparation Time: 10 minutes
Marinating Time: 1 hour
Serves 6

1 lb (500 g) conch meat
1 cup chopped sweet onion
2 tsp lime juice
2 cups chopped grapefruit sections
salt, pepper and Hot Sauce (page 148) to taste

Mince the conch. Combine it with the other ingredients, tossing to mix well. Marinate in the refrigerator for at least 1 hour before serving.

Note: The conch is a large marine snail found only in tropical waters and therefore comes ready-cooked.

FLORIDA

APPETIZERS
SOUPS
SALADS
ENTREES

FLORIDA

**APPETIZERS
SOUPS
SALADS
ENTREES**

Calabaza Squash

Preparation Time: 30 minutes
Cooking Time: 2 hours
Preheat Oven: 325°F (160°C)
Serves 6–8

1 Calabaza squash, 8–10 lbs (4-5 kg)
½ cup butter
1 cup light brown sugar
2 Tbsp olive oil
2 cloves garlic, minced
2 Tbsp ground pork
1 large sweet onion, coarsely chopped
1 green pepper, chopped
4 cups chicken stock
3 tomatoes, chopped
1 lb (500 g) sweet potato, peeled and chopped
2 lbs (1 kg) taro root, peeled and chopped
1 lb (500 g) peaches, chopped
1 lb (500 g) mangoes, chopped
1 Tbsp dried oregano
salt and pepper to taste

Cut the top off the squash and remove the seeds as you would with a pumpkin. Liberally rub the inside with butter and brown sugar. Replace the top and bake for 1 hour.

Meanwhile, in a large stew pan, heat the olive oil and sauté the garlic for 5 minutes; stir in the pork meat and brown for a further 5 minutes. Add the onion and green pepper to the pan. Pour in the stock and bring to a boil. Add the tomatoes, sweet potato and taro. Return the contents of the pan to a boil then remove from the heat. Stir in the peaches and mangoes along with the oregano and seasonings. Combine well and ladle the mixture into the squash. Return the squash to the oven and bake for a second hour. To serve, ladle the stew out of the squash into bowls.

Grapefruit Timbales with Avocado Mustard

Preparation Time: 25 minutes
Cooking Time: 65 minutes
Preheat Oven: 400°F (200°C)
Cooling Time: 2 hours
Serves 4

1 cup chopped tomatoes
2 Tbsp olive oil
½ cup chopped sweet onion
¼ cup white wine
1 tsp sugar
dash of Tabasco sauce
2 Tbsp chopped fresh basil or
   1 Tbsp dry basil

2 eggs, beaten
½ cup heavy cream
4 grapefruit sections

Sauce:
1 ripe avocado
1 tsp lime juice
1 Tbsp powdered mustard
¼ cup heavy cream

Skin and chop the tomatoes. Heat the oil in a saucepan and cook the tomatoes and onion for 5 minutes until soft. Stir in the wine and sugar; simmer for 15 minutes. Remove the tomato/onion mixture from the heat and puree it in a blender or food processor until very smooth. Add the Tabasco sauce, basil, eggs and cream. Blend again until smooth.

Butter four timbale molds or ovenproof glass cups and arrange a grapefruit section in the bottom of each one. Fill with the pureed mixture to within ½-inch (1.5 cm) of the top. Stand the molds in 1-inch (2.5 cm) of hot water in a baking pan and bake for 45 minutes. Cool about 2 hours. Unmold the timbales.

Note: To unmold a timbale, run the tip of a paring knife around the inside edge of the mold. Place the mold upside down on a serving dish, hold both the mold and dish firmly together and shake once. The timbale should slip out easily.

Sauce:
In a small bowl, mash the avocado until smooth. Beat in the lime juice and mustard. Add the cream, stir and pour over the timbales.

Oysters in Cumin Sauce

Preparation Time: 5 minutes
Cooking Time: 7–8 minutes
Serves 2

½ lb (250 g) fresh or frozen oysters
1 tsp pepper
1 tsp chopped fresh lovage or
   ½ tsp dried lovage
1 Tbsp chopped fresh parsley or
   1½ tsp dried parsley
1 tsp chopped mint or
   ½ tsp dried mint
1 tsp cumin
1 Tbsp honey
1 Tbsp cider vinegar

Combine all the ingredients, including the oyster liquid, in a heavy saucepan. Stir gently while bringing to a boil. Lower the heat and simmer for 2–3 minutes. This makes a smooth, spicy hors d'oeuvre.

Orange Scampi

PHOTOGRAPH PAGE 223

Preparation Time: 10 minutes
Cooking Time: 15 minutes
Serves 2

4 Tbsp butter
1 clove garlic, minced
1 tsp pepper
12 shrimps, peeled and deveined
½ cup fresh orange juice
1 Tbsp lemon juice
1 tsp cornstarch
1 Tbsp chives, chopped

In a large skillet, melt the butter and sauté the garlic until brown. Add the pepper and shrimp. Toss gently and sauté for 5 minutes over medium heat. Remove the shrimp and set aside. Pour off the butter.

Add the lemon juice and orange juice to the skillet; stir in the cornstarch until dissolved. Heat, stirring constantly, until the sauce thickens. Add the shrimp and chives. Heat, stirring gently, for 10 minutes. Serve immediately.

Shrimp Turnovers

Preparation Time: 20 minutes
Cooking Time: 3 minutes
Preheat Deep Fryer: 375°F (190°C)
Serves 4

2 Tbsp butter
2 Tbsp chopped onion
2 Tbsp chopped leek
2 cloves garlic, minced
salt, pepper and Hot Sauce (page 148) to taste
2 Tbsp chopped pecans
½ lb (250 g) shrimp meat
puff pastry (page 230)
1 cup sour cream
1 egg, beaten

Melt the butter and sauté the onion, leek and garlic until soft. Stir in the seasonings, pecans and shrimp meat. Remove the mixture from the heat.

Cut the pastry into 3-inch (8 cm) rounds and place 1 Tbsp of the shrimp mixture on each round. Dot with a teaspoon of sour cream, brush the edge of the pastry with egg and fold it over. Crimp the edges with a fork and drop the turnovers into the deep fryer. Fry for 3 minutes until golden. Drain on a paper towel and serve hot.

Golden Cheese Puffs

Preparation Time: 10 minutes
Cooking Time: 4 minutes
Preheat Deep Fryer: 400°F (200°C)
Serves 6–8

1 lb (500 g) cheddar cheese
6 eggs
2 tsp chili powder
light oil for frying

Grate the cheese and melt it very gently in a heavy saucepan over low heat or in a double boiler over hot water. Separate the eggs; beat the whites until stiff peaks form; and set aside. Beat the yolks until smooth then stir them into the cheese. Mix well and remove from the heat. Stir in the chili powder. Fold in the egg whites and combine well to make a batter.

Heat 1-inch (2.5 cm) of light oil in a skillet or use a deep fryer. Drop the batter by the spoonful into the hot oil and fry for 3–4 minutes until golden. Drain the puffs on a paper towel and serve hot.

Cream-Filled Seafood Puffs

Preparation Time: 20 minutes
Baking Time: 45 minutes
Preheat Oven: 400°F (200°C)
Yield: 24

¾ cup water
6 Tbsp butter
1 cup flour
2 cups cooked, flaked fish
4 eggs
1 cup heavy cream
pinch of cayenne

In a saucepan, heat the water and butter to boiling point. When the butter is melted, blend in the flour. Beat the batter to a paste and remove it from the heat as soon as it forms a ball. Blend in the flaked fish. Add the eggs, one at a time, beating well, until a thick batter is formed. Use two teaspoons to form 1-inch (2.5 cm) balls. Place on a baking sheet and bake for 15 minutes then lower the heat to 350°F (180°C) for a further 15–20 minutes, until the puffs are golden brown. Cool slightly.

Whip the cream and cayenne together until fairly stiff. Spoon the cream into a kitchen syringe and inject each puff with approximately 1 tsp of the spicy cream.

FLORIDA

APPETIZERS
SOUPS
SALADS
ENTREES

Sloppy Joe's Bar, Hemingway's favorite, in Key West, Florida.

FLORIDA

MAIN COURSE

Feijoada

Preparation Time: 30 minutes
Soaking Time: overnight
Cooking Time: 2–3 hours
Serves 8–10

3 cups black beans
1 lb (500 g) dried beef
½ lb (250 g) bacon
5 cloves garlic, chopped
4 lbs (2 kg) pork roast
1 lb (500 g) smoked pork sausage
3 cups chopped onion
¼ cup chopped fresh parsley
2 chili peppers, chopped
1 leek, chopped
salt and pepper to taste

Soak the dried beans and beef overnight in separate bowls of water. Discard the water. Chop the beef into 1-inch (2.5 cm) pieces, mix with the beans and cover with cold water in a very large pot. Bring to a boil, lower the heat and simmer for at least 1 hour until tender.

Slice the bacon into 1-inch (2.5 cm) pieces and fry in a large skillet. Add the garlic and fry until soft. Cut the pork roast into 2-inch (5 cm) cubes and fry a few at a time with the bacon and garlic until browned on all sides. Put pork chunks in the pot with the beef and beans. When browned, fry the sausage in the same way. Combine the bacon, sausage and remaining ingredients with the pork, beef and beans in the pot. Stir and simmer for 1 hour. Adjust for seasoning and serve with rice.

Grapefruit Game Hen

Preparation Time: 15 minutes
Cooking Time: 45 minutes
Serves 4

1 large red grapefruit, peeled and seeded
1 Tbsp honey
½ cup white wine
1 tsp pepper
1 tsp fresh or dried thyme
2 Tbsp vegetable oil
1 Tbsp grated fresh ginger root
2 large game hens

In a blender, combine all the ingredients except the game hens and puree to a smooth sauce. Carefully cut the game hens in half down the middle; rinse them and place flat side down in a large heavy pan. Cover with sauce, boil, lower the heat and simmer for 20 minutes. Remove and arrange birds in baking dish. Pour over the hot sauce and place the dish under the broiler for 15–20 minutes until the birds are golden and the sauce bubbles. Serve at once.

Mango-Stuffed Chicken in Puff Pastry

PHOTOGRAPH PAGE 223

Preparation Time: 1 hour
Cooking Time: 1 hour
Serves 4

Puff Pastry:
2 cups flour
pinch of salt
cold water
1 cup cold butter

Filling:
4 large chicken breasts, boned
2 Tbsp chilled butter
¼ cup chopped walnuts
small bunch of chives, chopped
4 sprigs of French tarragon, chopped
1 Tbsp brandy
2 Tbsp heavy cream
pepper to taste
1 firm mango
1 Tbsp lemon juice

Puff Pastry:
In a bowl or food processor, mix the flour, salt and cold water to make a firm dough. Form the dough into a ball and refrigerate it for 10 minutes. Roll out the dough on a floured board until it is a ½-inch (1 cm) thick rectangle. Place ½-inch (1 cm) thick slices of cold butter in the center of the rectangle and fold over the top, bottom and both sides so that the butter is completely covered. Again roll the dough out ½-inch (1 cm) thick and fold into thirds. Repeat twice more. Chill the dough in the refrigerator for ½ hour.

When the dough is chilled and rested, roll out as before and fold it four more times. Return the dough to the refrigerator for another 10 minutes.

Filling:
Wash the chicken fillets and pat them dry. Cover with wax paper and flatten slightly with a mallet or knife handle. Set the chicken aside.

In a small saucepan, melt the butter and sauté the walnuts and chives for 5 minutes. Remove the pan from the heat and stir in the tarragon, brandy, cream and pepper.

Peel and quarter the mango. Place the mango sections in a shallow buttered baking sheet or casserole dish. Liberally coat each section with the walnut/herb stuffing. Carefully lay a chicken fillet over each mango section and mold it into a mound. Brush with lemon juice. Roll out the chilled pastry ⅛-inch (2.5 mm) thick and cut to cover each chicken fillet as neatly as possible. Trim off any excess pastry.
Bake the chicken at 350°F (180°C) for 1 hour.

CALAMARI WITH LIME PASTA, Recipe this page.

Calamari with Lime Pasta

PHOTOGRAPH THIS PAGE

Preparation Time: 30 minutes
Cooking Time: 30 minutes
Serves 4

Pasta:

1½ cups all purpose flour
2 Tbsp grated lime rind
¼ cup lime juice
2 eggs
1 hot red pepper, seeded and minced
1 Tbsp olive oil

Sauce:

¼ cup sherry
1 cup fish stock
1 lb (500 g) calamari (squid), cleaned and cut into rings
3 Tbsp butter
small bunch of chives, chopped
½ lb (250 g) okra, chopped
2 Tbsp grated lime rind
2 Tbsp flour
small bunch of fresh chervil

Pasta:
In a bowl or food processor, combine the semolina, flour, lime rind and juice, eggs and red pepper. Add olive oil as required to make a firm dough. Knead well for 10 minutes. Cover and let the dough rest for 30 minutes. Roll out or feed through a pasta machine until it is very thin — about ¹⁄₁₆-inch (1.5 mm) thick. Cut the dough into ⅛-inch (2.5 mm) wide strips and let them dry for 10 minutes.

To cook, bring 4 qts (4 lt) lightly salted water to a boil and drop in the pasta. Simmer for 7–10 minutes until "al dente". Drain the pasta and mix it with 1 tsp olive oil to prevent it from sticking together.

Sauce:
Combine the sherry and fish stock; bring to a boil. Add the calamari and simmer for 10 minutes. In a separate saucepan, melt the butter. Add the chives, okra and lime rind; stir-fry for 5 minutes. Thicken the mixture slightly with the flour then stir in the calamari and stock. Stir well, bring to a boil and serve with the hot pasta. Garnish with chopped chervil.

FLORIDA

MAIN COURSE

A sunset is one of the many attractions which put the Florida coastal regions in great demand by tourists.

FLORIDA

SWEETS

On The Rocks

Preparation Time: 2 minutes
Serves 2

2 cups beef consommé (liquid)
1 cup vodka
1 Tbsp lime juice
ice

Mix the ingredients together and serve in a glass over ice on a very hot day.

Chocolate Rum Tarts

Preparation Time: 20 minutes
Chilling Time: 1 hour
Serves 8

8 puff pastry tart shells (page 230)
1 oz (30 g) unsweetened chocolate
3 eggs, separated
1 cup sugar
¼ cup dark rum
1 envelope unflavored gelatin
¼ cup cold water
1 cup heavy cream
powdered sugar

Bake the tart shells at 350°F (180°C) for 15 minutes. Remove them from the oven and allow them to cool.

Melt the chocolate in the top of a double boiler over hot (not boiling) water. Beat the egg yolks with the sugar until they are smooth then stir in the rum. Dissolve the gelatin in the cold water and add it to the melted chocolate, stirring continually until the chocolate and gelatin are fully combined. Beat the chocolate mixture into the egg yolk mixture. Whip the egg whites until stiff and fold them in. Whip the cream until stiff and fold it in. Spoon the filling into the tart shells and chill for at least 1 hour. Dust with powdered sugar before serving.

Florida Sunrise

Preparation Time: 5 minutes
Macerating Time: 1 hour
Serves 2–6

6 large strawberries, chopped
1 orange, peeled and chopped
3 Tbsp sugar
3 Tbsp lime juice
¾ cup cognac
1 bottle champagne

Combine all the ingredients except the champagne in a punch bowl. Cover and let the mixture sit for 1 hour. Pour the well-chilled champagne over the fruit; stir and pour immediately into chilled glasses.

Coffee Kahlua Custard

Preparation Time: 10 minutes
Cooking Time: 30 minutes
Preheat Oven: 375°F (190°C)
Serves 6

4 eggs
2 cups milk
⅔ cup honey
1 cup strong black coffee
chocolate-coated coffee beans
½ cup Kahlua

In a blender, whisk the eggs until creamy. Add the milk, honey and coffee; mix until smooth.

Butter 6 individual custard cups or molds. Sieve the custard mixture then pour it into the prepared dishes. Place the custard cups in a baking dish containing about 1-inch (2.5 cm) of hot water. Bake for ½ hour or until just set. Allow the custards to cool.

Garnish with chocolate coffee beans and pour over the Kahlua.

The custards may be served in their cups or unmolded onto a serving plate. To unmold, run a knife around the top edge of the custard then stand the cup in hot water for a few seconds. Put a serving plate over the custard and invert the plate and mold together quickly. If the custard does not come free the first time, a sharp tap on the base of the mold will release it.

Sand sculpturing at Treasure Island, Florida.

Left: AVOCADO ICE CREAM, Recipe this page. *Right:* PEPPERED STRAWBERRIES, Recipe this page.

Peppered Strawberries

PHOTOGRAPH THIS PAGE

Preparation Time: 5 minutes
Cooking Time: 1 hour
Serves 4

1 pt strawberries
1 tsp white pepper
2 Tbsp icing sugar
1 Tbsp chopped fresh mint

Hull the strawberries, cut them in half and put them in a bowl. Sprinkle with pepper, sugar and finely chopped mint. Toss gently and let sit for 1 hour at room temperature. Toss again after ½ hour.

Avocado Ice Cream

PHOTOGRAPH THIS PAGE

Preparation Time: 5 minutes
Cooking Time: 1 hour
Serves 2

2 ripe avocados
3 Tbsp lime juice
¼ cup sugar
1 cup vanilla ice cream
sprig of mint

Peel, pit and mash the avocados. In a blender, blend in the lime juice, sugar and ice cream. Beat well. Store in the freezer.

To serve, scoop into glass serving dishes and top with fresh chopped mint.

Key Lime Pie

Preparation Time: 20 minutes
Cooking Time: 40 minutes
Preheat Oven: 375°F (190°C)
Serves 6

Shell:
3 Tbsp butter
¼ cup sugar
1½ cups graham cracker crumbs
½ cup chopped almonds

Filling:
3 eggs
4 limes, juiced
½ cup sugar
½ cup heavy cream
¼ lb (125 g) butter, melted
grated rind of 4 limes
whipped cream for garnish

Cream the butter and sugar then stir in the graham cracker crumbs and almonds. Press the crumb mixture onto the bottom and sides of a 9-inch (23 cm) pie pan to form a shell. Chill for 20 minutes.

Beat the eggs until light and frothy; combine with the lime juice, sugar and cream. Beat well. Stir the melted butter into the egg mixture along with the grated rind. Mix well and gently pour into the pie shell. Bake for 35–40 minutes, until the filling is set. Cool completely. Garnish with piped whipped cream.

FLORIDA

SWEETS

Hawaii

To think of Hawaii is to think of tropical days, fragrant flowers, exotic fruits and relaxed living; a tourist haunt of international acclaim.

Not widely known is the fact that there is one Hawaiian island where people aren't expected to eat anything for the next 10,000 years.

Windsurfers in full flight on the famous waves at Maui, Hawaii.

HAWAII

INTRODUCTION

The reason is simple. Unless mermaids are fact and not fiction, nobody does or can live on it, as this island is still 3000ft under the sea!

The island is called Lo'ihi and is a volcanic growth discovered in 1986, via a specially made underwater vehicle from Woods Hole oceanic laboratories.

Back to the Hawaii you can visit. These islands boast one of the most beautiful climates in the world with gentle south sea breezes tempering hot days and balmy evenings — a paradise of year-round summer (no winter — just a wet season).

Now the 50th state, Hawaii was a monarchy until 1893. The history is colorful with awe-inspiring highlights. For example, the people of these islands were mostly Polynesians who arrived some 2,000 years ago from other parts of the Pacific.

Each island became its own community and, like communities everywhere, they didn't get on too well to start with. It took 10 long years of bitter inter-island wars before King Kamehameha was able to unify the islands into one cohesive group.

James Cook was the first white man to chart the islands — which he named the Sandwich Islands after the Earl of Sandwich, first lord of the British Admiralty of the time. It was also to be Cook's final resting place following an altercation between his crew and the natives when the latter made their point with spears. These early years of contact with the civilized world was a typical good news/bad news period for the islanders. Traders brought not only new technology to the Hawaiians but many diseases previously unknown amongst the islanders. As a result, thousands died from ailments such as measles and influenza.

With a climate ideal for American-developed pineapple, sugar cane and cattle plantations, it was logical that Hawaiian agriculture be pointed in this direction. The proud Hawaiians were far from keen to handle menial tools like hoe and plough; it simply wasn't in their easy-going nature. To solve the problem Chinese and Japanese laborers were brought in around the turn of the century and, naturally, other nationalities followed. The subsequent intermingling of races (the Hawaiians had considerably more enthusiasm for love than work) has produced a stunningly beautiful race of people.

Only eight of the twenty-strong island group are part of the state of Hawaii, the other twelve being administered by the Department of the Interior. Each of the major islands of the state are special.

Oahu, on which Honolulu is situated with its beautiful beaches, skyscraper hotels, night spots and imposing Diamond Head watching over all, is the tourist capital. Hawaii is the largest of the islands with beaches varying from white through gold, gray, green and black and two regularly active volcanoes. Not widely known is that this island has one of the largest cattle ranches in the United States.

Maui, named after a Polynesian god, has a huge volcanic crater to the south and is a hideaway for many of our artists and celebrities. Kauai, known as the "Garden Island", boasts dramatic green canyons and ridges and is an obvious target location for movie makers and holiday makers alike. Molokai, known as the "Friendly Island" because of the courtesy with which people greet visitors, is the adventure island with camera safaris to the private breeding compounds supplying the world's zoos and a 2,774 acre wildlife refuge.

Lannai is the center of the Dole pineapple industry, where hundreds of acres are given over to growing pineapples. Niihau, owned by the Robinson family since 1864, is an island with little contact with the outside world and is a fortress of traditional Hawaiian language and customs, virtually undisturbed by modern times. Lastly, Kahoolawe is a windswept and unpopulated island off the south western coast of Maui.

While preparing exotic dishes like Red Pepper Soufflé with Crab Sauce or Guava Macadamia-Glazed Ham, you will be able to conjure up the sights, smells and sound of this beautiful island group with its mix of races, customs and culinary variety and convey the feeling of Hawaii to those included in the "Luau" you will create.

Top: LEMON CHICKEN WITH DEEP-FRIED RICE, Recipe page 246. *Bottom:* CHICKEN WINGS IN GINGER, Recipe page 248.

HAWAII

**APPETIZERS
SOUPS
SALADS
ENTREES**

Red Pepper Soufflé with Crab Sauce

Preparation Time: 20 minutes
Baking Time: 20 minutes
Preheat Oven: 425°F (220°C)
Serves 4

3 sweet red peppers, seeded and finely chopped
1 medium onion, minced
1 tsp Tabasco sauce
2 Tbsp flour
4 eggs, separated
2 Tbsp butter

Crab Sauce:

½ lb (250 g) crab meat
1 Tbsp lemon juice
2 Tbsp white wine
2 Tbsp heavy cream
2 Tbsp cornstarch

Soufflé:

Combine the peppers, onion, Tabasco and flour in a bowl; mix thoroughly. Beat in the egg yolks. Beat the egg whites until stiff and fold them into the pepper mixture. Butter 4 small soufflé molds and spoon the mixture into them. Bake for 20 minutes. Serve immediately with the crab sauce.

Sauce:

While the soufflés are baking, blend together all the sauce ingredients. Heat them gently in a saucepan, stirring occasionally until the mixture thickens slightly.

Spinach Rolls

Preparation Time: 30 minutes
Baking Time: 30 minutes
Preheat Oven: 350F (180°C)
Yield: about 30 rolls

1 bunch fresh, large-leaved spinach
2 Tbsp olive oil
2 Tbsp minced shallots
1 lb (500 g) ground lean pork
1 red pepper, seeded and chopped
½ tsp pepper
pinch of salt
1 Tbsp lemon juice

Sauce:

¼ cup tomato sauce
½ tsp hot sauce
1 Tbsp lemon juice
1 Tbsp olive oil

Separate the spinach leaves, wash thoroughly and trim the stalks. Place the leaves flat, one at a time, in the bottom of a heavy saucepan. When all the leaves are layered, cover them with boiling water and let stand. After 30 seconds, drain off the water; the leaves should now be limp. Allow them to cool.

Heat the olive oil in a skillet and sauté the shallots and ground pork for 2–3 minutes; remove from the heat. Add the chopped red pepper, black pepper, salt and lemon juice; mix well. Place 1 Tbsp of the pork mixture on each spinach leaf and roll up each one tightly. Lay the spinach rolls on a baking sheet close together to prevent them from unrolling.

Blend together the tomato sauce, hot sauce, lemon juice and olive oil; mix until smooth. Pour this sauce over the rolls and bake them for ½ hour.

Note: This dish may be prepared in advance and kept in the refrigerator overnight until you are ready to bake it.

Stuffed Lychee Nuts

Preparation Time: 15 minutes
Cooking Time: 5 minutes
Serves 6–8

1 lb (500 g) cooked or canned lychee nuts
¼ lb (125 g) cream cheese
2 Tbsp ginger conserve or jelly
½ cup pineapple juice
¼ cup sugar
½ tsp ground ginger

Drain the lychees. Cream the cheese and ginger conserve. Stuff each lychee with the cheese mixture and set aside in a warm dish.

Simmer the pineapple juice, sugar and ground ginger until the sauce becomes syrupy. Pour over the stuffed lychees and serve warm.

Fried Corn

Preparation Time: 10 minutes
Cooking Time: 7 minutes
Serves 4

1 cup corn niblets, cooked
1 onion, chopped
1 stalk celery, chopped
2 Tbsp chopped fresh cilantro
1 hot pepper, minced
1 egg, beaten
2 Tbsp flour
3 Tbsp peanut oil

Mix all the ingredients except the oil in a bowl or food processor and mix until stiff. Heat the oil to 375°F (190°C) in a wok or large skillet. Drop the corn batter by tablespoonsful into the hot oil and fry for 4 minutes on one side; turn and fry for 3 minutes on the other side. Drain and serve hot.

BANANA SOUP AND TOASTED MANGO SANDWICH, Recipe this page.

Banana Soup and Toasted Mango Sandwich

PHOTOGRAPH THIS PAGE

Preparation Time: 30 minutes
Serves 4

Soup:
1 qt (1 lt) milk
1 cup heavy cream
4 large ripe bananas
½ tsp nutmeg
1 Tbsp lemon juice

Combine all the ingredients in a blender and beat until very smooth. Chill in the refrigerator for ½ hour.

Sandwich:
4 thick slices white bread
4 Tbsp butter
½ cup heavy cream, whipped
1 tsp lemon juice
1 Tbsp sugar
1 cup mango pulp
3 tsp cinnamon
3 Tbsp sugar

Trim the crusts from the bread and melt 1 Tbsp butter in a skillet. Fry 1 slice of bread until golden on both sides. Set it aside and fry the other 3 in the same way. Whip the cream until it is thick then beat in the lemon juice and sugar. Pour in half of the mango pulp and beat again. Repeat until all the mango pulp is incorporated and the mixture is quite stiff.

To serve, sprinkle the toast liberally with cinnamon and sugar. Spread the fruit and cream mixture thickly over the toast and dust lightly with cinnamon. Serve at once with the chilled banana soup.

Water Chestnut Puffs

Preparation Time: 5 minutes
Cooking Time: 5 minutes
Serves 4

1 cup water chestnuts
1 egg
1 pt (½ lt) milk
1 tsp baking powder
pinch of pepper
pinch of cinnamon
flour
oil for frying

Mix the first six ingredients together in a blender or food processor until very smooth. Add just enough flour to make a thick batter. Heat the oil in a skillet to about 375°F (190°C). Drop teaspoons of batter into the hot oil and fry for 4–5 minutes until golden. Drain and serve hot.

HAWAII

APPETIZERS
SOUPS
SALADS
ENTREES

HAWAII

APPETIZERS
SOUPS
SALADS
ENTREES

Steamed Buns

Preparation Time: 30 minutes
Rising Time: 1 hour
Cooking Time: 30 minutes
Yield: 18 buns

1 package active dry yeast
2 tsp sugar
¾ cup warm water
2 Tbsp vegetable oil
2½ cups flour
¼ cup sesame seeds

Dissolve the yeast and sugar in the warm water; let it froth for 10 minutes. Stir in the oil and flour; mix to form a soft dough. Turn the dough onto a floured board and knead it for 10 minutes until it is very smooth. Roll the dough into a long sausage shape, about 1-inch (2.5 cm) thick. Cut it into 1-inch (2.5 cm) slices. Pat each slice into a ball; arrange the dough balls on a bamboo or metal steamer, 1-inch (2.5 cm) apart. Cover the buns with a damp towel and let them rise for 1 hour.

Sprinkle the buns with the sesame seeds and steam them for ½ hour.

Note: If you do not have a steamer, you can effectively steam the buns in an egg poacher, 4 at a time.

Creamed Potatoes with Macadamia Nut Butter

Preparation Time: 20 minutes
Cooking Time: 25 minutes
Serves 4

4 or 5 medium-sized potatoes
½ cup heavy cream
1 bunch chives, chopped
pinch of salt
¼ cup butter
½ cup ground Macadamia nuts
freshly ground pepper

Peel, slice and boil the potatoes for 15 minutes until just tender. Drain them and mash or puree. Stir in the cream, chives and salt to taste and return to the pan. Keep warm over low heat.

Melt the butter and stir in the ground Macadamia nuts. To serve, mound the mashed potatoes onto serving plates. Make a depression in the center of each mound and place a tablespoon of the nut butter in the hollow. Liberally sprinkle the potato mounds with finely ground black pepper before serving.

Coconut Soup

Preparation Time: 20 minutes
Cooking Time: 20 minutes
Preheat Oven: 350°F (180°C)
Serves 4

2 coconuts
4 cups chicken consommé
1 Tbsp ground coriander seed
pinch each of nutmeg, cayenne, sugar
1 tsp grated lemon rind
turmeric

Drill the coconut eyes with a hammer and screwdriver; drain and reserve the milk. Break the coconuts and cut out the meat. Place one cup of the coconut meat in a blender with 1 cup of the consommé; blend until smooth. Pour this mixture into a pan with the rest of the consommé, the reserved coconut milk, the coriander, nutmeg, cayenne and sugar. Simmer for 20 minutes.

Chop or slice the remaining coconut meat and bake it for 20 minutes until toasted. To serve, strain the soup into bowls. Sprinkle each with the toasted coconut, lemon rind and a pinch of turmeric.

Hot Melon Salad

Preparation Time: 15 minutes
Cooking Time: 10 minutes
Serves 4

1 large honeydew melon
1 cup diced fresh pineapple
1 cup sliced banana
½ cup Macadamia or cashew nuts, coarsely chopped
½ cup cooked shrimp meat
2 Tbsp butter
2 Tbsp wildflower honey
4–5 fresh chilies, seeded and chopped
¼ cup lemon juice

Cut off the top third of the melon. Then cut deep Vs all around the melon to create a "crown." Discard the seeds. Remove the rind from the severed top of the melon and from the triangles that were cut from the crown. Cut these melon pieces into 1-inch (2.5 cm) chunks and place them in a large bowl. Add the pineapple, banana, nuts and shrimp meat.

Melt the butter in a saucepan; stir in the honey, chilies and lemon juice. Simmer for 10 minutes. Strain this sauce over the fruit in the bowl and toss well. Heap the fruit and shrimp mixture into the melon crown. Serve with coconut soup as above.

Ancient Gods at Hale-o-Keawe heiau in Hawaii.

The magnificent Kalalau Valley at Kauai, Hawaii.

HAWAII

MAIN COURSE

Lemon Chicken with Deep-Fried Rice

PHOTOGRAPH PAGE 239

Preparation Time: 15 minutes
Cooking Time: 10 minutes
Preheat Deep Fryer: 375°F (190°C)
Serves 4

4 deboned chicken breasts

Marinade:
1 Tbsp soy sauce
2 Tbsp sherry
1 tsp grated fresh ginger root
1 tsp grated lemon rind
1 tsp sugar

Batter:
1 egg white
2 Tbsp flour
2 Tbsp lemon juice

Sauce:
½ cup chicken stock
¼ cup sugar
2 Tbsp lemon juice
2 Tbsp cornstarch

Cut the chicken into ½-inch (1 cm) strips and place them in a bowl. Combine in a blender the soy sauce, sherry, ginger, lemon rind and sugar; beat until smooth. Pour the mixture over the chicken strips, mix well and marinate for ½ hour.

Beat the egg white until stiff, then beat in the flour and lemon juice. Drain the chicken strips, dip them in the batter and deep-fry them for 5 minutes until golden brown.

Pour any leftover marinade into a saucepan and add the chicken stock and sugar. Heat to a boil and stir well. Dissolve the cornstarch in the lemon juice and stir into the sauce. Lower the heat and heat gently, stirring, until thickened. Pour the sauce over the fried chicken strips and serve hot with Deep-Fried Rice.

Deep-Fried Rice

PHOTOGRAPH PAGE 239

Preparation Time: 4 minutes
Cooking Time: 5 minutes
Serves 4

4 cups cooked brown rice
2 Tbsp chopped fresh parsley
½ cup seeded and chopped sweet red pepper
1 egg, beaten

Combine all the ingredients in a bowl and stir to form a sticky mixture. Drop by the tablespoonful into hot oil (375°F) (190°C) and deep-fry for 4–5 minutes until just golden. Drain and serve the rice balls hot with Lemon Chicken.

Tropical Game Hens

Preparation Time: 20 minutes
Cooking Time: 15 minutes
Baking Time: 20 minutes
Preheat Oven: 400°F (200°C)
Serves 4

2 large game hens
1 Tbsp vegetable oil
1 clove garlic, minced
1 onion, chopped
1 tsp turmeric
2 tsp grated fresh ginger root
2 chilies
2 tsp coriander
1 tsp cumin
2 Tbsp lemon juice
1 cup coconut milk
1 cup chopped fresh pineapple

Split the game hens lengthwise and put them in a heavy pan. Cover them with boiling water, lower the heat and simmer, covered, for 12–15 minutes. Remove the hens from the stock and arrange them in a baking dish.

In a skillet, melt the vegetable oil; sauté the garlic and onion for 3–4 minutes until soft. Add the spices and lemon juice; stir well. Add the coconut milk and pineapple; bring the mixture to a boil. Pour the hot sauce over the game hens and bake for 20–25 minutes until brown.

Sweet & Sour Sausages

PHOTOGRAPH PAGE 247

Preparation Time: 10 minutes
Cooking Time: 10 minutes
Serves 8

1 lb (500 g) cocktail sausages
2 cups pineapple cubes
½ lb (250 g) snow peas

Sauce:
1 Tbsp soy sauce
1 Tbsp cider vinegar
½ cup guava jelly
½ tsp powdered mustard
½ tsp grated fresh ginger root
1 Tbsp light brown sugar
1 Tbsp cornstarch

Combine each cocktail sausage with a pineapple cube; wrap the combination with a snow pea and secure with a toothpick. Place in a saucepan.

Combine the sauce ingredients in a blender and mix until smooth. Pour over the wrapped sausages. Heat slowly until the sauce boils, then lower the heat and simmer for 5 minutes. Serve hot or cold.

Top: STUFFED PAPAYAS, Recipe this page. Bottom: SWEET & SOUR SAUSAGES, Recipe page 246.

Stuffed Papayas

PHOTOGRAPH THIS PAGE

Preparation Time: 25 minutes
Baking Time: 45 minutes
Preheat Oven: 350°F (180°C)
Serves 4

2 Tbsp butter
1 onion, chopped
1 clove garlic, minced
2 slices bacon, chopped
2 cups diced cooked chicken
1 Tbsp lemon juice
½ cup white wine
3 tomatoes, peeled and chopped
2 large firm papayas

1 green apple, sliced
¼ cup ricotta cheese
paprika
Hot Sauce (page 148)

Melt the butter in a saucepan and add the onion, garlic and bacon. Sauté for 5 minutes until the onion is soft; stir in the chicken, lemon juice, wine and tomatoes. Simmer for 5 minutes.

Peel the papayas, cut them in half lengthwise and scoop out the seeds. Arrange the papaya halves on a baking sheet, cut side up and heap the chicken mixture onto each half. Decorate each with apple slices and a tablespoon of ricotta. Sprinkle with a pinch of paprika and bake 40–45 minutes. Serve with hot sauce.

HAWAII

MAIN COURSE

HAWAII

MAIN COURSE

Guava Macadamia-Glazed Ham

Preparation Time: 15 minutes
Cooking Time: 2 hours
Preheat Oven: 325°F (160°C)
Serves 6–8

4–5 lbs (2–2.5 kg) ham roast
1 cup guava pulp
1 Tbsp grated orange rind
2 Tbsp dark brown sugar
1 tsp grated fresh ginger root
¼ cup chopped Macadamia nuts
1 Tbsp cornstarch
¼ cup orange juice

Bake the ham for 1 hour. Mix the guava, orange rind, brown sugar and ginger in a saucepan; bring to a boil. Remove the ham from the oven and pour off the fat. Brush liberally with the guava sauce. Return the ham to the oven to bake for 1 hour longer, basting every 15 minutes.

Set the ham on a serving platter. Combine the sauce, drippings and Macadamia nuts in a saucepan and bring to a boil. Simmer for 5 minutes. Dissolve the cornstarch in the orange juice and stir into the sauce. Continue to heat and stir until the sauce thickens. Pour some of the sauce over the ham and serve the rest in a side dish.

Chicken Wings in Ginger

PHOTOGRAPH PAGE 239

Preparation Time: 5 minutes
Cooking Time: 25 minutes
Serves 4

1 Tbsp peanut oil
2 Tbsp grated fresh ginger root
1 clove garlic, minced
8 chicken wings
1 Tbsp soy sauce
2 Tbsp sugar
1 Tbsp cornstarch
3 Tbsp rice wine or sherry
2 Tbsp sesame seeds

Heat the peanut oil in a wok or skillet until almost smoking. Stir-fry the ginger, garlic and chicken wings together for 2 minutes. Add the soy sauce and sugar; mix well. Dissolve the cornstarch in the wine and add to the wok. Bring to a boil, then reduce the heat and simmer for 15–20 minutes, until the wings are done. Sprinkle the chicken with sesame seeds and serve hot.

Polynesian Spare Ribs

Preparation Time: 10 minutes
Cooking Time: 80 minutes
Serves 6–8

4–5 lbs (2–2.5 kg) country-style pork Spare Ribs
1 onion, chopped
1 Tbsp pepper
1 bay leaf

Sauce:
2 Tbsp ground coriander seed
2 cloves garlic, minced
1 tsp pepper
pinch of salt
¼ cup sugar
2 Tbsp vinegar
2 Tbsp soy sauce

Place the ribs in a heavy saucepan and add the onion, pepper and bay leaf. Cover with boiling water and simmer over low heat for 1 hour or, until tender. Remove the ribs from the stock and drain them.

In a small saucepan, mix all the sauce ingredients and bring them to a boil. Liberally brush the ribs with the sauce then grill or broil them for 20 minutes using medium heat and basting frequently. Serve the ribs hot with extra sauce.

Beef Teriyaki

PHOTOGRAPH PAGE 249

Preparation Time: 10 minutes
Marinating Time: 1 hour
Cooking Time: 7 minutes
Serves 6

2 lbs (1 kg) sirloin tip steak

Sauce:
¼ cup Miri (sweet saki) or sherry
¼ cup soy sauce
1 tsp sugar
2 tsp grated fresh ginger root
1 tsp grated fresh horseradish

Cut the steak diagonally into strips ¼-inch (½ cm) thick. (For easier cutting, chill the meat in the freezer for 20 minutes.)

Combine all the sauce ingredients in a bowl or blender and mix until very smooth. Marinate the meat in the sauce for 1–2 hours.

To cook, thread the beef strips onto skewers and grill or broil them over high heat for 3 minutes. Liberally brush the meat with sauce and cook on the other side for 3–4 minutes. Serve hot with chopped watercress, shredded lettuce and sliced raw mushrooms.

Left: SPRING ROLLS, Recipe this page. Right: BEEF TERIYAKI, Recipe page 248.

Spring Rolls

PHOTOGRAPH THIS PAGE

Preparation Time: 1¼ hours
Deep Frying Time: 4 minutes each
Serves 12

Filling:

½ lb (250 g) pork shoulder, cut into very thin strips
1 tsp cornstarch
1 lb (500 g) fresh bean sprouts
5 Tbsp vegetable oil
3 slices fresh ginger root
½ lb (250 g) shrimp meat
½ tsp salt
1 Tbsp rice wine or sherry
¼ lb (125 g) mushrooms, sliced
2 leeks, chopped
½ tsp sugar
1 Tbsp soy sauce

Wrappers:

1 egg, beaten
2 cups flour
pinch of salt
cold water
1 egg, beaten

Filling:

Slice the pork, sprinkle it with cornstarch and set it aside. Rinse the bean sprouts and pat them dry. In a wok or large skillet, heat 1 Tbsp of the oil to 375°F (190°C) (moderate). Fry the ginger for 5 minutes. Remove and discard the ginger and raise the temperature to 425°F (220°C) (hot). Add the shrimp, salt and wine; stir-fry for 1 minute. Remove the shrimp and set aside. Add another tablespoon of oil to the pan and stir-fry the pork for 2 minutes. Set the pork aside. Stir-fry the mushrooms and leeks for 2 minutes. When all the ingredients have been stir-fried, toss them together in a bowl with the sugar and soy sauce.

Wrappers:

To make the spring roll wrappers, beat together the egg, flour and salt. Gradually add enough cold water to make a stiff dough. Turn the dough onto a floured board and knead it well for 10 minutes. Roll out the dough with a rolling pin or pasta maker until it is paper thin. Cut it into 6-inch (15 cm) squares.

To Assemble:

Place about 3 Tbsp of filling in the center of each wrapper. Fold up the bottom corner. Fold up both sides and roll up tightly to make a sealed package. Continue making the rest of the rolls until all the dough has been used. Brush the rolls with the beaten egg and deep-fry them at 375°F (190°C) for 4 minutes until golden brown. Drain and serve hot.

HAWAII

MAIN COURSE

HAWAII

SWEETS

Macadamia Nut Burnt Cream Crisps

PHOTOGRAPH PAGE 251

Preparation Time: 25 minutes
Cooking Time: 30 minutes
Preheat Oven: 325°F (160°C)
Chilling Time: 1 hour
Broiling Time: 10 minutes
Yield: 12 crisps

Crisps:
1 cup Macadamia nuts
¾ cup sugar
3 egg whites

Cream:
1 cup milk
3 egg yolks
¼ cup sugar
1 tsp vanilla
1 cup heavy cream

3 Tbsp light brown sugar

In a food processor or blender, grind the Macadamia nuts into a paste. Gradually beat in the sugar and egg whites until smooth. Butter a baking sheet. Pipe or spoon the mixture to form 2-inch (5 cm) round tart shells, slightly depressed in the center. Bake for ½ hour. Cool slightly then loosen the shells from the baking sheet with a spatula.

Scald the milk in a saucepan. Beat the egg yolks, sugar and vanilla in a bowl or blender until creamy. Gradually beat in the hot milk. Return to the pan and reheat over low heat, stirring con-

stantly, until the custard thickens. Remove from the stove, cover and cool the custard. Whip the cream until stiff. When the custard has reached room temperature, fold in the cream and spoon the mixture into the crisp tart shells. Chill the crisps in the refrigerator for at least an hour.

Just before serving, sprinkle each crisp with ½ tsp brown sugar and place under the broiler at 400°F (200°C) for 10 minutes or until the sugar melts and the cream just starts to brown. Serve immediately.

Sweet Finger Wontons

PHOTOGRAPH PAGE 251

Preparation Time: 40 minutes
Cooking Time: 5 minutes
Yield: 36 wontons

Wrapping:
1½ cups flour
1 egg, beaten
pinch of salt
cold water

Filling I:
1 cup shredded fresh coconut
¼ cup coconut syrup
1 tsp grated lemon rind

Filling II:
½ cup chopped Macadamia nuts
1 Tbsp chopped candied ginger
1 Tbsp lemon juice
1 Tbsp dark brown sugar

Filling III:
½ cup dried sliced bananas
1 Tbsp chopped candied ginger
1 Tbsp lemon juice
1 Tbsp honey

Icing sugar

Combine the flour, egg and salt in a bowl or food processor. Add enough water to make a stiff dough. Turn the dough onto a lightly floured board and knead well for 10 minutes. Cover and let the dough rest for 10 minutes while you prepare the fillings.

To make any of the fillings, mix the ingredients in a bowl or food processor and set aside.

Roll out the dough paper thin or pass it through a pasta machine. Cut it into 3-inch (8 cm) squares. Place 1 Tbsp of filling in the center of each square, roll up the squares tightly and twist the ends like candy wrappers. Deep-fry the wontons, a few at a time, at 375°F (190°C) for 5 minutes until golden brown. Cool. Sprinkle the wontons with icing sugar and serve them warm. If they cool off, they may be reheated in a 300°F (150°C) oven for 10 minutes, then dusted again with sugar.

A beautiful dancing girl performing at the Polynesian Cultural Center in Oahu, Hawaii.

Top: SWEET FINGER WONTONS, Recipe page 250.
Bottom: MACADAMIA NUT BURNT CREAM CRISPS, Recipe page 250.

Festive

Many nations have the same major festive days, such as Christmas, Easter and birthdays, while others have days of festivity common only to that country. For example, the Russians do not celebrate birthdays but Saint's Days. Each child is traditionally named after a saint and he or she is given presents to celebrate their name rather than the day of their birth.

Feasts and festivals are thought to have originated with superstitious pre-historic man, whose reliance on nature was virtually total. Any method of appeasing the elements must have seemed like a good idea and with the turning of the seasons, different spirits and gods would have to be pleased to ensure the safety of the people and their environment. Objects in nature that he did not understand were also targets for worship, such as the sun which gave him light and warmth.

As civilizations developed, their feasts and festivals became more ritualistic and elaborate. Romans and Greeks held games and fairs during their festivals.

With the coming of Christianity, many of the old feast days and customs became integrated into this new religion. Christmas day is believed to be the date of a pagan festival and mistletoe is traced back to the British Druids who used it as a charm.

Christmas Yule Log (recipe — this section) is named after the huge oak log burnt once a year by the Normans and Anglo-Saxons to honor Thor, the god of thunder.

Although Christmas is celebrated around the world, most countries have their own traditions which have been incorporated into the festival.

In France, children put their shoes on the doorstep so the Christ Child can fill them with presents. In some parts of France every member of the family must help to bring in the Yule Log which must burn from Christmas to New Year's Day.

Children in most South American countries believe the wise men bring their Christmas presents. In China, Santa Claus is called Sheng Tan Lao Ren (which translates to Holy Birthday Old Man). In the Philippines a special Christmas dish called 'colacion' is prepared, and with one or two members staying home to serve any visitors, the rest of the family go out to enjoy their colacion with friends.

Easter, similarly, has traditions in every country in which it is celebrated and Hot Cross Buns are in nearly all cases, part of that tradition (recipe — this section). In Belgium, children make nests of hay and hide them in the garden for the Easter bunny to fill. In Greece and Rumania people tap red eggs together as an Easter greeting when they meet.

In the Ukraine, Easter is celebrated for two weeks. Holy week is observed with reverence and the week after Easter is full of celebration and dancing. They are famous for their beautifully painted Easter eggs and each village has its own design.

In Syria, beggars are invited into churches; their feet are washed in memory of Christ's bathing of the disciples' feet and each are given gifts.

These are just a few of the many customs and traditions of our two major Christian Festivals. All of them make the joy of these occasions greater and bring us closer together as a family or nation.

Festive occasions, whether religious or not, are usually a marvellous excuse to eat delicacies savored only rarely. What Christmas would be complete with Mince Pies (Traditional Mincemeat & Rum and Mincemeat Muffins — recipe this section). A feast of the proportions of Christmas would be lost without a homemade Christmas Cake (recipe this section).

All the recipes in this chapter are guaranteed to please a feasting crowd and make this festival more memorable for all who partake.

A little boy innocently enjoying Christmas.

HOT CROSS BUNS, Recipe this page.

FESTIVE

SWEETS

Hot Cross Buns

PHOTOGRAPH THIS PAGE

Preparation Time: 25 minutes
Rising Time: 2¼ hours
Baking Time: 25 minutes
Yield: 12

Dough:
¾ cup warm milk
⅓ cup sugar
2 packages active dry yeast
3½ cups all-purpose flour
pinch of salt
½ tsp cinnamon
½ tsp mace
½ cup melted butter
2 eggs, beaten
½ cup currants

Cross:
2 Tbsp flour
2 Tbsp milk
½ tsp vanilla

Glaze:
¼ cup warm honey

Stir the warm milk, sugar and yeast together in a mixing bowl; allow to stand for 10 minutes until the yeast is frothy. Gradually stir in the flour, salt, spices, butter, eggs and currants. Turn the dough onto a lightly floured board and knead it for 5 minutes. Place the dough in a clean bowl, cover it, and let it rise for 1½ hours in a warm place.

Turn the dough out and knead it again for 5 minutes then divide it into 12 balls. Grease 2 cookie sheets and place the balls of dough 2 inches (5 cm) apart. Let rise a second time for 45 minutes. When the buns are ready to bake, preheat the oven to 400°F (200°C).

To make the cross, blend together the flour, milk and vanilla to a smooth paste. Spoon the mixture into a wide syringe or piping bag and decorate each ball of dough with a cross. Bake for 15 minutes. Remove from the oven.

Brush each bun liberally with warm honey and set aside to cool. Hot cross buns should be eaten fresh; any left over may be split and toasted the following day.

Mole de guarjolote (Turkey Mole)

Preparation Time: 30 minutes
Cooking Time: 2 hours
Serves 10

12–14-lb (6-7 kg) turkey
½ cup drippings or lard

Sauce:
2 Tbsp olive oil
3 onions, chopped
2 cloves garlic, minced
½ cup seedless raisins
2 oz unsweetened chocolate, chopped
1 tsp cinnamon
½ tsp each of anise, cumin, cloves
3 Tbsp red chili powder
6 cups turkey stock

Garnish:
1 cup tortillas, broken
¼ cup sesame seeds

Cut the turkey into pieces. Heat the dripping in a large skillet and brown the meat well on all sides. Remove the turkey to a large heavy pan. Cover it with water and bring to a boil. Reduce the heat and simmer covered for 45 minutes.

Add the olive oil to the dripping in the skillet. Stir in the onion and garlic. Cook for 5 minutes then add all the raisins, chocolate, spices and stock. Remove the turkey from the broth and cut away all the meat. Set aside. Add the turkey bones and giblets to the sauce, stir well and simmer for ½ hour.

Arrange the turkey meat in a deep casserole or baking dish. Remove the bones from the sauce. Puree the sauce and pour it over the turkey meat. Sprinkle with the broken tortillas and sesame seeds. Bake for ½ hour at 400°F (200°C).

Traditional Mincemeat

Preparation and Cooking Time: 2½ hours
Yield: 6 quarts (6 lt)

2 lbs (1 kg) ground beef
1 lb (500 g) beef suet
3½ lbs (1½ kg) apples, peeled, cored and chopped
2 lbs (1 kg) seedless raisins
1½ lbs (750 g) currants
¾ cup candied citron
¾ cup candied lemon peel
2 lbs (1 kg) light brown sugar
1 Tbsp salt

1 cup molasses
3 cups apple cider
1 tsp mace
1 Tbsp cinnamon
1 Tbsp ground cloves
1 Tbsp allspice
2 tsp nutmeg
1 lb (500 g) walnuts, chopped
¼ cup lemon juice
1 cup brandy

Place the meat in a very large saucepan with just enough water to cover and simmer for ½ hour. Drain the meat and return it to the pan. Add all the remaining ingredients except the lemon juice and brandy. Bring the mixture to a boil, reduce the heat and simmer for 1½ hours, stirring occasionally. Stir in the lemon juice and brandy. Ladle the mincemeat into sterilised jars. Seal, cool and store. Allow the mincemeat to mature for at least 6 weeks before using.

Caribbean Black Cake

Preparation Time: 30 minutes
Cooking Time: 2½ hours
Ripening Time: 6 weeks–2 months

3½ cups currants
2½ cups seedless raisins
2 cups seeded raisins
1¼ cup candied citrus
1½ cups dried figs, chopped
1 cup cooked prunes, pitted and chopped
1 cup glazed cherries
1 cup pitted dates, chopped
½ cup candied orange peel
1 cup whole blanched roasted almonds
3 cups dark rum
1 cup butter
2 cups brown sugar
2 Tbsp each of cinnamon, allspice, nutmeg
5 eggs
2 cups flour
2 Tbsp baking powder

Combine all the fruit, the nuts and the rum in a large bowl. Cover and let stand for 1 week, stirring occasionally.

Cream the butter, sugar and spices. Beat in the eggs, flour and baking powder. Fold in the fruit/rum mixture. Mix well. Line 2 loaf pans with greased paper and pour in the batter. Place the pans in a shallow dish of hot water and bake at 275°F (140°C) for 2½ hours. Cool, remove from the pans and discard the paper. Sprinkle the cakes with rum and wrap tightly. Store the cakes in an air-tight container. Sprinkle them with rum once a week; keep them at least 1 month before cutting.

FESTIVE
SWEETS

FESTIVE

SWEETS

Christmas Cake

Preparation Time: 20 minutes
Cooking Time: 1½ hours
Preheat Oven: 325°F (160°C)
Serves 12–15

1 lb (500 g) butter
2 cups sugar
½ tsp baking powder
¼ cup sliced almonds
1½ cups seedless raisins
1½ cup sultanas
1½ cups currants
1½ cups candied mixed fruit
½ cup candied cherries, chopped
1 tsp cinnamon
½ tsp nutmeg
½ tsp mace
1 cup brandy
6 eggs, separated

Cream the butter and sugar together in a very large mixing bowl. Add all the other ingredients except the eggs. Mix thoroughly. Separate the eggs and stir the yolks into the cake mixture. Beat the egg whites until stiff and fold them in.

Liberally butter and flour a large loaf pan and pour in the cake batter. Bake for about 1½ hours. Test for doneness with a toothpick. Cool slightly and turn out onto a wire rack to cool completely. Store the cake in a tight container. If the cake gets a little dry, brush it with sherry.

Pompion Pie

Preparation Time: 10 minutes
Cooking Time: 30–35 minutes
Preheat Oven: 350°F (180°C)
Serves 6–8

shortcrust pastry for a single-crust pie
1 Tbsp butter
1 onion, chopped
½ cup cooked ham, chopped
14 oz (440 g) can pumpkin
¾ cup sour cream
1 egg, beaten
1 tsp thyme
1 tsp oregano
1 pinch of anise
salt and pepper to taste
6 strips of bacon

Line a 9-inch (23 cm) pie plate with shortcrust pastry and bake in a preheated oven for 10–12 minutes.
Meanwhile, melt the butter in a saucepan and sauté the onion until soft. Toss in the chopped ham and stir until coated with butter.

In a bowl, stir together the pumpkin, sour cream, egg, herbs and onion/ham mixture. Stir just until mixed; do not puree. Pour this mixture into the baked pie shell and decorate with bacon strips. Bake for 15–20 minutes.

Place the pie under the broiler for 5 minutes or until the bacon sizzles. Remove and allow to cool slightly; if served too hot, the pie will be runny. It can also be served cold.

Rum Mincemeat Muffins

Preparation Time: 10 minutes
Cooking Time: 20 minutes
Preheat Oven: 375°F (190°C)
Yield: 12 muffins

1½ cups flour
¼ cup sugar
2 tsp baking powder
pinch of salt
½ cup butter
½ cup apple juice
2 eggs, beaten
1 cup mincemeat (page 225)
½ cup dark rum
12 sugar cubes

Mix the dry ingredients in a bowl. Set aside. Melt the butter in a saucepan. Add the apple juice and beaten eggs to the butter. Stir the liquid into the dry ingredients then add the mincemeat. When just mixed, spoon into well-greased muffin tins, filling them about ⅔ full. Soak the sugar cubes in the rum and place one cube on top of each muffin. Bake for 20 minutes. Serve warm.

Christmas Yule Log

PHOTOGRAPH PAGE 257

Preparation Time: 20 minutes
Baking Time: 20 minutes
Preheat Oven: 350°F (180°C)
Assemble: 10 minutes
Serves 8

4 oz (125 g) unsweetened chocolate
⅔ cup all-purpose flour
pinch of baking soda
pinch of salt
4 eggs
1 cup sugar
2 Tbsp water
1 cup heavy cream, whipped

Melt the chocolate in a double boiler over hot (not boiling) water or in a heavy saucepan over low heat.

CHRISTMAS YULE LOG, Recipe page 256.

Combine the flour, baking soda and salt. Set aside. Beat the eggs and sugar together until smooth. Add the water and mix well. Pour the egg mixture into the melted chocolate and combine. Pour the liquid ingredients into the dry ingredients and mix thoroughly.

Line a 15-inch (30 cm) by 10-inch (25 cm) jelly roll pan with wax paper and pour in the mixture. Smooth the top with a knife and bake 20 minutes.

Sprinkle a clean tea towel with powdered sugar and roll up the cake in the towel. Cool.

Whip the cream and sugar together until stiff. Unroll the cake and spread it with the sweetened cream. Reroll without the towel and set on a platter. Decorate with Chocolate Icing.

Chocolate Icing

1 oz (30 g) unsweetened chocolate
¼ cup butter
2 cups powdered sugar
2 Tbsp milk
½ tsp vanilla

Slowly melt the chocolate with the butter in a double boiler over hot not boiling, water. Beat in the sugar, milk and vanilla; mix to a smooth paste. Use a knife or spatula to spread the icing over the chocolate roll. Score the surface with a fork to make it resemble bark. Frost with icing sugar if desired.

FESTIVE

SWEETS

FISH

To many Americans, fish is not just a food but more a way of life and almost a culture.

We are lucky. Fish abound in our long coastal stretches and in the big inland waterway networks which comprise the hundreds of lakes and rivers of the hinterland.

Fishing is one of the biggest national sports in the country and is as American as apple pie. Camping trips up river, the log cabin on the lake, the house on the beach, are part of the American way of life. Linked to that way are no less than 2200 different species of fish.

Fish is also a major source of protein and has been used as such since prehistoric times. The following is a short guide to the more popular table varieties.

Haddock

A deep water fish found in the American Atlantic. The flesh is white and flaky with a delicate flavor, and is a lean fish. It may be baked whole, with or without stuffing. Filleted, it is fried, poached or boiled. Haddock is also smoked and is very popular in this form. It is boiled and then dressed with a sauce or oil and lemon dressing. First place the haddock in water, bring to the boil, then remove and discard the water. Replace with fresh water or milk and cook through on moderate heat. This removes the strong salty, smoked flavor.

Cod

Atlantic Cod is the most commercially important fish, and is fished on a vast scale. It is a large fish and can weigh up to 80 lbs, so is usually sold in fillets or steaks. Small cod of 3 to 4 lbs is also available. It has a white firm flesh and is suitable for cooking by any method. The most popular way is battered and fried, it is also favored for fish casseroles, soups and chowders. Dried salted cod has been the staple food of many cultures. Salted cod must be soaked in 6 changes of water before cooking.

Mackerel

Is a very popular fish, both for its fine flavor and the sport involved in catching it. It is mostly found along the Atlantic coast and into the Gulf of Mexico. Some species are also found in the warm waters of the Pacific Coast. As it has a high oil content, broiled without fat is the best method of cooking. It may also be baked or poached with some tart ingredient such as white wine, vinegar, tomatoes, lemons or gooseberries, to counteract the oiliness. It is sold cut into fillets or steaks.

Herring

The Herring supports a vast commercial industry, being one of the most abundant sea fish. In America it is fished in both the Atlantic and Pacific waters. It is a highly nutritious fish with a high oil content and high in vitamins and calcium; it is also an inexpensive fish. Because of its high oil content it bakes well, either stuffed or on a bed of potatoes and other vegetables, and may be poached or broiled. It is also sold in a cured, pickled or smoked form as Bismark herrings, rollmops and kippers.

Ocean Perch

A rock fish found along the Pacific Coast. It is an important commercial fish. It is a slightly oily fish with a moist flesh and a delightful taste. Ocean Perch is a good all-round fish being suitable for all cooking methods. It is delightful poached whole then served with oil and lemon dressing or mayonnaise. Ocean perch is sold whole or cut into steaks, depending on size.

Trout

Is a fish which has a small resemblance to the salmon. There are many varieties, some living solely in fresh water and some migratory. Rainbow trout is the most adaptable variety, being raised by aquaculture to fill streams and rivers. It is a good sporting fish and provide excellent eating, having a moist firm flesh, usually pink in color and a sweet mild flavor. Trout is suitable for all cooking methods and is usually cooked whole.

FISH

Red Snapper
There are many species of snapper in American waters; the most popular, as a table fish, is the Red Snapper. It is a white fleshed fish with a firm texture and fine flavor suitable for all methods of cooking. Its popularity as a table fish makes it highly sought after, therefore expensive at the market place. It may be cooked whole, baked, grilled or barbecued or cut into steaks or fillets and broiled or pan-fried. Grey snapper and yellow-tail snapper are also good but not as delicate as the red snapper.

Sea Bass
Is an excellent table fish. It is a lean fish with a white firm textured flesh and fine flavor. It has also the advantage of having few bones and so is usually cooked whole. Large fish may be poached in court-bouillon or baked. Smaller fish are best broiled whole. There are many species of Sea Bass in North American waters and the Black Sea Bass, found off the eastern coast, is the finest. Freshwater bass is also a popular table fish.

Flounder
Is a flat fish which has its eyes on the one side of its body. Flounder is a delicate textured fish with an excellent flavor. It is best grilled or pan-fried whole and served with a lightly seasoned butter sauce. Large fish are sold filleted which are used in many ways, and can be served with most of the classic fish sauces. Flounder is similar to Sole which is not readily found in American waters. Most Sole in the markets are imported, therefore expensive. Flounder may be successfully substituted in any recipe.

Halibut
Is the largest of the flat fish and is usually sold as cutlets or fillets. The texture is dryer than sole and flounder so it is better to cook it with a sauce, in a casserole or baked. It may be cut into chunks and skewered to make fish kebabs. Marinate first, and brush with marinade while on the barbecue or under the broiler. The California Halibut and the larger Pacific Halibut are fished along the West Coast of America. They are a highly desirable sport fish as well as a table fish.

Salmon
Salmon is considered the "king of fish". It is a marine fish which swims up freshwater rivers to spawn then returns to the sea. It is a very strong swimming fish which gives anglers a chance to test their skills.
Salmon has a pink firm yet moist flesh and a subtly superb flavor. It is best poached whole in court-bouillon and served hot or cold with a good mayonnaise. To bake, wrap in buttered foil and place in a moderate oven. Salmon steaks or fillets may be pan-fried or broiled; use mild flavorings and seasonings.

Catfish
The Bullhead Catfish is native to the fresh waters of North America. The many varieties found throughout the country include the Blue Catfish, a large fish with a fine flavor which is highly valued as a sporting fish as well as a table fish. The Yellow Bullhead, Brown Bullhead and Channel Catfish are other popular varieties. Catfish may be broiled, barbecued, pan-fried or baked.

Pacific Barracuda
Known also as California Barracuda. It is a large active fish sought after by anglers more for the sport involved than the table. The annual sport catch nears the million mark.
Fresh barracuda steaks, grilled with lemon butter and a dash of pepper is a meal that will not be forgotten. Its flavor is such that only the simplest cooking method is necessary.

Whitefish
It is also known as Lake Whitefish and is one of the most valuable freshwater fish in North America. They occur in large rivers and lakes in Alaska, Canada, Great Lakes and North New England. They are a slightly oily fish, their flavor is superb and they are considered a delicacy. Unfortunately the number of fish landed each year is decreasing due to the deterioration of the habitat and depletion of stocks.
White fish may be baked, broiled or poached, avoid highly flavored additions.

Seafood was around long before the advent of trawler nets and lobster pots, though this diet for early "waterfront" man was based on oysters and other molluscs.

It wasn't because he had million-dollar tastes; he had no implements to catch anything else from the sea.

For much the same reason, the first settlers in Virginia and Plymouth sought the rich nutrients of oysters.

One settler wrote "we fed upon nothing but oysters for eight weeks space, having no other allowance at all."

The Pilgrim fathers at Plymouth were astonished at the quantity and quality of lobsters and crabs found on the beach.

With a little tuition from the Indians, the settlers also discovered the delights of clams and how to bake them. Shellfish, once the cheapest food, and consequently the main diet for many people, is, these days, quite the reverse.

Oysters

Oysters are a marine bivalve mollusc, which has been eaten by man since very early times. Their delightful flavor and texture give oysters great gastronomic merit. Natural oyster beds cannot provide the quantity needed to satisfy the demand of today; oyster farming has ensured a supply of quantity and quality. Oysters are gathered from special beds where they have been carefully cultivated. Oysters are most popular served au natural, or in oyster or seafood cocktails. The large American oysters do not have the delicate flavor of the smaller varieties. They are often cut up and cooked. Many internationally acclaimed recipes for oysters were created by American chefs, such as Oysters Kilpatrick, Oysters Rockefeller.

Mussels

Mussels are edible molluscs found in all oceans. They enjoy great popularity and are sometimes referred to as "the oysters of the poor". It is important to be sure that the mussels you buy are absolutely fresh, or if you gather them yourself they are gathered from unpolluted waters. Fresh mussels have tightly closed shells, if some are open, lightly tap the shell with your fingers; if they close they are safe, it shows the mussel is still alive. Discard any that remain open.

Scrub each shell with a brush and cut off the beard or tufts, which protrude from the closed shell then rinse well under running water. Cook mussels until shell opens. They may be served in their shell, or the meat removed and included in other dishes.

CRUSTACEANS

Crabs

Are a crustacean found off the Atlantic and Pacific coasts. If fresh raw crab is bought it should be alive and active. It must be killed just before cooking, through its nerve center. Insert a sharp pointed knife or skewer at several angles just above the mouth; the crab should die very quickly. Crabs may be boiled, baked or steamed. When cooked the meat is removed from the shell and may be eaten as is with a dressing, included in other dishes or mixed with a sauce. It may be placed back into the shell to serve.

Canned crabmeat is always available, remember to pick over the meat to remove any pieces of shell or sinew.

Crawfish

Is a large crustacean also known as the spiny lobster. It is like the lobster but has whip-like antennae instead of the large claws. The meat is very much like lobster, although not quite as delicious, and is prepared and used in the same way.

When selecting any of the crustaceans at the market, go for the medium sized. This will give you a better ratio of meat to shell and value for money. If bought live choose one which is heavy in relation to size, this shows that they are not long out of the sea. Crawfish tails are sold fresh and frozen and are a good buy for there is little to discard.

Lobster

The lobster is a large salt water crustacean found only in the Northern Hemisphere.

Fresh raw lobster must be alive and active when bought and must be killed just before cooking. Stabbing the lobster through the nerve center just behind the head is one way. Another way is to place it in a large pot of cold water and bring it gently to the boil. When the water reaches 70°F the lobster faints and dies almost immediately showing no discomfort. The cold water method produces a more tender lobster.

If the lobster is to be broiled it must be killed by the stabbing method, then cut in half down the center, brushed with melted butter or oil and place under the broiler or on the barbecue.

Clams

Clams are a shellfish which live in wet sand and can be gathered at low tide. They are found on the Atlantic coast in the northern states. New England is famous for its large clams. Autumn is the best season for clams, although they are found all year round. Fresh clams are tightly closed or will close when touched. Discard any that float or have broken shells. Soak clams in salted water for 30 minutes then rinse again to rid them of sand.
East Coast clams have a soft shell and are best for eating raw or lightly steamed. The West Coast clams have a hard shell, are smaller and have a more succulent flavor.
Clams may be added to stews, served with various sauces, made into soup or the famous chowders. Clam bakes are a traditional American feast.

Cockles, Winkles and Whelks

Cockles are small molluscs found mainly in estuaries. They are at their best in winter. Cockles are boiled and eaten with vinegar. They also make excellent soup. Winkles are small, round black shells which are inhabited by a sea snail. They are also called periwinkle. Winkles are boiled in salted water for 10 minutes. The snail is extracted with a pick then served with vinegar or lemon juice, salt and pepper.
Whelks are spiral shelled molluscs similar to the winkle and are cooked and served the same way.

Scallops

Are tasty molluscs, in America they are mainly found on the Northern Atlantic coast. The best scallops come from England and Ireland and many are exported to the United States. The American scallop is smaller and does not have as good a flavor.
Scallops are usually sold already shucked, and are available fresh or frozen. They may be cooked in many ways; lightly poached and served in a white sauce, baked in white wine, dipped in batter and fried, or threaded on skewers and broiled or barbecued. Scallops should only be lightly cooked over moderate heat as they become tough if cooked too long.

CRUSTACEANS

Shrimps

Are small crustaceans which inhabit sandy seabeds. Outside America they are known as prawns. Many varieties are fished from the seas around America, they can differ in size, color, and flavor. The best quality shrimps come from the cold waters of the North Atlantic. The large or even jumbo size from the East Coast are excellent for making shrimp or prawn cutlets, and for broiling. The tiny shrimp from the West Coast are sweet and tender, and are excellent for shrimp salads, cocktails and hors-d'oeuvres. No matter what the size, shrimps are always a popular delicacy on the menu.
Fresh cooked shrimps are always firm and dry. Fresh raw shrimps are firm, glossy and have no unpleasant odor. Remember that 1 lb of shrimps in the shells yield ½ lb or 1 cup of shelled shrimps.

Crayfish

Is a freshwater crustacean found in the rivers and lakes of Europe and America. The species found in the U.S.A. is slightly different to the European species, being much smaller. The flesh is firm and delicately flavored and it is better to serve them as simply as possible to maintain that delicacy. Barbecued or boiled and served with a dressing are perhaps the best methods. Live crayfish should be cooked as soon as possible after catching.

Scampi

Scampi is a crustacean which is a miniature member of the lobster family. It looks like a lobster but is the size of a large shrimp. The body covering is stronger than the shrimp and more difficult to remove than the prawn. They are almost transparent when raw and turn pink when cooked. It is the scampi tails that are eaten, there is no meat in the upper part of the body. The scampi meat is unbeatable for flavor. Scampi tails may be bought frozen. Few fresh scampi are available in our markets as they are fished in Atlantic waters.

VEGETABLES

Food would be dull indeed without the color, taste and texture of vegetables; neither would we be so healthy, as vegetables are a powerful source of essential nutrients and fibre.

Initially, the choice of vegetables in the evolving civilized world was confined to what grew naturally in an area. Then traders started carrying different vegetables to new locales where they were not known. These were planted to widen the scope of available vegetables in the area. The turn of this century saw big strides forward in vegetable cultivation to achieve greater yields and better resistance to plant disease, insects and climates via hybrid species. Much of it was the work of Gregor Mendel, an Augustinian monk who in the 1860's carried out experiments in plant crossing. Sadly, his notations were largely ignored until 1900 when horticulturalists, realizing the benefits, carried on his work, resulting in the wide choice of vegetable species we know today.

Carrots

Are one of the very early vegetables used, which originated in South West Asia and entered the Mediterranean area in ancient times. It is used in soups, stews and casseroles. It can become a more exciting vegetable when cooked with herbs, spices, dried fruits, fruit juices or with honey or brown sugar glaze. Grated raw carrot is a popular addition to salads.
Carrots are extensively used for processing and made into carrot juice. They are valued for their high Vitamin A content.

Turnip

One of the first vegetables to be transplanted and cultivated from its wild form. It originated in South West Asia and was a staple food of ancient civilizations. Its mild sweetish flavor combines well with potato to make a purée or soup, and it gives a delicate flavor to stews and casseroles. Roast turnips are an alternative to potatoes and boiled turnips make an interesting substitute for potato salad. Turnips are a good source of potassium and a fair source of Vitamin C and calcium.

Artichokes

Grew wild around the Mediterranean area in ancient times. They only enjoyed a short period of popularity by the Roman nobility, the common folk would not touch them. With the fall of Rome they became a forgotten vegetable until rediscovered by Florentine cooks in the 14th century who created dishes using them. Artichokes are a vegetable loved by a few who know them, yet unknown to many. Better known and used are the canned artichoke hearts which can be used in salads and many other dishes.

Watercress

Originated in Western Asia and Southern Europe and has been enjoyed in the same form since ancient times to the present day. The plant has a long stem with small sprigs of green leaves. The sprigs are plucked from the main stem and used in salads, chopped to color and flavor dressings, sauces and mayonnaise. It has a fine peppery flavor which enhances the foods with which it is combined. It may be lightly boiled and served as a green vegetable or used in soups. Watercress is a good source of Vitamin C and calcium.

Broccoli

Originated in Italy and has been enjoyed for thousands of years. In its original form broccoli had large branching leaves with no clearly defined main head. It is a vegetable which is very popular today. Lightly poached, steamed or stir-fried are the best ways of cooking broccoli, combined with an oil and lemon dressing, creamed horseradish and mayonnaise, or cheese sauce. It is also blanched and served in salads. Broccoli is the most nutritious of vegetables with a high Vitamin A, C and B content and high in protein, calcium and iron.

Brussels Sprouts

Brussels sprouts are a relative newcomer to the vegetable world. They originated in the 13th century in Belgium, the result of development by Belgium horticulturists from the cabbage, one of the oldest known vegetable plants. Brussels sprouts should be lightly cooked as overcooking produces a strong aroma. Add a piece of celery to the cooking pot to reduce the strong aroma. Brussels sprouts are a very nutritious vegetable, being high in Vitamins A, C, B1 and mineral content.

VEGETABLES

Cucumbers

It was known to grow in India about 3,000 years ago, and was also enjoyed in ancient Egypt, Greece and Rome. In the 15th century, Columbus planted them in Haiti. There are many species which include the green cucumber, the small Lebanese or the long Italian, the white apple cucumber and the prickly skinned Gherkin cucumber which is used for pickling. They are mainly used raw as a salad vegetable and are included in cold soups and dips. Cucumbers are a fair source of potassium and calcium.

Lettuce

Lettuce first appeared about 550 B.C. where it was eaten as a cooked vegetable in Egypt and Persia. The most popular species is the cabbage lettuce of which there are many varieties, the difference between them being the season of cultivation and the method; open ground or under glass. The best known is the Iceberg lettuce which was developed in the United States in 1930s, The Cos or Romaine is an oval shape and has a mild sweet flavor and may be eaten cooked or raw. Lettuce is a good source of most minerals and vitamins.

Fennel

Originated in the Mediterranean area. The base of the stem is the edible portion and the leaves are used as a herb. Fennel has a mild aniseed flavor and a crunchy texture which is delightful when added raw to salads. It is a popular vegetable in French and Italian cooking, such as provincial type dishes. Fennel may be steamed and served with a cheese sauce, braised with tomatoes, onions and garlic, and added to meat casseroles. Fennel is a fair source of calcium and iron.

Asparagus

Asparagus has always been classed as an elite vegetable. The nobility of ancient Rome considered it a delicacy. The asparagus we have today was the milder flavored plant from Eastern Europe. Varieties include the green asparagus with a thick or thin stem, white, and violet green asparagus. Fresh asparagus are best when lightly poached or steamed and served with a hollandaise sauce or vinaigrette dressing. The green asparagus is a good source of Vitamins A and C and many minerals.

Spinach

Originated in the Caucasus and Persia and by the 7th century was established in China, later it appeared in Europe. Spinach is not to be confused with Swiss chard which has a wide white stem. Spinach has a delicate flavor and can be included in many dishes. It is cooked with just the water that clings to its leaves after washing, in a covered pan until it is just wilted. Spinach may be served raw in a salad. Dill and nutmeg both enhance the flavor of spinach. It is an excellent source of Vitamins A and C.

Beetroot

Is a relatively new plant, developed around the Mediterranean about the 15th century, from a wild species that grew close to the sea. In the 18th century the sugar beet was developed from the beetroot. Cook beetroots, drain and cool a little, then slip the skin off with the hand. They may also be peeled then grated or slivered and sautéed in hot butter. The beetroot tops are an excellent vegetable, cook as for spinach. Beetroot is a good source of Vitamin C and potassium, and the leaves are high in Vitamin A.

Aubergine

Known also as eggplant as some varieties are egg shaped. It is indigenous to tropical Asia and from the 5th century BC was recorded as being used in China. It came into the Mediterranean area via the Arab world and later into Europe. It may be fried, baked, grilled or added to stews and casseroles. Eggplant needs to be well cooked before it releases its delightful flavor, crisp eggplant has no flavor. Before frying sliced eggplant, soak in salted water for 20 minutes and pat dry. This prevents it soaking up a lot of oil during frying.

Okra

Originated in Northeast Africa and crossed the Red Sea into Arabia. It became a favourite food of the Arabs who took it to the Meiterranean and North Africa. It was grown in the Ivory Coast and featured in the ritual foods of the local religion. The slaves brought it to America and now features prominently in Cajun cooking. For best results wash okra, peel around the conical top, then sprinkle with vinegar and spread in the sun for 30 minutes. Cook as desired. This treatment prevents a gelatinous substance from developing during cooking.

NEW WORLD VEGETABLES

There was something missing from the world's food table right up to the 16th century — individuality.

Culinary skills had improved during the Renaissance but essentially they were no more than a mix of well tried ideas and ingredients.

All that changed with the discovery of the Americas and all the new foods found there. Out of the Americas came the Italian tomato sauces to top the pizza or serve with pasta.

The French developed French fries and pomme parisienne and the Swiss, their rosti. Austrians created the chocolate coated gateau, the Germans developed potato salad and dumplings; curries of India were hotted up with chili as were the satays of Asia, and Africa found tuberous roots of the cassava, a saviour for their peoples. In Sweden the people were tempted by Janson's newly discovered "temptation".

Virtually every nation adopted something from the new world and made it their own which, if nothing else, gave the world's food tables the individuality they needed.

Potato

When the potato was first sighted in Peru, none realized the impact it was to have in the daily diet of much of the population of the world. This did not happen immediately, for although first grown in Spain about 1555 and England about 1584, it was not until the early 1700s that it began to be established as a food. For the next 60 years it fought many suspicions and fears as to its suitability as a food. By the end of the century it became firmly established as a staple food in the cuisines of many nations. It is interesting to note that North America received the potato via England when English colonists took it to Virginia. The versatility of the potato cannot be matched by any other vegetable. Many are the ways it may be prepared, countless are the recipes it is included in, and just as prolific are the varieties of potatoes which have been developed to suit most climates, seasons and soil conditions. Our most popular varieties are the Katahdins and the Idaho or Burbanks.

Beans

Are native to Mexico and Guatemala and have become a favorite vegetable of many lands. They are called by many names, but they are all cultivated varieties of the same species. These include snap, string, french and butter beans, which are yellow in color. We now have the stringless bean.

Beans are mostly served as an accompaniment to main meals, they may be included in many vegetarian dishes where they provide necessary protein. Beans are a fair source of vegetable protein and a good source of Vitamins A and C.

Zucchini

Zucchini is one of the numerous varieties which developed from the squash which is native to Central and South America, and was growing in North America long before colonization. Easy cross-pollenization accounts for the numerous shapes, sizes and colors of the squash. The zucchini is classed as a summer squash as it has a tender skin and does not need to be peeled. It has a mild flavor and is suitable for inclusion in many cooked dishes as well as being eaten raw in salads.

Zucchini is a fair source of vitamins and minerals and is low in calories.

Pumpkin

Is also a member of the squash family. It is classified as winter squash and has a hard skin which is usually peeled. It may be cooked with the skin on as the skin softens on cooking. The large pumpkin has a more developed flavor than the young squash. It may be boiled or baked and made into soup. It was one of the new foods introduced by the friendly Indians to the first settlers. One must not forget the traditional pumpkin pie made with this vegetable. Pumpkin is an excellent source of Vitamin A and has a fair mineral content.

Peppers

Belong to the genus "Capsicum" from tropical South America. When they became known in Europe after the voyages of Columbus, the flavor of cuisines changed. In America peppers are known as sweet, green globe or bell peppers. They all refer to a variety of the same vegetable which may be green, red or yellow, and bell or long in shape.

They have a sweet peppery flavor and are cooked in meat and vegetable dishes or eaten raw in salads. Peppers have a high Vitamin C content.

Sweet Potato

Although found in Central America at the time of Columbus, the exact origin of the Sweet Potato is not known. It was introduced into Spain and later, England and Asia. Sweet potatoes have their own delicious flavor; simply boiled or roasted is enough. They are an excellent accompaniment to lamb, pork, ham and turkey. They may be made into a soup or mashed and formed into patties with a crumb coating and fried. Sweet potatoes are a high source of Vitamin A and potassium.

Tomato

For over 100 years after its introduction into Europe the tomato was grown only as an ornamental plant. Records show that around 1750 it entered the cooking pot and by 1800 Sicily sent the first crop of tomatoes to markets in Naples and Rome. Serious cultivation of the tomato began at the beginning of the 20th century. Tomatoes are grown throughout the year, but the summer tomatoes are the most flavorsome. They are also an excellent source of Vitamin C.

Sweet Corn

Corn, or maize, originated in Central America and Mexico. The variety known as Sweet Corn and used as a fresh vegetable is different from the corn or maize which is ground into flour or made into cornflakes. The best way to eat sweet corn is lightly boiled, broiled or barbecued on the cob. For convenience, corn kernels off the cob are available tinned or frozen. Puréed kernels make tasty sauces to serve over other vegetables. Sweet Corn contains many vitamins, minerals and some protein and is highly valued for its fibre content.

Avocado

Originated in tropical Central and South America. It was planted in other tropical areas in Asia, and in Spain. It was not until the beginning of the 1900s that serious cultivation began in America and the West Indies. There are hundreds of cultivated varieties of avocados. Avocado is served with a vinegar or lemon dressing, it goes well with all seafood, chicken and veal. It is sometimes included in sweet dishes. Avocados are high in monosaturated fats, and a good source of Vitamins A and C.

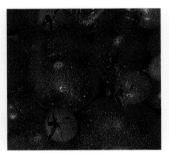

Chili

Chili also belongs to the genus "Capsicum"; it is a smaller and hotter variety having a greater amount of capsaicin, the ingredient which gives it a hot burning taste. It traveled to many places, but it was in India and Asia that it had the greatest impact. Chili may be bought fresh or dried and ground into a powder. If using fresh chili, remember to wash your hands well immediately after handling as the volatile capsaicin which remains on the fingers can burn eyes and mouth if touched.

Cassava

Is a tuber or root vegetable found in South America. It was taken to Spain in the 16th century and from there to Africa and Asia. It became a staple food of the African people and is also used extensively in Asia. It is a vegetable rich in starch from which tapioca is made. Tapioca is used to thicken soups and to thicken milk puddings. Cassava is high in protein and calcium.

Choyote

Is a native of Mexico and Central America. It is a member of the squash family. It is also called choko, Mirliton or just vegetable pear. It is a bland vegetable that may be cooked with more flavorsome ingredients to give extra flavor. Boiled or steamed and served with a cheese sauce, it makes a tasty entrée or side dish. It may be added to stews and casseroles or baked with other vegetables. Choyote contains Vitamins A and C and has a fair mineral content.

Jerusalem Artichoke

Is an irregular shaped tuber which is native to North America. It was taken to France in 1607 and from there into Holland and England. There are many theories on how it received its name, artichokes because it resembles the flavor of globe artichokes, but Jerusalem — it still remains a mystery. It has a delicate sweetish flavor and is an excellent addition to stews and casseroles. It may be boiled with the skin on if the tuber is young. It contains a fair quantity of vitamins and minerals and has a mild laxative effect.

HERBS

Herbs are a gift from nature that transform our food into culinary delights. These plants have volatile oils which are released into the foods imparting their particular aroma to the food.

They have been used throughout history for medicinal and culinary purposes. The first formal herb gardens were planted by monks in their monasteries and the nobility in their castle grounds.

Herbs must be used carefully to achieve subtle results. Delicately flavored herbs should be added towards the end of cooking time, just long enough to release the oils, for, if added too soon, the flavor will be lost.

Herbs should enhance the flavor of the main ingredient and not overpower it, therefore take care with the quantity of herbs used; more may be added later if desired flavor is not achieved.

Fresh herbs may be stored up to a week in the refrigerator. Place them stem down in a tall enough jar with one inch of water in the bottom. Cover with a lid or plastic wrap. They must be kept covered as the cold air dehydrates the leaves and they wilt.

Basil

A delightful herb to use in salads, egg dishes and particularly with tomatoes which suit its spicy aroma. They darken quickly after cutting so, if adding to a tomato salad, use the small whole leaves and do not chop them. Basil may be used dried in cooking, the fresh is only used in salads. Basil is said to aid digestion and many make a tea with the leaves. Basil is often referred to as the kingly herb.

Bay Leaf

An essential ingredient in a "bouquet garni." It has a robust flavor, one leaf is enough to flavor a stew or casserole. It should be added at the beginning of cooking time and simmered with the food. Bay leaf is used to flavor stocks, soups, stews, casseroles, and savory mince. It may be added to marinades. The bay leaf may be used fresh, if you have your own tree, but is mostly used in the dry form. To dry bay leaves, hang a branch in a cool place in a draught. When leaves have turned grey-brown, strip the branch and store. Bay leaf, or laurel, is the herb of victor

Purslane

Is a fast-growing succulent which grows in moist, warm climates. There are two species, the summer and winter purslane. It has small, thick leaves on a thick, fleshy stem. Both the leaves and stem are used. Purslane has an almost acidic flavor which gives a delightful tangy taste to any salads it is included in. Try adding it to marinated mushroom salad or tomato and cucumber, as well as a green salad. It may be chopped finely and added to cream cheese, to give a different taste to mayonnaise or to lift the flavor of mashed potato.

Mint

There are many varieties of mint, the most commonly used variety is the spearmint. Mint has a cool and refreshing taste and so is often added to fruit cups and long drinks. It is used to flavor meat dishes and various egg and vegetable dishes. In fact, if you like mint you will use it anywhere. Mint has been in use since ancient times. It was used to make mint tea and the ancient Greeks considered it "a cooler of the blood and refreshment for the brain."

Dill

Is a very popular herb. It has a distinctive somewhat pungent flavor that goes well with lettuce salads and spinach dishes. Added to yoghurt or sour cream it makes a fine flavored dressing for potato salads, cucumber dishes and fish dishes. Its fine, feathery leaves are great for garnishing. It is best to snip the leaves with scissors instead of chopping with a knife.

Sorrel

Is a herb with a sharp tangy flavor. It is used mainly to flavor sauces and soups. It may be puréed and added to mayonnaise and sour cream to make sorrel dressing for potato or pasta salads. The sorrel purée may be added to cream cheese to make a dip. To make the purée, cook the sorrel leaves as you would spinach, then process in a blender or pass through a sieve.

Borage

Has a mild peppery flavor and is mainly used very finely chopped in green salads. Traditionally, it was used to spice fruit punches or wine cups. Older leaves can be used chopped in stocks and soups. Borage is said to have originated in the Middle East. It has built a reputation as being able to "make men and women merry and glad", perhaps through its association with the wine cups. The Welsh name for borage is 'Llanwellys' which means "herb of happiness."

Chervil

Chervil has a fine delicate leaf which should not be cooked for more than 10 minutes otherwise the fine flavor will be lost. It is used to flavor fine delicate sauces but mostly used chopped and sprinkled over vegetables, fish or poultry. It is one of the famous "fines herbes" used in French cooking. The Greek origin of its name 'chairephyllon' makes it the herb of joy.

Rosemary

Rosemary has a fresh resinous flavor although quite strong and pungent. It combines well in dishes that include garlic. It is suited to lamb, beef and pork dishes and a little added to vegetable casseroles imparts a fine flavor. It can be made into a tea and is helpful in treating nervous headaches, and it is said to stimulate the memory. This is how it came to be known as the herb of remembrance.

Marjoram

Its sweet subtle aroma makes it an essential component of many dried herb mixes, but it is a herb best enjoyed when used fresh. It is a herb which suits most meat and poultry dishes egg and cheese dishes, and is used in sausage making. Mythology tells us that the herb acquired its sweet fragrance when Aphrodite touched it. Perhaps that is why Shakespeare referred to it as the herb of grace.

HERBS

Savory

A herb with a distinctive flavor very popular in sausage-making and for meat stuffings. It is most often used to flavor bean or pulse dishes for it is said to have a two-fold effect: it gives flavor, and aids the digestion. It can be obtained fresh or dried; its flavor is far superior when used fresh. Savory is suitable for all meat and vegetables.

Sage

Sage was first used as a medicinal herb, and was often added to rich foods to aid with digestion.
It has a strong flavor and only a small amount should be used. It is an ingredient in the dried herb mix.
Sage originated around the Mediterranean and was popular for making sage tea, as it still is today. Pour one cup of boiling water over one teaspoon dried sage, cover and steep for a few minutes then strain and serve with honey. It soothes the nerves and induces sleep.

Thyme

There are several varieties, but garden and lemon thyme are the most popular culinary herbs.
Garden thyme has a savory, pungent flavor which is suited for use with strong dishes such as soups, stews, casseroles, meat pies and hamburgers.
Lemon thyme is a milder flavour and is suitable for use with chicken, fish, omelettes and light vegetables.
Thyme may be used fresh or dried, but remember to use far less of the dried herb as the flavor is more concentrated in this form.

Tarragon

Tarragon has a tart flavor, yet spicy aroma. It is one of the most sought-after culinary herbs. Tarragon is well suited to flavor fish and shellfish, and the fresh leaves make a suitable garnish. Tarragon is an excellent herb to use with chicken, turkey and veal. It is essential in the flavoring of classic French sauces such as Béarnaise and is often seen steeped in bottles of vinegar. You may make your own tarragon vinegar by immersing tarragon sprigs in a bottle of vinegar.

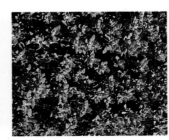

SPICES

There is a certain wicked charm surrounding spices that goes back to ancient times. What spices there were in Europe were brought by Arabs along the trade routes from India and Asia, and they were expensive.

By the middle of the first century AD, the Romans were able to sail new and larger vessels through the Red Sea to bring spices back from India. This trade with the Orient was later supported by the opening of the Silk Road, along which the Romans ferried back ginger, 'cassia' (cinnamon) and other goods from China.

The Byzantines, and later the Venetians, prospered by continuing the trade following the fall of Rome.

As both the Portuguese and the Dutch were sailing around Africa to get to India for these lucrative products, the Spanish commissioned Columbus to find a shorter route. In the course of it, Columbus found something even greater than spices — the Americas. Nevertheless, what would an apple pie be without cloves in it?

Cloves

Are the best known of all the spices, they are the flower buds of a tree belonging to the myrtle family and are pink when picked. The best cloves come from Madagascar and Zanzibar.

Cloves are pungent and aromatic and are used to flavor both sweet and savory dishes; stewed fruits, pot roasts, marmalades, chutney and pickles to name a few. Only a small pinch of ground clove or two or three whole cloves are necessary.

Cinnamon

Is the bark of a small evergreen tree which belongs to the laurel family. It grows in Ceylon and South India. Paper thin strips of the bark are peeled off and rolled into a light quill or stick and left to dry. It is then cut into cinnamon sticks or ground into powdered cinnamon. A piece of cinnamon stick may be added during cooking to meat stews, mince, curries, milk custards and stewed fruits, then removed before serving. Powdered cinnamon may be added to cakes, biscuits and pastries and sprinkled over milk puddings and toast.

Mustard

Is the seed of the mustard plant and is native to England, Europe and parts of Asia. Mustard is sold in many forms. Black or white mustard seeds can be sprinkled over salads and cooked vegetables. Mustard powder can be added to mayonnaise, white sauce, stuffed egg, dips or salad dressings. Ground mustard is added to curries and other dishes. Jars of mustard paste can be used for serving with cold meats. These include the English mustard, which is very hot, French mustard which is mild and very flavorsome and German mustard which has a strong, hot flavor.

Cumin

Is the tiny, aromatic fruit of a herb-like plant. The fruit is so small it is usually referred to as a seed. It is indigenous to Egypt but from early times has been cultivated in the Middle East and India. It is used extensively in Middle Eastern dishes and in Asian cuisine. It is an important ingredient in curry powder blends and garam masala. It is used to flavor beef and lamb stews, meat balls and kebabs. Cumin is sold in either whole seed form or ground.

Turmeric

Turmeric is a member of the ginger family, native to parts of Asia. The root is dried and ground to a powder which has a warm, slightly bitter taste, and a yellow color. It is used in curry blends and gives that warm golden color to curry dishes. It is also used to color and flavor rice, devilled eggs and mayonnaise. It is added to mustard powder for flavor and color, and is an ingredient in pickles.

Paprika

Is the dried condiment made from the sweet red pepper. The original variety of pepper came from Central America. It was taken by the Turks into Hungary. There they developed a variety of red pepper with a sweet, smoky flavor and called it Paprika. It features prominently in the Hungarian cuisine, flavoring and coloring their famous national dishes, Goulash and Paprika Chicken. It is used for its color and flavor in many other dishes. Today, it is much in demand by microwave cooks to color food which does not brown in the microwave oven.

SPICES

Nutmeg

Is the kernel of the plum-like fruit of the Myristica fragrance tree which grows mainly in Indonesia and Malaya. The outer part of the kernel is ground into a spice called Mace which is milder in flavor. The inner kernel is the nutmeg, which is sold whole or ground. It is better to buy the whole nutmeg and to grate it on a fine grater when needed. Grated nutmeg is used to flavor milk puddings, eggnog, spinach, asparagus and meat dishes.

Vanilla

Is the long, black bean pod from a climbing tropical orchid, Vanilla Planifolia. It originally came from Central America. The pods are picked before they are completely ripe, plunged into boiling water then before they dry are shut in tins where their aroma develops.
Vanilla pod is sold in a sealed file. It can be added to milk or fruit while cooking, then removed and put away for re-use. If a pod is closed in a container with sugar, the sugar will be impregnated with the vanilla flavor. Vanilla essence is an extract from the vanilla pod.

Cardamom

Is the seed of a plant which belongs to the ginger family; it is native to India. The seeds are enclosed in a small pod the size of a pistachio nut. The pod may be infused in milk to give a delightful flavor to custards. It is usually pulverized, with the small seeds enclosed, to a powder and used to flavor curries, meat and vegetable dishes. Cardamom is also used in fruit cookery, as it gives a delectable flavor. The Arabs add a little ground cardamom to their finely ground coffee before brewing.

Ginger

Ginger has been an essential ingredient in Indian and Asian foods since the earliest times. It is the root of a reed-like plant. It has a peppery piquant flavor and is used to flavor meat, chicken and vegetable dishes. Green fresh ginger is grated or thinly sliced and cooked in with the foods. Root ginger is the sun-dried root which is ground into a powder. It is used in cakes and biscuits and goes well sprinkled on to pumpkin, carrots and sweet potato. Ginger is sold preserved in syrup and crystalized. Chocolate-coated ginger is a real delicacy.

Pepper

Pepper is the universal spice and one of the first ever to be used and traded. The Arabs traded pepper from India to the ancient world. Later, the Romans built ships to sail from the Red Sea to India to bring back the precious spice, which was becoming scarce. By the middle of the first century AD, Indian merchants, depleted of spices, had to look to South East Asia for supplies.
Pepper is the fruit of the Piperaceae plant. Black pepper comes from the unripe berries which are dried with the outer skin intact. White pepper is from the ripe berries with the outer skin removed.

Saffron

Comes from the stigmas of the flowers of the Saffron Crocus. About 80,000 flowers are required to make 1 lb of saffron and the stigmas must be plucked by hand from each flower, then dried. It is understandable why true saffron is the most expensive spice. It originated in Corycus, in present day Turkey, and spread to Persia and China, then westward into Europe. Saffron was highly prized in ancient times. It imparts a delicate flavor and a pale, golden color to foods. It is the traditional spice in bouillabaisse, paella and Cornish saffron cakes.

Allspice

The dried berry of a tree native to Central America and the West Indies, sometimes called Jamaica pepper tree. The berries are ground to a powder which gives an aroma resembling a mixture of cloves, nutmeg and cinnamon. That is the reason it was given the name allspice when discovered in the 16th century. It is not to be confused with mixed spice. Actually the flavors of the two do differ; allspice has a more peppery flavor. It is used in many meat and mincemeat dishes, egg, fish, cheese and vegetable dishes, and a little in fruit cakes.

Juniper Berries

Are the berries of the Juniper shrub which grows wild in Europe and England. Juniper berries are used to flavor gin. They are also used in marinades, and to flavor venison and game birds and are often used in bean dishes. The berries are dried and used whole, not ground, and are added during long, slow cooking. Six berries simmered in a stew give a flavoring equivalent to 1/4 cup of gin.

FRUITS

Expressions like "the apple of her eye" and "an apple a day keeps the doctor away" are pointers to the inherent goodness of fruit.

All fruit is subject to change through cross-breeding as science searches to create bigger, better or hardier varieties. This is not new, however, as cross-breeding fruit has been practised since the Middle Ages.

The attraction of cross-breeding is in the improvement of the appearance, texture and taste of different fruits plus more bountiful and hardier crops, with better handling and storage characteristics.

So far nobody has been able to produce a skinless or ready peeled grape, though seedless grapes are now common. Yet strange things have happened in the search for new growing techniques.

For example, one grower produced square tomatoes to make "ideal" sandwiches. Square tomatoes proved impossible to handle or transport. Back to the growing board.

One result of cross-breeding developments is that many original species of fruit have now vanished.

We have listed some of the less familiar fruits — some old and some new.

Gooseberry

There are two varieties, one is indigenous to Western and Central Europe and the other, called Cape Gooseberry, comes from Peru. The latter is enclosed in a paper-like lantern which peels off to expose the berry.

Both varieties are similar in taste. They have a sweet tart taste and may be eaten fresh or stewed. Because of their tartness they are used to accompany rich dishes such as goose, venison and tongue. Gooseberries are available canned in syrup and are also made into jam.

Lychees

Are a small, round fruit with a pinkish, hard skin which is brittle and therefore easy to remove. They have a sweet, delicately perfumed flavor. Lychees originated in China and are now grown in other hot climates. Few are grown in the U.S.A.; those in the market place are imported. They are, however, available canned in syrup. Lychees give a wonderful fragrance to fruit salads and fruit cocktails and can be added to main-course salads. Stuffed with a cream-cheese mixture they make interesting hors d'oeuvres.

Kiwi Fruit

Is native to China and Japan, and is also called Chinese gooseberry. In 1906 it was taken by a missionary to New Zealand and was renamed kiwi fruit. Various commercially viable varieties of the kiwi fruit were developed and by 1960 they became a sought-after fruit around the world. California is the main production area in the U.S.A. Kiwi fruit has a sweet, tangy flavor. They may be eaten as is, or cut and added to fruit salads. They are excellent for cheeseboards and for accompanying and garnishing meats and seafood.

Strawberries

Wild strawberries of many varieties have always grown on the European and American continents. Repeated attempts to cross wild strawberry varieties to produce a larger and more sturdy fruit were for a long time unsuccessful. It was by chance that strawberry plants from Virginia and from Chile were placed in the same strawberry patch in Brittany, France. The plants were successfully crossed.

From this new variety many more varieties have been developed. Their uses are many, including jams, cold and hot desserts, ice creams, drinks and salads.

Date

Date is the fruit of a variety of palm tree, grown in the Middle East as early as 3,000 BC. It is now grown in many other places, including California and Arizona. The date has always been an important source of food for the people of North Africa and the Middle East. Dried dates are exported all around the world from these areas. Fresh dates from California are now readily available. They are large, juicy and sweet and are considered a delicacy. They are delightful eaten as is, tossed into vegetable salads or served with a cheeseboard.

Pawpaw

The pawpaw was first seen growing in tropical America although it is not known if it originated there. It was taken to the tropical areas of Asia where it thrived.

Ripe pawpaw has a sweet taste with a slightly musky aroma. It may be eaten peeled and sliced, included in fruit salads and is refreshing when sliced or diced and set in orange jello.

The pawpaw is also known by the name papaya.

FRUITS

Persimmon
A delightful fruit, not very well known, which originated in China and Japan. They are now grown in many sub-tropical areas. Their sweet, fragrant flavor only develops when the fruit is completely ripe or over-ripe. Before this stage it is unsuitable for eating because of the high tannin content, which disappears on ripening. The fruit is sold when unripe and has to ripen before eating. This may be hastened by putting it in a paper bag with a ripe pear, banana or apple. The persimmon has a soft, pulpy flesh and is eaten by spooning out the pulp.

Fig
The fig is native to the Eastern Mediterranean area. Since biblical times it has featured as an important food. There are many varieties of figs, some have green skin with either pink or white centers and some purple skin with a deeper pink center. The fig has a sweet, fragrant taste and is best eaten chilled. It is an edible garnish for platters of ham, salami and smoked turkey; a single serve of the same makes an interesting starter. Figs were first introduced into California and now grow extensively in the warmer states of the U.S.A.

Mango
Today the mango is a highly prized fruit. Its delicate flavor has made it an extremely popular fruit. It is indigenous to East India and Malaysia. It was first introduced into Africa in the 10th century. The Portuguese introduced it into Southern Africa and Brazil around 1700 and it was later grown in the West Indies. Florida plantings date from 1825. Many varieties have been developed, the stringless variety is now the most popular.
It is popular in mango mousse, mango ice cream and yoghurt. The poorer quality fruit may be used to make mango chutney.

Guava
The guava is a fruit indigenous to tropical America. It is now grown in the Southern U.S.A. and South East Asia. The many varieties include white, pink or deep red fleshed fruit with a green or yellow skin.
It is a sweet, fragrant fruit and must be fully ripe for the best flavor. It is used as is or cut and added to fruit salads and platters, made into mousses or ice cream. Its beautiful and unusual color is very effective when used as a garnish.

Mangosteen
It is a rare fruit grown in a few select places. It is indigenous to Malaysia and is grown throughout South East Asia. It is now being cultivated in Central America and Brazil, but only in limited areas where climate and soil conditions are suitable. It is imported from these areas to the U.S.A. markets.
The flavor of the fruit is superb and it has been given the title "queen of fruits". It is a luxury fruit, and its limited supply makes it expensive.

Star Apple
An interesting fruit with an interesting shape. A cross-section slice of the fruit forms a five-pointed star, hence the name. It has a pale, yellow flesh and is sweet and aromatic to taste. The larger fruit are the most delicious. Smaller, less sweet fruit may be simmered with sugar for a compote or sliced and used in sweet and sour dishes.
The star apple is usually sought after for garnishing, as its color and shape make stunning arrangements possible for both sweet and savory dishes.

Loquat
Those who have a loquat tree in the back garden will be familiar with this fruit. Up until now it did not have great commercial possibilities.
The loquat is native to China and Japan and now grows in various sub-tropical areas. Varieties have been developed with better commercial qualities, so they are appearing more regularly in the market place.
It is eaten fresh as is, cut up and added to fruit salads or made into compote or jam.

Melon
It is difficult to identify the various melons as there are a vast number of species and one may be substituted for another in certain recipes Melons are generally divided into four groups: Cantaloupe Melon — which has a segmented or bumpy skin with an orange or greenish flesh; Net Melon — with a light-colored network-marking on the skin and an apricot flesh; Winter Melon — with a smooth, pale green or whitish skin and a green flesh, often called Honeydew Melon; Watermelon — a green skin and a red, crunchy textured flesh.

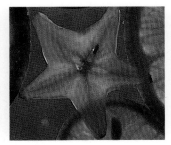

EDIBLE FLOWERS

Flowers almost literally speak for themselves for they constitute the world's only international language able to convey feelings between people irrespective of mother tongue.

Behind the romance of flowers is logic; the unique sensory combination of scent and sight in a single blossom can convey a message more succinctly and more eloquently than any other medium. Ancient Eastern and Western cultures discovered, flowers can also add real magic to food. Only in recent years has the art re-emerged as a culinary fashion through restaurant trends such as the Japanese inspired Nouvelle Cuisine, where edible flowers are used to add a subtle dimension to both flavor and visual appeal of the meal or dish.

Edible flowers are used to flavor sugar, syrups, sweet sauces and liqueurs; they can be simmered in soups and stews or baked into cakes and cookies. Selected flowers can be candied, pickled, frittered, made into jams and jellies or simply eaten raw as an enhancement to salads. The prospects for new creations with edible flowers are endless and limited only by the sensitivity and imagination of the chef.

Use this guide to the edible characteristics of particular flowers to add your own touch of distinction in food preparation.

Rose

The petals from any fragrant, fully grown rose may be used. They may be tossed through salads; steeped in vinegar to give it a fragrance; used as a garnish for cold fruit soups; candied to garnish sweets and frozen into ice-blocks to use in long drinks. They may be infused in milk to make scented milk puddings and used to make rose petal jam. Rose petal punch is made by soaking the petals in water and a little sugar. The liquid is strained off and mixed with champagne or white wine, with a few fresh petals for garnish.

Violets

Crystalized violets on top of a delightful cake or ice-cream, is a familiar sight to many people. Violets tossed into potato and apple salad or a pale green salad are both good to look at and eat. They are also used to make violet scented vinegar and violet butter. Violets may be simmered in a syrup to pour over sweets and fruits and the small petals when added to a strawberry or lemon soufflé give a stunning effect.

Violet sprays are used to garnish elegant entrée dishes and all kinds of cold desserts.

Jasmine

Jasmine has a sweet scented, somewhat overpowering perfume. Its main culinary use is to make Jasmine tea. The flowers are dried and blended with tea leaves.

Jasmine tea should be brewed and served without milk so the delightful flavor can be appreciated. Jasmine flowers are also used in oriental cookery and confectionery.

Jasmine flowers are a beautiful garnish for cakes and sweet pastries.

Carnation

Is one of the ingredients of the formula for the liqueur Chartreuse. It is also steeped in white vinegar, to make a delicately scented dressing.

Carnation petals may be tossed into a variety of salads and fruit salads. They are also simmered with water and sugar to make a syrup.

Zucchini Flower

The zucchini flower is very popular in Mediterranean cuisine. The young zucchini is cut with the flower still attached and gently steamed.

The vivid yellow of the flower and green of the zucchini make an attractive vegetable accompaniment.

Larger flowers are stuffed with a rice or cheese stuffing and cooked in a sauce.

Orange Blossom

Fresh orange blossom was once popular as a decoration for wedding cakes. The small flowers may be tossed over a salad or floated in fruit sauces to serve with desserts. Orange flower water is a popular flavoring in Middle Eastern cuisine. It is used to flavor syrups and milk puddings. Fresh blossoms can be simmered in milk before the milk is strained and used to make various custards.

EDIBLE FLOWERS

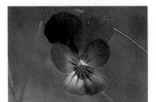

Nasturtium

Is the better known edible flower. The leaves have a mild, peppery flavor which resembles watercress. It is also known as Indian cress, referring to the Peruvian Indians, for it originated in Peru. When brought to Europe by the Spaniards its culinary use was soon discovered. The leaves are used for sandwich fillings and added to tossed salads. The flowers are also added to many salads or used alone as a flower salad, mixed with chopped chervil and an oil and lemon dressing. Nasturtium flowers make a beautiful garnish

Marigold

It is a strongly scented flower and should be used sparingly. It can be used in place of saffron in rice dishes and a few petals tossed into a salad will give a piquant flavor.

A handful of marigold petals can be added to almost any vegetarian dish, cooked or raw, to give color and a slightly nutty flavor.

Marigold petals are also added to custards to give a golden color and a subtle flavor. Dried petals are pulverised and added to soups.

Mimosa

These blossoms which resemble small, yellow puffs may be used to garnish many foods. As they are quite delicate, do not toss into the food, but pluck the blossoms off their stem and scatter over salads, quiches and au gratin dishes. They are useful to garnish microwave dishes which lack the golden color of oven-cooked foods.

Borage

The flower of this herb is used for culinary purposes just as much as the herb. It is a very attractive and unusual flower with brilliant blue petals and prominent black anthers. They are floated on top of many drinks, are excellent to garnish a punchbowl and are scattered over salads just before serving.

They may be brushed with egg white and sprinkled with superfine sugar to garnish swirls of cream on cakes and desserts.

Lavender

May be used to flavor fruit jellies, especially apple jelly. It is used in marinades for venison and other game and also in stews. Only a small amount is used, for the perfume is quite strong. Quince stew, with a small sprig of lavender, has a delightful flavor and scented sugar may be made by placing a sprig of lavender in a jar of sugar for a few days. The sugar can then be used to make cakes and biscuits or to sprinkle over fruit.

Chrysanthemum

Chrysanthemum petals are used in salads and sprinkled over vegetable dishes. Choose any color which will contrast with the vegetable color.

They may also be added to sauces and egg dishes. Small flowers may be used to garnish iced cakes and frozen desserts.

Elder

The strongly aromatic, white Elder flowers are used to make wines and cordials. They are also used to flavor cooked fruits, particularly gooseberries. The dried flowers are made into a tea which has a soothing quality.

Elder flower fritters are made with the heads of elder flowers. They are washed in salted water and dried, then dipped in a batter and deep-fried in hot oil.

Sprinkle with sugar before serving.

Scented Geranium Flowers

Flowers of the scented geranium plant are used as well as the leaves. They give a special flavor to stewed apples and quinces and to apple and quince jelly. The petals of the flowers may be added to the jellies when bottling, giving a decorative effect as well as flavor.

Scented geranium flowers are a different variety of geranium to the usual geranium flowers found in the garden.

GAME

Wild birds, boar, bear, deer or any other animal hunted for food is known as game, though it is difficult to know which came first — the word or the sport. It is hard to believe that in the days when hunting was essential to stay alive, that catching dinner would have been thought of as a game.

Every cloud has a silver lining, they say, and in the dark ages of essential hunting, the good news was that huge forests were rich in game and therefore food supply was plentiful.

As forests became smaller and game grew less populous in direct proportion to the expanding human race, hunting as a general means of survival was simply outmoded.

Thus heralded a new age of game breeding; farms systematically produced the necessary meat and poultry. The "game" aspect of this produce was simply removed, which is why beef and chicken are not game produce.

But you can't keep a good hunter down, even when there's no real need for this. So, in a neat about turn, specialist farms created produce — like duck and pheasant — systematically bred and reared for numbers and then let free for the hunting season.

This, coupled to the limited supply of natural wild game available, plus the various legal protections which surround game stock during breeding seasons, has led to cuisines based on game being thought of as a gourmet food only for those with big enough bank accounts to pay the price.

In reality, game is truly a gourmet food, but no longer because of price. Game farming now makes this desirable produce available all year round and there is no reason why you shouldn't include duck, pheasant and venison on your regular menu list.

Pheasant

Pheasant is a game bird of great reputation. Its distribution is almost world-wide, having spread naturally or artificially from its native area, China. George Washington introduced the pheasant into the U.S.A. in the late 18th century, and it took 100 years through more importation and natural multiplication for their numbers to become significant. They are now farmed commercially for the market.

Pheasant needs to be hung three to 10 days, depending on age, before dressing and cooking. This tenderizes the bird and intensifies the flavor. Birds which are sold frozen have been hung before freezing. If buying fresh, dressed pheasants, check with the supplier as regards to hanging time.

There are many recipes for pheasant. The cooking methods used are usually roasting, braising or pot roasting.

Rabbit

Rabbit would be the most readily available game to both the hunter and the shopper. As they frequent almost all areas from north to south, the hunter can always "bag a rabbit". Nowadays they are bred in hutches for the table and are thus easy to find in the marketplace.

Rabbit has a fine textured and lightly gamey flavored meat. The wild rabbit has a better flavor than the hutch rabbit, while the latter has a whiter and more tender meat.

To joint a rabbit, cut off the legs at the joints, then cut the hind legs in half through the bone. Cut the body crosswise into five or six pieces. Wash well in water with two tablespoons of vinegar added, then rinse and pat dry. Moist heat cooking methods such as braising or casseroling are best suited for rabbit. Marinating tenderizes the rabbit as well as adding flavor.

Partridge

The partridge is slightly smaller than the pheasant and the flavor is more delicate. The true partridge is not native to the United States — the name partridge is given to the ruffed grouse in the north and to the massena quail in the south.

Partridges, like all game birds, benefit from hanging. Young birds need to be hung for three to four days, older birds for six to seven days.

Older birds are best marinated then braised or casseroled. Younger birds may be roasted or slowly broiled. Larding the birds with pork fat or basting with butter during cooking will help to keep them moist and tender.

Venison

Venison is a term used for any antlered animal whether it be moose, elk or deer. The male or buck is more flavorsome than the doe. Venison is available at specialty game shops either fresh or frozen.

Moose meat is a fatty meat and is cooked like pork. Elk and deer resemble beef in texture although they have a richer flavor and a darker colored meat. For roast venison, use the leg, rump shoulder or saddle. These need to be larded before cooking (except moose) as the meat has virtually no fat and will tend to dry if not larded. Pork or ham fat is best to use, bacon fat has too strong a flavor. For best results place the larded joint in a marinade for 12 hours or up to two days. The tender cuts of young venison — steak, chops, loin — may be cooked without marinating. These may be sautéed, pan-fried or braised.

Bear

Bear meat is dark in color, strongly flavored and tougher than other game meat. It is not readily available except in northern states and Alaska. However, game shops could provide frozen cuts if ordered in advance.

Moist heat methods of cooking are needed for bear meat, as the long, slow cooking in moisture will tenderize the meat. For large cuts, cook in a dutch oven, on the hot plate or in the oven. Smaller cuts or pieces may be casseroled, braised or stewed. For best results, marinate the bear meat for at least 24 hours in an oil based marinade before cooking. Add an acidic ingredient such as vinegar, tomato or wine to help tenderize the meat.

GAME

Quail

Quail is the smallest of the game birds. It is a migratory bird and is usually found in great numbers on the eastern shores of the Mediterranean and Red Seas at the end of summer. Quail is now farmed commercially in many countries including the U.S.A. and can be enjoyed all the year round.

Quail should be cooked within 24 hours of killing. Frozen quail is available and must be defrosted in the refrigerator. As the birds are small, this does not take very long.

Quails are succulent and tender and full of flavor. They may be broiled, roasted or skewered and placed over hot coals. Baste frequently during cooking and take care not to overcook. They may be served in exotic sauces using cream wine and tart fruit such as grapes and gooseberries. Allow two quails per person for a main course serve. Quail eggs are also available. They are considered a delicacy and may be served in many interesting ways.

Wild Duck

Wild duck can be obtained by going out and shooting your own. Excess catches are usually traded around the areas where they are hunted. The flavor of wild duck depends on their feeding ground. Shallow water types usually feast on nearby grain fields, the deep-water or diving duck feed on aquatic vegetation, and some of these feed on fish. Those that have a high fish diet have a fish flavor which can be eliminated by placing apples, onions, grapes or lemon in the cavity before cooking. Wild ducks have a superior flavor to domestically bred ducks. Wild ducks may be roasted, braised or casseroled.

CEREALS

'Ceres' was the goddess to whom the Romans offered prayers for the protection of their wheat crop; thus the origin of the word cereals.

For thousands of years, seven cereals have been classed as the staple food of man and different cultures depended on one or two of them for their nourishment. Wheat was the cereal of Southern Europe and the Middle East; rye and oats of Northern Europe. Millet was important to Africa, rice to Asia and maize was the cereal of the Americas.

As the population of the world expanded, cereal cultivation had to increase. Strains and varieties of cereals were developed to suit different climatic conditions and to produce an optimum grain; new areas were found which were suitable for cereal growing. The Midwest is but one example where our pioneers began cultivation and made it into one of the best cereal growing areas of the world.

Maize

This amazing grain was found already in systematic cultivation in many parts of South, Central and North America, at the time of European discovery of the Americas.

Its importance as a staple food was soon recognized by the old world when it was taken there in 1520. Within 50 years it was being grown in Europe, Africa and Asia.

Maize has many uses — cornmeal, flour, polenta, the ever popular cornflakes and popcorn, to name a few. The sweet corn variety is a popular vegetable.

Oats

Oats were cultivated in Northern Europe from 1,000 BC. It was first noticed as a weed in the wheatfields and was usually pulled out and fed to the horses. At times when the wheat crops failed, the people took to eating the oats. In the Celtic lands, oats were always appreciated and used mainly as a food. The Scots love their oatmeal porridge and the Welsh love their oatcakes. Now oats are enjoying a new revival as a health food. It is sought after for its high fibre content and its ability to lower blood cholesterol.

PULSES

Pulses are ideal to lay your hands on, not for measuring a heartbeat, but as an economical food which costs little, stores extremely well and contains a lot of protein.

Pulse is the seed of edible leguminous plants and is usually a term applied to dried peas, beans and lentils. Together with various grains, these were the staple food of the ancient world and still are in many areas of the world. Pulses tend to be incomplete in protein content though, as they do not contain all of the essential amino acids. The solution is simple; combine the pulse with nuts and cereals to fill in the amino acid gaps.

Pulses are recognized as a first class source of nutrition as they also contain valuable minerals, vitamins and, additionally, have a high fibre content with all the benefits that this implies. They are also fat-free and the indications are strong that pulses effectively reduce blood cholesterol levels.

Pulses rate highly as a health food, and interesting, tasty dishes can be produced by combining pulses with assorted spices, herbs and vegetables.

Garbanzo or Chick-Pea

Is a leguminous plant native to West Asia. It is listed amongst the oldest foods in the diet of peoples from the Mediterranean area through to India and is still widely used in the cuisines of that area. There are several varieties Garbanzos are used in soups, stews and casseroles, boiled and used in salads or puréed to make the popular dip hommus. Pre-soaking is necessary before cooking; they must then be boiled for about 1 hour or simmered for 2 hours. Canned garbanzos are now available.

Haricot Bean

Small, oval bean, white in color, native to Central America. It can vary in size but is always the same plump kidney shape. It is also known as white bean, navy bean and great northern. It is a popular pulse in many cuisines. The French use it in their cassoulet and it is the bean used to make Boston Baked Beans. This famous dish from New England is the forerunner to canned baked beans in tomato sauce.

Pre-soak the beans for several hours then cook for 1 or 2 hours, according to recipe.

Rice
Rice originated in South East Asia. It was growing in the area surrounding Thailand around 3,500 BC. Asians serve it at every meal either boiled or steamed and as fried rice. The people of the Middle East have their pilaf, the Italians have risotto and the Spanish their paella.
Rice products include rice flour and ground rice for use in puddings, cakes and as a thickening for sauces. Rice puffs and bubbles for breakfast cereals and crisp rice cakes or biscuits are now in demand for gluten free and low calorie diets.

Wheat
Wheat was first cultivated about 7,000 BC in Mesopotamia. The prairies of the United States are considered one of the best wheat growing areas of the world. Wheat is milled into flour for bread making and other baked products. The hard durum wheat is used to make semolina which is used to make pasta. Wheatgerm and bran are used in breakfast cereals and muesli. The whole wheat grain may be boiled and used in many dishes and salads. Burghul, which is wheat that has been soaked then dried and crushed, is cooked as a pilaf or soaked and mixed with parsley to make tabouleh.

Rye
It is believed that Rye originated in North Eastern Europe. It was first noticed growing as a weed in the wheatfields. The further north wheat was planted, the more rye was present until ultimately it was to become the staple cereal of Northern Europe. Rye is a very hardy plant, very resistant to cold and can grow in the poorest soils. Rye flour is rather greyish in color and the bread made from it is dark, with a distinctive flavor and can keep fresh for a long time. Rye breads have a lower carbohydrate content than wheat breads and are favored for diabetic and slimming diets.

Barley
One of the first grains grown by man. Systematic cultivation began about the same time as wheat. Barley was used as a bread flour, but its low gluten content produces a hard loaf. It is usually combined with wheat flour in bread making. The starch content of barley is converted into sugar by fermentation and is made into malt. This is used in many commercial products such as packet soups and sauces. It is used to make malt breads and also a flavoring in drinks. Barley is used to make malt vinegar, but its most famous use is in the making of whiskey.

Lentils
Lentils are the seeds of a small, branching plant which is native to the Middle Eastern area. Lentils have been used as a food since biblical times. Brown or green lentils are larger than most others and do not disintegrate during cooking. Use them in stews and casseroles. Red lentils are smaller and usually disintegrate, so are suitable for soup or purée dishes. Lentils do not require pre-soaking before cooking. Lentils are an excellent source of vegetable proteins and feature in vegetarian diets.

Split Peas
Dried peas which are split in half. There are two kinds — green and yellow, although their taste does not differ very much. Dried split pease have been used as a food since early times.
Split peas are mainly used in soups or served as a purée. The famous English or Irish dish, pease pudding, is a purée made with green split-peas and the Greek dish, fava, is a purée made with yellow split peas.
Split peas may be soaked for a few hours before cooking as this will shorten the cooking time. Yellow split peas do not need pre-soaking.

Red Kidney Bean
This kidney shaped, dark red bean, was a staple food in Central and South America in pre-Columbian times. Now widely used worldwide, it is favored for its color and slightly sweet flavor. Kidney beans may be dark red, or pink to maroon in color. They are used for making bean salads and are included in the famous Texan dish chili con carne.
Kidney beans must be pre-soaked, then boiled slowly for 1½ hours. Tinned kidney beans are cooked and ready to add to any dish. They need to be rinsed before use.

Soya Bean
Originated in China and has been an important food in Asian cooking for many thousands of years. They are an important source of protein, being the only complete vegetable protein. Soya beans are made into many products: bean curd which resembles white cheese in appearance; soya milk, used as a milk substitute which is favored by many because it contains no fat. The beans are also used to make condiments notably soy sauce; they are ground into flour and an oil is extracted from them. These products are much in demand in Western countries for health diets.

NUTS

In many ways, nuts can be thought of as emergency rations provided by nature. They are, after all, ready packed in handy containers and are easily gathered, stored or carried. Almost every kernel is a tiny powerhouse packed with protein. Nuts combine particularly well with all other vegetables in supplying essential amino acids.

Hardly surprising, then, that nuts have been a universal food in all societies throughout history from the time when man's predecessors were presumably swinging between the very trees and shrubs that provided this handy nourishment (assuming Darwin is right about our origins).

As a result, nuts are present in almost every aspect of cooking from soups to sauces; savories to sweets.

Nuts have a high oil content and this may be extracted for use as cooking oil. It is expensive and is mainly used in tiny quantities as a flavoring.

Ground nuts make excellent thickening for sauces as well as garnishes, while whole kernels are the ideal "nibble" to serve with drinks especially when salted, spiced or both.

Almond

Is one of the most popular nuts world-wide. There are two types: bitter almond — which is distilled into an essence; the sweet almond — which is eaten raw or used in cooking.

Sweet almonds are sold in the shell or shelled. They are also sold either with the skin on or blanched. To blanch almonds, pour boiling water over them and stand for a minute then rub the skins off. To sliver or flake the blanched almonds, place them in a bowl of hot water to keep them soft while you are working, they will regain their crisp texture on cooling.

Pistachio

A most interesting nut, prized for its pleasant flavor and delightful green color. Attractive as a garnish when sprinkled over ice cream, gateau and custard desserts.

When fresh, they have a purple outer skin under the shell and a pale, yet distinctive, green colored nut. They lose their color if kept for a long time.

Pistachio nuts are native to Asia Minor and are also grown in the Mediterranean area. Now being grown in areas of the United States, supplies are still restricted and as a result they are an expensive nut.

Chestnut

Chestnut is the only nut which has to be cooked before it is eaten. It has a tough outer skin which is removed while the nut is still warm. Chestnuts may be roasted over hot coals or under the broiler or boiled. Slit the outer skin with the point of a sharp knife before roasting so that they will not explode. Chestnuts may be used in stuffings, cooked with meats and used as a vegetable. Boiled chestnuts can be made into a purée and used as a filling for cakes and meringues or to make the famous sweet Mont Blanch.

Marrons glacé, considered a great delicacy, are chestnuts which have been preserved whole in a heavy sugary syrup.

Filbert

Is a style of hazelnut native to the Mediterranean area. Filberts are named after St. Philbert, a French monk whose feast day in August coincides with the ripening period of these nuts.

Filberts may be eaten whole, raw or slightly roasted, or chopped and used in cookies and cakes. They are finely ground for use in baking and in sauces.

There is little difference between filberts and hazelnuts, and more often than not, one name is used for either nut.

NUTS

Pecan

The pecan is native to North America. Its species is a relative of the walnut and it resembles the walnut in flavor and texture. The two nuts are interchangeable in most recipes.

Pecans are a good eating nut, either plain or toasted with spices. They are used in cookies, nut breads, cakes and ice creams. They may be added to stuffings and included in vegetarian dishes. Their main claim to fame is in the traditional Pecan Pie, which is also very popular outside the United States.

Pecan nuts, too, have become very popular outside America, and are now being grown in Australia and South Africa.

Macadamia

The macadamia nut is native to Australia but its recognition as a superior eating nut came from Hawaii. The tree was taken to Hawaii and planted and its instant popularity soon developed into large scale cultivation of the nut.

It is a round nut with a very hard outer shell. The nut has a rich buttery flavor and a delightful, crunchy, yet soft, texture. It has a very high oil content which gives it its rich flavor and special texture. The macadamia is mainly eaten as a cocktail nibble, slightly roasted and lightly salted or plain. It is occasionally used in confectionery.

TEA & COFFEE

Wars have been waged and nations conquered over tea and coffee and both probably rate as being the world's most prevalent beverages.

Tea or coffee can be a humble drink or an art form that hallmarks the level of etiquette in both guest and host alike. Use a mug, but don't be one and ignore the social significance of either beverage for coffee mornings, afternoon tea parties, etc.

Tea

Tea is the world's most popular beverage. It is an evergreen shrub of the camellia family which, in its wild state, can grow to a height of 30 feet. The cultivated plant is pruned to a bush so that the leaves can be easily picked. The leaves are dried and processed and used to brew the hot beverage.

Tea is native to China and Japan and has been used in those countries as a beverage for thousands of years. It was taken to Europe by the Dutch in 1610 and to England in 1644, where tea-drinking quickly became the fashion. The tea plant was introduced into India and Ceylon early in the 19th century and by 1864 was being exported from there to England. India and Ceylon or Sri Lanka, as it is now known, are the largest tea exporters in the world.

Tea: Production and Use

Only the first two tip leaves on the end of each twig are plucked for fine tea. The third and fourth leaves are used for coarse tea. There are two types of tea — green and black. For green tea, the leaves are dried immediately after picking, which gives the brew made from them a soft, mild flavor. Black tea, which is more robust in flavor, is allowed to ferment in its natural moisture before being lightly roasted and slowly dried. Black tea is the more popular of the two.

There is only one species of tea plant but there are many varieties of flavor depending on the locality and soil where it is grown, the age of the leaf and the processing methods. As many as 30 varieties may be blended to make a particular brand of tea.

To Make Tea:

Warm the pot by rinsing with hot water and add 1 teaspoon of tea leaves for each cup. Pour on the water as soon as it comes to the boil. Allow the tea to infuse for not less than three minutes and not more than five minutes. Serve with milk and sugar if desired or plain with a slice of lemon.

Iced Tea

This popular way of serving tea originated in the United States. It was first served at the St.

Louis World's Fair in 1904. Use twice the amount of tea leaves indicated for the hot beverage, strain over ice-cubes in a tall glass. Add lemon slices and mint leaves and sweeten to taste. It can also be made by making tea in the normal way, strain and chill, or soak the leaves in cold water for 12 hours then strain and chill. Spiced iced tea and tea punches are very refreshing. It is more convenient to make them with tea bags.

Fruity Tea Refresher

Serves 3
4 cups orange juice
4 tea bags
juice of 2 lemons
1 cinnamon stick
6 whole cloves
⅛ teaspoon grated nutmeg
lemon peel
lemon slices for garnish

Place orange juice in a saucepan and bring to the boil. Remove from heat and add remaining ingredients except lemon peel. Cover and infuse for 5 minutes. Remove tea bags and allow to cool. Strain and chill. Serve in suitable glasses garnished with lemon slices.

Spiced Iced Tea

Serves 4
4 tea bags
6 teaspoons sugar
1 cinnamon stick
¼ teaspoon grated nutmeg
1 long piece lemon rind
6 cups boiling water

Place all ingredients into a heat-proof jug and pour on the boiling water. Cover and stand 10 minutes. Strain and cool. Serve over crushed ice in tall glasses.

Coffee

The coffee plant originated in Abyssinia, or Ethiopia, as it is known today. It is said that the stimulating qualities of the plant were first discovered when a shepherd noticed that his sheep, after eating from a certain shrub, remained awake and active all night. The shrub was the coffee plant. Legend also tells us that the first person to drink coffee was the Mufti of Aden, who in the beginning of the ninth century heard about the stimulating bush from herdsmen. Desiring to remain awake and alert during prayers and meditation, he made a brew of the small berries of the plant and found the result very satisfactory. The use of coffee spread from Aden to Mecca and Medina, and throughout the Middle East.

By 1550 this new beverage had reached Constantinople, the capital of the Ottoman Empire, where the first coffee house was established in 1554. The Turkish ambassador to the French court in 1669 made the beverage fashionable when he offered it to all who visited him. By 1671 Marseilles had the first coffee house in Europe and, a year later, a coffee house opened in Paris. By 1683 Vienna, which is famous for elegant coffee houses, had opened her first one.

The demand for the new beverage prompted a Frenchman, Desclieux, to plant coffee in Martinique and later French Guiana. From there it spread to Central America and Brazil. The Dutch established plantations in Java by 1720.

Coffee: Production and Use

Coffee beans are classified into 3 main types: Arabica, which produces the finest coffee and has a low caffeine content; Robusta, which is a strong high caffeine type but of inferior quality; Liverica, which is a highly productive variety but mediocre in flavor. The blending of many different beans from various places in the world enables coffee merchants to create an infinite range of flavors. Variation of flavors is also achieved by the degree of roasting of the coffee bean. A light roast gives a full yet mild flavor, while heavier roasts produce strong coffee with a varying degree of bitterness according to the degree of roasting.

Preparing Coffee:

The coffee bean may be freshly ground at home using a coffee grinder. Grind only the amount needed as required. Coffee may also be purchased already ground and packed in vacuum packs which keep it fresh. On opening, the contents should be transferred to a dry jar or container with a tightly-fitting lid. Always remember to replace the lid immediately after measuring out the ground coffee.

There are many types of equipment for coffee making on the market; follow the manufacturer's instructions for best results. Coffee may be also brewed in an enamel, china or heat-proof jug or pot. Place 1 good tablespoon per cup of water into the container and pour over the measured amount of boiling water which has been allowed to come off the boil for a few seconds. Stand covered for 5 to 10 minutes then gently pour through a fine strainer taking care not to disturb the sediment in the bottom of the jug. Coffee should never be boiled as it acquires a strong, bitter taste. Coffee may be served black or with milk or cream. For special coffee, add a little liqueur to the cup. Strong black coffee should be served in demi-tasse cups.

Iced Coffee

Iced coffee is a very refreshing way to enjoy coffee. Make a brew of coffee and allow to cool, or dissolve instant coffee in a small amount of hot water and then fill with cold water. Serve in a tall glass over crushed ice. Whipped cream may be swirled on top or add a scoop of vanilla ice cream.

Cardamom Coffee

Cardamom gives a delightful flavor to coffee. Grind a cardamom pod with coffee beans or add a pinch of ground cardamom to the pot. It is used for both hot or iced coffee.

Vienna Coffee

Pour freshly brewed hot coffee into large cups and swirl a generous amount of whipped cream on top. Dust the cream lightly with ground nutmeg.

Hot Chocolates, Sodas and Shakes
Hot Chocolate

When the Mexican Aztec Indians fancied a cup of hot chocolate, a beverage to which they were particularly partial, there was no such thing as "instant" anything. First the cocoa beans had to be carefully roasted over an open fire. These were then pounded to a powder to which was delicately added ground flowers and water.

Making hot chocolate is considerably easier these days. Instant drinking chocolate is readily available in a prepared powdered form or it can be made by melting choc-bits or block chocolate in hot milk.

The strength of the chocolate should be decided by your taste and this is varied by using all milk, milk-to-water ratio or milk and cream. Other tasty variations are to top the drink with whipped cream, float marshmallows and/or add a touch of sparkle by including rum, brandy or your favorite liqueur.

Hot Chocolate Toddy
Serves 3
2 cups hot chocolate
1 cup strong black coffee
sugar to taste
¾ cup brandy
¾ cup cream, whipped
Combine the chocolate and coffee in a large jug, sweeten to taste with sugar. Whip with a whisk until frothy. Stir in the brandy and pour into mugs. Top each with a dollop of whipped cream.

Sodas

In the 1950's American teenagers used to perch on bar stools surrounded by giggling friends, cheerfully sucking soda through a straw.

The drugstore era, popularized soda drinks — though most of these pull-on soda tap havens have now almost vanished. But soda remains one of the greatest hot weather drinks for the whole family.

The recipes are easy, requiring no more than bottled club soda or lemonade to add that lip-tickling effervescence. Ensure that the bottled soda or lemonade is well chilled or add crushed ice to the glass for best results.

Chocolate Soda
1 tablespoon chocolate topping or syrup
¼ cup milk
1 scoop vanilla ice cream
1 small bottle club soda, chilled
Place chocolate topping or syrup in a tall glass and stir in the milk. Add a good scoop of ice cream then pour in the chilled soda until the glass is almost filled. Serve with a long handled spoon and drinking straw.

Ice Cream Soda
1 tablespoon vanilla or maple syrup
1 large scoop vanilla ice cream
1 small bottle club soda or lemonade, chilled
Place syrup in a tall glass, add the ice cream and slowly pour on the chilled soda. Serve with long handled spoon and drinking straw. Variations: Other flavours to use include — lime, orange, passionfruit, mango. Ginger ale may be used in place of soda or lemonade.

Strawberry Soda
1 tablespoon strawberry topping or syrup
¼ cup sliced fresh strawberries
1 scoop strawberry ice cream
1 bottle club soda or lemonade.
Place the strawberry topping or syrup in a tall glass and add the fresh strawberries. Add the ice cream and gently fill the glass with the chilled soda or lemonade. Serve with a long handled spoon and drinking straw; garnish with whole strawberry.

Ginger Ale Soda
1 scoop pecan ice cream
1 small bottle ginger ale, chilled
mint leaves to garnish
Place ice cream in a tall glass and top with the chilled ginger ale. Garnish with mint sprig, serve with drinking straw.

Shakes

Milk shakes might be a modern idea (another product of the American drugstore era) but to a dedicated milk shake freak these rich, creamy drinks are sheer heaven.

For a long time it wasn't possible to make real milk shakes at home as the whisks were available only as commercial models. Now you can make your own shakes with domestic units, wand mixers and even blenders. The secret is to use only chilled milk or your shake won't froth.

Milk Shake

½ teaspoon vanilla extract
1 cup milk, chilled
1 tablespoon vanilla ice cream
Combine all ingredients in a milk shaker or blender and mix until frothy. Pour into a tall glass and serve.

Caramel Thick Shake

2 tablespoons caramel sauce or topping
½ cup yoghurt
½ cup milk, chilled
Place all ingredients in a blender and mix until thick and frothy. Serve immediately.

Banana Milk Shake

1 ripe banana
2 teaspoons sugar
1 cup chilled milk
1 tablespoon ice cream (optional)
Cut banana and place in a blender jar. Add sugar and a little milk and blend until the banana is a smooth purée. Add milk and ice cream, if using, and blend until mixture is thick and frothy. Serve immediately.

Strawberry Milk Shake

1 tablespoon strawberry topping
1 cup chilled milk
1 small scoop strawberry ice cream
Place all ingredients in a milk shaker or blender and mix until thick and frothy. Serve immediately.

Malted Milk Shake

¼ teaspoon vanilla extract
2 teaspoons malt
1 cup milk, chilled
1 small scoop ice cream
Place all ingredients in a milk shaker or blender and mix until thick and frothy. Serve immediately.

Chocolate Milk Shake

2 teaspoons drinking chocolate
2 teaspoons sugar
¼ cup warm milk
¾ cup chilled milk
1 scoop chocolate ice cream
Mix drinking chocolate, sugar and warm milk to a smooth paste and pour into a blender and add chilled milk, blend until frothy. Pour into a tall glass and add ice cream. Sprinkle top with drinking chocolate powder and serve immediately.

HOT CHOCOLATE SODAS & SHAKES

LEMONADES COLD & HOT PUNCHES

Lemonade

Few things can be so American as homemade lemonade. Children would set up sidewalk stands selling lemonade for pocket money and remember how there always used to be a lemonade stall in the fairground on Founders' Day?

Bottled lemonade is obviously more convenient, but it really doesn't compare with the homemade product served ice-cold fresh. Here's how to make your own original American lemonade.

Lemonade I

Serves 15

1 lb (500 g) sugar
8 lemons
½ pint (2 cups) boiling water
chilled water or soda to mix

Place the sugar in a wide bowl. Lightly grate the rind of the lemons into the sugar using the fine side of the grater. With your hands rub the rind into the sugar, the coarse crystals bruise the rind and release more of the aromatic oils from the rind. Pour over the boiling water and stir until the sugar is dissolved.

Juice the lemons and strain into the cooled sugar syrup. Chill well. To serve pour ⅓ cup lemon syrup into a tall glass. Add ice cubes and top with chilled water or soda water. Garnish with a slice of fresh lemon.

The lemonade may be mixed in the same proportion in a large jug. The syrup base which is not used may be stored in the refrigerator for 2 days or frozen if needed to keep longer.

Lemonade II

Serves 15.

4 lemons
1 lb (500 g) sugar
½ pint (2 cups) water
chilled water or soda to mix

Peel the rind of the lemons thinly in a long coil. Use a sharp knife or a potato peeler and take care not to peel too deeply. Trim off any white pith from the strips as this will give a bitter taste. Place lemon rind in a saucepan and add the pint of water. Bring to the boil and then simmer for 5 minutes. Add the sugar and stir until sugar has dissolved, then slowly simmer for 10 minutes. Allow to cool then strain into a suitable container. Juice the lemons and add to the syrup. To serve pour ¼ lemon syrup into a tall glass. Add ice and top with chilled water or soda. Garnish with a fresh lemon slice.

Cold Punches

A refreshing cold punch served at a gathering caters for those who do not partake of alcoholic drinks or prefer only mild alcoholic drinks. The punch may be made non-alcoholic or with some alcohol added.

The requirement is a good base. This could be cold tea or a lemonade or orangeade syrup base. Added to this is one or a variety of fruit juices — fresh, tinned or frozen — and pieces of thinly sliced or dried fruits. Just before serving, place in the ice cubes and top the punch with a carbonated water such as sparkling mineral water, soda water, ginger ale or root beer.

Float a garnish of fruit slices or even a flower or two on top. Red or white sparkling wine may be added if an alcoholic punch is required and for a stronger punch, gin or other spirits may be added. Serve in a large punch bowl with a ladle. If a punch bowl is not available a large transparent plastic bubble bowl may be used. For an extra touch, decorative ice cubes may be made by freezing pieces of fruit in the ice trays with the water. You may flavor the cubes with sherry or whiskey, using not more than 2 tablespoons per tray.

Pineapple Punch

Serves about 30

2 cups strong, hot tea
1 cup sugar
¾ cup lemon juice, chilled
2 cups orange juice, chilled
2 tablespoons lime juice
1 cup small fresh mint leaves, washed
1 can pineapple slices, including juice
5 pints (2½ lt) chilled ginger ale
4 pints (2 lt) soda water
crushed ice

Into a large bowl, combine the hot tea and sugar. Stir until sugar has dissolved. Add the lemon, orange and lime juices then add the mint. Stir well and refrigerate for 2 hours or more.

Just before serving strain the mixture into a large punch bowl. Cut 6 of the pineapple slices into small pieces and leave 2 whole. Add to the punch including the juice from the can. Pour in the ginger ale and soda water; add the crushed ice. Garnish with fresh mint sprigs and serve.

Champagne Strawberry Punch

Serves about 30

½ lb (250 g) fresh strawberries
¾ cup sugar

3 bottles chilled champagne
2 cups crushed ice

Wash and hull the strawberries and cut into slices. Reserve 1 cup of sliced strawberries. Place remainder into a punch bowl and sprinkle with the sugar. Allow to stand for 30 minutes; stir occasionally. Just before serving, add the crushed ice and pour in the champagne. Stir well and add the cup of reserved strawberries. Serve immediately.

Hot Punches

Ideal to serve at fireside gatherings and at the ski lodge. The most famous American hot punch is the hot Eggnog traditionally served on Christmas Eve.

Eggnog

Serves 20

8 eggs, separated
¾ cup sugar
¾ cup bourbon
½ cup brandy
3½ cups hot milk
ground nutmeg
¾ cup heavy or whipping cream

Place egg yolks and sugar in the large bowl of an electric mixer. Commence beating at low speed then increase to high speed and beat until mixture is thick and lemon colored. Scrape bowl frequently. Reduce speed and gradually beat in the bourbon and brandy. Pour into a large bowl or punch bowl. Stiffly beat the egg whites until soft peaks form, then with the same beaters, beat the cream until stiff peaks form. Into the punch bowl, pour the hot milk then quickly fold in the egg whites and cream, using a wire whisk. Sprinkle nutmeg lightly over the top and serve immediately in punch cups or mugs.

Mulled Wine

Serves 8

1 cup water
⅓ cup sugar
4 cloves
1 stick cinnamon
1 orange, thinly sliced
1 lemon, thinly sliced
1 bottle red wine
fresh lemon slices for garnish

Place the water, sugar and spices into a saucepan and bring to the boil; simmer for 5 minutes. Add the orange and lemon slices, then add the wine and simmer for 5 minutes more. Carefully ladle into punch cups or mugs, removing cloves and cinnamon stick as you ladle. Garnish each with a fresh lemon slice and serve immediately.

Hot Fruit Glögg

Serves 6 to 8

2 cups apple juice
1 cup grape juice
2 tablespoons sugar
1 stick cinnamon
4 cloves
1 long piece orange peel
1 cup gin
⅓ cup raisins
⅓ cup slivered almonds

Combine juices, sugar, spices and orange peel in a saucepan, bring to the boil and then simmer for 5 minutes. Add the gin and simmer 2 minutes more. Divide the raisins and almonds between 6 punch cups. Remove the cinnamon cloves and orange peel and pour the glögg into the cups. Serve immediately.

LEMONADES COLD & HOT PUNCHES

COCKTAILS

Cocktails

Forget notions that cocktails are for evening only; champagne cocktails and daiquiris are both examples of smart drinks for the other end of the day, i.e. breakfast entertaining.

Cocktails are said to originate in America (originally as aperitifs) and used to be defined as short mixed drinks comprising two or more liquid ingredients shaken or stirred with ice to promote blending and chilling.

But a cocktail these days is also a long drink, often exotically garnished to add both colorful appearance and subtle flavors. Long cocktails tend to be daytime drinks, and that's anywhere between breakfast and dinner.

Setting up a home Cocktail Bar
Cocktail-making requires a set of equipment necessary to achieve a good result. It is advisable that when you purchase these, they are used solely for cocktail-making.
1. A *Cocktail Shaker*:
Necessary to mix the ingredients well and produce a smooth drink.
2. A *Stirring Glass and Spoon*:
For mixing stirred drinks.
3. A *Hawthorn Strainer*:
To place over the glass when it is necessary to strain drinks through the ice.
4. *Cocktail Glasses*:
Should be clear and unetched to allow the color and presentation of the drink to be clearly seen.

Mixing
Shake: Cocktails which are shaken are those which are made naturally opaque by the ingredients such as cream, fruit juice, egg white, e.g. Alexander.
Stirred: Cocktails which are stirred are those which are naturally clear, e.g. Martini.

Measures
Common measures, and their equivalents, used in cocktail recipes:

10 drops	= 1 dash
6 dashes	= 1 teaspoon
5 teaspoons	= 1 fluid ounce (30 ml)
half nip	= ½ fluid ounce (15 ml)
nip	= 1 fluid ounce (30 ml)
double	= 2 fluid ounces (60 ml)
jigger	= 1½ fluid ounces (45 ml).

Basic Bar Stocks

When setting up a home cocktail bar it is not necessary to have a large variety of drinks to begin with. The following will provide a good basic stock.

Spirits	Liqueurs
Vodka	Creme de Cacao
Gin	Creme de Menthe
Dry Vermouth	Cherry Brandy
Sweet Vermouth	Cointreau
Brandy	Tia Maria
Bourbon	Curacao
Rum	Angostura Bitters

Carbonated drinks such as soda and tonic water, lemonade, lime cordial, dry ginger ale and cola should also be on hand. Buy small bottles so there will be little waste. Canned fruit juices for long drinks can include tomato, apricot, pineapple and orange. Again, it is advisable to have stocks of small cans.

Cocktails

Brandy Alexander
1 cup crushed ice
1 jigger brandy
½ jigger Creme de Cacao
½ jigger whipping cream
Place ice in a cocktail shaker and pour over remaining ingredients. Shake well together. Strain into a cocktail glass.

Grasshopper
1 cup crushed ice
1 jigger heavy cream
1½ fluid ounces (45 ml) white Creme de Cacao
1 jigger Creme de Menthe
Place ice in a cocktail shaker and pour over the remaining ingredients. Shake well and strain into two cocktail glasses. Garnish side of glass with mint sprig and cherry.

Pink Lady
1 cup crushed ice
1 jigger lemon juice
1 jigger gin
1 egg white
1 dash grenadine
Place ice in a cocktail shaker and pour over the remaining ingredients. Shake well and strain into two glasses. Garnish with lemon slice.

Martini
1½ cups crushed ice
2 jiggers gin
1 teaspoon dry vermouth
2 stuffed green olives
Place ice in stirring glass and pour in the gin and vermouth. Stir well with stirring spoon then strain into two chilled cocktail glasses. Place an olive in each and serve.

Stinger
1 cup crushed ice
1 jigger brandy
½ jigger white creme de menthe
Place ice in stirring glass and pour in the brandy and white creme de menthe. Strain into a cocktail glass. Garnish and serve.

Long Drinks

Taken literally, you can go to any lengths with long drinks but as a rule long drinks are a cocktail given greater volume by adding mineral water, soda, tonic, lemonade, orangeade or juice, cola or ginger ale.

Long drinks should be served in 10-12 oz glasses (highball, for example) and can be garnished with cherry, mint sprig, orange or lemon slice/peel, cucumber or strawberries.

Garnish is often placed on the side of the glass for eye appeal.

Construction of a Cocktail or Mixed Drink
1. *Base*
Main ingredient is the major proportion; it is usually the spirit.
2. *Modifier*
Ingredient to tone down the base. It is usually fruit juice, fortified wine, liqueurs or egg.

3. *Flavor*

Ingredients in this group are those used to give a specific flavor such as bitters, vermouth and liqueurs Only a dash or small portion is used.

4. *Color*

Liqueurs which have a choice of color are used, e.g. blue Curacao, green Creme de Menthe and Chartreuse, red Cherry Brandy and brown Tia Maria.

Long Drinks

Tom Collins

1 nip lemon juice
1 jigger gin
1 teaspoon sugar syrup
1 dash angostura bitters
soda water

maraschino cherry and lemon
twist of lemon for garnish
Place ice in a cocktail shaker. Pour in the lemon juice, gin, syrup and bitters. Shake well and strain over ice cubes in tall glass. Add soda to fill glass. Garnish and serve.

Pink Pussycat

1 nip cherry brandy
1 fluid ounce (30 ml) heavy cream
1 fluid ounce (30 ml) cherry juice
lemonade
Place ice cubes in a tall glass. Pour in the cherry brandy, cream and cherry juice. Stir well with a long spoon and fill glass with lemonade. Garnish with maraschino cherry and serve.

COCKTAILS

WINES

If a true elixir exists, it is likely to bear a label denoting a special bin or year as, suffice to say it would have to be a wine.

Most people appreciate that the heady juice of the grape can add romance to a dinner for two, a sparkle to a special occasion or simply make any meal complete no matter how sophisticated or simple the fare.

You do not need to be a connoisseur to enjoy wine, but it helps to have some idea of basic characteristics when making a wine selection.

It is also worth noting that the American wine industry, although young by European standards, was started in California in 1769 when Franciscan monks planted the first vines for sacramental use. We now have 29 wine producing States, though California is by far the largest. Many of the wines from this State are considered to rank with the best in the world.

Appetizer Wines

Appetizer wines or aperitifs are served before the meal to stimulate the appetite. Mixed cocktails are also served before a meal but many people find them too strong and prefer the more traditional appetizer wines.

Sherry

Sherry is a fortified wine, which means it has been made stronger with the addition of extra alcohol during its manufacturing process. This gives it a more concentrated flavor as well as a higher alcohol content. Dry sherry is best to serve as an appetizer, although sweet sherry is often preferred by some. Spain is accredited with being the home of sherry making and Spanish sherry is labeled simply "sherry." Sherry style wines from other countries have to be labeled with the country of origin.

Vermouth

Is also a fortified wine. The term vermouth covers a range of wine based drinks, flavored with herbs and other aromatic substances. There are many varieties, both red and white, dry and sweet. Most of the better known vermouths are from France or Italy. French style vermouth is dry and clear in color and Italian style vermouths are sweet and amber to red in color. Cinzano and Campari are two popular Italian styles, the former being rather bland and the latter slightly bitter in flavor. Vermouth may be drunk straight, with soda or mixed with spirits to make a cocktail.

Table Wines

This term is given to the red, white or rosé wines which are served to accompany a meal. The identification of table wines can be confusing if one does not know how to read the label.

Table wines are classified in two ways — Generic wines or Varietal wines — and are labeled accordingly.

Generic Wines

Are made to a style of wine using a blend of different grape varieties. The style of wine produced is named after a European wine district that gained fame and recognition for its particular wine, such as Hock, Moselle and Burgundy. The name is the only similarity with the authentic wines of the area for there is no

guarantee in Generic wines that the same grape varieties as the original were used. Generic wines are usually cheaper, massed produced wines, made on a blend of different grape varieties with the must (the infermented liquid) sometimes being transported from other areas.

Varietal Wines

Are named after the grape used in their making such as Semillon, Chardonnay, Cabernet, and must contain 75% of that grape in the wine. Varietal wines are the premium wines and therefore more expensive than the Generic Wines.

Red Wine

Generic varieties include Claret, Burgundy, Rosé, Chianti and Lambrusco. Varietal varieties include Barbera, Cabernet Sauvignon, Chelois, Concord, Petite Sirah, Pinot Noir, Ruby Cabernet and Zinfandel — (produced only in California).

A full bodied red wine such as Burgundy, Pinot Noir, Petite Sirah is usually served with fully flavored meat dishes such as roasts, grilled steaks and rich casseroles. Light, dry red wines such as Claret, Ruby Cabernet and Zinfandel, go well with lighter meals, cold meat platters, quiches and egg dishes.

Red wines should be served at room temperature. Light reds and rosé may be slightly chilled. Full bodied red wines need to be uncorked I hour before serving to allow certain scents and odours to be removed and others to develop.

White Wines

Generic varieties include Hock, Moselle, Chablis, White Burgundy and Sauternes. Varietal varieties include Rhine Riesling, Semillon Tokay, Sauvignon Blanc, Chardonnay, Chenin Blanc, Pinot Blanc, Delaware and Sylvaner.

White wines are very popular and seem to be preferred to red. They go well with light type meals such as fish, soups, poultry and salads. White wines can be dry, semi and sweet and are served chilled. The sweet white wines need more chilling than the dry.

Dessert Wines

As the name suggests, these wines are served at the end of the meal and are much sweeter and fuller than aperitif wines. They are served to accompany sweets, cheese platters and fruits, or without accompaniments to finish off a meal. Dessert wines are fortified wines, but some heavy, sweet table wines are also suitable to use as dessert wines.

Port Is perhaps the best known dessert wine. This wine style originated in Portugal but is now produced in most of the wine districts of the world. It is a strong, sweet deep red wine. Ruby and tawny port types are the younger ports which mature in the casks and are bottled. They do not improve or age any more after bottling. These are the less expensive types. Vintage port is aged in wood for 2 years and then bottled. Most of the maturing process takes place in the bottle and improves with age. It is necessary to decant a vintage port before serving, taking care not to disturb the sediment. Vintage ports are not ready to drink for at least 15 years; it is consequently expensive.

Madeira Comes only from the island of Madeira. It is a deep amber colored wine which is full bodied and sweet. It is frequently used in the making of desserts and used in sauces. There are also two varieties of dry Madeiras.

Masala Is based on the strong white wine of Sicily and is a medium bodied, sweet amber colored wine.

Muscatel and **Tokay** are also popular dessert wines which resemble Sherry, and Angelica, which resembles Port.

Sparkling Wines

These are the delightful bubbly wines sought after for many a merry occasion. Champagne is on the top of the list; Sparkling Burgundy and Spumante are other famous varieties.

Sparkling white wines made in the champagne style or "methode champenoise" are many, but the only sparkling wines entitled to be labeled champagne are those made in the legally designated area of Champagne in France.

Sparkling wines are generally white wines although there are a few rosé and red available. They should be served well chilled. They may be served at any time to accompany any course from aperitif to dessert, and mix well to make punches and long drinks.

BRUNCH & LUNCHEON

Brunch

In truth it was started by people getting up so late they missed breakfast and couldn't wait until lunch for something to eat. Inevitably it was called brunch, a fashion that has become so popular that it is now almost an institution.

Apart from being the only way to satiate indulgent teenagers, brunch is an excellent way to entertain friends and business associates at a civilized hour, avoiding both the bustle of breakfast and the formality of dinner. Brunch can be a wonderful mixture of dishes as just about anything goes (and goes down well). A variety of interesting breakfast dishes — the

ones we don't normally have time for — and light lunch recipes can be served together and thoroughly enjoyed.

There is no need to serve complicated recipes — variety is the key to a good brunch. Plenty of fresh fruits, juices, eggs (several different recipes can be used), tomatoes, mushrooms, bacon, ham and sausages, quiche, lasagna, salads, waffles, pancakes, bagels, croissants, muffins — the list is almost endless.

Drinks can be a real adventure — Buck's Fizz (orange juice and champagne), Strawberry Champagne Cocktail, Screwdriver, Bloody Mary to name but a few and, of course, plenty of fresh coffee and tea.

Brunch Buffet
Serves 12

	Page
Summer Morning Apple Juice	58
Phyllo Cheese Rolls	204
Scrambled Eggs with Sour Cream and Red Caviar	59
Celery and Horseradish Cream	58
Orange Nut Pancakes with Honey Butter	92
Hot Coffee	

Weekend Brunch
Serves 4

	Page
Hot Grapefruit	96
Scrambled Eggs with Beef	148
Stuffed French Toast	178
Hot Coffee or Tea	

Celebration Brunch
Serves 8

	Page
Florida Sunrise	234
Nut Omelette	202 (4 quantities)
Pesto Bread	202 (2 quantities)
Yoghurt Cheese with Hot Nut Topping	136
Hot Coffee or Tea	

Luncheon

Luncheon parties do not have to be fancy and vastly extravagant. Simple and delicious are often the watchwords for a successful luncheon (witty guests help so try to invite at least one).

Whether your luncheon is to be a formal affair or a relaxing meal on the patio, take heed of a few hints that will make the preparation easier.

Decide whether it's to be a sit-down or buffet style meal and plan your dishes to suit the occasion. There's nothing nicer than light, cool dishes in summer and hot, filling meals on a cold winter's day.

If you decide to try out something new, test it on the family first — hopefully they will give an honest opinion — it will give you valuable practice before the party.

Do as much of the work as possible in advance, make as many of the dishes as you can and set your table the day before. Details such as salads and flowers for the table can be prepared the morning of the party. This way you can guarantee that you'll enjoy yourself as much as everyone else will.

Committee Lunch
Serves 10

	Page
Pepper Mousse with Apple	203 (2 quantities)
Shrimp Crepes with Lime Sauce	109 (2 quantities)
Orange Herb Salad	123
Bourbon Pecan Pie	194
Coffee	

BRUNCH & LUNCHEON

Order of Work
Preparation the day before:
1. Prepare the pepper mousse and refrigerate.
2. Prepare and bake the pecan pie.
3. Prepare and cook the crépes. Stack with waxed paper between each crépe and refrigerate.
4. Prepare mini rolls for the salad.
5. Prepare lime sauce for the crépes.

Morning of luncheon:
1. Wash salad herbs and spinach, wrap in a tea-towel and refrigerate to crisp. Segment the oranges.
2. Arrange table.
3. Prepare shrimp filling, fill crépes and place in oven dish.
4. Unmould the pepper mousse and arrange with garnish onto individual plates. Refrigerate until serving time.

10 minutes before guests arrive:
1. Place crépes into slow oven to reheat.
2. Reheat lime sauce, place in the oven with crépes to keep hot.
3. Combine all salad ingredients and toss with dressing.

Business Luncheon
Serves 8

	Page
Smoked Salmon with Bacon and Watercress Cream	38
Chicken Poached in Plum Sauce	208 (2 quantities)
Jerusalem Artichokes with Peas	43
Creamed Potatoes with Macadamia Nut Butter	242
Peach Cream Brulee	134

Order of Work
Day before luncheon:
1. Prepare and arrange on the platter, ready to serve, the Smoked Salmon and Watercress Cream. Cover with plastic wrap and refrigerate.
2. Prepare Peach Brulee, in individual dishes if desired, and refrigerate.

Morning of luncheon:
1. Prepare and place chicken in oven.
2. Set table.
3. Prepare Creamed Potatoes.
4. Prepare Jerusalem Artichokes with Peas.

ENTERTAINMENT

Tea Parties

Morning and afternoon tea parties are rapidly gaining pace as a light, but fun way, to entertain at home. Both can be occasions in themselves (you don't have to play bridge!).

Morning tea is usually served around 11am while afternoon tea is timed for either 3 or 4pm. A selection of dainty sandwiches, biscuits and cakes is the usual fare, but the cake selection for afternoon tea should be more elaborate.

Morning Tea

	Page
Ruby Throated Hummingbird Cake	138
Polvorones	137
Rose Straffole	136
Jelly Roll	176
Sally Lunn Coffee Cake	194
Oatmeal Orange Muffins	194
Plum Scroll	217

Afternoon Tea

	Page
Chocolate Cake with Tangerine Curd	140
Grape and Kiwi Slice	136
Rum Babas with Almond Glaze	178
Orange Cream Cheese Brandy Snaps	196
Chocolate Rum Tarts	234

Morning and afternoon teas may be served buffet style or seated around a table. When setting the table for sit down tea parties, the cups are placed to the left of the hostess so that she may pour the tea and pass it around to the guests.

Dinner Parties

The arrangement of dinner parties can take many forms, from the informal sit-down, to the formal. There are varying degrees of formality depending on what can be managed by the hostess in regard to serving the meal. For a strictly formal dinner party, help will be required in the kitchen and in the dining room to serve the meal. Buffet dinner parties are a good way to get around serving problems.

Informal Dinner

Informal dinners are a lot less stressful, but still require considerable effort. The courses may be pre-served in the kitchen and placed before each guest as full plates. Alternatively, and easier, place the courses in the center of the table on serving dishes for the guests to help themselves. The first method is more demanding on the hostess who has to keep prancing out to the kitchen.

Informal Buffet Dinner

Informal buffet dinner parties are popular for the understandable reason that they are probably the easiest to organize and manage, especially if there is a large number of guests to cater for.

The food should be tastefully displayed with serving ware and hot dinner plates at the ready, so guests can help themselves with assistance from the host and hostess. Once served, the guest should proceed to a previously arranged place setting at a table. A large single table or several small tables (card tables, for example) are equally acceptable. It isn't a bad idea to have the appetizer ready served on the table and only the entrée served from the buffet. The dessert course can be table or self served. Menus should be the same as for a conventional sit-down dinner with a soup or appetizer, entrée with accompaniments and a dessert. The bigger the occasion, the wider the selection of menu dishes.

Formal Dinner

Organising a formal dinner isn't easy, so don't expect it to be. It requires skill, knowledge and dedication. If yours is to be a sit-down, strictly formal dinner party, you will need high quality help in both the kitchen and dining room. It's worth remembering that an acceptable way around the serving problem is to have a buffet dinner party instead. Strictly formal dining is a sophisticated occasion and is best not attempted on any scale unless the household boasts the required appointments and experienced staff is available.

On these occasions, both the host and the hostess must know what is expected of them. Equally important is guest management; they will need to know what is expected of them also. Classic formal service once included eight or more courses, but now it is acceptable to have three or four. Even so, precision and timing is essential for the service to flow smoothly. Drinks and hors d'oeuvres should be offered in the "salon" and it isn't until all the guests are assembled that the invitation to enter the dining room is offered. The host should help seat the guests according to the positioned place cards. The first course, having been served in advance, will be waiting.

The table setting will already have been checked with each position having wine goblets for both red and white wine; a water goblet plus a champagne goblet. Cutlery (decided by the menu) will be set from the outside in, and individual salt and pepper shakers should be placed above the plate. When all have finished the first course, plates are removed by the server from the right.

Wine is also poured from the right, though following courses are served from the left.

Informal Dinner Menu

	Page
King Crab Royale	18
Game Hens in Orange Sauce	26
OR	
Coffee Glazed Crown Roast of Lamb	208
Cauliflower with Huntington Sauce	124
Hot Sweet Yard Long Beans	42
Lemon Delight Bread Pudding	178

Informal Buffet Dinner

		Page
1st Course	Salmon Baked in Cider	27
2nd Course	Pheasant with Fruit Stuffing	68
	Pursalane Mint and Apple Salad	102
3rd Course	New York Trifle	114
	OR	
	Chocolate Mint Fondue	94

Formal Dinner

		Page
1st Course	Cream of Sorrel Soup	39
2nd Course	Stuffed Baked Lobster with Lime	63
3rd Course	Beef with Walnut and Orange Stuffing	46
	Leeks with Broccoli Sauce	44
	Baby Carrots with Bourbonaisse	185
	Hot Mustard Beans	185
4th Course	Rose Petal Herb Salad	58
5th Course	Blueberry Sorbet	72

ENTERTAINMENT

ENTERTAINMENT

Coffee and Dessert

It's in vogue to entertain with minimum fuss and effort, so why not invite a few friends round AFTER dinner for coffee and dessert? This idea also has particular appeal as a pleasant top to an evening at the theatre, a business meeting or just for the hell of it.

Most people have a sweet tooth and here's a great chance to indulge it. To keep the timetable easy, preparations can be made well in advance, the table laid in the afternoon and the sweets in place or waiting in the refrigerator. You will go up an instant grade in the hostess league by magically appearing with a selection of two or three delights like shoo fly pie or lime mango beignets. Liqueurs will go well with the coffee.

	Page
Rum Babas with Almond Glaze	178
Doughnuts with Kahlua Custard	96
Traditional Strawberry Shortcake	116
Lime Mango Beignets	176
Shoo Fly Pie	194
Crab Apple Cream Pie	32
White Chocolate Cheese Cake	73
Blackberry Pie	176
Cafe Diable	140

Cocktail Party

A cocktail party is a convenient way to honor social obligations when a large number of people are involved. It is also a popular form for business and promotional functions.

A selection of savories, both hot and cold, are served. They should be small enough to eat in one or two bites as no plates are used. Family members or waiters circulate with platters of savories; a buffet may also be set out with the cold savories and dips. Have bowls of nuts, crisps and dips with crackers set around the room on occasional tables. A bar should be arranged where a variety of alcoholic and non-alcoholic drinks are available. Calculating the amount of food necessary is usually difficult. If you allow ten savouries per person, 5 hot and 5 cold plus a number of dips with crudites, nuts and potato crisps, you will be sure your guests will not go hungry. A small sweet in the form of petits fours may be served at the end.

It is also a signal that the party is over and it is time to go. Cocktail parties usually begin between 6 and 7 pm and should only continue for 2 hours. If you intend your guests to stay longer into the evening then do not serve the sweets, but instead a more substantial dish could be served about 8 pm. This could be a plate of curry or other meat dish which can be eaten with a fork. When you feel it necessary to end the party, close the bar and bring out the sweets; only one variety is necessary.

Suggestions for a Cocktail Party

	Page
Phyllo Cheese Rolls	204
Catfish Rolls with Lemon and Sour Cream	174
Oysters in Cumin Sauce	226
Guacamole	149
Golden Cheese Puffs	227
Nasturtium Leaf Rolls	224
Shrimp Turnovers	227
Stuffed Dates	136
Mint Truffles	217

To Open a Champagne Bottle

1. Cut metal foil in a straight line under wire carriage and remove top part.

2. Tilt bottle away from you, keeping thumb on top of the cork, untwist the wire and gently remove.

3. With your fingers firmly around cork and neck, rotate bottle with other hand. Pull bottle down gently as you twist. Cork will ease out and will not pop.

Special Receptions

There is always some occasion for a special reception on a grand scale. These are held to celebrate family events such as a Graduation, Birthday Party, Engagement or Wedding. Many people are invited, there may be dancing and entertainment provided, depending on space; but one thing is always present, a grand buffet table with many and varied dishes. These occasions require meticulous planning. If this is done properly then the function will run smoothly and will give great satisfaction to the organizer. Planning should begin weeks before. Time spent at a desk with pen and paper will save many hours of work and wear and tear of nerves.

1. Begin with the guest list and invitations. This will establish the number to be catered for.
2. Plan a menu that will be within your budget and range of skills.
3. Decide which foods you wish to order cooked from outside suppliers and place your order early to avoid disappointment. Also, place orders for cuts of meat and special fruits or vegetables that are usually difficult to obtain, so you will have the time to select an alternative if not available.
4. Check your stocks of glasses, plates, flatware and place orders to hire any you may need. Tables and chairs may also be hired, not to forget a large coffee urn.
5. Make a list of alcoholic drinks you will need and keep your eye open for specials. If you begin to stock pile early you will save money.
6. Decide on your color scheme and order or hire table cloths well in advance. Yards of inexpensive material may be purchased cheaply to make cloths; colored sheets are good to use. Order paper serviettes to match or contrast with the cloths.
7. Flower arrangements also need thought and attention, you must place orders early to avoid disappointment.
8. Refrigerator space and freezer space may be a problem. These also may be hired; you will need to install them 3 days before the function.
9. A marquee in the garden may be the answer to a space problem. There are firms who will set one up for you and take it down afterwards; they are not expensive.
10. Don't forget the music.
11. Waiters and kitchen assistants will also be needed. Contact a catering service, usually the people who hire out serving ware can also provide this need.
12. You may feel the hiring is a large expense. Get quotes early so you will have time to make your choice. You can then compare this cost to the cost of having your celebration at a hotel or reception house. You will find it is more economical to have it at home as well as being more relaxed and enjoyable.
13. Shop for dry stores weeks in advance so as to save your time for the perishables.

Selection of Menu

To begin you will need a small selection of hors d'oeuvres, not too many so as not to kill the appetite for the food to come. Finger food such as canapes, dips, nuts and crisps are sufficient.

For the buffet, have a selection of cold meat platters and three or four salads. Vary the salads from a green tossed salad, pasta or rice salad, potato salad to a good coleslaw. Cold, cooked vegetable salads with an orange and onion, give a splash of color to the table.

Seafood dishes give a touch of extravagance. A shrimp fountain, or a large poached salmon, beautifully garnished, taste good and look attractive.

Filling dishes are needed to fill a crowd. Hot lasagne, cannelloni or ravioli are always popular.

A large, glazed ham is always an eye catcher on the table. Try the Baked Ham with Apricots and Chinese Mushrooms, page 113. Roast Chicken cut into pieces served hot or cold are always goers. You may like chicken pieces wrapped in pastry such as the Mango Stuffed Chicken in Puff Pastry on page 232. Desserts are usually the extravagant finale to a celebration buffet. Have a selection of two or three, plus a platter of fresh fruits. The fruits may be displayed in a large watermelon basket to make a stunning centerpiece.

ENTERTAINMENT

Celebration Buffet Menu

		Page
Hors d'oeuvres	Nasturtium Leaf Rolls	224
	Phyllo Cheese Rolls	204
	Guacamole (with crackers)	149
Buffet	Game Paté	25
	OR	
	Goose and Mushroom Paté	85
	Mexican Salad Caesar	147
	Peanut Potato Salad	205
	Devilled Nut Salad	205
	Village Salad	103
	Bourbon and Praline Ham	192
	Chicken and Creamed Curried Coconut	65
	Pecan Rice	175
	Asparagus in Tangerine Sauce	104
Dessert	Orange Cups	218
	Passionfruit and Ice Cream	115
	Pavlova	141

STORAGE GUIDE

Food Storage

A tidy storage cupboard will save you time and money so it's worth making the effort.

Purpose-made storage containers are good but expensive; by employing a little imagination, they are also unnecessary.

One of the benefits of the "packaged" age we live in is that manufacturers have to provide their products in containers that ensure a good shelf life. Re-cycle these and you will have free storage containers. Remember this when you shop — Is the container going to be useful? You will be amazed how many are.

Coffee Tins Buy a large 2 lb tin of coffee. It comes in a strong tin with a tightfitting lid, suitable for storing cracker biscuits, Sao biscuits, etc.

Coffee Jars Make wonderful store jars. Buy the same brand and size and collect the jars. They have good screw top lids and an attractive shape. Remove the label by soaking in hot water. Soon you will have a uniform set of store jars. If you want jars of graded sizes, just move to the next size down, concentrate on buying that size for a few months until you accumulate a number. Within a year you can have a uniform set of graded sizes for free.

Plastic Ice Cream Containers Although not airtight, they can be handy for refrigerator storage.

Biscuit Tins have always been used for storing cakes as well as biscuits. Many firms still sell biscuits in large deep tins; you will do well to collect a few.

Dry Ingredients

Baking Powder or Baking Soda
If bought in a tin, it may remain in the tin, but always make sure the lid is replaced tightly. Keep in a dry, cool cupboard away from range or water-heater. If bought in a packet, transfer into screw top jar.

Bouillon Cubes
Place in screw top jar after opening packet, store in the door of the refrigerator. Will keep for 6 months.

Coconut
After opening place into screw top jar, store in cool, dry place.

Coffee
After opening vacuum pack, empty contents into a jar. Always keep tightly closed. Will keep indefinitely.

Coffee – Instant
Store in cool cupboard in its own tin or jar. Always make sure lid is replaced tightly immediately after use. It will deteriorate quickly if not closed properly.

Dried Fruit
Store unopened, pack in a cool dry place. When opened, place contents in screw top jar. Store in refrigerator in hot weather.

Flour
Unopened, place in a cool dry place; opened, empty into a large tin with tightfitting lid. In very hot weather store in the bottom of the refrigerator.

Olive Oil
If bought in a tin, empty into glass bottles with screw top. Will keep 6 months and more in a cool place.

Packet Soup & Sauce Mixes
Do not buy in large quantities. Use before use by date. Store in cool, dry cupboard.

Pasta
After opening, transfer to airtight container. Will keep for months.

Pulses
Transfer contents of packet to store jar with tightfitting lid and store in a cool, dry place. In hot weather, place jar in the refrigerator.

Rice
Will keep indefinitely in a closed container in a dry place.

Salad Dressings
Will keep for 6 months unopened in cool place. Once opened, store in refrigerator.

Salad Oil
Will keep well if in a glass bottle, with tight lid, in a cool place.

Salt
Empty into store jar with tightfitting lid.

Sugar — Brown & White
Place in tight-lidded jar or bin.

Yeast — Active, dry
Place unopened sachets in a screw top jar and place in the refrigerator. Will keep for 4 months. Check date on packet before you purchase to make sure it is well within the expiry date.

Dairy Products

Butter
Keep covered in refrigerator. Butter absorbs refrigerator odors easily; remove from wrap and place in a covered container. Wash container before refilling with a new pat of butter.

If purchased in its own tub, always replace the lid. If lid becomes bent or cracked, cover with plastic wrap.

Buttermilk

Unopened, will keep for 2 weeks in refrigerator; if opened, will keep for one week.

Cheese

Cottage and Ricotta: Buy fresh product, and in quantity needed for immediate use, as they only keep for 4 to 5 days. Keep covered as they taint easily.
Cream Cheese and Neufchatel: Will keep in the refrigerator for about 10 days if in an unopened pack. If opened or purchased from a bulk pack, keep in a bowl with a loose cover or plastic wrap. If tightly closed in a container, the cheese sweats and develops a yellowy tint on the surface and a strong odor. If this occurs the surface may be scraped away and the remainder used.
Sliced Cheeses: Keep refrigerated in its package for 2-3 weeks.
Mature Cheeses: Place in a covered container and refrigerate. Will keep for over a month.

Cream

Make sure the cream you buy is fresh, it will keep in the refrigerator for one week.

Eggs

Refrigerated, they will keep for 1 month. Egg whites may be stored in a covered jar for 1 week. Egg yolks, if unbroken; place in a small bowl, cover with water and plastic wrap. They will keep, refrigerated, for 4 days.

Milk

Will keep refrigerated for 1 week. Do not return any small unused quantities of milk to original container as bacteria will spread to remaining milk and cause it to go "off" quickly.

Yogurt

Will keep in refrigerator for one week to ten days.

Fresh Meat, Fish and Poultry

Fresh Meat

All fresh meats should be kept in the refrigerator for only two or three days. If longer storage is needed, place in the freezer.

Processed Meats

Vacuum packed bacon, frankfurters or ham, if left unopened, will keep in refrigerator for one week to 10 days. When opened, store loosely wrapped in wax paper for three days.

Fish

Fresh fish of all kinds is best cooked on day of purchase, but will hold over for one day. Keep wrapped to prevent odor being absorbed by other foods in refrigerator.

Poultry

Wrap loosely and refrigerate, will keep 2 to 3 days.

Home Freezer Foods

Packing Meat

Wrap small cuts, steaks and chops individually in a light, plastic wrap. Pack required number into freezer bags, arranging evenly and as flat as possible so they will have good contact with cold surfaces. Extract air from the freezer bag with a vacuum freezer pump, or by pressing the pack from the sealed end towards the open end, then secure end with a twist tie or fold back and tape down. Label each package. Large roasts are treated in a similar way. Trim off excess fat before freezing, as remaining oxygen in the pack accelerates the oxidization of fat, giving the meat an "off flavor", after prolonged storage. Protect large cuts with an extra freezer bag to prevent tears while in freezer and protect meat from freezer burns, which is the dehydration of exposed surfaces. Meat produce already frozen should be placed as packed in a second bag and placed in freezer immediately.

Frozen Meat Storage Times

Recommended period of storage at 30°F (15°C) or for good eating quality.

Beef

Joints, solid	8 months
Joints, rolled	6 months
Steaks, stew meat	6 months

Lamb and Mutton

Joints, with bone	6 months
Joints, boned and rolled	4 months

Veal

Joints	6 months
Chops and other cuts	4 months

Pork

Joints	4 months
Chops and other cuts	2 months
Lean minced meats	2 months
Sausages and fatty minced meats	1 month
Bacon, commercially vacuum packed only	1 month
Ham, vacuum packed	1½ to 2 months

Chicken and Poultry

Chicken and Turkey whole	1 year
Chicken and Turkey pieces	6 months
Duck, Goose, whole	6 months

STORAGE GUIDE

CALORIE GUIDE

Calorie Guide

Obesity is embarassing, but more importantly, a potential killer; two good reasons for avoiding it. This doesn't mean you have to become a pantry paranoid. The key words are common sense and moderation.

We can't do much about your common sense, but this calorie guide will certainly help you with moderation. If you do get carried away, don't panic, simply adjust your diet the other way for a couple of days. As a rule, high calorie foods are rich in sugar and fats and should not be adopted as a daily diet. Save them for special occasions as a treat.

The figures used are based on an average adult serving and standard cup measures are sometimes quoted.

Food	Calories
Almonds, shelled, 1 cup	850
Apple, raw, medium size	117
Apple, baked	200
Apple dumpling	240
Apple juice, 1 cup	120
Apple sauce, ½ cup, sweetened	130
Apple sauce, ½ cup, unsweetened	50
Apricot nectar, canned, ½ cup	70
Apricots, sweetened, canned, 2 halves	40
Apricots, fresh, 2 whole	35
Artichokes, globe, 1 cooked	70
Asparagus, steamed, 8 stalks	20
Asparagus soup, creamed, canned, 1 cup	160
Avocado, ½ medium	190
Bacon, cooked, 1 strip	45
Banana, 1 medium	100
Banana cream pie, 1 serve	300
Beans, baked, canned, ½ cup	155
Beans, fresh green, cooked, ½ cup	15
Beans, kidney, cooked, ½ cup	115
Bean sprouts, raw, ½ cup	10
Beef, corned, 3 oz	185
Beef, fillet, 4 oz	400
Beef, hamburger, 1 patty	200
Beef, rib roast, 1 serve	400
Beef, 12 oz	150
Beetroot, cooked, ½ cup	30

Food	Calories
Berry pie, 1 serve	400
Berries, fresh, black and blue, ½ cup	64
Boston cream pie, 1 serve	240
Brazil nut, 1 shelled	30
Bread, commercial, 1 slice, ½" thick, white or wholemeal	60-64
Bread pudding, ½ cup	200
Broccoli, cooked, 1 serve	30
Brownie, 1 slice	95
Brussels sprouts, cooked, ½ cup	30
Butter, 1 square, ¼" thick	70
Buttermilk, 1 glass, 8 oz	90
Cabbage, shredded raw, 1 cup	20
Cake, cheese, 2" slice	350
Cake, chocolate layer, 1 slice	400
Cake, plain, 1 slice	50
Cake, cup, 1 frosted	130
Cake, pound, 1 slice	450
Cantaloupe, 1 average slice	60
Carrots, cooked, ½ cup	25
Cashew nuts, ¼ cup	100
Catsup, 1 tablespoon	17
Cauliflower, cooked, ½ cup	25
Cheese, Camembert, 1 wedge	115
Cheese, cheddar, 1 oz	70
Cheese, cottage, plain, ½ cup	86
Cheese, cream, 1½ oz	160
Cheese, Parmesan, 1 tablespoon, grated	25
Chicken, fried, ½ breast	155
Chicken pie, 1 individual 4½"	535
Chicken salad, ½ cup	200
Chocolate, 1 oz	144
Chocolate, sweet, 1 oz	155
Chocolate eclair, 1 average	320
Chocolate malted shake with ice cream	502
Chocolate soda	255
Cinnamon bun, 1	200
Cocoa with milk, 1 cup	240
Coconut custard pie, 1 slice	320
Coffee with 1 sugar, 1 cup	25
Cola drink, 1 glass, 12 oz	145
Coleslaw with Mayonnaise, ½ cup	85
Cookies, 1 chocolate chip	50
Corn kernels, canned, ½ cup	70
Corn bread, 1 slice	140

Food	Calories
Corn cob, 1 medium	100
Corn soup, creamed, ½ cup	100
Cornflakes, ¾ cup	75
Crabmeat, canned, 3 oz	80
Cream, light, 1 tablespoon	20
Cream, sour, 1 tablespoon	25
Cream, heavy, 1 tablespoon	55
Cream soups, canned, 1 cup	200
Cucumber, 12 slices	10
Custard, ½ cup	155
Custard pie, 1 slice	325
Dates, 4	85
Doughnut, sugared	180
Duck, roast, 1 serve	300
Egg, boiled or poached	80
Eggnog, ½ cup	200
French dressing	85
French toast	170
Fruit cocktail, canned, ½ cup with syrup	100
Gingerbread, 1 slice	170
Goose, roast, 1 serve	425
Grapefruit, ½	45
Grapefruit juice, unsweetened, 1 cup	100
Gravy, thick, 3 tablespoons	180
Griddle cakes, 2	150
Ham, baked, 3 oz	245
Herring, pickled, 1 piece	220
Honey, 1 tablespoon	65
Ice cream, commercial, plain, ½ cup	165
Jam or jelly, 1 tablespoon	60
Lamb, roast leg, 1 serve	250
Lamb chop, broiled, 4 oz	400
Lemon meringue pie, 1 slice	350
Lentil soup, 1 cup	250
Liver, calf, fried, 2 oz	110
Lobster, broiled, small	300
Loin chop, cutlet, 1 medium, fried	190
Macaroni cheese, ½ cup	220
Macaroni cooked plain, ½ cup	80
Margarine, 1 tablespoon	100
Meat loaf, beef and pork, 1 slice	265
Milk, condensed, ½ cup	490
Milk, whole, 1 cup	160
Milk, skimmed, 1 cup	90
Muffin, corn, medium	125
Muffin, English, 1 large	140
Mushrooms, fresh, 10 small	15

Food	Calories
Oatmeal, cooked, 1 cup	120
Olive oil, 1 tablespoon	125
Orange, 1 medium, fresh	65
Orange juice, fresh, 1 cup	110
Pancake, 1, 4"	60
Peaches, canned, 2 halves with syrup	85
Peanut Butter, 2 tablespoons	190
Pea soup, creamed, 1 cup	270
Peas, fresh, frozen, cooked, ½ cup	56
Pineapple fresh, 1 slice	40
Pineapple juice, 1 cup, sweetened	135
Popover, 1	100
Pork roast, 1 serve	300
Potato, 1 medium, baked, boiled	90
Potato, sweet, baked, 1 medium	155
Potatoes, french fried, 10 pieces	155
Potatoes, mashed with milk and butter, 1 cup	185
Prunes, sweetened, ½ cup	205
Pumpkin pie, 1 slice	320
Raisins, ¼ cup	107
Red snapper, baked, 1 serve	183
Rhubarb, stewed, ½ cup	190
Rice, brown or white, ½ cup, cooked	100
Salami, dried, 1 oz	130
Salmon, poached, 3½ oz	200
Sardines, canned in oil, 3 oz	175
Sausage, pork, 2 oz	125
Scallops, fried, 6	425
Shortcake with cream, 1 slice	350
Shrimp, boiled, 5 large	70
Spaghetti, plain, cooked, 1 cup	155
Spare ribs, cooked, 6	250
Spinach, cooked, ½ cup	25
Spinach soup, creamed, 1 cup	240
Sugar, 1 tablespoon	50
Tartare sauce, 1 tablespoon	100
Tomato cream soup, 1 cup	250
Turkey roast, 3½ oz	290
Waldorf salad, 1 serve	137
Walnuts, ¼ cup	50
Watermelon, 1 average slice	90
Wheatgerm, 1 tablespoon	25
White sauce, ¼ cup	106
White fish, 1 serve	100
Yoghurt, plain, ½ cup	65
Zucchini, cooked, 1 cup	40

MEASURES & CONVERSIONS

Weights and Measures

American standard measures have been used throughout this book. Weights and measures are rather daunting to the novice cook. Some are deterred from progressing with the recipe when they find they are short by ½ oz or 1 oz of some ingredient. Weights and measures in most recipes are intended as a guide only to help the cook determine how much to buy to make the recipe. In most cases a little more or less of even the main ingredients will not affect the success of the finished product. Only in structured recipes such as pastry products, cakes, breads, etc., are accurate measurements necessary, and even then if you are a ½ oz short on sultanas, your fruit loaf will still be a success. It is the ratio of shortening to flour to liquid content which is the most crucial in these types of recipes.

However, weights and measures seem to cause more problems between nations than to individual cooks, because although we now exchange our culinary material, we do not agree on our standards of weights and measures. As the cup measure is one of the most popular ways of measuring quantities along with the table and teaspoon it seems these three have been singled out to cause all the confusion. An American cup contains 8 fluid oz while an English cup is 10 fluid oz. The Australian cup is 250 ml which is the same as the American cup. The English and Americans agree on a 14.8 ml tablespoon while the Australians have a 20 ml tablespoon — but the good news is; we all agree on a 5 ml teaspoon. You are now all confused! The following chart will give you the English and Australian equivalents to the American standard measure.

Liquid Measures

IMPERIAL fl oz	METRIC ml millilitre	CUP AND SPOON fluid ounce
⅙ fl oz	5 ml	1 teaspoon
⅔ fl oz	20 ml	1 tablespoon
1 fl oz	30 ml	1 tablespoon plus 2 teaspoons
2 fl oz	60 ml	¼ cup
2½ fl oz	85 ml	⅓ cup
3 fl oz	100 ml	
4 fl oz	125 ml	½ cup
5 fl oz	150 ml	(¼ pint) 1 gill
6 fl oz	180 ml	¾ cup
8 fl oz	250 ml	1 cup
10 fl oz	300 ml	(½ pint)
12 fl oz	360 ml	1½ cups
14 fl oz	420 ml	1¾ cups
16 fl oz	500 ml	2 cups
20 fl oz	600 ml	(1 pint) 2½ cups
35 fl oz	1 litre	(1¾ pints) 4 cups

Cake Pan Sizes

	Imperial	Metric
Loaf Pans	9 x 5 in	23 x 12 cm
	10 x 3 in	25 x 8 cm
	11 x 7 in	28 x 18 cm
Round Cake Pans	6 in	15 cm
	7 in	18 cm
	8 in	20 cm
	9 in	23 cm

Quick Reference Conversion Table

All measurements are equal to the American standard cup and spoon measure.

USA & CANADA	ENGLAND	AUSTRALIA
1 cup (8 fl oz)	= ¾ cup (approx 7½ fl oz) − 3 teaspoons (½ fl oz)	= 1 cup (250 ml)
1 tablespoon (14.8 ml)	= 1 tablespoon (14.8 ml)	= ¾ of a tablespoon (15 ml) use 3 teaspoons (15 ml)
1 teaspoon (5 ml)	= 1 teaspoon (5 ml)	= 1 teaspoon (5 ml)

Dry Measures

All the measures are level, so when you have filled a cup or spoon, level it off with the edge of a knife. The following scale is the "cook's" equivalent, it is not an exact conversion of imperial to metric measurement.

IMPERIAL	METRIC
oz = ounces	g = grams
lb = pounds	kg = kilograms
½ oz	15 g
⅔ oz	20 g
1 oz	30 g
2 oz	60 g
3 oz	90 g
4 oz (¼ lb)	125 g
5 oz	155 g
6 oz	185 g
7 oz	220 g
8 oz (½ lb)	250 g
9 oz	280 g
10 oz	315 g
11 oz	345 g
12 oz (¾ lb)	375 g
13 oz	410 g
14 oz	440 g
15 oz	470 g
16 oz (1 lb)	500 g (0.5 kg)
24 oz (1½ lb)	750 g (0.75 kg)
32 oz (2 lb)	1000 g (1 kg)
3 lb	1.5 kg
4 lb	2 kg

Oven Temperatures

The centigrade temperatures given here are not exact; they have been rounded off and give a guide only. Follow the manufacturer's temperature guide, relating it to oven description given in the recipe. Remember gas ovens are hottest at the top, electric ovens at the bottom and convection-fan forced ovens are usually even throughout. We have also included Regulo numbers for gas cookers which may assist.

	C	F	REGULO
Very slow	120	250	1
Slow	150	300	2
Moderately slow	160	325	3
Moderate	180	350	4
Moderately hot	190/200	370/400	5/6
Hot	210/220	410/440	6/7
Very hot	230	450	8
Super hot	250/290	475/550	9/10

Length

IMPERIAL	METRIC
in = inches	mm = millimetres
ft = feet	cm = centimetres
¼ in	5 mm .5 cm
½ in	10 mm 1.0 cm
¾ in	20 mm 2.0 cm
1 in	25 mm 2.5 cm
2 in	5 cm
3 in	8 cm
4 in	10 cm
5 in	12 cm
6 in	15 cm
7 in	18 cm
8 in	20 cm
9 in	23 cm
10 in	25 cm
11 in	28 cm
12 in (1 ft)	30 cm

MEASURES & CONVERSIONS

Cup and Spoon Replacements for Ounces

In this table t represents teaspoonful, T represents tablespoonful and C represents cupful. The 8 oz cup or 250 ml cup has been used in the calculation.

INGREDIENT	½ oz	1 oz	2 oz	3 oz	4 oz	5 oz	6 oz	7 oz	8 oz
Almonds,									
ground	2 T	¼ C	½ C	¾ C	1¼ C	1⅓ C	1⅔ C	2 C	2¼ C
slivered	6 t	¼ C	½ C	¾ C	1 C	1⅓ C	1⅔ C	2 C	2¼ C
whole	2 T	¼ C	⅓ C	½ C	¾ C	1 C	1¼ C	1⅓ C	1½ C
Apples, dried									
whole	3 T	½ C	1 C	1⅓ C	2 C	2⅓ C	2¾ C	3⅓ C	3¾ C
Apricots,									
chopped	2 T	¼ C	½ C	¾ C	1 C	1¼ C	1½ C	1¾ C	2 C
whole	2 T	3 T	½ C	⅔ C	1 C	1¼ C	1⅓ C	1½ C	1¾ C
Arrowroot	1 T	2 T	⅓ C	½ C	⅔ C	¾ C	1 C	1¼ C	1⅓ C
Barley	1 T	2 T	¼ C	½ C	⅔ C	¾ C	1 C	1 C	1¼ C
Bicarbonate of									
Soda	1 T	2 T	⅓ C	½ C	⅔ C	¾ C	1 C	1 C	1¼ C
Breadcrumbs,									
dry	2 T	¼ C	½ C	¾ C	1 C	1¼ C	1½ C	1¾ C	2 C
soft	¼ C	½ C	1 C	1½ C	2 C	2½ C	3 C	3⅔ C	4¼ C
Biscuit Crumbs	2 T	¼ C	½ C	¾ C	1¼ C	1⅓ C	1⅔ C	2 C	2¼ C
Butter	3 t	6 t	¼ C	⅓ C	½ C	⅔ C	¾ C	1 C	1 C
Cheese, grated,									
lightly packed,									
natural cheddar	6 t	¼ C	½ C	¾ C	1 C	1¼ C	1½ C	1¾ C	2 C
processed									
cheddar	5 t	2 T	⅓ C	⅔ C	¾ C	1 C	1¼ C	1½ C	1⅔ C
Parmesan,									
Romano	6 t	¼ C	½ C	¾ C	1 C	1⅓ C	1⅔ C	2 C	2¼ C
Cherries,									
glacé, chopped	1 T	2 T	⅓ C	½ C	¾ C	1 C	1 C	1⅓ C	1½ C
whole	1 T	2 T	⅓ C	½ C	⅔ C	¾ C	1 C	1¼ C	1⅓ C
Cocoa	2 T	¼ C	½ C	¾ C	1¼ C	1⅓ C	1⅔ c	2 C	2¼ C
Coconut,									
desiccated	2 T	⅓ C	⅔ C	1 C	1⅓ C	1⅔ C	2 C	2⅓ C	2⅔ C
shredded	⅓ C	⅔ C	1¼ C	1¾ C	2½ C	3 C	3⅔ C	4⅓ C	5 C
Cornflour	6 t	3 T	½ C	⅔ C	1 C	1¼ C	1½ C	1⅔ C	2 C
Coffee,									
ground	2 T	⅓ C	⅔ C	1 C	1⅓ C	1⅔ C	2 C	2⅓ C	2⅔ C
instant	3 T	½ C	1 C	1⅓ C	1¾ C	2¼ C	2⅔ C	3 C	3½ C
Cornflakes	½ C	1 C	2 C	3 C	4½ C	5¼ C	6¼ C	7⅓ C	8⅓ C
Currants	1 T	2 T	⅓ C	⅔ C	¾ C	1 C	1¼ C	1½ C	1⅔ C
Custard Powder	6 t	3 T	½ C	⅔ C	1 C	1¼ C	1½ C	1⅔ C	2 C
Dates,									
chopped	1 T	2 T	⅓ C	⅔ C	¾ C	1 C	1¼ C	1½ C	1⅔ C
whole, pitted	1 T	2 T	⅓ C	½ C	¾ C	1 C	1¼ C	1⅓ C	1½ C
Figs, chopped	1 T	2 T	⅓ C	½ C	¾ C	1 C	1 C	1⅓ C	1½ C
Flour,									
plain or self-									
raising	6 t	¼ C	½ C	¾ C	1 C	1¼ C	1½ C	1¾ C	2 C
wholemeal	6 t	3 T	½ C	⅔ C	1 C	1¼ C	1⅓ C	1⅔ C	1¾ C
Fruit, mixed	1 T	2 T	⅓ C	½ C	¾ C	1 C	1¼ C	1⅓ C	1½ C
Gelatine	5 t	2 T	⅓ C	½ C	¾ C	1 C	1 C	1¼ C	1½ C
Ginger,									
crystallised pieces	1 T	2 T	⅓ C	½ C	¾ C	1 C	1¼ C	1⅓ C	1½ C
ground	6 t	⅓ C	½ C	¾ C	1¼ C	1½ C	1¾ C	2 C	2¼ C
preserved, heavy									
syrup	1 T	2 T	⅓ C	½ C	⅔ C	¾ C	1 C	1 C	1¼ C
Glucose, liquid	2 t	1 T	2 T	¼ C	⅓ C	½ C	½ C	⅔ C	⅔ C
Golden Syrup, Corn									
Syrup	2 t	1 T	2 T	¼ C	⅓ C	½ C	½ C	⅔ C	⅔ C
Haricot Beans	1 T	2 T	⅓ C	½ C	⅔ C	¾ C	1 C	1 C	1¼ C
Honey	2 t	1 T	2 T	¼ C	⅓ C	½ C	½ C	⅔ C	⅔ C
Jam	2 t	1 T	2 T	¼ C	⅓ C	½ C	½ C	⅔ C	¾ C
Lentils	1 T	2 T	⅓ C	½ C	⅔ C	¾ C	1 C	1 C	1¼ C
Milk Powder,									
full cream	2 T	¼ C	½ C	¾ C	1¼ C	1⅓ C	1⅔ C	2 C	2¼ C
non-fat	2 T	⅓ C	¾ C	1¼ C	1½ C	2 C	2⅓ C	2¾ C	3¼ C
Nuts, chopped	6 t	¼ C	½ C	¾ C	1 C	1¼ C	1½ C	1¾ C	2 C
Oatmeal	1 T	2 T	½ C	⅔ C	¾ C	1 C	1¼ C	1½ C	1⅔ C
Olives,									
whole	1 T	2 T	⅓ C	⅔ C	¾ C	1 C	1¼ C	1½ C	1⅔ C
sliced	1 T	2 T	⅓ C	⅔ C	¾ C	1 C	1¼ C	1½ C	1⅔ C
Pasta, short (e.g.,									
macaroni)	1 T	2 T	⅓ C	⅔ C	¾ C	1 C	1¼ C	1½ C	1⅔ C
Peaches,									
dried & whole	1 T	2 T	⅓ C	⅔ C	¾ C	1 C	1¼ C	1½ C	1⅔ C
chopped	6 t	¼ C	½ C	¾ C	1 C	1¼ C	1½ C	1¾ C	2 C
Peanuts,									
shelled, raw,									
whole	1 T	2 T	⅓ C	½ C	¾ C	1 C	1¼ C	1⅓ C	1½ C
roasted	1 T	2 T	⅓ C	⅔ C	¾ C	1 C	1¼ C	1½ C	1⅔ C
Peanut Butter	3 t	6 t	3 T	⅓ C	½ C	½ C	⅔ C	¾ C	1 C
Peas, split	1 T	2 T	⅓ C	½ C	⅔ C	¾ C	1 C	1 C	1¼ C
Peel, mixed	1 T	2 T	⅓ C	½ C	¾ C	1 C	1 C	1¼ C	1½ C
Potato,									
powder	1 T	2 T	¼ C	⅓ C	½ C	⅔ C	¾ C	1 C	1¼ C
flakes	¼ C	½ C	1 C	1⅓ C	2 C	2⅓ C	2¾ C	3⅓ C	3¾ C
Prunes,									
chopped	1 T	2 T	⅓ C	½ C	⅔ C	¾ C	1 C	1¼ C	1⅓ C
whole pitted	1 T	2 T	⅓ C	½ C	⅔ C	¾ C	1 C	1 C	1¼ C
Raisins	2 T	¼ C	⅓ C	½ C	¾ C	1 C	1 C	1⅓ C	1½ C
Rice,									
short grain, raw	1 T	2 T	¼ C	½ C	⅔ C	¾ C	1 C	1 C	1¼ C
long grain, raw	1 T	2 T	⅓ C	½ C	¾ C	1 C	1¼ C	1⅓ C	1½ C
Rice Bubbles	⅔ C	1¼ C	2½ C	3⅔ C	5 C	6¼ C	7½ C	8¾ C	10 C
Rolled Oats	2 T	⅓ C	⅔ C	1 C	1⅓ C	1¾ C	2 C	2½ C	2¾ C
Sago	2 T	¼ C	⅓ C	½ C	¾ C	1 C	1 C	1¼ C	1½ C
Salt, common	3 t	6 t	¼ C	⅓ C	½ C	⅔ C	¾ C	1 C	1 C
Semolina	1 T	2 T	⅓ C	½ C	¾ C	1 C	1 C	1⅓ C	1½ C
Spices	6 t	3 T	¼ C	⅓ C	½ C	½ C	⅔ C	¾ C	1 C
Sugar,									
crystalline 1A	3 t	6 t	¼ C	⅓ C	½ C	⅔ C	¾ C	1 C	1 C
Super Fine	3 t	5 t	¼ C	⅓ C	½ C	⅔ C	¾ C	1 C	1¼ C
Confectioners	1 T	2 T	⅓ C	½ C	¾ C	1 C	1 C	1¼ C	1½ C
moist brown	1 T	2 T	⅓ C	½ C	¾ C	1 C	1 C	1⅓ C	1½ C
Sultanas	1 T	2 T	⅓ C	½ C	¾ C	1 C	1 C	1¼ C	1½ C
Tapioca	1 T	2 T	⅓ C	½ C	⅔ C	¾ C	1 C	1¼ C	1⅓ C
Treacle	2 t	1 T	2 T	¼ C	⅓ C	½ C	½ C	⅔ C	⅔ C
Walnuts,									
chopped	2 T	¼ C	½ C	¾ C	1 C	1¼ C	1½ C	1¾ C	2 C
halved	2 T	⅓ C	⅔ C	1 C	1¼ C	1½ C	1¾ C	2¼ C	2½ C
Yeast,									
dried	6 t	3 T	½ C	⅔ C	1 C	1¼ C	1⅓ C	1⅔ C	1¾ C
compressed	3 t	6 t	3 T	⅓ C	⅓ C	½ C	⅔ C	¾ C	1 C

GLOSSARY OF FOOD & COOKING TERMS

à la	In the style of.
à la carte	According to the menu. Diners select individual dishes which have their price stated.
Age	To allow to mature. Meat and game are aged by hanging to render them more tender. Cheese and wines are aged to improve flavor.
al dente	Italian term used to describe pasta and rice that is cooked until it is just firm to the bite.
Almondine or Amandine	Dishes made or garnished with almonds.
Antipasto	The Italian name for hors d'oeuvres or appetizers. Usually consists of cold cuts of ham, salami, olives, artichokes and salad ingredients.
Aperitif	An alcoholic drink taken before a meal to stimulate the appetite.
Appetizer	A small piquant dish served before the main meal to stimulate the palate.
Aquavit	An alcoholic drink distilled from potatoes or grains.
Aspic	A savory jelly prepared from reduced, clarified stock of meat, poultry or fish. It can be purchased in powdered form. It is used to make vegetable jelly molds; to glaze fish and cold meats.
au lait	A French term meaning served with milk.
au gratin	With a brown surface. The dish is coated with a white sauce, sprinkled with breadcrumbs and browned in the oven.
au naturel	In a simple style or uncooked.
Baba	A rich yeast cake soaked with a syrup and flavored with rum.
Bake	To cook food in an open pan in the oven.
Bake Blind	To bake pastry cases, large or small, without their fillings. Place greased or waxed paper over the raw pastry in the pie plate. Fill with a dry ingredient such as rice, macaroni or dried beans and bake. Remove paper and filling five minutes before completion of cooking time to allow pastry to brown.
Baking Powder	A leavening agent added to flour to make products rise. It is a combination of alkaline baking soda and a dry acid with a starch ingredient to act as a buffer between the two.
Baking Soda	Also a leavening used in conjunction with an acid ingredient such as sour cream or buttermilk in baking.
Ballottine	A piece of meat, poultry or game which is boned, stuffed and rolled into the shape of a bundle, then cooked.
Barbecue	To cook foods over hot coals.
Baste	To spoon hot fat or liquid over food as it roasts or poaches, to keep it moist and juicy.
Batter	A mixture made with flour, egg and liquid which may be thick or thin according to use. Some fried foods are dipped in a batter before frying. Other batters are made into pancakes, crêpes and pikelets.
Bavarian	A cold, molded dessert made with gelatin, eggs, cream or custards and flavorings such as chocolate or fruit purée.
Béarnaise	A rich sauce made with butter, egg yolks and vinegar; flavored with chervil and tarragon. It is served with steaks or beef tenderloin.
Beat	To make a mixture smooth with rapid, regular motions using a spoon, wire whisk or electric mixer. Beating also incorporates air into foods. Cream is beaten to make it thick.
Bechamel	A white sauce enriched with egg and sometimes cheese.
Beignet	A light textured fritter which is deep-fried.
Beurre Blanc	A white sauce prepared from a reduction of butter, shallots, white wine and vinegar. It is served with fish.
Beurre Manié	A paste of butter and flour in equal quantities used to thicken soups, stews and sauces. It is dropped into the liquid in small pieces and beaten after each addition.
Bind	To moisten a mixture with eggs, milk or a sauce, to hold the ingredients together.
Bisque	A thick, rich cream soup usually made with shellfish and puréed vegetables.
Blanch	To place food in cold water and quickly bring to the boil then remove. This is done to whiten foods or lighten their color, or to remove strong odors. It also means to plunge foods into boiling water for less than a minute and then plunge into cold water to refresh. This is done to brighten the color of vegetables which are served crisp, eg. vegetable sticks and crudites. Fruit and nuts are blanched to remove skins. Place into boiling water for a few seconds then remove and skin.
Blend	To mix together thoroughly, two or more ingredients. It has also come to mean to place foods in an electric blender until it is puréed or minced.
Blintz	A thin pancake filled and folded into a parcel.
Boil	To cook food over high heat in liquid in which bubbles rise constantly to the surface.
Bombe	A dessert of ice cream or custard mixtures frozen in a spherical mold.
Bone	To remove bones from meat, fish and poultry.
Bonne Femme	French term meaning cooked in a simple or housewifely style. A dish cooked in this style has a garnish of fresh vegetables and herbs and usually includes mushrooms.
Bouchée	A tiny puff pastry cup similar to a vol-au-vent which is filled with a savory or sweet filling.
Bouillon	A clear seasoned broth made from meat or chicken, used as the base for soups and sauces.
Bouquet Garni	A bundle of several herbs usually consisting of a few sprigs of parsley, a sprig of thyme and a bay leaf, tied together so that it may be removed easily from soups and stews.
Braise	To cook slowly in a covered pan with a small amount of liquid. Food may be browned first in a small amount of oil or butter.
Bread	To coat foods with breadcrumbs, cracker crumbs or cornmeal, before frying.
Brochette	Food cooked on a skewer.
Broil	To cook food by direct heat on a rack over or under a hot element, or over charcoals.
Broth	The same as stock; liquid in which poultry, meat or fish have simmered.

Canapé — Plain or toasted bread or crackers topped with a savory mixture and garnish. Served as a hors d'oeuvre.

Caramelize — To heat sugar in a heavy based pan until it liquefies and develops a caramel color and flavor.

Carotene — A yellow-orange pigment found in orange-colored vegetables and fruits such as carrots, pumpkin and mangoes. It is converted to Vitamin A in the body.

Carve — To cut meat or poultry into slices or serving pieces.

Cassata — An ice cream mold consisting of different flavored and colored ice creams, enriched with fruits and nuts.

Casserole — A cooking utensil made from heat resistant glass, earthenware or metal, with a lid designed for long, slow cooking of meat and vegetables in the oven or on top of the range. The word casserole also denotes the food cooked in it.

Celeriac — A variety of celery which is cultivated for its bulbous, turnip-like root. It is cooked and eaten as a vegetable or added to soups and stews for flavor.

Cereal — The grain of certain grasses which have a farinaceous quality and are edible. Specifically wheat, oats, barley, rye, maize and millet. Cereal also means breakfast food preparations made from these grains.

Chafing Dish — A pan used for cooking food or keeping food hot at the table, usually heated by a spirit lamp or butane gas.

Chantilly — French term for cream which has been lightly whipped, sweetened and flavored with vanilla.

Charcuterie — French term for a shop where various pork products are sold. Nowadays also contains other cold meat products.

Chill — To refrigerate or let it stand in ice or iced water until cold.

Chine — To scrape the meat from the bone or portion of the bone and in some cases to remove the bone completely.

Chop — To cut food into small pieces with a knife or using a blender or food processor.

Chorizo — A Spanish sausage, very spicy, sold fresh or smoked.

Chou Pastry — A light pastry puff with a hollow center which is filled with sweet custard, cream or savory fillings.

Chutney — A highly seasoned relish of fruits; herbs and spices.

Cigarette Russe — A crisp cylinder-shaped sweet biscuit served with ice cream, mousses or cold soufflés to give a texture variation.

Clarify — To make a liquid clear by removing sediments and impurities.

Coagulate — To change from a fluid into a thickened mass; usually refers to the cooking of protein foods, eg. egg cookery.

Coddle — To cook slowly in simmering water. Usually applies to eggs which are cooked in their shell until the white changes from transparent to slightly opaque.

Coat — To dip foods into flour, crumbs, sauce or chocolate etc. until covered.

Cobbler — A pudding made from fruit and thickened syrup topped with a biscuit or cake topping and baked.

Colander — A rounded double-handled strainer used to drain off liquids. It is large and therefore suitable to drain large quantities that do not fit in a strainer.

Colette — A chocolate petit four.

Compote — Fruit cooked in a syrup to help retain its shape.

Condiment — An aromatic substance which is added to food to enhance its flavor. Usually it refers to additions at the table such as sauces, catsup and prepared mustard.

Convenience Foods — Refers to packet or canned preparations that are part or fully prepared eg. packet soups, sauces and cakes.

Court Bouillon — A liquid flavored with bay leaf, onion, celery, salt and pepper and sometimes wine, in which fish is poached.

Cream — To mix butter or other shortening and sugar until the sugar is dissolved and the mixture is light, fluffy and cream in color.

Crêpe — A thin, delicate pancake which is filled with sweet or savory fillings.

Croissant — A crescent shape roll made from a rich yeast dough.

Croquette — A preparation of cooked and minced meats, fish or poultry bound with a thick, white sauce, crumbed and shaped into balls or rectangular shapes, then deep-fried.

Croûte — A piece of bread, fried or toasted, on which prepared meat or small savories can be served.

Croutons — A small cube of bread, toasted or fried, used as garnish for soup or stews.

Crudite — A thinly cut stick or piece of raw vegetable, eaten with a dipping sauce. Served as an appetizer.

Crumb — To coat foods with flour, egg and breadcrumbs to form a protective cover for foods which are fried.

Cube — To cut into small half or quarter inch cubes.

Cuisine — A national or regional manner of preparing food; a general cooking style.

Curing — The process of salting and smoking meat and fish as a means to impart a particular flavor.

Curry — A highly flavored dish or sauce of Indian origin, containing a mixture of spices.

Custard Powder — A combination of corn starch, coloring and egg powder used to add to sweetened milk to make custard.

Decaffeinate — To remove the caffeine from coffee.

Decant — To pour any liquid from one container into another. Some wines are decanted so as to remove the sediment.

Decoration — The enhancing of the appearance of a finished sweet product for serving.

Deep-fry — To cook food in sufficient hot oil to allow the food to float.

Deglaze — To lift pan juices from a saucepan, frypan or baking dish with a little water, stock, juice or wine. The resulting liquid is used as the base for a sauce for the dish.

Dehydrate — To remove the water content from food stuffs.

Demitasse — A half-sized cup used to serve black coffee.

Deveining — To remove the feeding tract from prawns. After removing the shell make a shallow slit down the back of the prawn and lift the tract with a fine toothpick.

GLOSSARY OF FOOD & COOKING TERMS

Dhal A well seasoned lentil purée served with curries.

Dice To cut food into small, even-sized cubes or pieces.

Dijon Mustard A prepared mustard made in the style of the mustards made in Dijon France. It is made without the seed husk which is used in other mustards. It can be mild or highly seasoned.

Dilute To reduce in strength by adding water or other liquids.

Dissolve To mix an ingredient such as salt, sugar, gelatine into water until it disappears into the water and becomes one with it. Starches do not dissolve, they disperse.

Dolmades A stuffed roll of vine leaves or cabbage leaves. A meat and rice filling is used for both or a rice and pine nut filling is used only for vine leaves. They are simmered in a little water or stock.

Dot To scatter bits of butter or margarine over the surface of foods.

Dredge To coat food by dusting, sprinkling or rolling it in flour, cornstarch, sugar or confectioner's sugar.

Dress To mix salad or other foods with dressing or sauce.

Dressed Vegetables Vegetables to which additional ingredients have been added to enhance color, flavor, texture and to make them a more complete dish.

Dressing A mixture which is added to foods to add moisture and flavor such as salad dressings.

Dripping The fat and juices that render off meat when it is cooked. When strained and cooled the solid part can be used to fry foods.

Durum A hard wheat variety used to make pasta.

Dutch Oven A large cooking utensil made of cast iron. It has a lid and is used to cook large cuts of meat on top of the range eg. pot roast.

Éclair A finger-shaped length of chou pastry filled with whipped cream or cream patissiere and coated with chocolate.

Egg Wash A mixture of egg and milk or water, used for brushing over savory pastries and doughs to produce a sheen and golden brown color.

Emulsion A combination of two ingredients that don't combine permanently with each other and need the aid of a third ingredient. An example is oil and vinegar; in the making of mayonnaise, it needs egg yolk to act as the emulsifier.

En Croûte A French term meaning enclosed in pastry.

Entrée The main course of a meal.

Escalope A thin slice of veal cut from the leg or rump and flattened. It also refers to pork.

Escargot An edible snail, imported from France and served in the shell.

Espagnole A basic brown sauce made from brown meat stock, vegetables, herbs and wine. It is used as a base to make other sauces.

Essence A flavoring substance usually made by distillation.

Extract See "Essence".

Falafel A patty made from ground chick peas and spices which is deep-fried. Of Middle Eastern origin.

Fillet A piece of meat, fish or poultry which is boneless or has all bones removed.

Fine Herbes A mixture of fresh herbs — parsley, taragon, chives and chervil — which are finely chopped and used to flavor egg dishes and sauces.

Flambé To pour warmed alcoholic beverage over food and ignite when serving.

Flan An open pastry case baked in a fluted ring, filled with a sweet or savory filling.

Flute To make decorative indentations around pastry edges.

Fold To combine whisked mixtures with other ingredients by using a gentle circular motion over and under the mixture and not around, using a large metal spoon.

Fondant A thick creamy sugar paste which is used as icing and is the base of many confections.

Fondue A dish consisting of cheese melted in wine or chocolate and a little cream into which pieces of bread, fruit or cake are dipped and eaten.

Fool A cold sweet consisting of a fruit purée folded into whipped cream or custard.

Frappé A drink made with crushed ice, cream and sweetened fruits.

Freeze Dried A method of preserving food by rapid freezing, then drying.

Fritter Food dipped in batter and deep-fried.

Frying A quick method of cooking food in a small amount of hot fat or oil. Only tender foods are fried.

Galantine A dish made from boned out poultry which is stuffed and pressed into shape, then poached or baked. When completely cold it is coated with a chaud-froid sauce, elaborately decorated and coated in aspic.

Game Wild animals or birds hunted and killed for food. Today many are raised on game farms to supply the market.

Gammon The lower end of a side of bacon, or a smoked or cured ham.

Garam Marsala A mixture of spices from North India used to add flavor to curries and other foods.

Garnish A trimming added to a savory dish before serving to enhance its appearance.

Gâteau An elaborate cake made with a sponge or pastry base, filled with a cream filling of some kind. Nuts, glacé fruits and fresh fruits may also be used in the filling. It is covered in cream, icing or chocolate and decorated attractively.

Gelatin A protein obtained by rendering down connective tissues from slaughtered animals. It is a faintly amber, colorless, odorless and tasteless substance which when dissolved in hot water, and added to other liquid ingredients, sets them into a jelly.

Genoese A rich sponge cake with a higher butter content than normal sponges. Used in the making of Gâteau and petits fours.

Glaze To coat with a glossy mixture.

Grate To rub food on a grater to produce fine or coarse particles.

Grease To rub the surface of a dish with fat to prevent food from sticking.

Grecque, à la Prepared in the Greek style ie. with olive oil, lemon juice and fresh herbs.

Griddle	A thick flat iron plate used on top of the range to cook food.
Grissini	Italian bread sticks which are long, slender and crisp.
Gruel	A thin, light porridge made by boiling oats or barley in water or milk.
Haggis	A traditional Scottish dish made from a rich forcemeat of sheep's tongue, liver, heart and oatmeal which is packed into the cleaned out stomach of a sheep and cooked.
Halva	A Middle Eastern confection made with butter, sugar, honey, nuts and ground sesame seeds or semolina.
Hash	A dish of ground, fresh or cooked meats, poultry or fish which is fried or baked with potatoes, onions or other vegetables.
Herb Butter	Softened butter to which finely chopped herbs have been added. Used to serve with grilled meats and fish.
Hibachi	A small portable charcoal grill.
Hogget	The meat of a young sheep, from 10 months to 1 year old.
Hoisin Sauce	A spicy sauce made of soya paste, yellow beans, garlic, sugar and vinegar. It is used in Asian cooking.
Hollandaise	A rich sauce made with butter, egg yolks, lemon juice or vinegar and seasonings. It is usually served with eggs , fish and vegetables.
Homogenized Milk	Milk which has been forced at high pressure through a fine screen to break the fat globules into fine particles, which remain suspended in the milk and do not separate.
Hors d'oeuvres	Small savory foods served as an appetizer.
Horseradish	A cultivated plant with a pungent acrid root which is ground and used as a flavoring.
Infuse	To steep foods in a liquid until the liquid absorbs their flavor.
Jardiniere	French term meaning a garnish of vegetables.
Julienne	A method of cutting vegetables and other foods into thin, matchstick size pieces.
Kahlua	A coffee flavored liqueur.
Kebab	Cubes of meat and vegetables threaded on skewers and cooked over a charcoal fire.
Kelp	Dried seaweed used in Japanese cookery.
Knead	To work dough until it is smooth and elastic.
Kugelhopf	A rich yeast cake from Alsace.
Kulich	A traditional Easter cake made in Russia. It is a rich yeast dough flavored with saffron and baked in a tall narrow tin.
Ladle	A long handled utensil with a bowl at the end used to serve liquids such as soups, sauces or punches.
Lard	The white fat of pork, rendered and sold in solid form. It is used as a shortening to make pastry and biscuits and as a frying medium.
Larding	Threading strips of fatty pork or bacon onto the surface of lean meats before roasting.
Lemon Balm	A lemon scented herb of the mint family, used in stuffings and salads.
Lentil	Edible seed of a leguminous plant used in soups and purées. It is a source of protein.

Liaison	A substance used to bind or thicken sauces and soups.
Macaroon	Sweet biscuit made with egg, sugar and almond meal or coconut. They are very crisp and are often used to give texture to other sweet dishes.
Macedoine	A mixture of vegetables cut into small even shaped dice.
Macerate	To soak or infuse fruit in a syrup, liqueur or spirit to improve its flavor.
Maison	To indicate that the dish on the menu is a speciality of the restaurant.
Maître d'hôtel	The head waiter in a restaurant.
Marbling	The distribution of fat in the muscular tissue of a cut of meat.
Marinade	A flavored liquid into which food is placed for some time to give it more flavor and to tenderize. Marinades include wine and lemon juice or fruit juices mixed with oil, herbs and seasonings.
Marinate	To allow food to stand in a marinade.
Mask	To cover or coat cooked food evenly with a sauce, jelly or mayonnaise.
Matzo	A biscuit of unleavened bread, eaten by Jewish people during the Feast of the Passover.
Mayonnaise	A cold sauce made with egg yolk and oil, beaten into an emulsion. It is flavored with vinegar or lemon juice and seasonings and is often used as the base for other sauces.
Medallion	A piece of food, usually meat, cut into an oval or round shape.
Melba toast	Very thinly sliced bread which may be toasted or baked in a moderate oven until dry and slightly colored. Used to serve with patés, dips and mousses.
Menu	A list of dishes written in the order that they are to be served at a meal.
Meringue	A mixture of stiffly beaten egg white and sugar beaten until thick and glossy then baked in a slow oven.
Meunière	With sauce of butter, lemon juice and parsley. Usually refers to fish cooked in this way.
Mince	To cut into very fine pieces using knife, food grinder, blender or processor.
Mirepoix	A mixture of diced root vegetables and celery used as a base for cooking meats, fish and shellfish. Also used to flavor stews and sauces.
Miso	A soya bean paste made from the fermentation of cooked soya beans, wheat or rice, and salt.
Mix	To combine ingredients with a circular motion until evenly dispersed.
Mocha	Flavoring of coffee and chocolate.
Mornay	A dish covered with a thick white sauce, browned under the griller. Cheese is often sprinkled on top before browning.
Mortar	A heavy bowl made of marble, stone or metal in which foods such as herbs, spices and nuts are pounded with a pestle.
Mold	To form food into a shape either by hand or to set in a receptacle of the desired shape.
Mousse	A cold dessert made light in texture with the addition of whipped cream or beaten egg white.
Mousseline	A sauce enriched with whipped cream.

GLOSSARY OF FOOD & COOKING TERMS

Muesli — A breakfast cereal consisting of uncooked rolled oats, wheatgerm, bran, chopped dried fruit and nuts.

Mull — To spice, sweeten and heat wine.

Muscat — A variety of grape with a very sweet flavor used to make a sweet white wine.

Napoletana — In the style of Naples; usually with tomatoes and garlic.

Nest — A basket shaped arrangement of food such as potato straws, meringue baskets and rice nests.

Nicoise — Cooked and served with olive oil, tomatoes, garlic and black olives.

Noisette — A small round cut of meat from the loin of lamb with fat removed and weighing approximately 3½ oz.

Normandy, à la — In the Normandy style. Always includes butter, cream, apples and cider or Calvados.

Offal — The edible internal parts of an animal — liver, tripe, kidney, brains, tongue, sweetbreads and heart.

Olive Oil — The oil expressed from the olive fruit.

Ossobuco — A traditional Italian dish. Thick steaks of unboned shin of veal are simmered in a sauce of wine, tomatoes and herbs.

Ouzo — An aniseed flavored liqueur from Greece.

Paella — A Spanish dish made from rice, chicken, shellfish and vegetables.

Panada — A thick mixture of butter flour and milk, used to thicken and bind various dishes such as croquettes, soufflés and rissoles.

Pan-fry — To fry food in a small amount of fat or oil.

Parboil — To boil partially or for a short time.

Pare — To peel fruits or vegetables.

Parfait — A dessert consisting of cream or ice cream, fruit and nuts.

Pasta — A dough of wheat flour, salt, water and egg, rolled and cut into many shapes. Pasta is a feature of the Italian cuisine.

Pasteurization — To destroy harmful bacteria in milk and juices by a process of rapidly increasing and decreasing the temperature.

Pastry Case — A shell of pastry baked before a pie or tart filling is added.

Peel — To remove outer skin of fruits and vegetables.

Percolator — A pot used to brew coffee.

Pestle — An instrument with a rounded end used to pound food in a mortar.

Pesto — A thick uncooked sauce made with fresh basil, garlic, pine nuts, Parmesan cheese and oil. It is usually served with pasta.

Petit four — A dainty bite-sized iced cake or biscuit usually served with coffee.

Pilaf — A dish of seasoned rice with vegetables or meat added.

Piquant — Agreeably pungent or sharp in flavor.

Pit — To remove seed from whole fruit.

Poach — To cook food over low heat in simmering water.

Potage — French term for soup, usually thick and well seasoned.

Potato Flour — Flour extracted from cooked potatoes, used as a thickening agent.

Pot Roast — To cook large pieces of meat by braising in a pot.

Prawn — A large shrimp.

Preheat — To heat oven to desired temperatures before placing in the food.

Profiterole — Tiny cream puff, filled with sweet cream, served as a dessert.

Prosciutto — Italian style spiced and cured ham, sliced paper thin for serving.

Purée — To make a smooth thick mixture from soft or cooked fruits, vegetables or legumes by passing through a sieve, or food mill or working in a blender or food processor.

Raised Pie — A savory pie made with a hot water crust pastry. It is filled with meat or poultry and cooked, then after cooking is filled through the top with stock which will set into a jelly. It is a traditional English pie.

Réchauffé — French term for dishes made from leftover foods.

Reduce — To reduce the volume of liquid by rapid boiling in an uncovered pan. This concentrates the flavor and thickens the liquid.

Refresh — To immerse blanched or cooked vegetables in cold water to halt the cooking process immediately. It sets the color of vegetables.

Relish — A condiment such as chutney, pickles and mustard, eaten with food to add flavor.

Render — To melt fat down into dripping.

Rollmop — A marinated fillet of herring wrapped around a pickled stuffing and served as an hors d'oeuvre.

Rotisserie — A revolving spit used for roasting meat, either in the oven or over an open charcoal fire.

Roulade — Food that is formed into a roll.

Roux — A mixture of butter and flour in equal proportions which forms the basis for most sauces.

Saddle — A cut of meat, usually lamb, veal or venison, which includes part of the backbone and both loins.

Sambal — An accompaniment or side dish served with hot curry dishes to give a refreshing interlude.

Scald — To heat liquid just below boiling point.

Shortening — Fat which is used in pastry and cake making. Butter, margarine, hydrogenated vegetable oils, lard and dripping are all classed as shortening.

Shred — To cut food into slivers or thin, fine pieces using a knife or cutter.

Shuck — To remove the meat of oysters, clams, etc; from their shells.

Simmer — To cook food in a liquid just below boiling point. The bubbles should form slowly and just break the surface.

Skim — To remove fat or scum from the surface of food.

Sourdough — A piece of fermented dough reserved from one baking to act as a starter for the next batch; gives a distinctive sour taste to the bread.

Steam — To cook food in a steamer over boiling water.

Stew — To cook food in a simmering liquid over low heat.

Sweat — To heat vegetables in a small amount of butter in a covered pan over low heat in order to soften them and release flavors without coloring.

Table d'hôte	Set-price menu in a restaurant consisting of several courses.
Textured Vegetable Protein	Known also as T.V.P. A food product made from vegetable protein sources, especially soya bean. It is used to replace animal protein in vegetarian diets.
Toast	To brown food by means of dry heat, eg. bread, almonds, coconut.
Tofu	A soya bean curd which resembles a thick set custard or white cheese, used widely in oriental dishes.
Toss	To mix food lightly with a lifting motion using a fork and spoon.
Truffle	Edible fungus black or white in color, which grows beneath the ground usually under large oak trees. They are mostly found in France and Italy. They are considered a rare delicacy.
Truss	To secure poultry with string and skewers to hold its shape while cooking.
Tournedos	A small thick slice of beef ternderloin approximately ½″ thick which is fried in butter and oil and served on a fried croute.
Trivet	A three-legged metal stand on which meat is placed in a roasting pan to keep it off the bottom of the pan and to allow air to circulate.
Tureen	A large, deep dish with a lid in which soup is served.
Turnover	A semicircle large or small pie made by folding a circle of pastry in half over the filling and sealing the edges before baking. Shortcrust or puff pastry may be used.
Unleavened Bread	A bread which has no raising agent. It is usually flat and crisp. It is made from flour of various kinds, salt and water. Also called flat breads, they include tortillas, chapatis and Lebanese bread.
Upside-Down Cake	A cake in which topping ingredients of fruit, nuts and brown sugar are placed at the bottom of the cake tin with the cake mixture on top. When cooked it is served upside down.
Vacherin	A classic French dessert made of circles of meringue stacked and formed into a hollow nest then filled with fruit, chantilly cream or ice cream.
Vandyke	To cut or shape foods with continuous V-shaped points to enhance their appearance. Tomatoes, hard boiled eggs, melons, grapefruit, oranges and lemons are prepared in this way.
Velouté	A rich, velvety white sauce made from chicken, veal, fish or vegetable stock, thickened with a roux of butter and flour.
Vent	An opening or slit made in the center of a pastry-covered pie to allow steam to escape from the filling during cooking.
Veronique	A dish prepared or garnished with white grapes, usually fish or chicken dishes. The term originated in the Italian town of Verona, where locally grown grapes are frequently used in cooking.
Vinaigrette	A piquant dressing made with a mixture of oil and vinegar, seasoned with salt, pepper and often flavored with garlic or fresh herbs. It is served over salads, hot vegetables, hot or cold meats or fish.
Vinegar	A sour liquid produced by the fermentation of malt or wine.
Wafer	A thin, crisp cake or biscuit. Also means to cut into very thin slices.
Wasabi	Green horseradish, used in Japanese cookery. It is available in a powdered form.
Whip	To beat to a froth with a wire whisk, fork or electric beater in order to incorporate air and produce expansion.
Whisk	Similar to whip. Refers also to a wire utensil used for whipping.
Wok	A large, round bottom metal cooking pan used in Chinese cooking.
Wonton	A small square of thinly rolled dough used in Chinese cooking. The dough is filled with a sweet or savory filling and then fried, steamed or boiled.
Yam	The starchy tuberous root of a plant.
Yogurt	A cultured dairy product made from milk and the introduction of a lactic acid bacteria which thickens the milk to a custard like consistency.
Zabaglione	A rich custard-like sweet of Italian origin, made with egg yolks, sugar and marsala.
Zest	The thin outer skin or peel of citrus fruits which contains the essential flavoring oils. Also called rind.
Zester	An implement for removing the zest from citrus fruits.
Zwieback	A crisp dry rusk made from a special bread dough which is baked then cut into slices and dried out in a slow oven. The word in German for "twice baked." The rusks are crushed into crumbs and used to coat foods or to make crumbed pie shells.

Black Bear in the Kenai Fjords.

INDEX

ABBREVIATIONS
OF ALL CHAPTERS

INDEX

INDEX

INDEX

INDEX

INDEX

INDEX

INDEX

INDEX

Beautiful traditional Architecture in San Francisco

Pictorial Credits

Photographs supplied by Light Images Inc., Mill Valley, California, USA.

Photographers:

Gene Anthony
Darryl Baird
Carol Barrington
Werner Bertsch
Scott Clemens
Bob Clemenz
George Dritsas
Bob Edwards
Joe Farrell
Greg Gawlowski
Cathy Gehm
Lauren Geise
Pat Harrington
Robert Harrison
Judy Houston
Judy Howard
Mike Howell
Kerrick James
Roz Joseph
Zigy Kalunzy
Rubin Klass
Montes Deuca

David Lawrence
John Luke
Fred Lyon
Arthur Montes De Oca
Brian Morrison
Roger Mulkey
Mark Newman
Woody Payne
Frank Pedrick
Doug Perrine
Photo Source
Tod Powell
Carl & Ann Purcell
Tom Raymond
J. Schaber
Jeff Schultz
Bob Thomason
David Ulmer
Robert Winslow
Pat Woeber
Joan Yokum
William H. Mullins

Photographs supplied by the Australian Picture Library.

Blumebild
M. Cook

Wetzel
Schick

Photographs supplied by the IMAGE Bank

Murray Alcosser
Marv Lyons

G. Cigolini
Luis Castañeda

Acknowledgements

Special thanks:

The Publisher wishes to thank their family and the many other people for making this book so successful.

Production:

Gas Graphics TGC Pty Ltd

173 Commonwealth Street,
Surry Hills, NSW 2010
Australia
Ann Alberts, Kay Barnes, Daphne Molony, Mark Swadling

Hartley & Marks Ltd.

3663 West Broadway,
Vancouver, BC V6R2B8
Canada

InterType Pty. Limited.

61 Albion Street,
Surry Hills, NSW 2010
Australia

Griffin Press Limited

262 Marion Road,
Netley, SA 5037
Australia

Also the following students involved in the Advanced Certificate in Home Science of Brookvale Technical College, N.S.W., who were very helpful in the excellent way they prepared food for the photography under the auspices of Ellen Argyriou.

Maxine Jenkins
Pam Glover
Kathryn Munro
Katrina Goulding

Tracey Pickworth
Sonya Richter
Melissa Brown
Amana O'Bryne
Lesly Newton

Suppliers

IMPERIAL GARDENS LANDSCAPE PTY. LTD.
CTS ENGINEERING PLASTICS DIV
CUT-TO-SIZE PLASTICS PTY. LTD.
DRONROAST PTY. LTD.
COUNTRY FURNITURE ANTIQUES
AUSTRALIAN EAST INDIA CO.
AUSTRALIAN FLY FISHERMAN
GOODWOOD SADDLERY
MR. BRASSMAN
HOSÉ ASTUDIO
ININI

JAMES MUSIC
PEARSONS FLORISTS
GAG GRAPHIC ART GALLERY
THE SLATE PEOPLE PTY. LTD.
MANLY-WARRINGAH FORMAL HIRE
ABC MARKETING
SYDNEY PROP CENTRE
LIFESTYLE IMPORTS PTY LIMITED
AUSTRALIAN ELIZABETHAN TRUST
STONECRAFT TILERS
AUSTRALIAN DUTCH EAST INDIA CO.
S.O.S. MARINE